ISHIKAWA

$1 00

A

# Teaching Science for Understanding

## A Human Constructivist View

This is a volume in the Academic Press
**EDUCATIONAL PSYCHOLOGY SERIES**

*Critical comprehensive reviews of research knowledge, theories, principles, and practices*

Under the editorship of Gary D. Phye

# Teaching Science for Understanding

## A Human Constructivist View

EDITED BY

### Joel J. Mintzes

*Department of Biological Sciences*
*University of North Carolina—Wilmington*
*and Department of Mathematics, Science and Technology Education*
*North Carolina State University*
*Raleigh, North Carolina*

### James H. Wandersee

*Graduate Studies in Curriculum and*
*Instruction*
*Louisiana State University*
*Baton Rouge, Louisiana*

### Joseph D. Novak

*Department of Education*
*Cornell University*
*Ithaca, New York*

ACADEMIC PRESS

San Diego    London    Boston    New York    Sydney    Tokyo    Toronto

Images © 1997 PhotoDisc, Inc.

This book is printed on acid-free paper. ∞

Copyright © 1998 by ACADEMIC PRESS

All Rights Reserved.
No part of this publication may be reproduced or transmitted in any form or by any
means, electronic or mechanical, including photocopy, recording, or any information
storage and retrieval system, without permission in writing from the publisher.

Academic Press
*a division of Harcourt Brace & Company*
525 B Street, Suite 1900, San Diego, California 92101-4495, USA
http://www.apnet.com

Academic Press Limited
24-28 Oval Road, London NW1 7DX, UK
http://www.hbuk.co.uk/ap/

Library of Congress Card Catalog Number: 97-80819

International Standard Book Number: 0-12-498360-X

PRINTED IN THE UNITED STATES OF AMERICA
97  98  99  00  01  02  QW  9  8  7  6  5  4  3  2  1

# Tikkun Olam

## On Improving the World

*It is not your obligation to complete the work,
neither are you free to desist from it.*

Rabbi Tarfon
Pirket Avot 2:20
Ethics of the Fathers

# Contents

# Theoretical and Empirical Foundations of Human Constructivism

## 1. THE PURSUIT OF A DREAM: EDUCATION CAN BE IMPROVED
### Joseph D. Novak

## 2. REFORM AND INNOVATION IN SCIENCE TEACHING: A HUMAN CONSTRUCTIVIST VIEW

*Joel J. Mintzes and James H. Wandersee*

## 3. RESEARCH IN SCIENCE TEACHING AND LEARNING: A HUMAN CONSTRUCTIVIST VIEW

*Joel J. Mintzes and James H. Wandersee*

# Theory-Driven Intervention Strategies

### 4. THEORY-DRIVEN GRAPHIC ORGANIZERS
John E. Trowbridge and James H. Wandersee

### 5. METACOGNITION AND CONCEPTUAL CHANGE
Richard F. Gunstone and Ian J. Mitchell

## 6. HISTORY AND PHILOSOPHY OF SCIENCE AND THE PREPARATION FOR CONSTRUCTIVIST TEACHING: THE CASE OF PARTICLE THEORY

Joseph Nussbaum

## 7. THE CASE FOR ANALOGIES IN TEACHING SCIENCE FOR UNDERSTANDING

Zoubeida R. Dagher

## 8. THE COMPUTER AS A POWERFUL TOOL FOR UNDERSTANDING SCIENCE

*Ron Good and Carl Berger*

## 9. USING HYPERMEDIA TO REPRESENT EMERGING STUDENT UNDERSTANDING: SCIENCE LEARNERS AND PRESERVICE TEACHERS

*Michele Wisnudel Spitulnik, Carla Zembal-Saul, and Joseph S. Krajcik*

## 10. SMALL GROUPS AND
## SHARED CONSTRUCTIONS
### M. Gail Jones and Glenda Carter

## 11. INTERACTIVE HISTORICAL VIGNETTES
### James H. Wandersee and Linda M. Roach

## 12. TALKING AND DOING SCIENCE: IMPORTANT ELEMENTS IN A TEACHING-FOR-UNDERSTANDING APPROACH

*Eleanor Abrams*

# Epilogue

## 13. EPILOGUE: MEANINGFUL LEARNING, KNOWLEDGE RESTRUCTURING, AND CONCEPTUAL CHANGE: ON WAYS OF TEACHING SCIENCE FOR UNDERSTANDING

*Joel J. Mintzes, James H. Wandersee, and Joseph D. Novak*

# Contributors

*Numbers in parentheses indicate the pages on which the authors' contributions begin.*

**Eleanor Abrams** (307), Department of Education, University of New Hampshire, Durham, New Hampshire 03824

**Carl Berger** (213), Educational Studies Program, School of Education, University of Michigan, Ann Arbor, Michigan 48109

**Glenda Carter** (261), Center for Research in Mathematics and Science Education, North Carolina State University, Raleigh, North Carolina 27607

**Zoubeida Dagher** (195), Department of Educational Development, University of Delaware, Newark, Delaware 19711

**Ronald G. Good** (213), Graduate Studies in Curriculum and Instruction, Louisiana State University, Baton Rouge, Louisiana 70803

**Richard Gunstone** (133), Faculty of Education, Monash University, Clayton, Victoria, 3168 Australia

**M. Gail Jones** (261), School of Education, University of North Carolina, Chapel Hill, North Carolina 27599

**Joseph S. Krajcik** (229), Educational Studies Program, School of Education, University of Michigan, Ann Arbor, Michigan 48109

**Joel J. Mintzes** (29, 59, 327), Department of Biological Sciences, University of North Carolina, Wilmington, North Carolina 28403 and Department of Mathematics, Science and Technology Education, North Carolina State University, Raleigh, North Carolina 27607

**Ian Mitchell** (133), Faculty of Education, Monash University, Clayton, Victoria, 3168 Australia

xv

**Joseph D. Novak** (1, 327), Department of Education, Cornell University, Ithaca, New York 14853

**Joseph Nussbaum** (165), Science Teaching Department, Weizmann Institute of Science, Rehovot 76100, Israel

**Linda Roach** (281), Department of Physical and Mathematical Sciences, Northwestern State University of Louisiana, Natchitoches, Louisiana 71457

**Michele Wisnudel Spitulnik** (229), Educational Studies Program, School of Education, University of Michigan, Ann Arbor, Michigan 48109

**John E. Trowbridge** (95), Department of Teacher Education, Southeastern Louisiana University, Hammond, Louisiana 70401

**James H. Wandersee** (29, 59, 95, 281, 327), Graduate Studies in Curriculum and Instruction, Louisiana State University, Baton Rouge, Louisiana 70803

**Carla Zembal-Saul** (229), Department of Curriculum and Instruction, Pennsylvania State University, University Park, Pennsylvania 16802.

# Preface

... quality over quantity; meaning over memorizing and understanding over awareness

The history of science education is replete with well-intended efforts to improve teaching and learning in elementary and secondary schools and, to a lesser extent, in colleges and universities. In North America, reform movements of the last 100 years have been driven largely by forces lying outside the teacher's traditional domain. For the most part, these efforts have been fed by broad-based social forces pitting proponents of the "academist" and "practicalist" traditions against each other. Among the most important of these social forces have been massive immigration waves and urbanization, military competition, struggles for gender and ethnic equity, and even economic survival. These forces have resulted in large-scale, cyclical, and at times disruptive shifts in curricular emphases and instructional practices. At centuries' end we find ourselves in the midst of yet another of these spasms.

To many classroom teachers, curricular and instructional changes mandated at the local, state, or national levels often seem arbitrary at best and poorly conceived at worst. Sometimes they appear to be nothing more than "band-aids" or expedient responses to political pressure. Why should a competent science teacher, with years of hard-won experience and knowledge gained through daily practice, implement ideas "hatched" by others? How can we determine whether recent recommendations by internationally prominent scientists and science educators offer anything better than those "tried and true" practices good teachers have employed for generations? What can the reflective science teacher do to select really effective strategies and distinguish them from the "snake oil" and panaceas peddled by those who have a political agenda, or worse, a financial stake in change?

In this volume we present a Human Constructivist model of science teaching and learning which offers an alternative to the hunches, guesses, folklore, and nostrums that have guided our profession for generations. In writing and editing this book, we have been motivated by an abiding conviction that the economic engine of the twenty-first century is likely to be substantially different from that of the twentieth; that the age of the agrarian/manufacturing society is rapidly disappearing, and that our primary roles in the future will depend on our collective capacities as meaning-makers and knowledge-builders. For those fortunate individuals who are well prepared, the advent of a "Knowledge Age" is an exciting prospect, and science teachers are clearly on the cutting edge of that revolution. However, teachers must be empowered with a framework of useful ideas and practical tools if they are to manage change wisely. This book is dedicated to helping science teachers empower themselves with state-of-the-art knowledge of theory, research, and practice.

## Human Constructivism

In recent years, much has been made in the popular press of the so-called "science wars." The phrase refers to an on-going debate between classically educated scientists who view their work as an objective effort to understand natural phenomena through direct observation of the physical world, and a new generation of scientists and philosophers who contend that science is more realistically seen as an effort to construct socially negotiated meanings. Within the constructivist camp are those "radical constructivists" who reject entirely the notion that scientific knowledge can be tested against an external reality, and the "social constructivists" who contend that reality itself is simply a product of social negotiation. Recently these esoteric questions, once the province of philosophers, historians, and sociologists, have begun to impact the science classroom, promising to change much of what teachers have done for generations.

In contrast to the notions of the radical and social constructivists, Human Constructivists take a moderate position on the nature of science. On the one hand, we find the views of classical "logical-positivists" intellectually indefensible; on the other, we think that many constructivists have created a relativistic mind-world that is ultimately self-defeating. We prefer instead a view of science that acknowledges an external and knowable world, but depends critically on an intellectually demanding struggle to construct heuristically powerful explanations through extended periods of interaction with objects, events, and other people. In its simplest form, we believe that human beings are meaning-makers; that the goal of education is to construct shared meanings and that this goal may be facilitated through the active intervention of well-prepared teachers.

## Teaching Science for Understanding

This book is an attempt to provide science teachers with a rational framework for making decisions about curriculum and instruction in the twenty-first century. In it we focus on ways that good teachers help students learn meaningfully. In our view, the decision to encourage *meaningful* rather than *rote* learning is the most important one a science teacher makes. In many ways, the decision reflects a set of values that favors quality over quantity; meaning over memorizing, and *understanding* over awareness. To us, rote learning and the conformity it engenders may be likened in some respects to a form of intellectual slavery. In contrast, we value and respect individual human minds and believe that, in a democracy, learners deserve an educational system that encourages, supports, and rewards divergent, creative thinking; deep understanding; and novel ways of solving problems. Further, we believe that such a system is ultimately in our best political, social, and economic interests collectively.

The book is composed of three sections. In the first section (Chapters 1–3), we introduce the theory and research on which our views are founded. The section begins with a chapter by Dr. Novak who recounts some of the important events that inspired his seminal contributions to science education and the critical role of David Ausubel's work in the evolution of his Human Constructivist perspective. It was Ausubel's remarkably insightful suggestion that, "the most important single factor influencing learning is what the learner already knows." This idea became the centerpiece of Novak's work.

In Chapters 2 and 3 we place Novak's ideas in historical perspective and elaborate on the research program his ideas have engendered. The program comprises a corpus of more than 3500 studies originating in virtually every country on Earth. These studies, in turn, have stimulated work on a set of powerful metacognitive tools for students, teachers, researchers, and other knowledge-makers in schools, corporations, and healthcare agencies in the United States and abroad.

Section II (Chapters 4–12) is authored by an internationally recognized group of leading researchers and practitioners and offers a set of new, theory-driven intervention strategies designed to encourage meaningful learning and knowledge restructuring in science. In our view, these chapters provide some of the best advice currently available on ways of teaching science for understanding.

Trowbridge and Wandersee (Chapter 4) discuss the "cartography of cognition" and present a set of graphic organizing techniques that includes concept maps, concept circle diagrams, vee diagrams, and other heuristically powerful approaches. In Chapter 5, Gunstone and Mitchell focus on conceptual change and metacognitive approaches in the teaching of physical science ideas. Nussbaum (Chapter 6) introduces his use of debates and conceptual conflict in teaching students about the particulate theory of matter. The use of several analogical strategies is described in detail by Dagher (Chapter 7), while Good and Berger (Chapter 8) provide an insightful overview of computers as powerful tools for constructing meaning in science disciplines. Recent advances in the use of hypermedia techniques are introduced by Spitulnik, Zembal-Saul, and Krajcik (Chapter 9), and the value of small groups and cooperative strategies is analyzed by Jones and Carter (Chapter 10). The section concludes with a chapter (11) by Wandersee and Roach describing a novel way to introduce the history of science into classroom discussions, and a discussion of "science talks" and "student as scientist" programs by Abrams (Chapter 12).

In the epilogue (Section III), we summarize the suggestions of these authors and present a model designed to help teachers reflect on and evaluate new ways of teaching science for understanding. In this concluding chapter we describe the essential differences between "assimilative," "reconstructive," and "integrative" teaching episodes and focus on the teacher as a catalyst in efforts to facilitate conceptual change. We conclude with a brief cautionary note on the potential misuses of technology in teaching.

## Our Audience

This book is intended primarily for science teachers, graduate students, teacher educators, curriculum developers, and researchers. However, it will be of interest to a very broad range of people who are concerned about the current state of science education and what we might do to improve it. For parents, school administrators, supervisors, school board members and other "stake-holders" in the educational system, this book provides a thorough-going treatment of the most significant problems in science teaching and learning and offers a wide-range of practical solutions.

## A Tribute

We dedicate this book to Professor Joseph D. Novak for his 40 years of service to the profession of science education. Dr. Novak retired from his position as Professor of Science Education and Biological Sciences at Cornell University in June of 1997. He has given to the field numerous insightful contributions to theory, research, and practice in science teaching and learning, and we look forward to his continued contributions in the role of Professor Emeritus.

# PART

# I

# Theoretical and Empirical Foundations of Human Constructivism

# The Pursuit of a Dream:
# Education Can Be Improved

JOSEPH D. NOVAK

*Cornell University*

## INTRODUCTION

Over the past four decades, the work that my graduate students, visiting professors, students of my students, and I have done has been gaining popularity around the world, especially in Latin countries and the Far East. The question is often asked of me: How did you decide to use the theories and pursue the studies you and your associates have done? There is no simple answer to this question, partly because, over time, the theories, methods, and ideas that have guided our work have changed. This change has not been random or arbitrary, but rather a function of our previous studies and new complementary contributions by scholars in a variety of disciplines. Nevertheless, there has also been a constancy in our work with a focus on the question: How can we help people become better learners? From early in my career to the present day, my belief has been that we can never make this a better world to live in unless we can develop better ways to help people "get smart." It has been my conviction over the years that education, both formal and informal, can be dramatically improved—if we can make the study of education more like the study of science, i.e., guided by theory, principles, and productive methodologies. In short, I believed we needed new and more powerful *paradigms*, to borrow Kuhn's (1962) term, to guide educational research and practice.

This chapter is an autobiographical sketch of my search for better ways to educate. It is necessarily an abbreviated autobiography, and I cite only a few people who contributed to our work, but I hope it can serve to illustrate, especially to students and younger faculty in education, that it is possible to improve education; we can pursue the dream that education can be improved. The other chapters in this book go on to present work done by former students and/or associates, plus some excellent work done by others—all of which point to support the idea that education, and especially science education, is being improved. The study of science can be *meaningful* to everyone.

## DEVELOPING A PASSION FOR LEARNING

My elementary school experiences were largely a frustration to me. Most of what was presented seemed repetitious, simple, and boring, while reading, especially oral reading to the class, was often embarrassing. The basal readers we used contained mostly nonsensical stories and often I would import a word, or the pronunciation of a word, to try to make sense of the reading. Coming out of the Great Depression, our home had very few books, and the family made no trips to the public library. I was highly curious about things, especially things related to nature, but there was little available at my reading level that presented the kind of information I needed to understand why plants grew, what made fire, what the sun and stars were. Science instruction was essentially nonexistent in my elementary school and math was mostly drill on simple repetitive textbook "problems."

By upper elementary school, my reading skills were better, but it was still difficult to find books at my level that *explained* how things worked. My brother, 5 years older and by then in high school, was helpful and encouraging, but his science and math courses did not deal adequately with theories and ideas; they presented mostly "facts" to be memorized. Except for a rather good physics course, the science I had in high school was predominantly memorization of word definitions and various "facts." Social science instruction was often worse, presenting few ideas and testing primarily for recall of dates, names, or other minutiae. Repeatedly I wondered throughout my schooling: Does education have to be so dull, so lacking in meaning or significance? And I recall some of my classmates struggling with what seemed to me the simplest of problems. Wasn't there a better way to help them learn?

Also about this time I was struck by the observation that many of my classmates appeared to have almost no capacity to reason things out. Were they just born stupid or were they being miseducated? I thought then that a good percentage of their problems could derive from poor education. I began to realize that I was fortunate to have a dad who, although he completed only four years of education in an eastern European village school, kept encouraging me to try to figure out on my own how things worked and why things were the way they were. If I misbehaved, his punishment was usually to cause me to reflect on why what I did didn't make sense. "Well," he would say, "if it doesn't make sense, don't do it!" Often it would have been less painful to get a spanking, but that was not his way, at least not with me.

When I was 13 years old, I began working after school and Saturdays, first shining shoes and then waiting on customers and pressing clothes in a dry cleaning shop. Working 20 or more hours per week took time from what could have been valuable learning experiences, but it also taught me to use my time efficiently, especially when I began college as a full-time student and working 35 to 40 hours per week. It was my good fortune to have the great University of Minnesota easily accessible to me, so I could live at home and continue work in the dry cleaners, covering all of my expenses.

I discovered "pocket books" in college and began to collect books (most costing 25 cents or less) on every subject, including some of the literary classics. George Gamow's books on science and similar books became a passion for me. Often I was less interested in my course textbooks than in the various other books I was reading. I did acquire an interest in teaching and proceeded to take courses to certify as a science and mathematics teacher. I also became interested in history and other social sciences and took coursework beyond the college requirements. By my senior year in college, I became passionate about learning, especially in science, and read extensively. I also began to help out in a plant physiology laboratory and began some of my own experimental work. Science became very exciting to me. Several of my botany professors were excellent mentors and helped me to gain confidence in my capabilities as a science student.

In contrast to my work in science and social sciences, I found my studies in education courses to be deeply troubling. These courses lacked viable theories and principles, and so much that was presented as theory or principles failed the criterion my dad had taught me to apply—they just didn't make sense, not in terms of their logic or coherence or in terms of their application to the real world. My year of internship in secondary science teaching was satisfying in terms of the students' receptivity to powerful ideas of science, but frustrating in terms of all the constraints the "system" placed on the kind of teaching I wanted to do. It was also evident that the system could not be changed by working in a classroom, so when I was offered a teaching assistantship in the Botany Department at the University, I jumped at the opportunity to pursue further studies in sciences and education.

## GRADUATE STUDY IN BOTANY AND EDUCATION

Housed in the botany building, and doing work as a teaching assistant in botany and a research assistant in plant physiology, I also pursued studies in my major field, Education. Again, I found course work in botany and other sciences exciting, but courses in education, with the exception of statistics and a course in higher education by Professor Ruth Eckert, largely trivial at best or borderline nonsense at worst. For example, an "advanced" course in educational psychology, "Theories of Learning", used the popular textbook by Hilgard (1948), but all the theories presented were *behavioral* theories. Piaget, for example, was not mentioned. No cognitive learning theories, such as Bartlett's (1932, 1958), were mentioned. My conclusion was that the theories of learning presented were at best relevant to pigeons, rats, or cats, which were the experimental subjects in most studies, and perhaps for rote memorization tasks such as learning nonsense syllables. I argued vehemently with my course professor that I thought the theories presented were nonsense in terms of human learning; his defense was that he was using the most popular book in the field. Why, I wondered, do apparently intelligent people subscribe to such nonsense! I saw it as a classic case of the Emperor's New Clothes, where only the childlike naive could see that the emperor was naked. And it would be another decade before Ausubel's (1963) *Psychology of Meaningful Verbal Learning*, which strongly influenced my thinking, would be published. So I chose to design my thesis research using a cybernetic model, based largely on the writings of Norbert Weiner (1948, 1954).

The philosophy courses I took were strongly rooted in the *positivist* tradition, with criteria for truth and falsification the hallmark of rigorous, logical thinking. Minnesota was world famous as a center for "logical positivism," and my professors were some of the founding fathers of the center. Bright and distinguished as they were, I could not buy what they were selling. My experiences in the Botany laboratories did not square with their ideas; "truth" or "proof" appeared very illusive at best, and again I wondered why smart people could believe these things. I saw much more validity in ideas such as Conant's (1947) *On Understanding Science*. Later, Conant's disciple, Thomas Kuhn (1962), would publish his now famous *Structure of Scientific Revolutions* and help to advance what is now known as *constructivist* epistemology that is gaining popularity today. We shall discuss epistemological issues throughout this book.

My thesis research attempted to compare gains in "problem solving ability" for students enrolled in a conventional lecture–laboratory botany course with those who received regular course materials augmented with study guides to accelerate their progress. This allowed for a 6-week period devoted totally to individual research projects selected by the students. The idea was that individuals needed experience in real problem-solving activities to gain competence in problem solving. I recognized that 6 weeks was a small part of the lifespan of my students, but I thought some significant gains could be possible.

A major task was to design what I hoped would be a "content neutral" problem-solving test, since I did not regard any of the so-called "critical thinking" or "problem-solving" tests available to have validity for my study— and some published studies questioned whether these tests had any validity at all. This took much of my time for several months, including tryout and evaluation of earlier versions. In the end, I believe I did devise a complex paper-and-pencil test that validly and reliably measured aspects of individual's problem-solving ability, at least according to the criteria derived from the cybernetic theory of learning I was using. The test had some interesting psychometric properties that I reported later (Novak, 1961, 1977a, pp. 104–108).

While the "conventional" group had somewhat higher mean scores on the ACT test and "factual knowledge" tests, the "problem solving" group had a higher posttest mean score on the problem-solving test. Most of the mean differences were not statistically significant, including the latter (Novak, 1958). In retrospect, the results make sense; for viewed through our current "conceptual goggles," significant gains in problem-solving ability would require more and better organized relevant knowledge structures as well as better metacognitive processing—too much to expect under the best of circumstances in a 6-week period. Research results notwithstanding, the whole research experience, including preparation of a botany study guide with labeled photomicrograph (Novak, 1961), was enormously valuable and convinced me that difficult as the task may be, there can be a *science* of science education, and indeed, even a *science* of education. To help create new principles and theories that could lead to science of education was the exciting challenge that lay ahead.

After my first year of graduate studies, I married Joan, a girl I met in my chemistry lab during my sophomore year. She worked as a medical technologist for 3 years until our first child was born. Subsequently, we had two additional children in 3 years, and Joan was very busy being full-time mother and homemaker. Over the years, her love and emotional support helped to sustain me when personal or professional difficulties arose. Over the years I have increasingly come to appreciate my good fortune in having Joan's support, something few men and even fewer women have so constantly. Our children and now also our grandchildren have been a joy and source of pride.

## TEACHING BIOLOGY AND BIOLOGY TEACHERS

After completing my doctoral studies, I took a position in the Biology Department at Kansas State Teachers College at Emporia. In addition to teaching botany, biology, and plant morphology, I taught a course called Methods and Materials for Biology Teachers, taken by both preservice and inservice teachers. The latter course was essentially a review of the "big ideas" of biology with appropriate laboratory and field studies that could be easily replicated in schools. I was struck by how weak many of the teachers were in understanding basic concepts of biology and other sciences, evidenced also in a study we did on the recommended college preparation of Kansas science teachers (Novak & Brooks, 1959). In the latter study, we were surprised at how few science courses were regarded as "an absolute minimum" or "essential," mirroring, in part, the poor preparation of teachers in science found in an earlier study by Brooks and Baker (1957). This may also reflect the limited value of science courses where learning and testing involves rote memorization rather than understanding basic concepts. Anderson (1949) found that rote learning of science was the pattern employed in the preparation of most science teachers; he also found that there was little relationship between student achievement and the science preparation of their teachers. Memorization may be an effective learning strategy for getting passing grades in science or other courses, but it is very ineffective for acquiring the kind of disciplinary knowledge necessary for effective teaching. Why, then, were so many science teachers using a rote learning approach in their college preparation?

I enjoyed my time in the Biology Department at Emporia and felt fortunate to be there. After all, my major in the PhD program was Science Education. There was an interesting twist of fate that operated in my career. While a graduate student at Minnesota, an invitation was received in the Botany Department to send a representative to a conference in Michigan to study the "feasibility" of developing a new high school biology program. None of the professors were interested in going, so they asked if I wanted to go, since I was an "educator"—a label they used with derision, but also with a note of kindness toward me. I thought it was wonderful to go to a meeting—all expenses paid! The conference was directed by Richard Armacost, then editor of the *American Biology Teacher* (ABT), and Jack Karling, Head of the Biology Department at Purdue University. John Breukelman, the first editor of ABT and a founding father of the National Association of Biology Teachers (NABT), chaired the discussion group in which I participated for 10 days. Following this conference, a proposal was sent to the National Science Foundation to fund what became known as the Biological Sciences Curriculum Study (BSCS). Three new high school biology programs were subsequently developed.

Gil Liesman, who was my officemate in Botany until he graduated, brought the vacancy at Emporia to my attention; and who was the Chairman of Biology at Emporia? John Breukelman! In 1967, Armacost was killed in an auto accident and candidates for his position were sought. A former graduate student who studied with my major professor, and now Dean of Education at the University of Kansas, recommended me to Purdue. And who turned out to be the key decisionmaker for who would be hired for the position? Jack Karling! What remarkable things came from that early conference in Michigan—and much more was to follow as I became active in NABT.

When I moved in 1959 to Purdue University with a joint appointment in Biology and Education, my principal work was instruction in methods courses and intern teacher supervision, plus supervision of MS and PhD students. Here again I was surprised at how little *conceptual* understanding of biology and other sciences was evidenced in my certification candidates and also in many experienced teachers enrolled in our summer programs. During 1959–1962, the Department of Biological Science underwent a major curriculum overhaul, in which I participated as cochairman of the curriculum committee. Most of the existing introductory courses were scrapped and a new seven-semester sequence was developed, including Principles of Biology, Cell Biology, Developmental Biology, Genetics, and Ecology. All courses used examples from plants, animals, and microbes to varying degrees, and all placed major emphasis on understanding basic concepts. As teaching candidates emerged from the new program, there was a striking difference in their mastery of biology and related science concepts and their ability to use these in innovative independent research projects. Teaching candidates were now acquiring an understanding of basic biology concepts needed for effective teaching (Novak, 1963).

Another important change in my thinking and the work of my graduate students occurred in the early and mid-1960s. Our research studies were producing results that consistently pointed to the idea that information storage and information processing were not distinct brain functions, as cybernetic theory would suggest, but rather interdependent and related to the kind of learning approach utilized. As our "cybernetic paradigm" was beginning to crumble, David Ausubel (1963) published his *Psychology of Meaningful Verbal Learning*, presenting a new and exciting theory of learning that seemed to explain all the troublesome aspects of the data we had been gathering. By 1964, all of our research projects and also our instructional improvement projects shifted to the "meaningful learning paradigm" espoused by Ausubel. It was also in the early 1960s that I became familiar with Piaget's work through seminars with a colleague, Charles Smock, who had studied with Piaget. While our research group found much of value in Piaget's studies and developmental ideas, our data did not support his "developmental stages" ideas. Moreover, Piaget was a *developmental* theorist and we saw *learning* theory as more fundamental to understanding both learning processes and developmental processes. Ausubel's assimilation theory seemed to be more powerful and more parsimonious in explaining learning, learner success, and learner failures (Novak, 1977b).

During the later 1960s and 1970s there emerged what might be called the "battle of educational paradigms." In the world of psychology departments, behaviorism or behavioral psychology held a very firm hegemony, and any "mentalistic" theory of learning or development was suspect. Cognitive learning ideas were virtually shut out from the academy, and Ausubel had great difficulty getting many of his papers published in leading psychology journals. Mager's (1962) *behavioral objectives* were the only valid foundation for instructional planning in the eyes of psychologists and also in the eyes of many educators who failed to see the limiting psychological and epistemological foundations of behavioral objectives. In the world of science education, there was overwhelming acceptance of Piaget's ideas by almost the entire community. Our group at Purdue University and later (1967) at Cornell University was almost alone in our critical views regarding Piaget's theories and enthusiasm for Ausubel's ideas. So rigid and so dominant were many of the proponents of Piaget's ideas that *none* of the numeous research proposals I submitted to the National Science Foundation (NSF) or the U.S. Office of Education (USOE) were accepted for funding, at least not until 1978, when Mary Budd Rowe helped to steer one of my NSF proposals through her division. For 2 successive years, none of the research papers proposed by me and my students were accepted for presentation at meetings of the National Association for Research in Science Teaching.

By the mid-1970s, the "cognitive revolution" had begun in psychology departments and educational psychology programs. While behaviorism, and narrow interpretations of Piaget's work, remain alive and well in school and corporate settings, these are dying paradigms in the scholarly studies focused on human learning. The climate for the kind of work we were doing 30 years ago is now much improved. In fact, in 1978 I received my first NSF grant for a study dealing with the feasibility and value of using concept maps and Vee diagrams in junior high school classes (Novak, Gowin, & Johansen, 1983).

Throughout the 1960s and 1970s, when so much criticism of our work was prevalent from educationists and, to some extent, psychologists (although the latter with few exceptions ignored our work), my students and I were supported both intellectually and financially primarily by the science community. My students were often favored for teaching assistantships in science departments. We also received support from the U.S. Department of Agriculture Hatch program, the College of Agriculture and Life Sciences at Cornell University, and Shell Companies Foundation. So often I had occasion to be thankful for my affiliations with science departments and scientists, including Nobel Laureate scientists such as Roald Hoffmann and Kenneth Wilson. These associations provided much of the validation of our work during the 1960s and 1970s. My students, and a number of visiting professors, provided much of the caring and personal support anyone needs to pursue the difficult task of theory development to guide educational improvement.

## CREATING A THEORY OF EDUCATION

As our research and instructional improvement programs evolved, building heavily on Ausubel's (Ausubel, Novak, & Hanesian, 1968, 1978) assimilation theory of meaningful learning, several patterns began to emerge. First, it was clear that learners who developed well-organized knowledge structures were *meaningful* learners, and those who were learning primarily by rote were not

**EXAMPLES**

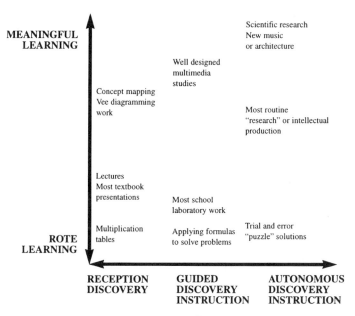

**FIGURE I**

The rote–meaningful *learning* continuum is distinct from the reception–discovery continuum for *instruction*. Both reception and discovery instruction can lead to rote learning *or* meaningful learning. School learning needs to help students move toward high levels of meaningful learning, especially in reception instruction that is the most common.

developing these structures and/or their knowledge included many misconceptions. Second, while experience with what Ausubel called "concrete empirical props" and science educators call "hands on experience," was important, it was also important to carefully clarify the meanings of words (or concept labels) and propositional statements. Much of this could be done by didactic or reception instruction, provided that it was integrated with appropriate experience. In agreement with Ausubel, our work showed the importance of distinguishing between *learning* approach and *instructional* approach. With regard to instruction, either reception instruction or inquiry (or discovery) approaches can be very rote or very meaningful learning experiences. This is illustrated in Figure 1.

A third pattern that was evident was that learners' approach to learning was somewhat related to their epistemological ideas, albeit the nature of the relationship even today remains problematic and is one of our continuing research concerns. We observed some tendency for those students who were most positivistic in their epistemology ideas to favor rote learning approaches, and those who were more constructivist tended to favor meaningful learning strategies. In any case, it was evident that philosophical issues, and especially epistemology issues, needed careful consideration in education.

Finally, it became increasingly evident that in educating we "reap what we sow." Instruction and evaluation emphasizing or favoring rote learning strategies lead to little improvement in learner's usable knowledge structures, whereas the reverse was the case when meaningful learning strategies were encouraged or favored.

Parallel to the evolution in psychology of learning in the 1960s and 1970s was an evolution in philosophy and epistemology. As already noted, some of this was sparked by Conant and later Kuhn, but then a cascade began, stimulated by people such as Toulmin (1972) and Brush (1974), and an unstoppable rush away from positivistic epistemologies occurred. More recent philosophers, such as Feyerabend (1988) and Miller (1989), argue for "realists" epistemology, and von Glasersfeld (1984) and others argue for "constructivist" epistemologies.

These parallel developments in psychology and philosophy encouraged me to take a try at synthesizing *a theory of education*. The dream I had as a graduate student in the early 1950s, that education could become more like science and be guided by theory and principles, seemed within reach. Given a sabbatical leave in 1973–1974, I had the time needed to attempt the synthesis that led to publication in 1977 of A *Theory of Education*. I had already organized a course called Theories and Methods of Education that afforded me the opportunity to share my ideas with students and visiting faculty, including the coauthors of this book, and I benefited from their criticisms, insights, and application of the *Theory*. In my view, progress in our research and instructional development programs accelerated significantly after we had a viable theoretical foundation to work from.

## A 12-YEAR LONGITUDINAL STUDY
## OF SCIENCE LEARNING

Given the "battle of paradigms" that was going on in the 1960s and 1970s, it seemed to our research group essential to determine what basic science ideas young children could understand and whether or not this understanding would facilitate future learning, as predicted from Ausubel's theory. However, my work with lower elementary school teachers as I was writing and testing science ideas in the early 1960s for our elementary science series, *The World of Science* (Novak, Meister, Knox, & Sullivan, 1966), indicated that most of these teachers did not understand or could not teach basic concepts of atoms, molecules, energy, and energy transformations, etc. Therefore, I decided to adopt an audiotutorial strategy we had developed with college botany students at Purdue University (Postlethwait, Novak, & Murray, 1964; 1972, Chapter 6) and use it to teach primary school children. An earlier sabbatical at Harvard University in 1965–1966 afforded me the time and resources to develop, evaluate, and refine several audiotutorial lessons working with first-grade (6- to 7-year-old) children. When I returned to Purdue University, we obtained some U.S. Department of Education funding through the Lafayette Public Schools and began further development, testing, and refining of audiotutorial lessons. When I moved to Cornell University in 1967, we obtained similar support through Ithaca Public Schools and also support from Shell Companies Foundations. By 1971, we had developed some 60 audiotutorial science lessons designed for children in Grades 1 and 2. Incidentally, when these lessons were placed in school learning centers rather than primary grade classrooms, even fifth- and sixth-grade students (10–12 years old) worked with the lessons with enthusiasm. Most teachers who took the time to work through the lessons found them "very enlightening."

Incidentally, our work with audiotutorial instruction in botany courses grew out of the labeled photomicrographs and other materials I developed for a Study Guide for my Ph.D. study. Postlehwait began using these photos and drawings to supplement taped comments for students who had missed lectures. Student response was so positive that he began to add lab demonstration materials and within a year, the traditional laboratory and much of the lecture material was dropped in favor of self-paced, audiotutorial study in a new "learning center" that was established in the Biology building. Hundreds of visitors came to Purdue to see the learning center in operation and Postlethwait's approach was replicated in many schools and universities around the world. Application of this instructional strategy in elementary school classrooms proved to be very successful, albeit we found we had to discourage classroom discussion led by the teacher on some topics to avoid introduction of teacher misconceptions, so prevalent at the elementary school level.

From our pool of 60+ audiotutorial lessons, we selected 28 for administration to children on a schedule of roughly one new lesson every 2 weeks. The lessons were carefully sequenced to provide for early introduction of basic concepts and progressive elaboration of these concepts in later lessons. Some modifications in lessons were made as they progressed over a 2-year period. Figure 2 shows a child working with materials in a carrel unit. Children were interviewed every 4–6 weeks to record their understanding of concepts presented. A group of 191 children were given this instruction during 1971–1973; we called this group the "instructed" group. A similar group of 48 children enrolled in the same classrooms with the same teachers, during the 1972–1974, 1 year later, did not receive the audiotutorial science lessons; we called this group the "uninstructed" group.

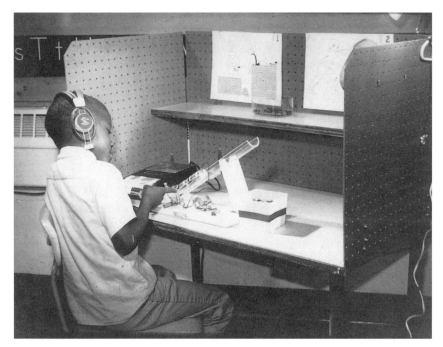

**FIGURE 2**
A 6-year-old child working in an audiotutorial carrel during our
12-year longitudinal study.

By the end of the second year of the study, when "instructed" and "uninstructed" students could be compared, it was evident that instructed students were benefiting from the lessons. After grade two, all students received instruction in science as delivered in Ithaca public schools. We did periodic interviews of both instructed and uninstructed children throughout their tenure in Ithaca schools, although for various reasons we had to limit subsequent interviews to concepts dealing with the particulate nature of matter, energy, and energy transformations.

During our first year of interviewing, we recognized the problem of interpreting interview tapes and transcriptions. Discerning patterns in changes in children's conceptual understandings from these tapes and/or transcriptions was overwhelming. We began to accumulate file drawers full of interview transcripts. It became obvious that we needed a better method or tool for representing children's cognitive structures and changes in cognitive structures. Reviewing again Ausubel's ideas and his theoretical principles, we decided to try to represent children's ideas as hierarchically organized frameworks of concepts and propositions. In short, we invented a new knowledge representation tool: *concept maps* were constructed from interview transcripts to represent the knowledge evidenced by the child. Figure 3 shows two concept maps constructed for one of our students; the upper map represents the student's knowledge in Grade 2 and the lower map represents the student's knowledge in Grade 12. It is evident that this child was learning science meaningfully and was elaborating her conceptual frameworks. Although both her Grade 2 and her Grade 12 concept maps show some misconceptions and missing concepts (e.g., the concept of space is missing in grade 12), it is evident that Cindy has been building and elaborating her knowledge of the nature of matter and energy.

From the time our first instructed children received instruction and were interviewed until the time when the last uninstructed students were interviewed in Grade 12, a period of 13 years had elapsed. Many graduate students participated in the study and both M.S. and Ph.D. students used some of the data for their thesis work. Finally, Dismas Musonda compiled data for the entire span of the study and his Ph.D. thesis served as a primary data base for a publication on the study. Because of the extraordinary nature of the study and data obtained, it was necessary to revise and resubmit the paper three times before it was accepted for publication (Novak & Musonda, 1991). In response to editorial requests, graphic presentation of the data was dropped, but one of the original figures is reproduced here in Figure 4.

Several remarkable things are shown in Figure 4. First, it is obvious that the instructed students showed fewer "naive" or invalid notions and more valid ideas than the uninstructed students. This difference was statistically highly significant and practically very important. We see that instructed students had less than half as many invalid notions and more than twice as many valid notions as uninstructed students. Furthermore, Figure 4 shows that instructed students became *progressively better*, both with regard to valid and invalid notions, but this was not the case for uninstructed students, especially from Grade 7 on when formal instruction in science began in Ithaca schools. These data strongly support the theoretical foundations for the study, namely that when powerful anchoring concepts are learned early in an educational program (Ausubel calls these "subsuming concepts"), they should provide a foundation for facilitation of later learning. Obviously this occurred. Since the instructed and uninstructed samples (by Grade 12) did not differ significantly in ability as suggested by grade-point averages and SAT scores (Novak & Musonda, 1991), the only factor that could account for the differences observed was the power of the early audiotutorial science lessons.

The content of the science lessons offered in Grades 1 and 2 was relatively abstract and certainly not commonly taught in these grades. The fact that these lessons had a highly facilitating effect on future learning indicates that they were learned meaningfully, at least for a substantial percentage of the students. Clearly these results cannot be explained with either behavioral theory (there was very limited reinforcement and rehearsal of ideas) or Piagetian

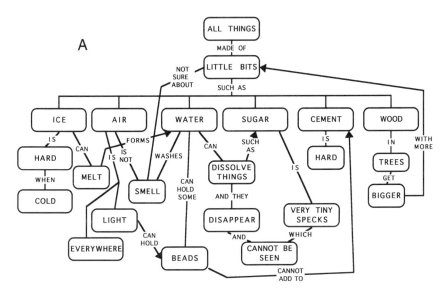

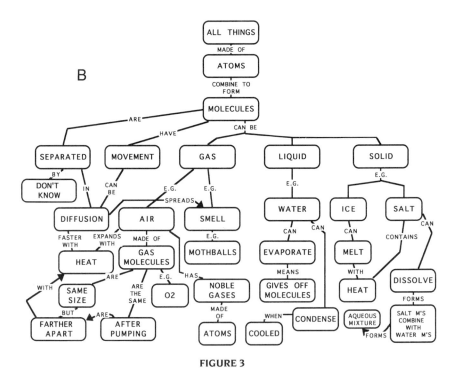

**FIGURE 3**

Concept maps showing changes in a child's understanding of the
particulate nature of matter from Grade 2 (A) to Grade 12 (B).

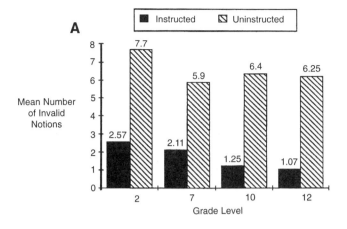

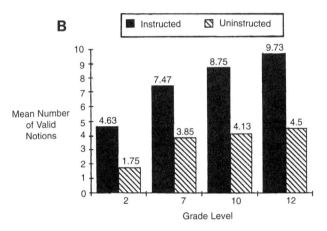

**FIGURE 4**

Bar graphs showing the frequencies with which "instructed" students (grey bars) and "uninstructed" (dark bars) evidenced naive notions about the structure of matter (A) and valid notions. Note that only the instructed students show continuous improvement over the years.

theory, which posits little success with abstract science concepts at ages six to eight (see, for example, Shayer & Adey, 1981). The results are consistent with results from more recent studies such as those of Matthews (1980) and Carey (1985). Our 12-year-study, the only one of its kind reported to date, clearly indicated that our program was on the right track, both theoretically and in terms of practical consequences for education.

It has been common in the sciences that the necessity for developing new tools for making or processing records obtained in research have led to practical applications. For example, development of oscilloscopes to study and record electromagnetic wave patterns led to the development of television. In an analogous manner, the concept mapping tool, as we developed it, proved to be a useful tool in many education applications. First, making concept maps from interviews has permitted us and others to observe specific changes in learners' cognitive structures with relative ease and a degree of precision that was not possible by reviewing interview recordings or transcripts alone. They are useful for identifying and remediating misconceptions or "alternative conceptions" (Novak & Musonda, 1991; Wandersee, Mintzes, & Novak, 1994; Mintzes, Wandersee & Novak, 1997). Subsequently, we and others have found that interviews in any knowledge domain can be better interpreted using concept maps, including interviews with consumers, patients, or counselors. Second, concept maps can help learners organize subject matter and facilitate learning and recall of any subject matter (Novak & Gowin, 1984; Novak & Wandersee, 1990). Third, concept maps can be a valuable evaluation tool—one I have used extensively in my own classes (Novak & Ridley, 1988). Fourth, they can be useful for teachers and other educators for organizing and planning instructional material (Symington & Novak, 1982; Novak, 1991). Fifth, they can identify cognitive-affective relationships that can be enormously helpful in counseling settings (Mazur, 1989). Sixth, they help in team building and reaching consensus on project goals and objectives (Edmondson, 1995). Seventh, they can enhance creative production, since creativity requires well-organized knowledge structures and an emotional proclivity to seek new interrelationships between diverse domains of knowledge. These and other applications of the concept mapping tool have had a major impact on our programs, including recent applications in corporate settings. Other knowledge representation tools will be discussed in Chapter 4.

## DEVELOPMENT OF THE VEE HEURISTIC

Much of our research dealt with instruction in science laboratories. A continuing problem observed was that students often proceeded through the laboratory work doing what was prescribed in the laboratory manual, but often not understanding *why* they were doing what they were doing nor what the meaning of their records, graphs, tables, charts had for understanding better the science they were studying. My colleague, Bob Gowin, had found this to be the case in other disciplines as well. Gowin's PhD work was in philosophy, and he maintained a strong commitment to understanding the structure of knowledge and the process of knowledge creation. Gowin (1970, 1981) first proposed five questions that need to be answered to understand the structure of knowledge expressed in any work:

1. *The telling question*. What is the telling question of the work?
2. *The key concepts. Conceptual structure*. What are the key concepts?
3. *Methods*. What methods were used to answer the telling question?
4. *Knowledge claims*. What are the major claims in the work?
5. *Value claims*. What value claims are made in the work?   (1981, p. 88)

These questions proved useful to our students in analyzing research papers or other documents and for interpreting laboratory work. However, the latter required that more attention was needed on the events or objects observed and on other epistemological elements such as the philosophy or epistemology guiding the inquiry and the "world views" held by the inquirer. In 1977, Gowin conceived a new way to represent all of the elements and to suggest their interrelationships. He created the "Knowledge Vee." This gradually underwent some modifications, and Figure 5 shows our current form of the Vee heuristic as used in our current work and definitions for 12 elements involved in the structure and creation of knowledge.

We proceeded to use concept maps and the Vee heuristic in many of our research studies and to aid in the design of instruction. While most students, teachers, and professors immediately see value in concept maps, it has been our observation that the Vee heuristic is more difficult to grasp. One reason for this may be that most of us are brought up in patterns of thinking about knowledge and knowledge discovery that are primarily positivistic in character. The highly fluid, complex process of knowledge creation represented in the Vee can at first be overwhelming. With time and effort, however, we have found that the value of the Vee heuristic is recognized and concept maps are seen as useful to represent some aspects of the Vee, namely the structure of concepts and principles guiding the inquiry (or the "left side") and the structure of knowledge and value claims (on the "right side"). I know of no other heuristic tool for representing the structure of knowledge, and I would predict that in 20 to 30 years, it may become more widely used in schools and corporations.

## LEARNING HOW TO LEARN

While writing the draft of A *Theory of Education*, I organized a new course, "Learning To Learn." Initially I thought the course would be appropriate for freshman and sophomore students, but mostly juniors and seniors enrolled. We had also found in earlier work with a special program for freshmen that very few Cornell students think they have problems learning. For the most part, they achieved predominantly A grades in their high school work, and even in most courses taken by freshmen. It is not until their sophomore or junior years at Cornell University, when they take courses where rote memorization will not suffice to get A grades, that students realize they must either

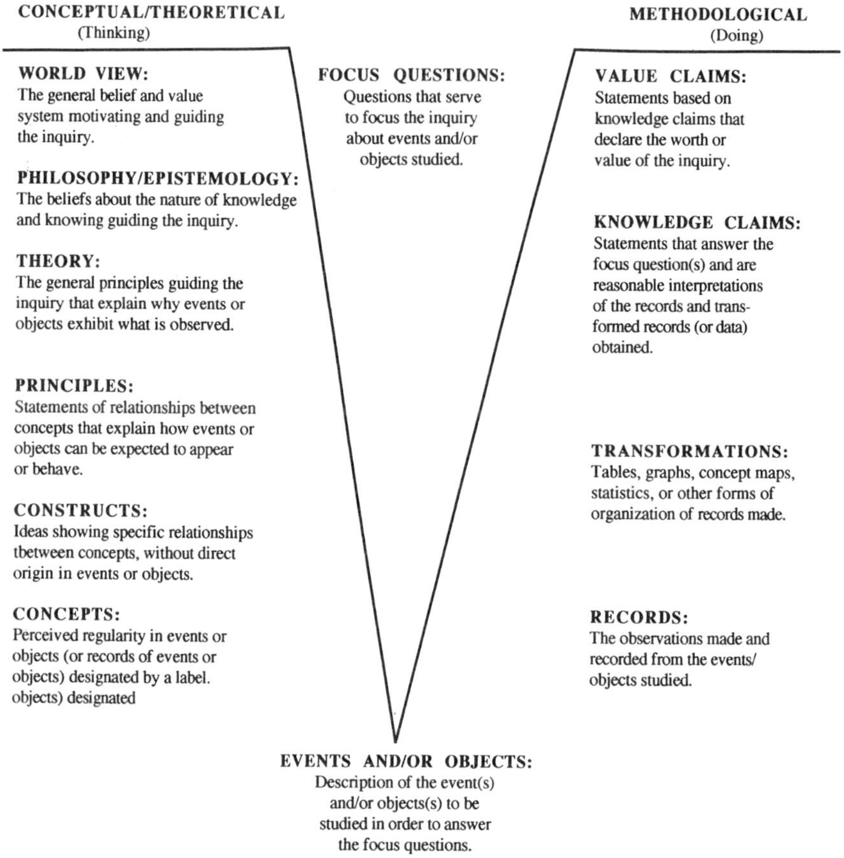

CONCEPTUAL/THEORETICAL                                              METHODOLOGICAL
(Thinking)                                                              (Doing)

**WORLD VIEW:**
The general belief and value
system motivating and guiding
the inquiry.

**FOCUS QUESTIONS:**
Questions that serve
to focus the inquiry
about events and/or
objects studied.

**VALUE CLAIMS:**
Statements based on
knowledge claims that
declare the worth or
value of the inquiry.

**PHILOSOPHY/EPISTEMOLOGY:**
The beliefs about the nature of knowledge
and knowing guiding the inquiry.

**KNOWLEDGE CLAIMS:**
Statements that answer the
focus question(s) and are
reasonable interpretations
of the records and trans-
formed records (or data)
obtained.

**THEORY:**
The general principles guiding the
inquiry that explain why events or
objects exhibit what is observed.

**PRINCIPLES:**
Statements of relationships between
concepts that explain how events or
objects can be expected to appear
or behave.

**TRANSFORMATIONS:**
Tables, graphs, concept maps,
statistics, or other forms of
organization of records made.

**CONSTRUCTS:**
Ideas showing specific relationships
tbetween concepts, without direct
origin in events or objects.

**CONCEPTS:**
Perceived regularity in events or
objects (or records of events or
objects) designated by a label.
objects) designated

**RECORDS:**
The observations made and
recorded from the events/
objects studied.

**EVENTS AND/OR OBJECTS:**
Description of the event(s)
and/or objects(s) to be
studied in order to answer
the focus questions.

**FIGURE 5**

Gowin's Vee showing key epistemological elements that are involved in the
construction or description of new knowledge. All elements interact with
one another in the process of constructing new knowledge or value claims
or in seeking understanding of these for any set of events and questions.

be less able than they thought they were before or they must be doing
something wrong in their studies.

At first, many of the students who enrolled in "Learning to Learn" were
essentially seeking better tricks for memorizing, taking notes, and preparing
for exams. They wanted a "quick fix" for their declining grade point average.
They were not looking for a course that would help them develop new ways
of learning and new insights into the nature of knowledge. The dropout rate
the first year or two from my course was about 30%. Most of those students
who persisted ended the semester with a new sense of empowerment over
their own learning. It was not uncommon for students to tell me they never

knew there was another way to learn other than rote memorization. They were grateful to me for "turning their lives around" as they gained skill and confidence in *meaningful* learning, aided, in part, by concept mapping and Vee diagramming tools. In 20 years of teaching this course, I never had a single student who completed the course who failed to gain skill and confidence in their ability to learn meaningfully. Some admitted they would continue to learn by rote in some courses—courses that were poorly taught or courses that held little interest for them. Many in later years have written to tell me that their high success in graduate studies would have been unlikely without "Learning To Learn."

The sorry fact is that Cornell University students are among the very best high school graduates. And yet, most of them have done most of their previous learning largely by rote. Studies of student learning approaches in this country and abroad have shown that similar patterns prevail in other countries (see Chapter 5). The result is that students may graduate from both high school and university, and yet very little of what they memorized is functional knowledge. For example, in a widely circulated video tape, A *Private Universe*, graduating seniors, graduate students, and faculty were asked to explain why we have seasons. Twenty-one of 23 persons interviewed at random could not give a satisfactory explanation—including one graduating senior who had just recently completed a course, "The Physics of Planetary Motion"! Obviously he had been learning almost totally by rote, as may have been the case for many others interviewed. The universality and pervasiveness of rote-mode learning patterns in schools and universities is astonishing, given our current knowledge of the limited value of such learning. As Pogo has said, "We have met the enemy, and the enemy is us"! Forty years after my own disappointing school learning experiences, I find that, for the most part, not much has changed. Why? What can be done about it? These remain nagging questions.

Although research on the value of the Vee heuristic for facilitating learning is not as extensive as that on the value of concept maps, our data indicates that secondary school and university students can benefit from using this tool (Novak, Gowin, & Johansen, 1983). Figure 6 illustrates how the question of "Why do we have seasons?" can be thought through using the Vee and associated concept maps. An interesting research project might be to assess the value of this kind of instruction in elementary, secondary, and/or college classroom setting.

There is hope for improvement of education in the future. I take heart in the fact that *Learning How To Learn* at this writing has been published in nine languages with other translations projected. The ideas and strategies that will be presented in this book are slowly taking hold, not only in the U.S. but also in countries around the world. The 350+ graduate students and visiting professors who have done theses or worked with me are everywhere in the world, and their students and their students' students (my "intellectual great grandchildren") continue to multiply and add their efforts to the slow pro-

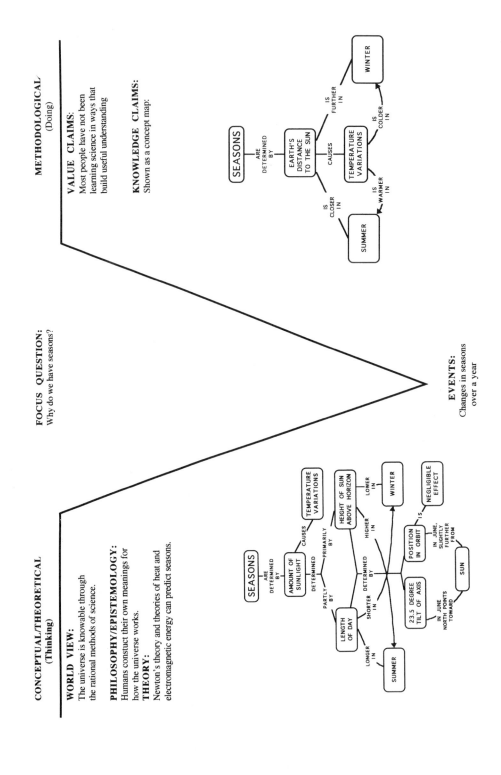

**CONCEPTUAL/THEORETICAL**
(Thinking)

**WORLD VIEW:**
The universe is knowable through the rational methods of science.

**PHILOSOPHY/EPISTEMOLOGY:**
Humans construct their own meanings for how the universe works.

**THEORY:**
Newton's theory and theories of heat and electromagnetic energy can predict seasons.

**FOCUS QUESTION:**
Why do we have seasons?

**METHODOLOGICAL**
(Doing)

**VALUE CLAIMS:**
Most people have not been learning science in ways that build useful understanding

**KNOWLEDGE CLAIMS:**
Shown as a concept map:

SEASONS — ARE DETERMINED BY — EARTH'S DISTANCE TO THE SUN — IS FURTHER IN — WINTER

EARTH'S DISTANCE TO THE SUN — CAUSES — TEMPERATURE VARIATIONS

TEMPERATURE VARIATIONS — IS COLDER IN — WINTER

EARTH'S DISTANCE TO THE SUN — IS CLOSER IN — SUMMER

TEMPERATURE VARIATIONS — IS WARMER IN — SUMMER

**EVENTS:**
Changes in seasons over a year

SEASONS — ARE DETERMINED BY — AMOUNT OF SUNLIGHT — CAUSES — TEMPERATURE VARIATIONS

AMOUNT OF SUNLIGHT — DETERMINED PRIMARILY BY — HEIGHT OF SUN ABOVE HORIZON

AMOUNT OF SUNLIGHT — PARTLY BY — LENGTH OF DAY

HEIGHT OF SUN ABOVE HORIZON — LOWER IN — WINTER

HEIGHT OF SUN ABOVE HORIZON — HIGHER IN / DETERMINED BY — POSITION IN ORBIT

POSITION IN ORBIT — IS — NEGLIGIBLE EFFECT

POSITION IN ORBIT — IN JUNE, SLIGHTLY FURTHER FROM — SUN

LENGTH OF DAY — SHORTER IN — WINTER

LENGTH OF DAY — LONGER IN — SUMMER

23.5 DEGREE TILT OF AXIS — IN JUNE NORTH POINTS TOWARD — SUN cess of educational reform. Thousands of others who embrace similar ideas are pushing for educational change, changes that move learners from the disempowering effects of rote learning to the empowering consequences of rich, meaningful learning.

For me, another source of optimism for future improvement of education is my belief that the theoretical foundations for education are improving. The growing consensus on the validity of constructivist epistemological ideas and cognitive learning principles suggest that the science education community and the education community in general are moving forward (Linn, 1987). My efforts to synthesize epistemological ideas and psychological ideas as they relate to the construction of knowledge were first published in 1987. Both disciplinary and personal knowledge is acquired through *Human Constructivism*. Further discussion of these ideas will be offered in Chapter 2.

Although we have been working with professors to apply the Vee heuristic and concept mapping to their research work for more than a decade, our first systematic effort to study the value of the Vee and concept maps as a tools to facilitate research and new knowledge creation began in 1993. We were fortunate to enlist the cooperation of Professor Richard Zobel who headed the "Rhizobotany group," a research group at Cornell University focused on the understanding of roots and root functions. Some of the preliminary findings were that even experienced researchers in the group had only a sketchy knowledge of the overall intellectual activities of the group. Concept maps and Vee diagrams helped the group see where individual projects contributed to broader research questions. Some of the researchers evidenced little knowledge of, or interest in, epistemological issues. A preliminary report on this work has been published (Novak & Iuli, 1995).

I began a revision of A *Theory of Education* during my sabbatical in 1987–1988, but pressures of other work required that I set this aside. During my sabbatical in 1994–1995, I resumed work on this manuscript; however, our research studies between sabbaticals and the initiation of work with corporations (described below) led me to restructure substantially the earlier work and to write essentially a new book. With the title "Learning, Creating, and Using Knowledge: Concept Maps as Facilitative Tools in Schools and Corporations" (Novak, in press), the manuscript is currently in production with Lawrence Erlbaum Associates, Inc. I believe this new book can provide a useful foundation for improvements in education in any field and in any context. In addition, this book, of which you are now reading the first chapter, should contribute to the improvement of science education.

---

**FIGURE 6**

A vee diagram for the question "Why do we have seasons?", showing a concept map on the left side that depicts a valid knowledge structure held by scientists and a concept map on the right side illustrating the typical knowledge structure held by children and adults.

## MY THIRD CAREER—HELPING
## CORPORATIONS LEARN

For some two decades, I have had occasional students with experience in business and had participated in meetings and seminars with persons from the business world. While I found individuals who saw the relevance of our work to business, they were predominantly from lower ranks in business organizations and their efforts to introduce the ideas and tools generally met with quick dismissal by upper-level management. In 1991, Alan McAdams, Professor in the Cornell Johnson School of Business and Management, invited me to coteach a course with him in the business school. For some years he had been an enthusiast of concept mapping, and he wanted to learn more about education. I was eager to learn more about business and the corporate world. We enjoyed good success with our new course (it received the highest student ratings for any course in the School) and taught it again in 1992. Most of the students were MBA candidates with 6 to 8 years of experience in the business world. As part of the course project activities, we worked with for-profit and not-for-profit organizations, using concept mapping and Vee diagrams as tools to better understand the structure and function of the organizations.

What we found was that all of the organizations studied had some serious problems in one or more of the following areas: personnel knowledge about the "mission" or strategic plan of the organization, functioning of individual units, barriers to communication, and failue or limited ability to learn as an organization. Both McAdams and I were struck by the energy and enthusiasm of our students for the work we were doing, but also by the resistance of most of the organizations to the implications of the findings from our studies. One thing became eminently clear to me: nonprofit and for-profit corporations *could* benefit significantly by applying ideas from A *Theory of Education* and *Learning How To Learn*. The problem was finding an organization with the right leadership to demonstrate the value of the tools and ideas.

There is the saying, "Nothing is more unstoppable than an idea whose time has come." Something very important has happened in the business world in the past decade—*globalization*. While it is true that worldwide trade has been part of the business world at least since prehistoric times, new transportation, communication, and other technologies have evolved to the point where almost any product can be made almost anywhere and shipped at relatively low cost everywhere. Suddenly, U.S. and other nation's businesses have found themselves head to head in competition with businesses all over the globe. In 1988, Prestowitz observed, in *Trading Places: How We Are Giving Our Future To Japan and How To Reclaim It*, that although the United States was once the economic giant of the world, we were rapidly giving this position to Japan. While he placed much of the blame on poor trade policies with Japan and other countries, there were other problems facing corporate America. Peter Senge (1990), Marshall and Tucker (1992), and Peter Drucker (1993) were among the business sages who were saying business will not get better until American corporations become better at learning and better at creating new knowledge. Nonaka and Takiuchi's (1995) book *The Knowledge Creating Company: How Japanese Companies Create the Dynamics of Innovations* has been "required reading" for many corporate executives.

Fortuitously, I had the opportunity in June of 1993 to meet an executive of a major U.S. corporation who was seeking "better tools" to facilitate research and development work. I held my first meeting with a research team in late December, 1993. The consensus was that concept mapping and the ideas I presented could be of value to Corporate R & D work. Another meeting was held in April, 1994, and gradually the number of scheduled meetings increased. I was faced with a difficult decision: Should I continue in the secure position of full professor at Cornell University and pursue only token efforts to apply our ideas in the corporate world or should I resign from Cornell and free myself to pursue my hunch that a better way for me to improve education in schools and universities may be to improve education and knowledge creation in corporations? I chose in July, 1995 to pursue my hunch.

So far, so good. At this writing, the receptivity and application of tools and ideas with at least one corporation has been accelerating. The "pilot programs" we have run show promise and have probably contributed to some new product development. As with all R & D work involving teams, it is difficult to assign value to one individual's contribution or to which strategies led to success. In the end, the *value* of our work will have to be a subjective judgment. There are some criteria that are empirical in nature, e.g., the number of members of research teams who ascribe significant value to concept mapping and related ideas, and this kind of data is being gathered. At this writing it is too early to be explicit in our knowledge claims regarding the value of metacognitive tools in corporate settings, but the overwhelming reaction has been positive.

Unfortunately, the necessity for confidentiality prevents me from discussing specific projects we have done and the kind of outcomes that have been derived from these projects. In time, this information can and will be released. It is also my hope that we can gather the best evidence possible in an enterprise that is not focused on research. If we can demonstrate significant gains using metacognitive tools to aid in improving the production of new knowledge and the use of knowledge in the corporate setting, one thing is certain. Global competitive pressures will require that almost all corporations must move to employ our strategies or similar strategies. The time frame for this to occur is a matter of years, not decades or centuries.

## CONTINUING THE PURSUIT OF A DREAM

There is much more to be done. At best, a very small fraction of learners in our world are engaged in predominantly meaningful learning practices, whether in schools, universities, or workplaces. While I remain skeptical of data that suggest American students are improving in their "critical thinking skills," there is a growing recognition that something is wrong with the way many students are being taught and the learning patterns that result from this. See, for example, the many research papers on student misconceptions available via Internet (Novak & Abrams, 1994). Probably no science educator in touch with the research believes that to be effective, all a teacher (or textbook) needs to do is to present the "facts." The extent to which learner- and teacher-held epistemologies influence the quality of learning is still recognized by only a minority of educators, but this situation appears to be improving rapidly. Just in the past 10 days while writing this chapter, I have been contacted for help by six researchers in the U.S. and other countries who are centering their research on questions of the relationship of learner epistemologies and success in meaningful learning.

So positive changes are occurring. I believe that if corporate America, and the corporate world in general, move to employ new ideas on knowledge creation and knowledge utilization, the entire process may accelerate enormously. For one thing, corporations may have the incentive—good profits at best and survival at the least—to move ahead in applying new educative tools and ideas. They could bring enormous resources, and their own examples, to bear on these problems—resources measured in the hundreds of *billions* of dollars! These long-term self-interests require that they help schools and colleges improve their educational practices. They can bring their resources to bear on current problems and needed educational innovations. These are revolutionary times in the business world, and this will, in due course, require, and help to bring about, revolutionary changes in education. This, I predict, shall happen in the next 20 years or so—about half of the time of my career in education. These are exciting times for educators and learners!

We cannot, however, rely on corporations to do the basic research needed to understand more effective ways to teach science and to educate science teachers. Most likely, these studies will be done in schools, colleges, and universities. There is now tremendous opportunities for young scholars who choose to pursue such work. It is to these people, especially the "new generation" of scholars, we hope this book can serve as a "handbook" of fundamental ideas and research approaches.

# References

Anderson, K. E. (1949). *The relative achievement of the objectives of secondary school science in a representative sample of fifty-six Minnesota schools.* Minneapolis: University of Minnesota, Unpublished dissertation.

Ausubel, D. P. (1963). *The psychology of meaningful verbal learning.* New York: Grune and Stratton.

Ausubel, D. P. (1968). *Educational psychology: A cognitive view.* New York: Holt, Rinehart and Winston.

Ausubel, D. P., Novak, J. D., & Hanesian, H. (1978). *Educational psychology: A cognitive view,* 2nd Ed. New York: Holt, Rinehart and Winston.

Bartlett, F. C. (1932). *Remembering.* Cambridge, UK: Cambridge University Press.

Bartlett, F. C. (1958). *Thinking: An experimental and social study.* London, UK: G. Allen.

Brooks, M. E., & Baker, W. N. (1957). A study of academic preparation of the secondary science teachers of Kansas. *The Science Teacher,* 24 (October), 277–280.

Brush, S. G. (1974). Should the history of science be rated X? *Science,* 183(4130), 1164–1172.

Carey, S. (1985). *Conceptual change in childhood.* Cambridge, MA: The MIT Press.

Conant, J. B. (1947). *On understanding science.* New Haven, CT: Yale University Press.

Drucker, P. F. (1993). *Post-capitalist society.* New York: HarperCollins Publishers, Inc.

Edmondson, K. M. (1995). Concept mapping for the development of medical curricula. *Journal of Research in Science Teaching,* 32(7), 777–793.

Feyerabend, P. (1988). *Against method.* London, UK: Verso.

Gowin, D. B. (1970). The structure of knowledge. *Educational Theory,* 20(4), 319–328.

Gowin, D. B. (1981). *Educating.* Ithaca, NY: Cornell University Press.

Hilgard, E. R. (1948). *Theories of learning.* Englewood Cliffs, NJ: Prentice-Hall.

Kuhn, T. (1962). *The structure of scientific revolutions.* International Encyclopedia of Unified Science, 2nd. ed. enlarged Vols. 1 and 2: Foundations of the University of Science, Vol. 2, No. 2. Chicago, IL: University of Chicago Press.

Linn, H. (1987). Establishing a research base for science education: Challenges, trends and recommendations. *Journal of Research in Science Teaching,* 24(3), 191–216.

Mager, R. F. (1962). *Preparing objectives for programmed instruction.* San Francisco, CA: Fearon.

Marshall, R., & Tucker, M. (1992). *Thinking for a living: Education and the wealth of nations.* New York: Basic Books.

Matthews, G. B. (1980). *Philosophy & the young child.* Cambridge, MA: Harvard University Press.

Mazur, J. N. (1989). *Using concept maps in therapy with substance abusers in the context of Gowin's theory of educating.* Ithaca, NY: Cornell University, Department of Education. Unpublished masters thesis.

Miller, R. W. (1989). *Fact and method: Explanation, confirmation and reality in the natural and the social sciences.* Princeton, NJ: Princeton University Press.

Mintzes, J., Wandersee, J., & Novak, J. D. (1997). Meaningful learning in science: The human constructivist perspective. In G. D. Phye (Ed.), *Handbook of academic learning.* Orlando, FL: Academic Press.

Nonaka, I., & Takiuchi, H. (1995). *The knowledge creating company: How Japanese companies create the dynamics of innovations.* Oxford, UK: Oxford University Press.

Novak, J. D. (1958). An experimental comparison of a conventional and a project centered method of teaching a college general botany course. *Journal of Experimental Education,* 26(March), 217–230.

Novak, J. D. (1961). The use of labeled photomicrographs in teaching college general botany. *Science Education,* 45(3), 122–131.

Novak, J. D. (1963). What should we teach in biology? NABT *News and Views* 7(2), 1. Reprinted in *Journal of Research in Science Teaching* 1(3), 241–243.

Novak, J. D., Meister, M., Knox, W. W., and Sullivan, O. W. (1996). *The world of science series.* Indianapolis, IN: Bobbs-Merrill.

Novak, J. D. (1977a). A theory of education. Ithaca, NY: Cornell University Press.

Novak, J. D. (1977b). An alternative to Piagetian psychology for science and mathematics education. Science Education, 61(4), 453–477.

Novak, J. D. (1991). Clarify with concept maps. The Science Teacher, 58(7), 45–49.

Novak, J. D. (1995). Concept mapping to facilitate teaching and learning. Prospects, 25(1), 79–86.

Novak, J. D., & Abrams, R. (eds.). (1993). Proceedings of the third international seminar on misconceptions and educational strategies in science and mathematics (August 1–4). Published electronically, Internet. Access: http://www2.ucsc.edu/mlrg

Novak, J. D., & Brooks, M. E. (1959). College preparation of science teachers. The Science Teacher, 26(7), 473–477.

Novak, J. D., & Gowin, D. B. (1984). Learning How To Learn. Cambridge, UK: Cambridge University Press.

Novak, J. D., & Iuli, R. I. (1995). Meaningful learning as the foundation for constructivist epistemology. In F. Finley, D. Allchin, D. Rhees, & F. Fifield (Eds.), Proceedings of the Third International History, Philosophy and Science Teaching Conference, Vol. 2 (pp. 873–896).

Novak, J. D., & Musonda, D. (1991). A twelve-year longitudinal study of science concept learning. American Educational Research Journal, 28(1), 117–153.

Novak, J. D., & Ridley, D. R. (1988). Assessing Student learning in Light of How Students Learn. Washington, DC: The American Association for Higher Education Assessment Forum.

Novak, J. D., & Wandersee, J. (1990). Co-Editors of Special Issue: Perspectives on Concept Mapping, Journal of Research in Science Teaching, Vol. 27(10).

Novak, J. D., Gowin, D. B., & Johansen, G. T. (1983). The use of concept mapping and knowledge Vee mapping with junior high school science students. Science Education, 67(5), 625–645.

Postlethwait, S. N., Novak, J. D., & Murray, H. (1964). The Integrated Experience Approach to Teaching Botany. Minneapolis, MN: Burgess.

Postlethwait, S. N., Novak, J. D., & Murray, H. (1972). The Audio-Tutorial Approach to Learning Through Independent Study and Integrated Experience, 3rd ed. Minneapolis, MN: Burgess.

Prestowitz, C. V., Jr. (1988). Trading Places: How We Are Giving Our Future to Japan and How To Reclaim It. New York: Basic Books.

Senge, P. M. (1990). The Fifth Discipline: The Art & Practice of the Learning Organization. New York: Doubleday/Currency.

Shayer, M., & Adey, P. (1981). Towards a Science of Science Teaching: Cognitive Development and Curriculum Demand. London, UK: Heinemann Educational Books.

Symington, D., & Novak, J. D. (1982). Teaching children how to learn. The Educational Magazine, 39(5), 13–16 (Australian).

Toulmin, S. (1972). Human understanding, Vol. 1: The collective use and evolution of concepts. Princeton, NJ: Princeton University Press.

von Glasersfeld, E. (1984). An introduction to radical constructivism. In P. Waxlawick (ed.), The Invented Reality (pp. 17–40). New York: Norton.

Wandersee, J. H., Mintzes, J. J., & Novak, J. D. (1994). Learning: Alternative conceptions. In Gabel, D. L. (ed.), Handbook on research in science teaching (pp. 177–210). A project of the National Science Teachers Association. New York: Macmillan.

Weiner, N. (1948). Cybernetics. New York: Wiley.

Weiner, N. (1954). The human use of human beings, 2nd ed. Garden City, NY: Doubleday.

# CHAPTER 2

# Reform and Innovation in Science Teaching: A Human Constructivist View

JOEL J. MINTZES
*University of North Carolina—Wilmington*

JAMES H. WANDERSEE
*Louisiana State University*

In some ways the decade of the 1990s has been an unsettling period for science teachers, occasioned by major new curricular proposals and innovative teaching strategies that promise substantial change in the coming years. But science education is no stranger to change. In fact, the history of science education in the United States is characterized by large-scale, recurring, and at times disruptive and detrimental shifts in curricular emphases and instructional practices at the elementary and secondary school levels (DeBoer, 1991; Duschl, 1990; Hurd, 1961; Montgomery, 1994). Typically these shifts reflect a response to some real or imagined threat posed by domestic or international circumstances in the political, social, economic, or military arenas. Although science teachers have not shouldered the entire burden of these external forces alone, they have suffered more disruption than others because of the acknowledged role of science and technology in service to the national defense and welfare.

How should the reflective science teacher respond as these external forces exert their powerful influence in the classroom? Are we obligated to blindly implement curricula and instructional strategies that we suspect are unproven and possibly ill conceived? What tools or resources do we have at our disposal to help us identify potentially useful practices in science education? Must we rely on our experience and intuition alone or do we have access to something more robust?

In this chapter we describe the origins of a Human Constructivist model of science teaching which can serve as an alternative to the hunches, guesses, and folklore that have guided our profession for over 100 years. In our view, understanding the historical and sociocultural contexts of reform and innovation in science teaching and recognizing the external forces that impact classroom practice are vital components of a professional education. But simply recognizing these forces is insufficient, teachers must be empowered with a framework of useful ideas and practical tools if they are to manage change wisely. Within the framework of a Human Constructivist view of learning, we hope to help science teachers empower themselves with state-of-the-art knowledge of theory, research, and practice. It is to these ends that this book is dedicated.

## RESTRUCTURING SCIENCE EDUCATION: THE PRE-SPUTNIK YEARS

As the decade of the nineties winds to a close, science teachers have been confronted by a host of new proposals aimed at "restructuring" the profession. Widely disseminated reports authored by nationally prominent scientists and educators have suggested a need to rethink the curriculum and reconsider a host of common practices classroom teachers have employed for years (American Association for the Advancement of Science, 1993; National Research Council, 1996; National Science Teachers Association, 1992). How should science teachers respond to these reform efforts?

In our view the primary responsibilities of the science teacher are to understand these calls for reform, to assess the motivations and objectives of reform leaders in historical and social context, and to evaluate the proposed changes in terms of their likely impact on student learning. In the final analysis our "bottom line" should focus on the extent to which any new proposal enhances *understanding* and *conceptual change* in the science classroom. To fail in these responsibilities is to relinquish control of our profession to others.

Recent historical work (DeBoer, 1991; Duschl, 1990; Montgomery, 1994) suggests that many of the reform efforts of the past 125 years have been driven by forces lying outside the teacher's traditional domain. Broad-based social forces buffeting the science curriculum include massive immigration waves, urbanization, military competition, struggles for ethnic and gender equity, and, most recently, economic survival. These forces have resulted in a cycle of change that pits proponents of the "academist" and "practicalist" traditions in American education against each other (Montgomery, 1994).

The effects of these cyclical struggles have been felt most directly in the kind of learning that dominates the science classroom.

In the years following the Civil War, science had not yet achieved a secure place in the American college curriculum which was heavily skewed toward classical studies, language, rhetoric, history, mathematics, and the arts. At the secondary school level science teaching, where it existed at all, was dominated by textbooks, rote learning, and recitation. A small number of lower schools experimented with ideas borrowed from influential Swiss and German thinkers, including Pestalozzi, Froebel, and Herbart, who emphasized the natural development of "mental faculties" through the study of common physical objects such as leaves, rocks, and insects. This focus ultimately became formalized in "object lessons," a type of teaching that stressed observation, direct manipulation, and even a certain level of experimentation.

During the decades of the 1870s and 1880s, with the rise of industry and technology and the rapid influx of semiskilled workers into the cities, our most prestigious colleges and universities gradually moved away from classical studies and came to embrace a broader curriculum that included aspects of the natural sciences. The Morrill Act of 1862 established land grant colleges that came to symbolize the use of "scientific knowledge" to solve agricultural and technological problems. Public enthusiasm for science and technology was reinforced by popular discussion of evolution and natural history led by luminaries such as Harvard's Louis Agassiz and later by Herbert Spencer. Seeking to offer technological solutions to urban and industrial problems, several institutions—notably Yale and Johns Hopkins—quickly expanded the study of science into full-fledged graduate programs modeled largely after those of the German university system. The growth of science in the colleges and universities ultimately became the single most important stimulus to science education at the elementary and secondary school levels.

As university-level science established itself, pressure grew to standardize college admissions policies and soon blue-ribbon committees were sought to formulate rigorous college preparatory programs at the high school level. In 1892 the National Education Association appointed a committee composed of university presidents and secondary school principals to examine "the proper limits" of secondary school subjects and "the best methods of instruction, the most desirable allotment of time . . . and the best methods of testing the pupils' attainment therein . . ." (National Education Association, 1893). The Committee of Ten, as it came to be called, was chaired by Harvard President Charles W. Elliot and was dominated by academic leaders that included the U.S. Commissioner of Education and the heads of several other prestigious institutions, including the University of Michigan and Vassar College, among others. A scientist by training, Elliot took particular interest in the work of the three conferences devoted to natural history, physics and chemistry, and the earth sciences. The conferences operated as subcommittees and were substantially controlled by disciplinary experts in the natural sciences.

The initial report of the conferences included a resolution that fully 25% of the high school curriculum be devoted to the formal study of natural science, a proportion that dropped to 20% in the final report of the Committee. The recommendations called for a rigorous introduction to virtually all branches of science over a 4-year period and strongly supported such innovations as double laboratory periods, Saturday morning laboratories, and extensive field trips; all designed to ensure that first-hand experience with natural phenomena replace the "book science" that had come to dominate secondary school instruction. Additionally the conference members strongly condemned classroom practices that encouraged rote learning and meaningless recitation.

The final report of the Committee of Ten is one of the most remarkable documents in the history of American education. It represents the first time that university-based scientists contributed substantially to the emerging debate on what schools teach and how they teach it. The sample "courses" suggested by the Committee offered a strong disciplinary view of science that stressed the structure of knowledge and the nature of scientific inquiry. The report was widely discussed among public school leaders; ultimately, however, its influence was short lived. It soon became apparent that the objectives of the Committee, to prepare students for further work at the nation's best colleges and universities, were largely antithetical to the goals of those who ran the public schools. The latter included a newly emergent group of professional educators who occupied principalships, superintendencies, and chairs in recently established university departments of pedagogy.

The Progressive movement in American schooling originated in the writings of several widely respected educators around the turn of the century; prominent among them were John Dewey (1899) and Francis Wayland Parker (1895), who in turn were strongly influenced by the work of the Prussian pioneer of experimental psychology Wilhelm Wundt and the Italian advocate of "child-centered" learning Maria Montessori. The Progressive movement itself encompassed a widely divergent and often contradictory set of guiding principles; foremost among them were the notions of "usefulness and vocational training" promoted primarily by Dewey and Parker and "efficiency" heralded by advocates of "scientific management and testing" such as G. Stanley Hall, Edward Thorndike, and Louis Terman. The common view among these reformers was the perceived need to create a curriculum that served social needs and met the practical demands of a growing workforce engaged primarily in manufacturing and industrial pursuits.

Ultimately these forces were given voice in a second remarkable document, the report of the Commission on the Reorganization of Secondary Education (National Education Association, 1918). In short, the report recommended a curriculum that focused on "the application of knowledge to the activities of life, rather than primarily in terms of the demands of any subject as a logically organized science." The goal of "complete and worthy living for all youth" was embodied in a set of seven "Cardinal Principles" that were to serve as the guiding elements of the curriculum. These elements included: health; command of fundamental processes (i.e., subject matter knowledge); worthy home membership; vocation; citizenship; worthy use of leisure; and ethical character. The Committee on Science, headed by Otis W. Caldwell of Columbia University Teachers College, supported a curriculum that focused on the application of scientific knowledge to problems of everyday life such as public sanitation, personal hygiene, the function and repair of electrical appliances, industrial and household chemistry, photography, and practical aspects of nature study.

In summary, over a brief span of some 25 years (1893 to 1918) the most well-regarded association of professional educators, the NEA, had presented two authoritative documents that offered vastly divergent, even antithetical visions of secondary school science. Although the recommendations of the Progressivists would never be fully implemented, they nonetheless held strong sway in curricular decisions for almost 40 years, culminating ultimately in the "Life Adjustment" movement of the 1940s and 1950s.

In retrospect two substantially unrelated events, the first hardly noticed outside the circle of professional educators and the second widely reported, point to 1957 as a signal year in American science education. The first event was the death of the exceedingly influential journal *Progressive Education*, the official organ of the Progressive Education Association. This event among several others sent an unmistakeable message to tenacious adherents that the era of "Life Adjustment" was over. The second was the successful launch of the Soviet spacecraft Sputnik, which occurred on October 4th. To many in the science education community the Soviet achievement became one of only a handful of "defining moments" in the recent history of the profession and provided a clear signal that significant change was in the offing.

## POST-SPUTNIK REFORM AND THE RISE
## OF LEARNING THEORY: SCIENCE EDUCATION
## IN THE 1950s AND 1960s

The late 1950s and early 1960s were conservative and anxious years, coming on the heels of the McCarthy era and preceding the social upheavals that accompanied our involvement in Vietnam. These were the years of Eisenhower and Kennedy, Donna Reed and *Leave it to Beaver*. Elvis Presley reigned as King of popular culture. Davy Crockett caps and hoola hoops flooded the stores. J. Edgar Hoover warned us about Communist subversion and U2 pilot

Francis Gary Powers was shot from the skies over the Soviet Union. Levittown burst at the seams as the first wave of "baby boomers" entered their teenage years. Khrushchev pounded his fists at the United Nations and sent missiles to Cuba. Little Rock exploded. Science fiction films exploited the national angst, depicting insidious invasions by unseen and terrifying forces lurking beyond our control (*Invasion of the Body Snatchers; The Day the Earth Stood Still; Forbidden Planet*). Richard Nixon ran and lost (1960), ran and lost (1962).

Looking back at the era, separated by a chasm of some 35 years, it would be difficult to overemphasize the impact of Sputnik on the American psyche in general and the scientific community in particular. Americans had the expectation that science and technology were the crowning glory of western civilization and nowhere did that crown glow brighter than in the United States. For many who witnessed those years, the morning headlines of October 5th remain etched indelibly in the mind: "Russian Moon Circles Earth; Sputnik II Ready." How could this happen? How could a "nation of peasants," constrained by a repressive social, political, and economic system, beat us into space? Needless to say, the Russian achievement occasioned much soul-searching and not a little finger-pointing.

To many historians, public reaction to the events of October 4th represents simply a culmination of fears about American decline that grew rapidly in the aftermath of World War II. America had grown soft and our schools were largely to blame. We needed a more rigorous curriculum to help us "regain our lead"; a curriculum that focused on producing world-class scientists and engineers; a curriculum designed by scientists themselves. The existing science courses were said to offer students "a rhetoric of conclusions" (Schwab, 1962) and failed to impart the excitement of science and an appreciation of the major conceptual schemes and methods of scientific inquiry. In fact, the curriculum reform movement had already begun before the launch of Sputnik. In the Spring of 1956 Jerrold Zacharias and several prominent colleagues at MIT had begun work on a new high school physics course. With substantial support from the National Science Foundation, the newly formed Physical Science Study Committee (PSSC) began a crash program of writing, editing, and preliminary trials. By the Fall of 1958 over 12,000 students were using the PSSC materials.

The effort in physics was followed in short order by similar work in chemistry and biology. Under the auspices of the American Chemical Society, work began at Reed and Earlham Colleges to develop a new high school chemistry course for talented students that would be called the Chemical Bond Approach (CBA). This effort was expanded the following year to include a second course intended for a wider range of students, the Chemical Education Material Study (CHEM Study) course. In 1959 the Biological Sciences Curriculum Study (BSCS) began its work at the University of Colorado and ultimately produced three versions of BSCS Biology. In subsequent years these efforts would be followed by NSF-sponsored programs in earth science and "integrated" physical science for the middle school, including Time, Space, and Matter (TSM), the Earth Science Curriculum Project (ESCP), and Introductory Physical Science (IPS).

Although the objectives of these secondary school projects have been repeatedly dissected and minutely analyzed over the past 40 years, the overall goal of the work was summed up rather succinctly in 1959 by Jack Easley; the projects were an attempt to "restore the primacy of subject matter" to the science curriculum. The new programs eliminated much of the emphasis on technology and social issues, replacing them with rigorous textbooks and laboratory exercises that focused on the structure of the disciplines and modes of scientific investigation. It has been suggested with much justification that the reform movement of the fifties and sixties was essentially a reversion to "the Committee of Ten program in unadulterated form" (Montgomery, 1994). This time however, curriculum developers left nothing to chance, aiming to produce "teacher-proof" materials that carried the imprimatur of well-known disciplinary experts at prestigious universities with funding from the National Science Foundation. The scientists were supported in their efforts by a small group of learning and developmental psychologists and curriculum theorists; foremost among them were Harvard's Jerome Bruner (1960) and Chicago's Joseph Schwab (1962).

Curriculum work at the elementary school level came several years later. Again with the support of the NSF, three programs were ultimately developed: Science—A Process Approach (SAPA), under the auspices of the American Association for the advancement of Science (1967); the Elementary Science Study (ESS), developed by the Educational Development Center of Newton, Massachusetts (1969); and the Science Curriculum Improvement Study (SCIS), headed by physicist Robert Karplus at UC Berkeley (1970). The three projects differed substantially in content, scope, and sequence but all three focused heavily on developing an understanding of the nature of scientific inquiry. The work at AAAS was influenced significantly by learning theorist Robert Gagne (1963) of Princeton University and encouraged children to investigate simple natural phenomena. The investigative approach was formalized in a series of 14 "process skills" (e.g., observing, measuring, quantifying) that became the driving force and unifying theme of the project. At Berkeley, Karplus and Thier (1968) developed their "Learning Cycle" approach based loosely on the research of Swiss developmental psychologist Jean Piaget.

Although some attempt had been made to ground previous curricular reforms in the writings of contemporary philosophers (e.g., John Dewey), the post-Sputnik reformers drew heavily instead on the emerging field of psychological learning theory. Some have suggested that the "empirical flavor" of psychology was more attractive to the scientists themselves than the ephemeral reflections of armchair philosophers.

Additionally, however, philosophy was just then emerging from its positivist worldview and significant breakthroughs awaited in the works of Kuhn (1962), Toulmin (1972), von Glasersfeld (1989), and others. Regardless of the reasons, the theoretical writings of Piaget, Bruner, Schwab, and Gagne provided the rationale for much of the curricular work during this period. Space does not permit a thorough review of the voluminous writings of these individuals; however, a brief synopsis of each is in order.

Jean Piaget has been called the most eminent developmental psychologist of our age. Trained as a malacologist (i.e., an expert in bivalved molluscs), he began his work with children as a test administrator in the laboratory of Theodore Simon, a colleague of Alfred Binet, the IQ inventor. At an early point, Piaget became fascinated with the errors children make on IQ tests and he subsequently spent the first decade of his remarkably long career studying children's explanations of natural phenomena (Piaget, 1929). Later he took up studies on the development of basic epistemological issues such as how children understand physical causality, space, time, and number (Piaget, 1965). Although his theoretical writing was remarkably influential, it is as an experimentalist that Piaget will be remembered in psychological and educational circles. Piaget's "clinical interviews" focused on simple but brilliant informal tasks such as pouring liquids of equal quantities into containers of different shapes. Based on childrens' interpretations of these events he constructed a set of ideas about the development of reasoning that relied heavily on logical formalisms and biological mechanisms. The centerpiece of his "genetic epistemology" is the well-known stage theory of cognitive development.

In short, Piaget viewed learning as a biological process characterized by successive periods of assimilation, accommodation, and equilibration. The extent to which each of these is engaged depends largely on the age of the individual, the corresponding stage in the maturation of logical reasoning abilities, and the nature of the learning task. For those concerned with the teaching of school science, the most critical event was seen as the transition between the so-called "concrete" and "formal" stages of development, said to occur during adolescence, in which logical "operations" such as hypothetico-deductive, combinatorial, probabilistic, and correlational reasoning become available. Thus Piaget placed great emphasis on general cognitive functions rather than the structure of domain-specific knowledge, and the task of the teacher was to ascertain the "readiness" of the learner or the "appropriateness" of the learning task. In retrospect, Piaget's scheme appeared remarkably robust; however, it failed to account for differences among individuals due to contextual variables or prior knowledge (Lawson, 1991). As Gardner (1987) has suggested:

> Piaget's grandiose claims have proved less robust than his experimental demonstrations. The logical formalisms underlying specific stages are invalid, the stages themselves are under attack, and his descriptions of the biological processes of stage transformation have eluded even sympathetic scholars.

Nonetheless, at the time Piaget's work proved remarkably influential in the science education community due in large part to the efforts of Jerome

Bruner and, later, to Robert Karplus. In many ways, Jerome Bruner was the right person in the right place at the right time. A professor of psychology at Harvard and Director of the newly established Center for Cognitive Studies (1960), he is commonly thought of as intellectual father, mentor, colleague, and host to researchers in such diverse fields as information processing (e.g., George Miller); human problem-solving (e.g., Allen Newell, Herbert Simon, and Ulric Neisser); language and cognition (e.g., Noam Chomsky); as well as history and philosophy of science (e.g., Thomas Kuhn). A developmentalist by training, to science educators his most memorable contribution was undoubtedly the conviction that "Any subject can be taught in some intellectually honest fashion to any child at any stage of development." It was Bruner, at an early stage, who promulgated Piaget's work among American educators. However, it is his work on inductive reasoning and problem-solving that provided the underpinnings of the new emphasis on "discovery learning" and "conceptual schemes."

Bruner (1960) suggested that much of intellectual development is characterized by a unique and successive set of cognitive representations which he called the enactive, iconic, and symbolic forms. Young children, he maintained, learn best through the physical manipulation of concrete objects, and maturation is a product of increasingly successful attempts to use abstract signs and symbols to represent objects and events. His work stressed the significance of evolving systems of inner logic in which experience is translated into language, the basis for all thinking. For curriculum developers, his most influential work, *The Process of Education*, stressed four themes: (1) that school learning should focus on the *structure* of the disciplines (e.g., "Grasping the structure of a subject is understanding it in a way that permits many other things to be related to it meaningfully. To learn structure, in short, is to learn how things are related." p. 7); (2) that even very young children may be introduced to scientifically important concepts in a *developmentally appropriate* fashion (e.g., ". . . our schools may be wasting precious years by postponing the teaching of many important subjects on the grounds that they are too difficult." p. 12); (3) that students should be encouraged to develop the *intuitive* and *analytic* skills of scientists by engaging in active scientific inquiry (e.g., "The schoolboy learning physics *is* a physicist, and it is easier for him to learn physics behaving like a physicist than doing something else." p. 14); and (4) that teachers need to encourage an *intrinsic interest* in the discipline as a way of motivating students (e.g., "Ideally, interest in the material to be learned is the best stimulus to learning, rather than such external goals as grades or later competitive advantage," p. 14).

Next to Piaget and Bruner, perhaps the most influential writer of the day was Joseph Schwab. Schwab undoubtedly did more than anyone else to encourage the teaching of science as a "process of enquiry." Although his work was not substantially grounded in learning theory per se, his prolific efforts especially in biology (Schwab, 1962) did much to change the textbook-bound classroom practices of the day. Schwab's primary concern was that school science had evolved into a series of recitations that conveyed the results of scientific investigation but failed to instill the logical, analytical, and tentative nature of the enterprise. To Schwab (1962), science was increasingly taught

> . . . as a nearly unmitigated rhetoric of conclusions in which the current and temporary constructions of scientific knowledge are conveyed as empirical, literal, and irrevocable truths (in which students are asked). . . . to accept the tentative as certain, the doubtful as undoubted, by making no mention of reasons or evidence for what it asserts. (p. 24)

As a prominent contributor to the *Biological Sciences Curriculum Study*, Schwab championed the role of the open-ended laboratory investigation ("enquiry into enquiry," p. 65) as a way of encouraging students to ask questions, make observations, record and transform data, and develop tentative conclusions. Much of what he pioneered in his *Biology Teachers' Handbook* (BSCS, 1963) was subsequently adopted by curriculum writers and textbook authors in chemistry, earth science, and physics, as well as those working on integrated science at the middle school and elementary school levels. As a result, many aspects of the so-called "hands-on" science approach can be traced to Schwab's early efforts.

Along with Schwab's efforts, the early work of psychologist Robert Gagne on inquiry methods (1963) had a substantial impact on the curriculum reform effort, especially at the elementary school level where the AAAS Science—A Process Approach was given over entirely to developing an understanding of "science process skills" (e.g., observing, classifying, communicating). The rationale for this approach emerges from Gagne's "hierarchy of learning levels," a set of ideas originally based on principles of behaviorism (Gagne, 1965) but later recast within a cognitive framework (Gagne, 1985). The basic notion is that the learning of complex skills and behaviors depends on learning a hierarchy of successively more complex skills. Solving problems, for example, depends on learning higher order rules which requires an understanding of defined concepts. That in turn rests on a set of concrete concepts which require an abilty to discriminate among similar objects and events.

Ultimately Gagne's ideas mushroomed into a full-blown effort to microanalyze learning tasks and produced a kind of technology of instructional design (Gagne, Briggs, & Wagner, 1988). In the early 1960s, however, Gagne's ideas lent credence to an elementary school science program that introduced simple process skills (e.g., measuring, inferring, predicting) in the primary grades and advanced skills (e.g., formulating hypotheses, controlling variables, interpreting data) in the intermediate and upper grades. The principal criticism lodged against this scheme was its failure to introduce and help children build frameworks of interrelated scientific concepts; as a result, the classroom work became a meaningless succession of "hands-on" activities devoid of understanding. This criticism was embodied in Ausubel's work in meaningful verbal learning.

## AUSUBEL'S COGNITIVE
## ASSIMILATION THEORY: 1963

The publication in 1963 of David Ausubel's work *The Psychology of Meaningful Verbal Learning* had little influence on the science curriculum reform effort of the 1950s and 1960s. By the time it appeared in print much of the early work at the secondary school level had already been accomplished and those working on the elementary school projects had previously committed themselves to a developmental perspective based largely on Piagetian ideas. Furthermore, it appears that Ausubel's ideas were substantially novel and not well understood by curriculum developers and researchers alike, requiring further elaboration in his 1968 work *Educational Psychology: A Cognitive View*. In the epigraph to that book Ausubel offered his now oft-quoted refrain: *The single most important factor influencing learning is what the learner already knows. Ascertain this and teach him accordingly.*

William of Occam, the fourteenth-century philosopher, observed that the most powerful scientific theories are those that are reducible to the smallest set of explanatory propositions. This notion of parsimony applies well to Ausubel's theory. Ausubel's theory offers a handful of concepts which, when linked together, provides a framework for explaining a vast array of seemingly unrelated events about teaching and learning. The most important of Ausubel's concepts includes the distinction between *meaningful learning* and *rote learning*. For Ausubel, meaningful learning is the nonarbitrary, nonverbatim, substantive incorporation of new ideas into a learner's framework of knowledge (or *cognitive structure*). For this to occur three criteria must be met: the material itself must have potential meaning (i.e., it is not a list of nonsense syllables); the learner must already possess relevant concepts to anchor the new ideas; and he or she must voluntarily choose to incorporate the new knowledge in a nonarbitrary, nonverbatim fashion. When one or more of these requirements are not met, rote learning ensues.

Students who learn by rote tend to accumulate isolated propositions in cognitive structure rather than developing the strongly hierarchical frameworks of successively more inclusive concepts that are characteristic of meaningful learning. The major limitations imposed by such isolated propositions are poor retention and retrieval of new ideas, potential interference in subsequent learning of related concepts, and inability to use new knowledge to solve novel problems. For these reasons meaningful learning is generally more productive unless the goal is to retain and retrieve verbatim knowledge (e.g., a telephone number, an address or a padlock combination).

Certainly in most school situations meaningful learning is the preferred outcome.

In Ausubel's view, much of meaningful learning can be explained by a process he calls *subsumption* in which new knowledge, composed of more specific, less inclusive concepts, is linked to more general and inclusive concepts and propositions that are already a part of the learner's cognitive structure. An example of this is when a student learns the structural parts of a cell and the functions of each. This kind of elaborative learning probably accounts for much of the nonrote knowledge acquisition that goes on in good science classes, resulting in a gradual accretion of domain-specific information.

But even this kind of positive learning experience has its limitations, the most important of which Ausubel calls *obliterative subsumption*. When learning results in a significant modification of concept meanings over time, it may inhibit recall of previously learned, less inclusive knowledge. It appears that the process of meaningful learning can be a "two-edged sword," producing a more robust and powerful framework of related concepts that enhances further learning. However, it may also result in failure to retrieve specific, less inclusive concepts and propositions. Unfortunately the use of multiple choice tests and similar evaluation mechanisms often puts a premium on just this kind of knowledge, thereby in effect discouraging the type of learning that teachers prize most.

In *superordinate learning*, new, more general, inclusive, and powerful concepts are acquired that subsume existing ideas in a student's framework of knowledge. This kind of learning can and often does result in a significant reordering of cognitive structure and may produce the kind of conceptual change that we typically experience in creative or particularly insightful moments. When a student first learns that gravity explains much about the behavior of falling bodies, he or she has had such an experience. It is now clear that this kind of learning is responsible for many of the revolutionary breakthroughs that Kuhn (1962) describes as "paradigm shifts."

Two additional concepts advanced by Ausubel provide useful descriptions of changes that occur as knowledge is restructured in the course of meaningful learning; they are *progressive differentiation* and *integrative reconciliation*. By progressive differentiation Ausubel refers to the gradual elaboration and clarification of concept meanings that occurs during subsumption and superordinate learning. In the strongly hierarchical knowledge structures that characterize much of science learning, progressive differentiation typically results in increasing levels of hierarchy and bifurcation or branching of central concepts. Individuals who have experienced successful episodes in meaningful learning generally display highly dendritic knowledge structures composed of many levels of hierarchy.

*Integrative reconciliation* is Ausubel's label for a process occurring during meaningful learning in which there is an explicit delineation of similarities and/or differences between related concepts. Students who learn the principles of biological classification, for example, eventually come to understand the differences and similarities between Protists and Monerans; both are unicellular or colonial forms but one is composed of prokaryotic cells and the other, eukaryotic cells. Those who learn meaningfully begin to form these kinds of cross-connections between related concepts and eventually develop well-integrated, highly cohesive knowledge structures that enable them to engage in the type of inferential and analogical reasoning required for success in the natural sciences.

An additional distinction that Ausubel makes in his early writings is that between *reception learning* and *discovery learning*. In reception learning, concepts and propositions are presented to the learner by an independent agent (e.g., a teacher, a computer, a film) whereas in discovery learning, the goal is for the learner to infer the most important concepts and to construct significant propositions independently. It is important to note that reception and discovery learning may be accomplished through either meaningful or rote processes. The distinction between reception vs discovery and meaningful vs rote learning has been a source of considerable confusion in the science education community.

Many of the influential writers of the post-Sputnik reform era (Bruner, 1960; Schwab, 1962) endorsed independent, inquiry-oriented teaching approaches, sometimes implying that only through such approaches could meaningful learning occur (Novak, 1977). As will become apparent in subsequent chapters, the authors of this book reject that notion and take the position that the meaningful/rote and discovery/reception distinctions constitute orthogonal continua. Simply put, meaningful learning may result from either a process of discovery or through interaction with well-designed instructional materials of a more traditional, didactic nature.


## COGNITIVE SCIENCE AND POSTPOSITIVIST EPISTEMOLOGY: SCIENCE EDUCATION IN THE 1970s AND 1980s

Although it would be grossly misleading to single out any one date that marked a culmination of the post-Sputnik reform effort, July 20, 1969, the day the world watched Neil Armstrong set foot on the moon, suggests itself as a tangible and widely heralded turning point. Although federal funding for NASA and other "big science" projects continued at significant levels for many years to come, money spent on science education at the elementary and secondary school levels began to dwindle rapidly thereafter. Public attention shifted in the ensuing years from science and technology to domestic issues, especially those laden with social and political significance.

The 1970s and 1980s were years of shifting political sands. The Vietnam war ground slowly to a close, the sexual revolution peaked and declined; the women's movement gained steam, and the events of Watergate transfixed a nation. To many, the era provided a time for national introspection; a period of consolidation and even reflection following a turbulent time of social and political change. Jimmy Carter offered many voters redemption and new hope; hope that would soon be mired in an oil embargo and a hostage crisis. With inflation soaring into double digits, Ronald Reagan was elected in a major repudiation of Democratic policy. The 1980s saw further retrenchment in education spending as priorities shifted once again to military preparedness. Curricular and instructional innovation in science education were largely confined to local initiatives. Multiculturalism and issues of gender equity came to the fore as did a movement to integrate science, technology, and social issues; a swing that some viewed as a reversion to progressive-era priorities. At decade's end the Communist bloc would fracture and soon thereafter the Soviet Union itself would collapse, splintering into a score of smaller nations.

Although federal funding for science curriculum work largely disappeared during this period, a substantial effort continued in the development of theory and research. With contributions from the emerging discipline of cognitive science, reinterpretations of the history and philosophy of science, and new insights from epistemology, science education began slowly to mature as a theory-driven field of inquiry. This process was substantially aided by international cooperation and a growing desire to shed some of the provincial concerns that had dominated local curriculum efforts.

Cognitive scientists generally agree that their newly emergent discipline was born at a symposium on information theory held on the campus of the Massachusetts Institute of Technology in September of 1956 (Gardner, 1987). However, the insights generated by this eclectic group of neuroscientists, linguists, psychologists, anthropologists, and computer experts did not significantly impact science education for two decades or more. Perhaps the most important contribution of cognitive scientists is the view that the human mind is an elaborate mechanism that processes information (Atkinson & Shiffrin, 1968). From this perspective, the human information processing system consists of three independent but closely linked memory systems (Figure 2): a sensory buffer, a short term (or working) memory (STM), and a long term memory (LTM).

The best available evidence suggests that sensory information is registered in localized cerebral centers (i.e., sensory buffers) for periods of microseconds and rapidly decays thereafter unless it is consciously attended to. Sustained attention to sensory data moves the information into short term memory which has been likened in some respects to the random-access memory (RAM) discs used in personal computers; both have limited space and the information stored within them is subject to loss unless "saved" (or rehearsed). In the case of STM, the storage capacity is thought to be about seven independent "chunks" of information (Miller, 1956) and these chunks decay within 15–30 sec. Unlike the personal computer, however, where information may be saved to a hard drive without modification, saving information to LTM requires substantial processing which typically results in significant change in the structural complexity and propositional validity of the new knowledge. The changes are a product of deliberate and conscious attempts to interpret, evaluate, compare, and contrast new knowledge with existing knowledge and to establish connections between the two. It is this processing of information that invests new knowledge with its meaning and ultimately determines its idiosyncratic structure and potential usefulness to the learner.

Among the most significant studies done by cognitive scientists are attempts to explore and compare the idiosyncratic knowledge structures of novices and experts in scientific domains (Chi, Glaser, & Farr, 1988). These efforts have looked into domains as diverse as problem solving in chemistry, genetics and Newtonian mechanics, propositional knowledge about dinosaurs and mammals, and skill in medical diagnosis and computer programming, to name just a few areas. The findings have produced some robust, if tentative, conclusions about the structure and use of knowledge in natural science. For example, it is now clear that: (1) experts tend to excel singularly in their domain of knowledge and that transfer to other domains is quite limited in most instances; (2) experts tend to see large meaningful patterns in their knowledge domain and this enables them to solve problems more quickly; (3) experts generally possess a strongly hierarchical, cohesive framework of related concepts and they represent those concepts at a "deeper," more principled level; and (4) experts typically have strong "metacognitive" or self-monitoring skills that enable them to diagnose and remedy errors in comprehension.

Along with the contributions of cognitive scientists, science education benefited substantially from new insights in the history and philosophy of science and a postpositivist view of epistemology. Perhaps the most significant ideas arising in history and philosophy were those that bear on the nature of conceptual change. The works of Thomas Kuhn (1962) and Stephen Toulmin (1972) address the nature of "radical" and "evolutionary" change in our understanding of natural phenomena.

As suggested earlier, the late 1950s and early 1960s was a time of great ferment at Harvard University. In addition to the ground-breaking work at the Center for Cognitive Studies, Harvard President James B. Conant engaged a group of eminent scholars in the development of a series of *Case Histories in Experimental Science* (1957) which sought to integrate ideas from the history of science into the science curriculum. Among the contributors to this work were some of the best minds in science education at the time including Jack Easley, Leo Klopfer, and Fletcher Watson. One lesser-known junior contributor was physicist-turned-historian Thomas S. Kuhn whose 1962 work *The Structure of Scientific Revolutions* had substantial impact on science education (and many other disciplines) some two decades later.

Kuhn is now regarded as perhaps the most celebrated proponent of the so-called "new philosophy of science." This view rejects the logical-positivist position that observation, the cornerstone of all science, is a neutral activity and embraces instead the concept of theory-ladenness of observation. The basic idea is that our perceptions of objects and events in the natural world are strongly dependent on our store of prior knowledge. In effect, we view the world through a pair of "conceptual goggles." These conceptual goggles, which Kuhn calls "paradigms," direct the kinds of questions scientists ask, determine the legitimate methods that scientists use, and guide them in evaluating experimental findings.

Much of the time scientists engage in a kind of "normal science" which consists largely of puzzle-solving activities that reinforce and solidify the prevailing paradigm. Occasionally, however, anomalies crop up that are not easily explained by the paradigm and it becomes necessary to "patch-up" or modify its basic tenets to accommodate some new observation. Scientists, however, are strongly reluctant to jettison an existing paradigm unless the anomalies are so numerous and overwhelming as to call into question the fundamental propositions upon which it rests. When this occurs a "scientific revolution" is ripe for the making and significant conceptual change may be expected. Many philosophers of science now view this kind of "radical restructuring" as a central feature of important breakthroughs in scientific investigation.

While Kuhn's work stressed the radical shifts in scientific understanding, the work of Stephen Toulmin (1972) viewed conceptual change as a gradual, elaborative, and "evolutionary" process. To Toulmin, prevailing paradigms are those that have successfully competed in the marketplace of ideas and have proven to be more robust in their explanatory potential than any alternative views. He suggested further that concepts manifest themselves in populations and that major conceptual shifts are a product of the displacement of one concept with another more powerful concept.

> What we need, therefore, is an account of conceptual development which can accommodate changes of any profundity, but which explains gradual and drastic change alike as alternative outcomes of the same factors working together in different ways. Instead of a *revolutionary* account of intellectual change, which sets out to show how entire "conceptual systems" succeed one another, we therefore need to construct an *evolutionary* account, which explains how "conceptual populations" come to be progressively transformed. (pp. 121–122)

As philosophers of science wrestled with problems of conceptual change, others concerned themselves more broadly with the basic epistemological issue of how we come to know the external world. Although Kuhn and others before him had suggested that the worldviews of scientists are filtered through a lens of prior knowledge, they concerned themselves less with "naive" learners and how young people and inexperienced adults make sense of objects and events in their everyday lives. To science educators of course the issue of "personal knowledge construction" becomes a matter of central concern.

Although Kelley (1955) had written extensively on the subject of personal constructs within the framework of personality theory, the most influential of recent writers has been Ernst von Glasersfeld (1989), whose radical form of "constructivist" epistemology has had a substantial impact on thinking, if not practice, in science education. Glasersfeld traces many of his views to the eighteenth-century Neapolitan philosopher Giambattista Vico, whose novel work first addressed such issues as the origin of conceptual certainty and the role of language in conceptual development. One of Vico's fundamental ideas is that human beings can know nothing except for the cognitive structures that they have put together for themselves.

In Glasersfeld's epistemology the ultimate criterion of useful knowledge is its *viability*. He rejects entirely the notion that knowledge can be tested against some external reality and settles instead for a test of *compatibility*. To the radical constructivist, the issue of validity or "correspondence to nature" in the traditional sense has no meaning; the central question is whether knowledge "enables us to cope" successfully within our range of experience. In addition Glasersfeld assigns substantial importance to the role of social interaction in the construction of personal knowledge. It is through such interactions that we synthesize much of what we know about the world.

Within this social constructivist framework Glasersfeld recognizes the role of the teacher and the importance of the teacher's own knowledge. He stresses that "knowledge cannot simply be transferred" through linguistic communication and that teachers must understand the way their students view the world.

> Hence it is essential that the teacher have an adequate model of the conceptual network within which the student assimilates what he or she is being told. Without such a model as basis, teaching is likely to remain a hit-or-miss affair. (p. 136)

It is this central insight by Glasersfeld, and others before him, that has been the stimulus for considerable research activity in science education over a period of some 25 years. At this time researchers have amassed a mountain of information concerning students' "alternative conceptions" of natural phenomena in biology, chemistry, physics, and the earth and planetary sciences (Wandersee, Mintzes, & Novak, 1994; Mintzes, Wandersee, & Novak, 1997). It is our view that this knowledge (Chapter 3) combined with disciplinary, metacognitive (Chapters 4 and 5), and domain-specific pedagogical knowledge (Chapters 6–11) has the potential to transform the classroom from a "training center" to a place where understanding and conceptual change are encouraged. This view is embodied in a theoretical synthesis that Novak (1993a,b) has called Human Constructivism.

## NOVAK'S HUMAN CONSTRUCTIVISM: THE NEW SYNTHESIS

> Educational research in general, and science education research specifically, stand today in a position comparable to that of chemistry in the 18th century . . . It is likely that substantial advances in education would result if we could develop models for learning (specifically learning of science) that have equivalent heuristic and, ultimately, practical value. (Novak, 1963)

Perhaps no other individual in recent years has played a greater role in the development of an intellectually defensible theory and practice of science teaching than Joseph D. Novak. Novak received the Ph.D. in botany and science education at the University of Minnesota in 1957. His doctoral work focused on problem solving in college-level botany (Novak, 1958) and was grounded in a cybernetic model of information processing (Wiener, 1954). Following a brief stint on the faculty at Kansas State Teachers College, he joined the biology department at Purdue University in 1959. There he worked with Samuel Postlethwait developing the highly successful "audio-tutorial" (A-T) teaching approach, a forerunner of computer-assisted instruction that was widely imitated at colleges, universities, and secondary schools around the country (Postlethwait, Novak, & Murray, 1972). In later years the A-T system would provide an enormously useful vehicle for the study of science learning.

While at Purdue Novak began a series of studies that focused on learning in several college level science courses. In his earliest work, he and several graduate students researched the effect of analytic ability on learning in a problem-based botany course (Murray, 1963) and in several college-level chemistry courses for science and nonscience majors (Taylor, 1966). The work showed that "high analytic" students tend to excell in competitive university environments. Reinterpreting these findings some 10 years later within the context of Ausubelian theory, Novak (1974) concluded that his high-achieving students were those who came to the learning task with a well-established framework of prior knowledge; that is, knowledge of specific relevant concepts in the science.

Reviewing the unpublished first draft of Novak's book (1974) reveals that the period between these two studies (1963–1966) was critical in his search for a theoretical framework to guide his research efforts. It is clear that three events were instrumental in his decision to adopt Ausubel's Cognitive Assimilation Theory. The first of course was the publication in 1963 of *The Psychology of Meaningful Verbal Learning*. Additionally however were opportunities to meet privately with David Ausubel at a 5-day conference on concept learning in October 1965 and a sabbatical at Harvard in 1965–1966 during which he attended Jerome Bruner's seminar on cognitive learning and began a series of studies on children's science learning using audiotutorial lessons.

Novak returned to Purdue for a year and then in 1967 he accepted a position at Cornell where he soon attracted a group of talented, hard-working graduate students. This nascent research group coalesced around the robust ideas elaborated in Ausubel's (1968) second book, *Educational Psychology: A Cognitive View*. Over the next 30 years, working at Ithaca with very little external funding, Novak built and sustained a strong theory-driven research and development program in science education that became a model for many others in the field. Among his most important achievements has been a theoretical synthesis combining insights based on Ausubel's theory (Ausubel, Novak, & Hanesian, 1978) with those derived from contemporary epistemology and the history and philosophy of science. This theoretical contribution has been complemented by a program aimed at designing practical tools to help students learn how to learn (Novak & Gowin, 1984).

Novak's position (Figure 1), which he has called Human Constructivism, is a view of meaning making that encompasses both a theory of learning and an epistemology of knowledge building. It offers the heuristic and predictive power of a psychological model of human learning together with the analytical and explanatory potential embodied in a unique philosophical perspective on conceptual change. It is our view that Human Constructivism is at present the most useful framework available to science teachers who are seeking to make rational decisions about curriculum and instruction and who wish to found those decisions on issues of *understanding* and *conceptual change*.

Although Novak's central ideas have been described elsewhere in some detail (Novak, 1985, 1987, 1988, 1989, 1993a,b; Mintzes, Wandersee, & Novak, 1997), we will attempt here to briefly summarize three of his most important assertions and to reflect a bit on their implications.

## Human Beings Are Meaning Makers

It is my view that the psychological processes by which an individual constructs his or her own new meanings are essentially the same as the epistemological processes by which new knowledge is constructed by the professionals in a discipline . . . creating new knowledge is, on the part of the creator, a form of meaningful learning . . . (Novak, 1993b)

Human Constructivists assert that the cognitive processes resulting in the extraordinarily creative work of Nobel laureates such as James D. Watson, Francis H. C. Crick, and Maurice Wilkins, codiscoverers of the DNA double helix, are essentially the same as those of a freshman biology student who is wrestling with his or her first exposure to molecular genetics. In both cases individuals construct meanings by forming connections between new concepts and those that are part of an existing framework of prior knowledge. It

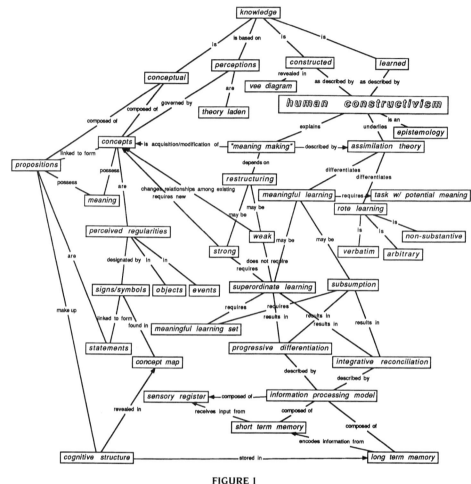

**FIGURE 1**
Concept map of Human Constructivism.

is this meaning making mechanism, embodied in a complex set of language symbol systems, that is the essential adaptation of the human species.

As of this writing, the science education community has been offered a host of "constructivist" epistemologies, each with its own "take" on the knowledge-building process. In our view, Novak's Human Constructivism is the only comprehensive effort that successfully synthesizes current knowledge derived from a cognitive theory of learning and an expansive epistemology, together with a set of useful tools for classroom teachers and other knowledge builders. In it Novak seeks to find unity among the processes of meaningful learning, knowledge restructuring, and conceptual change. As a result, to the Human Constructivist much of good school science and good scientific research produces learning that is gradual and assimilative in nature; it is caused by a cognitive process called subsumption and results in a "weak" form of knowledge restructuring and an incremental change in conceptual understanding. In addition, however, successful science students and scientists often experience particularly insightful moments that trigger a significant and rapid shift in conceptual understanding. This shift is a product of a radical or "strong" form of knowledge restructuring that results from superordinate learning. The principal product of this meaning making exercise is a strongly hierarchical, dendritic, and cohesive set of interrelated concepts; a conceptual framework.

One of the consequences of Novak's epistemological position is the need to rethink a central concept of the post-Sputnik reform era; the "Structure of a Discipline." How do we interpret this idea within a Human Constructivist framework? When Bruner, Schwab, and other reformers spoke of the importance of learning "structure," they often implied that scientists who are well schooled in a disciplinary perspective generally reach a kind of consensus about the meaning of its core concepts (Cole, 1992). Furthermore, the job of the teacher is to "convey" these meanings in a faithful manner to the next generation, but to do so in a way that stresses the tentative nature of the meanings and the open-ended, inquiring process that creates them. This optimistic yet essentially positivist view of the role of scientists, teachers, and learners carries within it something of an internal contradiction; namely that scientists create knowledge and learners consume it. Put somewhat differently, the assumption is that scientists come to know things in a qualitatively different way than students do. It is this central assumption that Human Constructivists reject.

Instead the Human Constructivist asserts that no two human beings, scientists included, construct precisely the same meanings even when presented with identical objects or events. As a result, our understanding of "structure" and how students might come to know it must be revised. This in turn demands a reconsideration of the goals of education and the methods teachers use in their interactions with students.

## The Goal of Education Is
## the Construction of Shared Meanings

> The almost infinite number of permutations of concept–concept relationships allows for the enormous idiosyncrasy we see in individual concept structures, and yet there is sufficient commonality . . . that discourse is possible, and sharing, enlarging and changing meanings can be achieved. It is this reality that makes possible the educational enterprise. (Novak, 1993b)

Human Constructivists reject the view that knowledge is a product that can be faithfully conveyed by teachers. Instead we substitute the idea that knowledge is an idiosyncratic, dynamic construction of human beings; that education attempts to bridge differences among people and that teachers are "middlemen" or negotiators of meaning. We further recognize that the process of negotiation implies a willingness and an ability to change and that conceptual change is governed by both gradual and radical events that are consistent with principles espoused in Ausubel's (1963) work. With Vygotsky (1962), we accept the notion that all learners are capable of change and that teachers have an ethical and professional responsibility to stretch the bounds of students' knowledge within some "zone" of modifiability.

Recognizing that conceptual change often involves the extremely time-consuming process of negotiation has significant implications for curriculum and instruction. For one thing, it means that fewer topics can be "covered" in the course of a typical school year and that great care need be taken in selecting and sequencing the concepts in a science curriculum. For another, it means that instructional methods must encourage active participation and substantial interaction among teachers and learners and that teachers themselves must be willing and able to change in response to social interaction with students.

One explanatory, or perhaps cautionary, note should be recorded here with respect to the negotiation of meanings and the expected outcomes of such a negotiation. Human Constructivists are realists; we recognize negotiation to be a process of "coming to terms." This does not imply, however, that all parties to a negotiation bring equally viable (von Glasersfeld, 1989) constructions to the negotiating table, nor that the goal of negotiation is to reach some kind of "compromise" in our understandings about objects and events in the natural world. Science is decidedly *not* about compromise nor even about reaching unanimity of opinion, though the latter might be viewed as a desirable long-range objective (Cole, 1992). Instead it is an ongoing struggle to construct robust, heuristically powerful explanations. Consensus, when it occurs, is usually confined to core principles and typically requires substantial negotiation over an extended period of time. Our assumption is that well-prepared teachers (and experienced researchers) might expect to have a decided advantage in any such negotiation; however, they, like all negotiators, need to recognize and admit to the limits of their own knowledge and recognize too, perhaps with some measure of humility, that "truth," like all epistemological concepts, is an elusive goal.

## Shared Meanings May Be Facilitated by the Active Intervention of Well-Prepared Teachers

What remains to be demonstrated are the positive results that will occur in schools or other educational settings when the best that we know about human constructivism is applied widely. To my knowledge, no school comes close to wide-scale use of such practices, even though there are no financial or human constraints that preclude this. (Novak, 1993b)

This book is about *understanding and conceptual change* and what teachers might do to facilitate these processes. In it we have invited a group of accomplished scholars to speak directly about novel intervention strategies that seem to have great potential and promise to substantially impact the way science teachers carry out their professional responsibilities. Among the proposed strategies are the use of graphic organizers, metacognitive tools, confrontation techniques, and targeted analogies. Additionally, there are chapters that describe the latest developments in microcomputer and hypermedia technologies, as well as the use of small groups, historical vignettes, and conversations about science.

We are greatly impressed with the wide range and potential value of these techniques. Nonetheless we encourage science teachers to evaluate each of the proposals carefully and critically, as we ourselves have done. As we have tried to show in this chapter, change is perhaps the only constant in science education and, as professionals, we have a significant responsibility to weigh new proposals in curriculum and teaching in light of their potential value to learners. In the final section of this chapter we suggest several questions that teachers might ask about new proposals in science education; questions that emerge from a Human Constructivist view of learning.

## THE PROMISE OF HUMAN CONSTRUCTIVISM

At the beginning of this chapter we promised a model of science teaching and learning that can serve as a rational alternative to the hunches, guesses, and folklore that have guided our profession for over 100 years. It is our view that the comprehensive model Novak calls Human Constructivism offers a set of guiding principles which, if conscientiously implemented, could substantially improve the quality of learning in elementary and secondary schools around the world. To assist teachers who may wish to implement the model, we propose a modest set of concrete questions focusing on the nature of knowledge, on the respective roles of teachers and learners, and on ways of organizing classroom experiences.

Increasingly, talented science teachers are being asked to take an active part in the selection of curricula, textbooks, and instructional materials. Rather than passive recipients of district-mandated curriculum guides and "teacher-proof" kits, these teachers are playing a central role in important decisions about curriculum and instruction. Accordingly, as teachers examine proposed reforms in the science curriculum and innovative teaching strategies for implementing those reforms, we suggest they ask themselves the following questions:

1. *On the nature of knowledge.* How do you think authors of the proposed reform/innovation might view the origins of scientific knowledge? Is

scientific knowledge viewed as a faithful reflection of the external world? A "tidy" bundle of eternal truths? Something to be "passed on" in unadulterated form? Does the knowledge of a scientist differ from that of a student? If so, how? What metaphors do you think the authors might use to characterize the way knowledge is represented in the learner's mind? Is it a "building"? A "snowball"? A "treasure chest"? What kinds of knowledge do the authors view as most important? Are they "skills"? Attitudes? Social implications? Concepts?

From the Human Constructivist perspective, knowledge is not a simple transcription of real world objects or events that can be faithfully communicated either from direct observation of nature itself or from one person to another. Instead, knowledge is an idiosyncratic, hierarchically organized framework of interrelated concepts that is "built up" by scientists and science students over time. The building of a unique conceptual framework is an active process that requires consciously connecting new knowledge to existing knowledge and testing it against one's *perceptions* of real world objects and events and the knowledge constructed by others. Fortunately, however, the unique frameworks so constructed are substantially overlapping; it is the overlapping nature of "core" knowledge in scientific disciplines that makes education possible. The most important knowledge that individuals can have are well-differentiated, highly integrated, domain-specific concepts; it is the structure of our conceptual frameworks that largely determines our success in using existing knowledge and the nature and quality of our subsequent learning experiences.

2. *On the role of teachers.* What metaphors do you think authors of the proposed reform/innovation might use to describe the primary role of the classroom science teacher? Is the teacher viewed as a "font" of knowledge? A "transmitter" of facts? An "arbiter" of disputes? What can be inferred about the authors' instructional views based on suggested activities in the teacher's guide? Are there any indications that the authors favor small group work? Independent learning? Whole-class activities? Interactive technologies? Do they suggest lectures? Discussions? Debates? How do they view laboratory and field investigations? Do the suggested investigations require thoughtful reflection? What are the authors' views about assessment? Do they favor "multiple-choice" tests? fill-ins? essays? portfolios?

Human Constructivists generally discourage teaching strategies that focus on the passive "reception" of knowledge. Lecturing with verbatim note-taking, film-watching, "cookbook"-style laboratory exercises, algorithmic approaches to "problem-solving," and independent work that stresses repetitive "drill" are examples of techniques that too often encourage rote learning. Instead, we favor approaches that demand active participation, intensive interaction, and thoughtful reflection. These activities may take the form of small, cooperative group work, debates, one-on-one conversations, demonstrations, or laboratories that introduce and attempt to resolve conceptual conflict, interactive technologies, and whole-class activities that provide context and encourage meaning-making, such as historical vignettes and the creative use of analogies, metaphors, and story-telling. We also think that students need to learn how to learn; for most individuals, this is not a skill that "comes naturally." The use of concept maps and other metacognitive strategies can help students to monitor and control their own learning. Finally, we recognize and acknowledge, with some regret, the well-known adage that "evaluation drives teaching and learning." Accordingly, we discourage assessment strategies like multiple-choice/true-false, fill-in and similar "objective" tests in favor of concept maps, essays, portfolios, verbal reports, and other methods that recognize, reward, and encourage meaningful learning.

3. *On the role of learners.* Do you think authors of the proposed reform/ innovation recognize, acknowledge, and value students' prior understandings? What metaphors might they use to characterize the student's role? Is he or she an "empty vessel"? A "blank slate"? A "pass receiver"? Are students viewed as passive partners or active agents? Are processes such as intensive interaction, negotiation, reflection, and risk-taking encouraged and rewarded? Do the authors recognize the importance of "learning how to learn"? Of empowering students with techniques for monitoring and controlling their own meaning making? Do they view meaningful learning as a time consuming activity? As an arduous effort to restructure knowledge? As an "endothermic" process required for conceptual change?

Human Constructivists value and respect the unique contributions of individual human minds as well as the essential aspects of a supportive social environment in the construction of shared meanings. To some extent we differ from the so-called "social" and "radical" constructivists in that we have spent a considerable amount of time thinking about thinking. As a result we offer a view of meaning making that stresses the significance of cognitive processes and the role of prior knowledge in the personal construction of new knowledge. We argue our view on both theoretical and "empirical" grounds. The research base, which now includes a mountain of evidence based on some 3500 studies in science education (Chapter 3), strongly suggests that science learners (and scientists themselves) harbor a vast array of alternative scientific views that are often strongly resistant to change. In contrast to the blank slate or empty vessel, we view the human mind as a unique and intricate framework (a hierarchical web) of interrelated concepts that enables human beings to "navigate" the complexities of life successfully. For most people, these frameworks are useful and strongly adaptive; typically they provide both a "rational" and an "emotional" foundation for decision making. As a result, the job of teaching new ideas becomes a matter of "conceptual change" and the profession of the teacher becomes a far more arduous role than was previously thought. It is clear now that learning requires considerably more time and effort than we used to think and, furthermore, that restructuring knowledge (as opposed to rote learning) is an activity that requires students to immerse themselves in the life of the mind as well as the "structure" of the canonical curriculum.

4. *On ways of organizing classroom experiences.* Do you think the authors of the proposed reform/innovation have given careful thought to scope, sequence, and coordination of classroom experiences? Is there adequate time in the normal school year and adequate resources at your school to implement the proposed ideas without encouraging rote learning? Are the proposed experiences appropriately sequenced to foster meaning making? Are they designed to help students bridge traditional disciplinary and subdisciplinary boundaries? Do they empower students to make decisions about their own learning? Do they adequately build on prior knowledge and prepare students for subsequent experiences? Do they encourage thoughtful reflection and the application of knowledge to solving novel, real-world problems?

To Human Constructivists there is much about the existing science curriculum that needs careful rethinking. In many ways, Americans now have a unique opportunity to do just that during the present period of *relative* calm in domestic and international affairs. And of course, as in previous times, there has been no shortage of reform proposals representing divergent viewpoints of professional and political groups. In our view it is important for teachers to carefully scrutinize these proposals through the lens of history and with knowledge of human learning and to evaluate them dispassionately in terms of their likely impact on understanding and conceptual change.

The history of science education has been one of cyclical change driven by external forces. This change has seen the repeated comings and goings of curricula guided by the Academist and Practicalist traditions in American education (Figure 2). In both traditions, substantial effort has been directed toward helping students make meaning out of objects and events in the natural world by linking them to central concepts in the sciences. In the Academist tradition, seen in the Committee of Ten report and the reforms of the 1960s, priority was given to establishing strong connections among the central concepts. This emphasis on the "structure of disciplines" often produced students who could manipulate signs and symbols well (e.g., $F=MA$) but had difficulty applying them to novel, real-world problems. In contrast the Practicalist tradition, seen in the Progressive-era reforms and the present-day STS movement, emphasized connections between disciplinary concepts and real-world problems. This deemphasis on disciplinary structure had the effect of raising students' "awareness" and concern for problems emerging in a technological society but typically failed to help them construct the knowledge necessary to understand the problems and contribute to their solution.

Human Constructivism promises a way out of this dilemma; a third way of organizing classroom experiences. It is our view that both the Academist

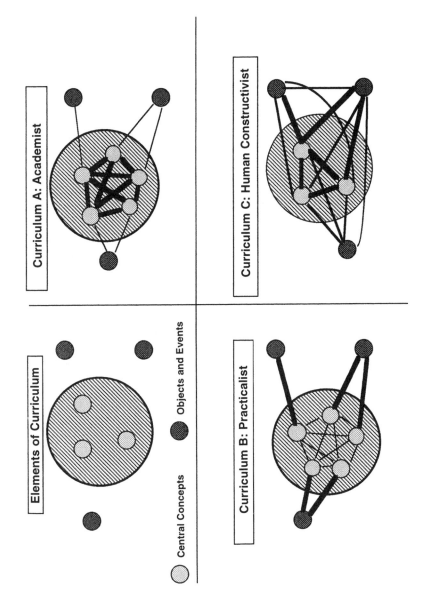

**FIGURE 2**

Curricular models in science education.

and Practicalist traditions have failed because they have sought to accomplish too much and as a result have actually accomplished very little. We subscribe to the notion that "less is more"; that a successful science curriculum focuses on only a handful of central concepts, the relationships among those concepts, and connections between those concepts and the objects and events of the natural world. In this view the primary objective of school science is *quality over quantity, meaning over memorizing,* and *understanding over awareness.*

## References

American Association for the Advancement of Science (1967). *Science—A process approach.* Washington, DC: Ginn and Co.

American Association for the Advancement of Science (1993). *Benchmarks for science literacy: Project 2061.* New York: Oxford University Press.

Atkinson, R., & Shiffrin, R. (1968). Human memory: A proposed system and its control processes. In K. Spence and J. Spence (Eds.), *The psychology of learning and motivation: Advances in research and theory,* Vol 2. New York: Academic Press.

Ausubel, D. P. (1963). *The psychology of meaningful verbal learning.* New York: Grune and Stratton.

Ausubel, D. P. (1968). *Educational psychology: A cognitive view.* New York: Holt, Rinehart and Winston.

Ausubel, D. P., Novak, J. D., & Hanesian, H. (1978). *Educational psychology: A cognitive view,* 2nd Edition. New York: Holt, Rinehart and Winston.

Biological Sciences Curriculum Study (1963). *Biology teacher's handbook.* New York: Wiley.

Bruner, J. (1960). *The process of education.* Cambridge, MA: Harvard University Press.

Chi, M., Glaser, R., & Farr, M. (1988). *The nature of expertise.* Hillsdale, NJ: Lawrence Erlbaum.

Cole, S. (1992). *Making science: Between nature and society.* Cambridge, MA: Harvard University Press.

Conant, J. (1957). *Harvard case histories in experimental science,* Vols. 1 & 2. Cambridge, MA: Harvard University Press.

DeBoer, G. (1991). *A history of ideas in science education: Implications for practice.* New York: Teachers College Press.

Dewey, J. (1899). *The school and society.* Chicago: University of Chicago Press.

Duschl, R. (1990). *Restructuring science education.* New York: Teachers College Press.

Easley, J. (1959). The physical science study committee and educational theory. *Harvard Educational Review,* 29, 4–11.

Educational Development Center. (1969). *Elementary science study.* Manchester, MO: Webster Division, McGraw–Hill.

Gagne, R. (1963). The learning requirements for enquiry. *Journal of Research in Science Teaching,* 1, 144–153.

Gagne, R. (1965). *The conditions of learning.* New York: Holt, Rinehart and Winston.

Gagne, R. (1985). *The conditions of learning,* 4th edition. New York: Holt, Rinehart and Winston.

Gagne, R., Briggs, L., & Wager, W. (1988). *Principles of instructional design,* 3rd edition. New York: Holt, Rinehart and Winston.

Gardner, H. (1987). *The mind's new science: A history of the cognitive revolution.* New York: Basic Books.

Hurd, P. (1961). *Biological education in American secondary schools 1890–1960.* Washington, DC: American Institute of Biological Sciences.

Karplus, R., & Thier, H. (1968). *A new look at elementary school science.* Chicago: Rand McNally.

Kelley, G. (1955). *The psychology of personal constructs.* New York: Norton.

Kuhn, T. (1962). *The structure of scientific revolutions.* Chicago: University of Chicago Press.

Lawson, A. (1991). Is Piaget's epistemic subject dead? *Journal of Research in Science Teaching,* 28, 581–592.

Miller, G. (1956). The magic number seven, plus or minus two: Some limits on our capacity for processing information. *Psychological Review,* 63, 81–97.

Mintzes, J., Wandersee, J., & Novak, J. (1997). Meaningful learning in science: The human constructivist perspective. In G. Phye (Ed.), *Handbook of academic learning*. Orlando, FL: Academic Press.

Montgomery, S. (1994). *Minds for the making*. New York: The Guilford Press.

Murray, D. (1963). The testing of a model for the interpretation of concept formation using college biology students. Unpublished Ph.D. dissertation, Purdue University.

National Education Association. (1893). *Report of the committee on secondary school studies*. Washington, DC: U.S. Government Printing Office.

National Education Association. (1918). *Cardinal principles of secondary education: A report of the commission on the reorganization of secondary education*. (U.S. Bureau of Education, Bulletin No. 35). Washington, DC: U.S. Printing Office.

National Research Council. (1996). *National science education standards*. Washington, DC: National Academy Press.

National Science Teachers Association. (1992). *Scope, sequence and coordination of secondary school science: The content core*. Washington, DC: NSTA.

Novak, J. (1957). A comparison of two methods of teaching a college general botany course. Unpublished Ph.D. dissertation, University of Minnesota.

Novak, J. (1958). An experimental comparison of a conventional and a project centered method of teaching a college general botany course. *Journal of Experimental Education, 26*, 217–230.

Novak, J. (1963). A preliminary statement on research in science education. *Journal of Research in Science Teaching, 1*, 3–9.

Novak, J. (1974). *Education: Theory and practice*. Unpublished manuscript. Department of Education, Cornell University, Ithaca, New York.

Novak, J. (1977). *A theory of education*. Ithaca, New York: Cornell University Press.

Novak, J. (1985). Metalearning and Metaknowledge strategies to help students learn how to learn. In L. West and A. L. Pines (Eds.), *Cognitive structure and conceptual change* (pp. 189–209). Orlando, FL: Academic Press.

Novak, J. (1987). Human constructivism: Toward a unity of psychological and epistemological meaning making. In J. Novak (Ed.), *Proceedings of the second international seminar on misconceptions and educational strategies in science and mathematics* (Vol. 1, pp. 349–360). Ithaca, New York: Department of Education, Cornell University.

Novak, J. (1988). Learning science and the science of learning. *Studies in science education, 15*, 77–101.

Novak, J. (1989). The use of metacognitive tools to facilitate meaningful learning. In P. Adey (Ed.), *Adolescent development and school science* (pp. 227–239). London: Falmer Press.

Novak, J. (1993a). A view on the current status of Ausubel's assimilation theory of learning. In J. Novak (Ed.), *Proceedings of the third international seminar on misconceptions and educational strategies in science and mathematics* (distributed electronically). Ithaca, New York: Department of Education, Cornell University.

Novak, J. (1993b). Human constructivism: A unification of psychological and epistemological phenomena in meaning making. *International Journal of Personal Construct Psychology, 6*, 167–193.

Novak, J., & Gowin, D. B. (1984). *Learning how to learn*. New York: Cambridge University Press.

Parker, F. W. (1895). Contribution to the discussion of Dr. C. C. Van Liew's essay on "Culture Epochs," National Society for the Study of Education first supplement. *National Herbart Society Yearbook*, 155–157.

Piaget, J. (1929). *The child's conception of the world*. London: Paladin, reprinted 1973.

Piaget, J. (1965). *The child's conception of number*. New York: Norton.

Postlethwait, S., Novak, J., & Murray, H. (1972). *The audio-tutorial approach to learning*. Minneapolis: Burgess.

Schwab, J. (1962). The teaching of science as Enquiry. In *The teaching of science* (pp. 1–103). Cambridge, MA: Harvard University Press.

*Science Curriculum Improvement Study*. (1970). Chicago: Rand McNally.

Taylor, M. (1966). The use of a model for the interpretation of concept formation in college chemistry. Unpublished Ph.D. dissertation, Purdue University.

Toulmin, S. (1972). *Human understanding, Vol. I: The collective use and evolution of concepts.* Princeton: Princeton University Press.

von Glasersfeld, E. (1989). Cognition, construction of knowledge, and teaching. *Synthese,* 80, 121–140.

Vygotsky, L. (1962). *Thought and language.* Cambridge, MA: MIT Press.

Wandersee, J., Mintzes, J., & Novak, J. (1994). Research on alternative conceptions in science. In D. Gabel (Ed.). *Handbook of research on science teaching and learning* (pp. 177–210). New York: MacMillan.

Wiener, N. (1954). *The human use of human beings.* Garden City, New York: Doubleday.

# CHAPTER 3

# Research in Science Teaching and Learning: A Human Constructivist View

JOEL J. MINTZES
*University of North Carolina—Wilmington*

JAMES H. WANDERSEE
*Louisiana State University*

The field of science education has benefited substantially from efforts to seek out and establish strong connections between theory, research, and classroom practice. It is our view that theory can provide a heuristically powerful set of guidelines for researchers and practitioners in science teaching; however, useful theory in turn needs to be continuously informed and modified by the results of empirical work and practical application. In Chapter 2 we explored several significant reforms and innovations in science teaching and looked briefly into some of the theoretical frameworks underpinning those efforts. In this chapter we wish to build on that foundation by focusing attention on the nature of research efforts in science education and how research can contribute to the improvement of classroom practice. In so doing our primary intent is to offer a general overview for those who are just beginning to explore the field. Our objective is to lend credence to the view, in contrast to that held by some "radical" constructivists, that empirical studies based on a strong theoretical framework and a fund of practical knowledge can provide an essential element of external validity to our work in science education.

## RESEARCH IN SCIENCE EDUCATION:
## A BRIEF HISTORY

Although reform and innovation in science teaching span a period of more than a century, much of the curricular work undertaken prior to World War I was not well informed by research efforts in the field (Curtis, 1926). And for good reason. Much of the research undertaken by science educators during this period was poorly conceived and generally primitive, even by standards of the day (Watson, 1963). In fact there is very little evidence that members of the Committee of Ten (1893) or the Commission on the Reorganization of Secondary Education (1918) even viewed education as particularly amenable to empirical investigation. Following the War, however, research in science education grew rapidly, culminating in the establishment in 1928 of an embryonic professional organization, the National Association for Research in Science Teaching (NARST).

Consistent with our historical view of reform and innovation in science teaching, we have found it instructive and convenient to organize our thinking about research by partitioning the period since World War I into three eras (Figure 1): the *Practicalist* period, comprising some 40 years between the publication of the "Cardinal Principles" (1918) and the launch of Sputnik (1957); the *Academist* period, dating from the Post-Sputnik reform (1958) to the epistemological revolution of the late 1970s; and the *Human Constructivist* period, beginning with the publication of Ausubel, Novak, & Hanesian's book (1978) and continuing to the present. Each of these eras has been characterized by a unique set of contemporary issues, by a strong group of leading theorists, and by a dominant epistemology that guided research activities of the day. Additionally, we find significant differences in the experimental designs, the investigative tools, and the analytic procedures employed by researchers. Most importantly, we discover that the questions occupying researchers evolved substantially over these periods and tended to reflect both the concerns of leading theorists and classroom practitioners of the day as well as those external forces that consistently impact the profession.

The period between the first World War and the launch of Sputnik was dominated by proponents of the Progressive Education movement, including among others Dewey, Thorndike, Binet, and Terman. These men were concerned with the practical issues of creating an efficient workforce, socializing a massive immigrant population, and fitting new arrivals into a demanding and rapidly expanding economy. As a result, much of the research during this period focused on measuring and testing of pupils and surveying the educational landscape. The emphasis was not so much on creating and evaluating innovative instructional strategies as it was on assessing the status quo and finding useful niches for diverse groups of people. The effort was decidedly utilitarian in outlook and stressed variables associated with efficiency, time management, adjustment to existing conditions in the workplace, and the development of "scientific attitudes."

| Era | Contemporary issues | Leading theorists | Dominant epistemology | Common research designs |
|-----|---------------------|-------------------|----------------------|------------------------|
| Practicalist (1918–1957) | Usefulness Efficiency Management Vocation/work Life adjustment Citizenship | Dewey Thorndike Binet Terman Cubberley | Rationalist/ utilitarian | Descriptive surveys Status reports Quasi-experimental designs |
| Academist (1958–1977) | Disciplinary structure Scientific inquiry Human development Behavioral change | Ausubel Bruner Gagne Piaget Schwab Skinner | Empiricist/ behaviorist | Nomothetic comparisons Correlational studies Experimental designs |
| Human constructivist (1978–    ) | Meaning making Understanding Conceptual change Knowledge structure Quality | Novak Vygotsky Kuhn Toulmin Glasersfeld | Postpositivist/ constructivist | Ideographic descriptions Cognitive probing Naturalistic designs Case studies |

| Research tools | Frequently-used data analyses | Exemplary research questions |
|----------------|-------------------------------|------------------------------|
| IQ and ability assessments Locally-constructed tests Surveys/questionnaires | Mean/standard deviation Simple descriptive | Attributes of science teachers and students Lecture vs laboratory vs demonstration Superstitious beliefs of science students Achievement measures Grade placement |
| Psychometric measurements Standardized tests Observation instruments | $t$-tests, ANOVA, ANCOVA $r$, $R$, multiple regression MANOVA, Factor Analysis Multivariate techniques | Behavioral objectives and taxonomies Individualizing instruction Curriculum evaluation Critical thinking/scientific attitude Classroom interaction Comparative teaching methods |
| Clinical interviews Concept maps Participant observation Ethnomethodology Classroom artifacts | Qualitative approaches Constant comparison | Conceptional development and cognition Ethnicity and gender effects Pedagogical content knowledge Cognitive intervention strategies Expert vs novice practice |

**FIGURE 1**

Trends in science education research.

Studies conducted during this period relied heavily on quasi-experimental research designs; others reported the results of extensive surveys and questionnaires addressed to teachers and school administrators. Typically, much was made of IQ measurements and assessments of intellectual ability and prior knowledge. Often this work depended on locally constructed tests and homemade instruments of questionable reliability and unknown validity. Published papers reported reams of descriptive statistics; unfortunately meaningful interpretations of these data were rarely attempted.

A review of research in science education for the period 1938–1947 (Boenig, 1969) offers a glimpse of 78 studies which, in the judgment of one influential science educator, Willard Jacobson of Columbia University Teachers College, "were done in a scholarly manner and which have been of significance in the field." In a preface to the volume, readers are informed that research articles included in the review were chosen by "distinguished science educators who were active in the field during the period being considered." It is reasonable to conclude that the studies summarized in the volume are among the best the field had to offer and a careful reading might provide some insight into the research questions science educators thought most important during the period.

Of the 78 studies included in the volume, approximately 50% were devoted to surveys and questionnaires that focused on current practice and the status of existing courses and programs. Examples include: "Trends in the Organization of High School Chemistry since 1920" (Hall, 1939); "Science Content in the Elementary School" (Gilbert, 1943); "The Opinions of Science Teachers and Their Implications for Teacher Education" (Burnett, 1941); "Science in General Education at the College Level" (Taylor, 1940); and "Science Sequence and Enrollments in Secondary Schools of the United States" (Hunter & Spohr, 1941). Another 20–30% of the studies reported on the development, administration, and results of testing procedures: "Complexity of Mental Processes in Science Testing" (Howard, 1943); "Knowledge of Science Possessed by Pupils Entering the Seventh Grade" (Matteson & Kambley, 1940); "The Measurement of Ability to Apply Principles of Physics in Practical Situations" (Wise, 1947); and "Superstitions of Junior High School Pupils" (Zapf, 1938). The smallest number of studies involved the experimental manipulation of classroom variables: "The Lecture-Demonstration Method versus the Problem-Solving Method of Teaching a College Science Course" (Barnard, 1942); "An Experiment in the Teaching of Genetics" (Bond, 1940); and "The Effectiveness of Laboratory Procedures" (Johnson, 1940).

The 20-year period following the launch of Sputnik saw remarkable change in the research activities of science educators. Among the most important events of this era were the establishment in 1963 of the first journal devoted entirely to research reports in the field (*Journal of Research in Science Teaching*) and the rapid expansion of graduate programs producing M.S. and Ph.D. recipients with the research skills necessary to tackle significant problems in science teaching and learning. Additionally, specialized research centers focusing on critical aspects of science education began to emerge; for example, Cornell University in learning theory; Harvard, Berkeley, and Chicago in curriculum development; the Universities of Minnesota, Michigan, Iowa, Texas, and Georgia in science teacher education. Virtually all of these developments were made possible by the rapid infusion of federal funds, especially from the National Science Foundation.

Reviewing research reports of this era one is struck by the extent to which empirical work was driven by the demands of curriculum reform and instructional innovation. These in turn reflected the national commitment to "catch up" with Soviet advances in the military, technological, and scientific arenas. A substantial amount of research activity focused on instructional improvement, student achievement and learning, and the education of science teachers.

As suggested in Chapter 2, the era was dominated by a reform movement that stressed the importance of learning the structure of scientific disciplines and the nature of scientific inquiry. These concerns were embodied in the writings of several influential theoreticians whose work focused on issues of human cognitive development and behavioral change. Foremost among them were Piaget, Bruner, Schwab, and Gagne.

Although Ausubel (1963) wrote during this period, his efforts were largely ignored by the science education research community. The zeitgeist favored instead an epistemology that was decidedly empiricist in theory and behaviorist in action. As a result, many researchers borrowed formal experimental designs from the agricultural sciences and strong quantitative tools from psychology and the other social and behavioral sciences. Much was made of psychometric issues such as "reliability" and "validity," and data analyses often depended on complex multivariate procedures including analyses of variance, multiple regression, and canonical correlation. In retrospect, it is doubtful that the basic questions posed by science education researchers warranted these powerful tools. Furthermore, it has been suggested with much justification (Novak & Gowin, 1984) that the use of these strong experimental designs and analytic procedures tended to obfuscate the central questions and to provide a veneer of scientism to an enterprise that lacked a cohesive theoretical framework.

Following up on the early research digests edited by Curtis (through 1937) and Jacobson (through 1957), the ERIC Clearinghouse for Science, Mathematics and Environmental Education at Ohio State University began publishing annual reviews of research in 1965. The *Summary of Research in Science Education* for the year 1972 (Novak, 1973) provides insight into some of the most influential research efforts of this period.

The Novak *Summary* abstracted and reviewed 231 studies of the more than 400 research reports published in 1972. Of these studies, the largest group (36 or approximately 15%) addressed the efficacy of innovative instructional methods with particular emphasis on "individualized" approaches based largely on the work of Benjamin Bloom (1971). These widely adopted, self-teaching approaches (e.g., audio tutorial, PSI) guided students through a set of "behavioral objectives" enabling learners to vary the instructional time required to reach a specified level of "mastery" in the discipline (Mintzes, 1975; Mintzes, Littlefield, Shaub, Crockett, Rakitan, & Crockett, 1976).

Three additional groups of studies each accounted for approximately 10% of the published work in 1972. These included: 25 reports on the science teacher, focusing on such issues as attitudes, behaviors, personality characteristics, and teacher education programs; 24 studies on Piagetian stage theory emphasizing replications of previous work and such issues as the effects of instruction, culture, and heredity on cognitive development and correlations between Piagetian stages and science achievement; and 21 studies that examined relationships between experimental treatments or student variables and learning in a variety of instructional settings.

Comparing these studies with those of the Practicalist era, one is immediately struck by the growth in sophistication of the research community. This growth is reflected in the types of questions posed, in the depth of probing achieved, and in the level of analytic ability and insightfulness demonstrated in the research reports. However, as Novak repeatedly noted throughout the *Summary*, the overwhelming majority (90% or more) of studies lacked any semblance of a theory base, and in the absence of such a framework there was very little that tied one study to another or provided much in the way of explanatory or heuristic value. As a result, the era produced a massive accumulation of research papers, many of which reported "no significant differences." This leads us to conclude that the 20-year period comprising the Academist era in science education research was marked by marginal advances in experimental technique but a general failure to tackle, and a clear failure to resolve, the most significant problems in the field.

In their chapter in the *Second Handbook of Research on Teaching*, Shulman and Tamir (1973) offer a number of insightful conclusions and prescient suggestions on the state of science education research in the mid-1970s. Summing up the research results accumulated in science education over the preceding decade, they conclude:

> One important characteristic of much of the literature in science education is the vast disparity between the profound and truly important nature of the questions raised by philosophers working in the field and the too-frequently trivial empirical studies conducted by empirical researchers in the field. For example, the enormous emphasis placed upon the importance of the structure of the subject matter should have generated far more empirical research . . . Instead we have a proliferation of theoretical pieces on this topic but precious little empirical study. (p. 1138)

Foremost among their suggestions for future research is an emphasis on studies of science-specific conceptual development:

There should also be an increase in a genre of basic research that is science-specific . . . like the cognitive development of science-relevant concepts in young children . . . The purpose would be to identify some general normative expectancies for the evolution of particular concepts around which curriculum developers and program writers could plan their creative endeavors. It would not really matter whether such conceptual developments were the products of ontogenic cognitive development or learning. The importance would be to provide general maps that would be useful for the activities of the curriculum developers. (p. 1139)

In retrospect this statement appears remarkably insightful (and it is); however, the comments of Shulman and Tamir were but one of many signs that the field of science education research had entered a critical period of transition. What was clear to researchers of the period is that they had expended a great deal of energy and an enormous amount of time and resources with few tangible results. Something had to change, and a description of that "something" will consume the remainder of this chapter.

Unlike the launch of Sputnik, which provided an unmistakably dramatic and much-heralded turning point, the transition to a Constructivist era in science education research proved to be a relatively gradual one. It was marked by a general dissatisfaction with previous research efforts and its chief proponents were armed with a newly emergent epistemological view (Driver and Easley, 1978). It was precipitated further by a spate of studies suggesting that even our brightest students were failing to develop a meaningful understanding of science concepts despite the best efforts of our ablest teachers and the creative work of our most thoughtful curriculum developers (Nussbaum & Novak, 1976; Novick & Nussbaum, 1978). Some have suggested it was even occasioned in part by economic competition with Japan and other east Asian nations (Wandersee, Mintzes, & Novak, 1994). Regardless of the precipitating events, the new effort in research was supported by an expansive vision of classroom practice and was grounded in a highly regarded cognitive view of learning (Ausubel, Novak, & Hanesian, 1978; Novak, 1977).

We have arbitrarily designated the year 1978 as a pivotal one in the transition to a Human Constructivist era in science education research. In contrast to the Academist period, the present era is marked by a concern for meaningful learning, knowledge restructuring, and conceptual change. Our efforts have been redirected toward ways of encouraging understanding and helping students construct well-differentiated and highly integrated frameworks of domain-specific knowledge in the natural sciences. As suggested in the previous chapter, this turn in our research agenda was heavily influenced by contributions from workers in the cognitive sciences and the history and philosophy of science.

In comparison to workers of the post-Sputnik period, contemporary researchers rely more heavily on naturalistic research designs, case studies, and qualitative measures of learning and understanding. The emphasis has shifted from psychometric tests to clinical interviews, concept maps, and participant observation. In general, science education research has moved from a psychological model to an anthropological model; from nomothetic comparisons to ideographic descriptions; and from complex, multivariate analyses to simpler data transformations. Some have suggested that present research efforts have offered a more "authentic" view of classroom problems and that results of these studies are more likely to impact the work of science teachers. Among the most pressing research issues are problems of conceptual change, ethnic and gender equity, teachers' knowledge, and exemplary practice. In our view some of the most significant studies of the past 20 years have focused on students' understanding of scientific concepts (Mintzes, Wandersee, & Novak, 1997). We will return to summarize the results of these studies after a brief introduction to several new tools that have had a remarkable impact on recent research in the field (Novak & Gowin, 1984).

## NEW TOOLS IN SCIENCE EDUCATION RESEARCH: THE CASE OF MARY A.

Over the past 20 years we have come to rely heavily on three remarkably powerful tools for exploring students' understandings of scientific concepts and documenting changes in those understandings. The tools were developed at Cornell University and have been employed in scores of studies since the mid-1970s; they are: Gowin's epistemological *vee diagram*, Novak's *concept map*, and a modified form of Piaget's *structured, clinical interview*. Additionally we have found value in several auxiliary tools, including: drawings, card sortings, and open-ended problem sets.

Since this book is intended primarily for teachers and graduate students who are just beginning to explore the field (and those who direct their thesis research), we will rely for our example on thesis work completed for the M.S. degree at a regional, comprehensive level I university (UNC-Wilmington). Our intention is to provide a case study of exemplary graduate student research in the hope that it might serve as a model for future students and their advisors.

### Mary's Vee Diagram

Normally in planning a thesis study our graduate students construct a set of successively more elaborate vee diagrams which are intended to help them identify a significant problem or *focus question* and to sort out the *conceptual* and *methodological* elements that are needed to further refine the problem and contribute to its solution. The technique was developed by Gowin (1981) to help learners "unpack" knowledge and value claims by explicitly delineating the route taken by a knowledge-maker from the inception of a study to its conclusions. In constructing a vee diagram our graduate students learn how theory-driven research proceeds from observing objects and events to making and transforming records, representing data, drawing conclusions and interpretations, generalizing the conclusions, and assigning value to them. The students also begin to recognize the critical interplay between the conceptual and methodological elements in a research study.

When Mary Arnaudin (1983) decided to focus her thesis study on students' understanding of human body processes, she constructed her first vee diagram. Subsequently, as a result of numerous conversations (many cups of coffee), much negotiation (an occasional sigh of exasperation), and further refinement, she settled on a cross-age study of students' "alternative conceptions" of the human circulatory system (Mintzes, 1984; Arnaudin & Mintzes, 1985). The vee diagram on which she based her study (Figure 2) identified her *focus question*: "How do students (ages 8–18) describe their understanding of the human circulatory system?" Since she wanted a reasonably strong representation of subjects across several age levels, the *objects* of her study became a group of over 500 students enrolled in local elementary, middle, and high schools and a regional campus of a state university.

At the outset it became clear that the success of the study would depend critically on Mary's ability to understand and use a set of *concepts* derived from two quite distinct domains of knowledge; that is, epistemology and learning theory as well as human anatomy and physiology. In our view, one of the principal limitations of science education research is the failure of would-be researchers to recognize that good work requires in-depth knowledge derived from the domains both of natural science and applied learning theory. Fortunately Mary had taken substantial coursework in human biology in her secondary school certification program (She had a B.S. in zoology and a second B.S. in science education) and had the opportunity to study learning theory for a semester with Joe Novak. During that semester she developed a strong *theoretical framework* and a practical *philosophy* of teaching based largely on Ausubel's ideas. She also had the opportunity to review and consolidate many of her ideas about the human circulatory system.

Based on her conceptual understanding of these domains we agreed that she would develop a research design composed of two phases: a naturalistic or qualitative phase wherein *records* would take the form of concept maps and tape recordings of clinical interviews, and a quantitative phase composed of student responses to a "multiple-choice" test. The basic idea was to explore and probe student conceptions inductively in phase I; to *transform* our records into a "conceptual inventory;" to develop a test based on the inventory, and finally to administer the test to 500 subjects in phase II. Clearly this research effort would be an ambitious undertaking, requiring a substantial amount of *recordkeeping* and multiple *transformations*. In the final analysis we wanted to be able to present the *results* in the form of

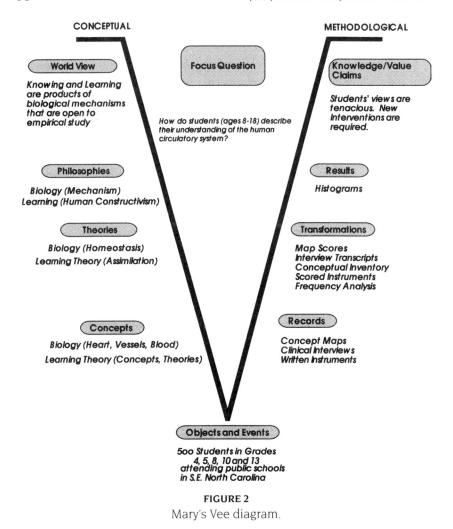

CONCEPTUAL                                                    METHODOLOGICAL

**World View**

*Knowing and Learning
are products of
biological mechanisms
that are open to
empirical study*

**Focus Question**

*How do students (ages 8-18) describe
their understanding of the human
circulatory system?*

**Knowledge/Value
Claims**

*Students' views are
tenacious. New
interventions are
required.*

**Philosophies**

*Biology (Mechanism)
Learning (Human Constructivism)*

**Results**

*Histograms*

**Theories**

*Biology (Homeostasis)
Learning Theory (Assimilation)*

**Transformations**

*Map Scores
Interview Transcripts
Conceptual Inventory
Scored Instruments
Frequency Analysis*

**Concepts**

*Biology (Heart, Vessels, Blood)
Learning Theory (Concepts, Theories)*

**Records**

*Concept Maps
Clinical Interviews
Written Instruments*

**Objects and Events**

*5oo Students in Grades
4, 5, 8, 10 and 13
attending public schools
in S.E. North Carolina*

FIGURE 2
Mary's Vee diagram.

histograms depicting the frequencies of student conceptions at each of the
designated age levels. We hoped that these results would enable us to develop an *explanation* of conceptual change within this domain of knowledge
and ultimately to offer a set of *knowledge* and *value claims* which might provide
guidance to teachers and curriculum developers in biology.

## Mary's Concept Maps

To begin her initial probe into students' understandings of the human circulatory system, Mary taught a group of 4th graders the concept mapping tech-

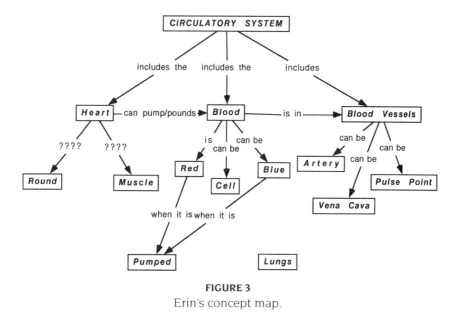

**FIGURE 3**
Erin's concept map.

nique and worked with them on the technique for 3 weeks prior to the investigation. Concept maps are two-dimensional, hierarchical, node-link representations that depict the major concepts and relationships found in a domain of knowledge. The technique was developed by Novak (1980) and his graduate students and has become a widely used strategy for assessing the structural complexity and propositional validity of knowledge in science-related fields (Novak & Gowin, 1984).

Following the initial training period, the children were given a set of eight concept labels (i.e., heart, blood, vessels, oxygen, food, cells, lungs, carbon dioxide) and were asked to construct a concept map on the human circulatory system (Figure 3). Carefully examining these maps, Mary quickly discovered that the children apparently understood a great deal about the circulatory system. For example, Erin seemed to know that the system includes the heart, the blood vessels, and the blood; the heart is a muscle that pumps blood; blood has cells and is contained within the vessels; and "artery" and "vena cava" are examples of blood vessels. In addition, however, it appeared that Erin subscribed to a number of "alternative conceptions": the heart is round; blood may be red or blue when it is pumped; the "pulse point" is a type of blood vessel (Arnaudin & Mintzes, 1986).

To find out whether these and similar ideas are also found in more mature students, Mary decided subsequently to work with a small group of college students enrolled in a first-year biology course for nonmajors. Here again she found an interesting and complex mix of scientifically

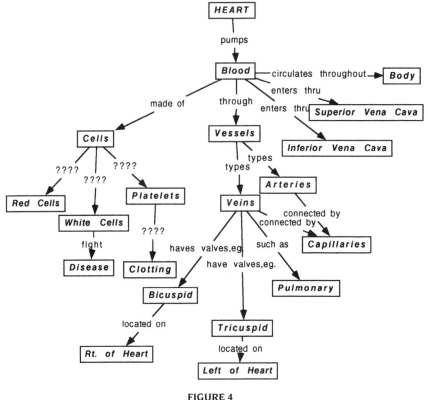

**FIGURE 4**
Jason's concept map.

acceptable ideas and misconceptions (Arnaudin, Mintzes, Dunn, & Shafer, 1984). After a series of three 1-hour lectures on the human circulatory system, Jason (Figure 4) depicted a reasonably sophisticated understanding of its structure and function but he also mixed up some significant details, confusing the bicuspid and tricuspid valves as well as venous and cardiac valves.

The results of the initial concept mapping study were tantalizing but Mary felt she might be able to explore students' understanding in greater depth by interviewing each of her subjects. It seemed to her that the concept maps were quite helpful in pinpointing potentially troublesome areas that could be probed in more detail through interactive techniques.

## Mary's Clinical Interviews

Using the concept maps as a point of departure, Mary developed a set of structured but flexible interview questions. Several of the questions asked students to draw pictures; another asked them to trace the course of a drop of blood through a plastic model of the human body; still another queried subjects on the sounds they heard as they placed a stethoscope to their chests. The complete interview protocols contained some 20 questions that probed into problematic areas revealed in the concept maps. However, the precise wording and ordering of these questions varied among subjects, enabling Mary to follow-up on promising leads as they developed in the course of the interview. As a result, no two interviews were precisely the same, each one generating a wealth of complex and enormously rich descriptive data. When these audiotaped interviews were transcribed and analyzed it became clear that Mary had found her way into a vast repertoire of alternative viewpoints about the structure and function of the heart, the blood vessels, and the blood itself.

One example is seen in the way students describe the circulatory pattern. When asked to show what happens to a drop of blood leaving the heart on a trip to the big toe, the students offered an interesting and revealing set of alternative viewpoints. Among the elementary school children, a significant number of interviewees subscribed to a view we have labeled the "one-way trip." In this view, blood leaves the heart and arrives at its destination directly, without passing through the lungs for oxygenation. Furthermore, once it arrives at its destination it does not return to the heart for another trip. Interestingly, among college students this view was quite rare; however, most of the freshmen Mary interviewed failed to understand the nature of the double (pulmonary and systemic) circulatory pattern. In another question aimed at eliciting students' understanding of the relationship of respiration and circulation, Mary asked students to explain what happens to the air we breath into our bodies (Figure 5).

At this point, Mary decided it was necessary to collate, summarize, and critically analyze the preliminary findings. Employing a "constant comparison" approach, Mary reviewed the concept maps and interview transcripts of all 50 students. This review resulted in a "conceptual inventory" describing the most frequent views of the structure and function of the heart, the blood vessels, and the blood. With these results in hand, she began to wonder how representative these findings might be of students in the local area. To answer this question she decided it would be necessary to construct a written instrument based on her inventory and to administer it to a cross-age sample of local students.

## Mary's Instrument

The paper-and-pencil instrument Mary developed contained a number of open-ended and forced-choice items (Figure 6). In several questions students were required to draw a structure or label a diagram. In others, they used their own language to describe a biological event or process. To satisfy

**Question: What happens to the air we breath into our bodies?**

1. Heart to lungs

    **Subject** (4th grade): See when, well, when you breath in the air it comes down and it goes through the heart and it comes to the lungs.

    **Mary:** Does it go anywhere else?

    **S:** No

    **M:** OK. So we breath it in, it goes to the heart and then to the lungs . . . why does it go to the heart?

    **S:** So, um, it can get to the lungs.

2. Mouth to lungs and out

    **M:** How does your body get air everywhere in it? You have any ideas about that?

    **S:** How does it get air?

    **M:** Uh-huh.

    **S:** You breath it in here (points to mouth in drawing); it goes down in here (points to lungs in drawing); then when you breath it out it comes back up.

3. From lungs via air tubes to rest of body

    **S:** (College freshman): (Drawing) Let's see, the air comes down your windpipe, this is your windpipe, then it goes through these lungs, then it goes to bronchiole tubes, then it goes to your air sacs and then it goes back out.

    **M:** OK, so you breath in, it goes into here (pointing) and it comes back out.

    **S:** Well . . . but see there're like these little bronchiole tubes that go all over your body. And they take it to all over your body and it goes back out.

    **M:** OK.

    **S:** I think in the lungs or bronchiole tubes it turns into carbon dioxide.

    **M:** (Later in interview) OK. so we have one system that takes air all over the body and another system that takes blood all over the body.

    **S:** (Nods yes)

    **M:** Is there any connection between these two organs, the heart and the lungs?

    **S:** I don't think so.

4. From lungs via blood vessels to heart to body*

    **M:** On your map you say the circulatory system starts with the lungs, what do you mean by that?

    **S:** Cause when you breath, the air goes in your lungs and from there everything starts.

    **M:** OK. Let's assume air gets to your lungs . . . then what happens?

    **S:** Air goes to these little sacs in your lungs, and blood's all in your lungs. It picks up the air and takes it to the heart and the heart pumps it to the rest of the body.

5. From mouth to windpipe to vein and out

    **S:** Oxygen comes in through the mouth, down the windpipe. It then goes to a vein that has a crack in it. When you breath out the dirty air goes out the crack and out the windpipe.

**FIGURE 5**

Mary's clinical interview transcript.

several members of her thesis committee, she ascertained the reading level (fourth grade) and $KR_{20}$ reliability estimates (.62) of her instrument. Finally, she administered the instrument to approximately 100 students at each of

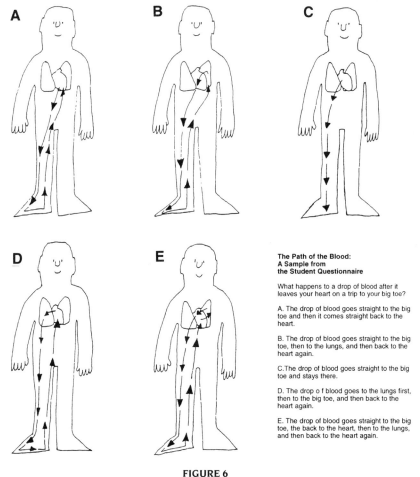

The Path of the Blood:
A Sample from
the Student Questionnaire

What happens to a drop of blood after it
leaves your heart on a trip to your big toe?

A. The drop of blood goes straight to the big
toe and then it comes straight back to the
heart.

B. The drop of blood goes straight to the big
toe, then to the lungs, and then back to the
heart again.

C.The drop of blood goes straight to the big
toe and stays there.

D. The drop o f blood goes to the lungs first,
then to the big toe, and then back to the
heart again.

E. The drop of blood goes straight to the big
toe, the back to the heart, then to the lungs,
and then back to the heart again.

**FIGURE 6**
An item from Mary's instrument.

five levels (fifth, eighth, and tenth grades, and college freshmen, both biology
majors and nonmajors). The data were transcribed and frequency and
×2 analyses were performed (Figure 7).

To finish this tale, we must report that Mary defended her thesis to a
somewhat indifferent and perplexed group of students and faculty and
fielded all questions with great alacrity. Several weeks later she was awarded
the Master of Science degree. That summer she presented the results to a
more enthusiastic and receptive audience at the first International Seminar
on Misconceptions in Science and Mathematics at Cornell University. In 1985
Mary received word that the paper based on her thesis had been reviewed by
the editorial board of *Science Education* and had been given its "Award of Merit"

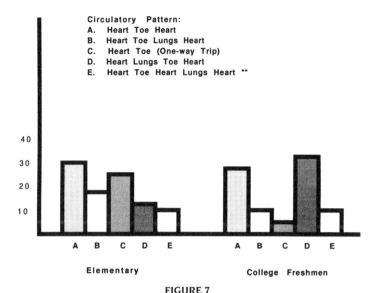

**FIGURE 7**

Frequencies of alternative conceptions: The human circulatory pattern.

in the "Outstanding Paper of 1984 Competition." In April of that year she flew to Cincinnati to receive the award at the annual meeting of the National Science Teachers Association. Ten years later portions of her research were incorporated into the PBS television program "A Private Universe." Today Mary serves as head of the education department at the Pisgah National Forest nature center and teaches at the community college level in western North Carolina. Her work has served as a model for many subsequent students (JJM).

## UNDERSTANDING AND CONCEPTUAL CHANGE IN SCIENCE: THE CURRENT RESEARCH AGENDA

In retrospect, we now recognize that Mary's study was but one effort in an avalanche of research on science understanding and conceptual change that began in the late 1970s and continues to the present day. This work has attempted to bridge the "vast disparity" that Shulman and Tamir (1973) saw between theory and empirical work in science education and has begun establishing, in their words, "some general normative expectancies for the evolution of particular concepts around which curriculum developers and program writers could plan their creative endeavors." A review of literature cited in *Science for All Americans* (1989) reveals that the authors of that widely disseminated report relied heavily on this new "genre of basic research" for empirical support.

Space does not permit a thorough review of this enormous research effort; however, we will attempt here to summarize some of its most important findings. Teachers and graduate students who want to familiarize themselves with research in this area in more depth should consult other sources (Mintzes & Arnaudin, 1986; Mintzes, Trowbridge, Arnaudin, & Wandersee, 1991; Mintzes, Wandersee, & Novak, 1997; Wandersee, Mintzes, & Arnaudin, 1989; Wandersee, Mintzes, & Novak, 1994).

To date, science educators have published over 3500 studies on students' understandings of scientific concepts (Pfundt & Duit, 1994). Based on this work and related work by researchers in the cognitive sciences we offer a set of 12 knowledge claims that have received substantial support through the efforts of thousands of researchers on every continent over a period of some 20 years (Figure 8).

In contrast to the assumptions of many science teachers, it is now clear that learners develop a set of well-defined ideas about natural objects and events even before they arrive at the classroom door. These ideas span the range of the formal scientific disciplines and seem to be found in equal frequencies among males and females, learners of all ages and ability levels, as well as cultural backgrounds and ethnic origins. Often these notions conflict with accepted scientific explanations and, most significantly, because they serve a useful function in everyday life, they tend to resist the efforts of even our finest teachers and most thoughtful textbook authors and curriculum developers. Unfortunately students' ideas often interact with knowledge presented in formal science lessons resulting in a diverse set of unintended learning outcomes.

Chapters 4–12 in this book describe a set of promising intervention strategies that attempt to address these difficult problems of understanding, offering assistance to those teachers who are committed to conceptual change. Before moving on to these strategies, however, we want to recite a few concrete examples of the types of "alternative conceptions" that students bring with them to their science classes.

In the physical sciences, the best documented examples come from the realm of Newtonian mechanics where, despite repeated instruction to the contrary, students continue to subscribe to a mix of Aristotelian and medieval views of forces acting on moving and stationary bodies. The basic misconception involves the relationship of force to motion, and for many students "motion implies a force" (Clement, 1983). This fundamental conceptual difficulty seems to rest on several underlying assumptions: (1) a force applied to an object causes motion in the direction of the force; (2) an object affected by a constant force moves with constant velocity; (3) the rate of motion is proportional to the magnitude of the force; and (4) in the absence of a force objects are at rest or are slowing down (Lythcott, 1985).

1. Learners are not "empty vessels" or "blank slates"; they bring with them to their formal study of science concepts; a finite but diverse set of ideas about natural objects and events; often these ideas are incompatible with those offered by science teachers and textbooks.

2. Many alternative conceptions are robust with respect to age, ability, gender, and cultural boundaries; they are characteristic of all formal science disciplines including biology, chemistry, physics, and the earth and space sciences; they typically serve a useful function in the everyday lives of individuals.

3. The ideas that learners bring with them to formal science instruction are often tenacious and resistant to change by conventional teaching strategies.

4. As learners construct meanings, the knowledge they bring interacts with knowledge presented in formal instruction; the result is a diverse set of unintended learning outcomes; because of limitations in formal assessment strategies, these unintended outcomes may remain hidden from teachers and students themselves.

5. The explanations that learners cling to often resemble those of previous generations of scientists and natural philosophers.

6. Alternative conceptions are products of a diverse set of personal experiences, including direct observation of natural objects and events, peer culture, everyday language, and the mass media as well as formal instructional intervention.

7. Classroom teachers often subscribe to the same alternative conceptions as their students.

8. Successful science learners possess a strongly hierarchical, cohesive framework of related concepts and they represent those concepts at a deeper, more principled level.

9. Understanding and conceptual change are epistemological outcomes of the conscious attempt by learners to make meanings; successful science learners make meanings by restructuring their existing knowledge frameworks through an orderly set of cognitive events (i.e., subsumption, superordination, integration, and differentiation).

10. The differential ability to solve problems in novel, real-world settings is attributable primarily to the advantages conferred on individuals possessing a highly integrated, well-differentiated framework of domain-specific knowledge which is activated through concentrated attention to and sustained reflection on related objects and events.

11. Learners who excel in the natural sciences habitually employ a set of metacognitive strategies enabling them to plan, monitor, regulate, and control their own learning.

12. Instructional strategies that focus on understanding and conceptual change may be effective classroom tools (Chapters 4–12).

**FIGURE 8**
A dozen knowledge claims about understanding and conceptual change in science.

In a now-classic study by Seattle high school physics teacher Jim Minstrell (1982), students were asked about the forces acting on a book lying flat on a table. In contrast to the widely held view that "objects at rest are not influenced by forces," the overwhelming majority of students attending this affluent suburban school recognized that downward forces (i.e., gravity) were indeed acting on the book; unfortunately, about half of them failed to understand that the table exerts an upward force on the book. Despite the best efforts of this 30-year veteran of the physics classroom, a large proportion of Jim's students (12 out of 27) remained unconvinced even after instruction to the contrary. Recently developed teaching strategies that rely heavily on the use of analogies (Chapter 7) and computer-assisted simulations (Chapter 8) seem to offer promising approaches to this problem.

In chemistry, another classic study by Novick and Nussbaum (1978) revealed that students have substantial difficulty understanding the particulate nature of matter. Israeli junior high school students who had been instructed on the topic in seventh grade were interviewed a year later on several aspects of the particulate model in the gaseous state. About 45% of them continued to rely on a continuous, "raisin-cake" model of matter. The underlying problem seems to be an inability to accept the idea that most of the space occupied by gases (as well as liquids and solids) is empty. The inescapable conclusion is that "pupils abhor a vacuum" and tend to fill it with "dust, air and smaller particles." In a follow-up study several years later (Novick & Nussbaum, 1981), similar views were found among high school and college students. One strategy that has been used with some success to teach the particulate nature of matter involves the use of debates and conceptual conflict (Chapter 6). Another approach employs small group discussions and cooperative learning (Chapter 10).

Biology students have difficulty with a wide range of concepts. In contrast to the physical sciences where problems of understanding often originate in the counterintuitive nature of the ideas, many of the conceptual hurdles in biology result from the necessity to integrate knowledge from several sources. Good examples of this are found in the knowledge domains of evolution (Good, Trowbridge, Demastes, Wandersee, Hafner, & Cummins, 1994) and ecology. Perhaps the most well-researched area in biology focuses on the notion of photosynthesis and the relationships between plants and animals in a closed ecosystem (Figures 9 and 10). Studies by Wandersee (1983) and Songer and Mintzes (1994) show that students of all ages have difficulty understanding the role of carbon dioxide as the primary source of plant biomass. That is, many students subscribe to the notion that plants obtain their food from the soil. In a closely related problem, learners typically experience conceptual problems with the issue of gas exchange. Most students seem to understand the dependence of animals on plants as a primary source of oxygen; they fail, however, to recognize that plants respire and thereby produce enough carbon dioxide to survive independently of animals.

## PLANTS GET THEIR FOOD FROM THE SOIL

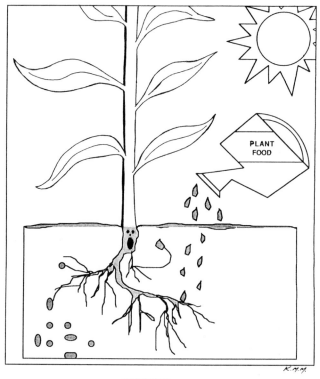

**FIGURE 9**
Where Do Plants Get Their Food? (Drawn by K. M. Markham).

This important finding was reported by Cathy Songer, a former graduate student who received her M.S. degree in 1993 (JJM).

Understanding complex biological issues such as photosynthesis and cellular respiration requires students to integrate knowledge from chemistry and physics and several other disciplines in order to construct a framework of ideas that applies to life forms. Several new teaching strategies offer opportunities to engage students in this kind of integrative activity; they include a range of graphic organizers (Chapter 4), metacognitive techniques (Chapter 5), interactive historical vignettes (Chapter 11), and one-on-one conversations (Chapter 12).

From a research perspective, it is clear that efforts to understand how students understand in the natural sciences are in an embryonic state. Well-designed studies that focus on changing students' ideas through instruc-

ALTERNATIVE CONCEPTION:

## PLANTS PERFORM ONLY PHOTOSYNTHESIS, NOT CELLULAR RESPIRATION

**FIGURE 10**
Can Plants and Animals Survive in a Closed Ecosystem?
(Drawn by K. M. Markham).

tional intervention are even newer. From the standpoint of a graduate student who is just beginning to explore this field, that is good news! It means that much remains to be done and that thoughtful, well-planned, well-executed, theory-driven research is sorely needed. But where to begin?

## TOWARD A NEW BEGINNING: FUTURE DIRECTIONS IN SCIENCE EDUCATION RESEARCH

In this concluding section we intend to drop some of the formalisms and "stuffiness" associated with academic writing and speak directly to teachers and beginning graduate students about doing research in science education.

In so doing we would like to offer some tips and practical suggestions for those who wish to contribute to our growing knowledge base on understanding and conceptual change in science. Each of us has served on editorial boards of several journals in the field and together we have amassed a combined total of some 50 years of research experience during which we have advised dozens of M.S. and Ph.D. students. We would like to share some of the practical knowledge we have put together and encourage you to think about these ideas and perhaps write to us with some of your own!

## Reading, Reflecting, and Discussing

As Human Constructivists we subscribe to the notion that "the single most important factor influencing learning is what the learner already knows." This conviction, combined with a rather traditional education in the natural sciences and many years in the classroom, has led us to value the knowledge of experienced teachers as well as researchers, but to do so in a critical and, we hope, constructive and reflective manner. Oftentimes students come to graduate school with a strong background in a science, a range of professional courses in education, and several years of practical classroom experience at the elementary or secondary school level. As a result, the typical graduate student has developed some well-defined and sometimes strongly held views about teaching and learning. This framework of prior knowledge serves as a "scaffolding" for virtually everything that happens in graduate school.

In this context, the first challenge a new researcher faces is learning to read the professional literature meaningfully; that is, learning to construct and reconstruct knowledge about science teaching and learning through a well-planned introduction to the theoretical and empirical foundations of the field. This kind of meaningful reading requires a substantial commitment of time, an opportunity and a willingness to reflect deeply on new knowledge, and a chance to share and negotiate meanings with a mentor and a small group of equally committed colleagues in a cooperative environment.

Although many graduate programs in science education require one or more courses in "research methods," our experience has been that these courses tend to focus primarily on issues such as experimental design and data analysis, often enrolling students from a wide range of disciplines. Certainly such an experience is useful, but it does not substitute for a well-planned program of reading that begins early in the program and is directed toward those who have a serious interest in science teaching and learning.

As a new graduate student in science education, we suggest that your reading include selections from the following areas: (1) History, Philosophy, Sociology, and Anthropology of Science (Atran, 1990; Cole, 1992; Conant, 1957; Kuhn, 1962; Toulmin, 1972); (2) Epistemology and Learning Theory

(Ausubel, Novak, & Hanesian, 1978; Novak & Gowin, 1984; von Glasersfeld, 1989; Vygotsky, 1962); (3) Cognitive Science (Carey, 1987; Gardner, 1985); and (4) Science Education (Driver, Guesne, & Tiberghien, 1992). Additionally, you will want to become a regular reader of the journals in the field. Among the journals you should read each month are several devoted to research, including: *International Journal of Science Education*, *Journal of Research in Science Teaching*, *Research in Science and Technological Education*, and *Science Education*. You may also want to keep up with those journals and magazines intended primarily for classroom practitioners such as: *The American Biology Teacher*, *Journal of Biological Education*, *Journal of Chemical Education*, *Journal of College Science Teaching*, *The Physics Teacher*, *School Science Review*, *School Science and Mathematics*, *Science and Children*, *Science Scope*, and *The Science Teacher*.

To aid you in locating relevant research articles you will need to become familiar with two computerized databases operated by the Educational Resources Information Center (ERIC), which is a national clearinghouse for published and unpublished materials in education. The Center maintains and updates *Journals in Education* for published articles and *Resources in Education* for unpublished articles, reports, curriculum materials, and proceedings of national and regional meetings. Virtually every college and university library maintains these materials in microfiche along with abstracts in hardcopy and electronic form. Access to the ERIC databases is also available through internet links. Additionally, the World Wide Web has numerous sites devoted to research in science education, among them is NARSTNET, which is operated by the National Association for Research in Science Teaching (Homepage address: http://science.coe.uwf.edu/narst/NARST.html).

Attendance at national and regional meetings of professional science education associations provides additional access to current work in the field. Among the meetings we regularly attend are those of NARST, the National Science Teachers Association (NSTA), National Association of Biology Teachers (NABT), American Educational Research Association (AERA), and American Association for the Advancement of Science (AAAS). Papers presented at these meetings are often on the "cutting edge" of recent research efforts and attendance at annual conventions will enable you to meet and exchange ideas with established researchers and graduate students at other institutions who share your research interests. In our experience, this kind of direct and often informal interaction can be strongly motivational and may even help you think through some of your ideas for a thesis or dissertation topic.

## Mapping and Diagramming

As you read, reflect on, and discuss the direction your research might take, we strongly recommend that you begin constructing a set of concept maps and vee diagrams that present your evolving ideas in visual form. The mapping and diagramming should begin as early as possible in your tenure as a graduate student and continue until you and your thesis committee agree on a thesis topic and a written paper. This ongoing effort to restructure your knowledge and present it in visual form accomplishes several purposes.

In the first instance it helps you clarify your thoughts and integrate your ideas from a variety of sources; for example, readings, discussions, direct observations and personal classroom experiences. For most of us, the "fuzzy" ideas that we conjure up need to be formalized, and the very act of formalizing them forces us to wrestle with subtleties and potential inconsistencies that inevitably crop up in our thinking. Fuzzy thinking is *not* a sign of poor thinking; it is a sign that says, "Caution: Knowledge Under Construction." Concept maps and vee diagrams can help to weed out the good ideas from the bad and to excise the ambiguities in our thinking.

Another way that mapping and diagramming help is by enabling us to share our ideas with others in a concise and timely manner. Good research is usually a product of many minds working together, negotiating meanings and arriving at some form of agreement that approaches consensus. (Check out the AAAS journal *Science*. You will find that single-author contributions are virtually nonexistent. Many articles have a dozen or more contributors). Any device that we can use to facilitate the sharing and negotiating of meanings is of potential value. These tools can be especially valuable to a graduate student who is working with a thesis committee composed of a number of individuals with diverse interests, skills, and intellectual commitments.

As we work through a significant problem our ideas about the problem, its significance and its potential solutions change. This is especially true of a research endeavor. In our experience it is rare for a thoughtful individual to "solve" the problem that he or she originally conceptualized. More often than not, the very act of working on the problem changes our perception of it, and typically the final destination of this problem-solving journey turns out to be far afield of that charted in our original map. In the course of this journey it is very important to keep track of where we started, the direction we took, and the significant turning points in the trip. One way to do this is through a succession of maps and diagrams which documents our thinking along the way.

The methods and results of our study will ultimately be embodied in a written document for others to see. In preparing the thesis, dissertation, or research paper, we have found that a concept map can provide a valuable way of graphically organizing our ideas in preparation for writing and offers a more flexible prewriting guide than a traditional outline. For those who have taken the time to restructure their knowledge in visual form over the course of several months, the final version of the concept map enables us to readily reconstruct our journey in the "linear" form generally preferred by graduate school deans.

## Broadening and Deepening

One of the common complaints about graduate work in science education is its parochial character. In many M.S. and Ph.D. programs, coursework emphasizes offerings available primarily in the School or College of Education. We think this is a mistake that serves to produce narrowly trained individuals possessing certain technical skills but sorely lacking the breadth and depth of knowledge that will be needed in coming years. As a teacher or graduate student in science education we strongly encourage you to think of yourself as a specialist in an interdisciplinary field that concentrates on understanding and conceptual change in science. To fulfill your role you will need to integrate a wide range of ideas from the natural and social sciences, as well as the arts and humanities.

If your previous education in a natural science discipline is inadequate, your first goal should be to address that deficiency. The work that contemporary science educators do requires depth of understanding in a specific science discipline. If you are enrolled in an M.S. program, you need the equivalent of at least a bachelors degree in biology, chemistry, physics, or earth science; if you are working toward a Ph.D., you need the equivalent of at least a masters. This recommendation for depth of knowledge is not a gratuitous one; it is borne of substantial research in cognition showing that "thinking" is contextually determined. If you wish to contribute to the improvement of science teaching and learning, you must prepare yourself to think like a scientist as well as a teacher.

In our experience, the most important contributions in science education come from people who know deeply, read widely, and learn to adapt ideas from many sources. In addition to your learning in a natural science discipline, you must continue your education in the social sciences, humanities, and the arts. The readings that engage you in an introductory seminar in science education may serve as entree to courses in those disciplines. We especially recommend courses that address issues in history, philosophy, and classical literature.

## Committing

As you read, reflect, and discuss; as you map and diagram; and as you broaden and deepen your understandings, you will eventually reach a point of commitment to a research problem and an approach to investigating that problem. Before you make that commitment, we suggest that you ask yourself the following questions about your problem:

Does the central problem grow out of and contribute to a broad-based theoretical and empirical framework that focuses on understanding and conceptual change in the natural sciences? Are the "focus questions" important? Are they "answerable" within the timeframe and the resources you have at your disposal? Do they apply across a wide range of contexts? Are the questions of concern to a diverse population of teachers, researchers, and school clientele rather than a local constituency? In designing your study, have you considered the important issues of students' prior knowledge, predominant learning modes, age, gender, ethnicity, culture, abilities, and interests? Are the answers likely to significantly impact classroom practice over an extended period of time?

In a recent publication (Wandersee, Mintzes, & Novak, 1994), we briefly outlined five promising areas of future research in science education. In our judgment, those who commit to one or more of these research agendas over an extended period of time are likely to make significant contributions to our understanding of science teaching and learning. We would encourage you to consider making a contribution to one of the following problems:

## Critical Junctures in Learning

Longitudinal studies have found that students typically traverse particularly critical periods in the learning of selected scientific concepts such as evolution, the particulate nature of matter, and the structure and function of cells, among others (Novak & Musonda, 1991; Pearsall, Skipper, & Mintzes, 1997; Trowbridge and Wandersee, 1994). For example, in one study (Pearsall, Skipper, & Mintzes, 1997) we discovered that the first few weeks in a college-level cell biology course is characterized by a radical or "strong" form of knowledge restructuring in that domain. By examining a set of successive concept maps drawn at 4-week intervals throughout the semester, we discovered that this period of major change involves the acquisition of entirely new superordinate concepts (such as "eukaryote" and "prokaryote") that substantially affects the way students think about cells. This period of radical restructuring is followed by subsequent periods of "weak" reorganization resulting from the more gradual and elaborative forms of learning that Ausubel and Novak call subsumption.

What happens to students who fail to restructure their knowledge during the early period? Might we expect to find similar periods of restructuring in other knowledge domains? Can metacognitive tools such as concept maps help students restructure their knowledge? From the perspective of Human Constructivism, studies such as these help us to understand conceptual change as a desirable epistemological outcome resulting from the orderly restructuring of knowledge that accompanies meaningful learning. The principal authors of the study, Renee Pearsall and Jo El Skipper, are high school biology teachers who received the M.S. degree in 1995 for their contribution. The presentation based on their theses was nominated for the annual "Paper of the Year" award at the 1996 annual NARST meeting. Related work on critical junctures in the learning of evolution constituted the core of John Trowbridge's doctoral dissertation. John, a contributor to this book, is' now an assistant professor of science education at Southeastern Louisiana University.

## Comparative Knowledge Structures

Studies by cognitive scientists have shown that novices and experts in scientific domains differ in the way they organize and use their knowledge (Chi, Glaser, & Farr, 1988). These differences may be important to science educators who are interested in documenting pathways of conceptual change. Only a few such studies have been devoted to comparing beginning and experienced students in formal learning environments (Smith, 1990; Markham, Mintzes, & Jones, 1994; Mintzes, Markham, & Jones, 1993); however, the results of these efforts are particularly intriguing. For example, in one study (Mintzes, Markham, & Jones, 1993) we found that freshmen college students completing an introductory biology course for nonmajors had radically different ways of organizing their thinking about "mammals" than seniors and graduate students finishing an advanced course in mammalogy (not surprising—but wait!). In a series of clinical interviews, 25 students enrolled in each of these classes were presented with line drawings representing a diverse group of 20 mammals and were asked to "tell me everything you know about a _____" (e.g., lion, manatee, bat). The propositions generated by these students were then analyzed for structural differences.

The results confirmed, as expected, that the experienced students were demonstrably more knowledgable about mammals; they offered twice as many scientifically acceptable propositions as the novices (Figure 11). The important finding, however, was revealed in a structural analysis of the propositions (Figure 12). The frequencies of propositions we observed demonstrate the emergence in the experienced group of a vast, new repertoire of implicit, superordinate concepts that reorders students' thinking. These superordinate concepts provide a parsimonious yet very powerful mechanism for conveying biological adaptations and phylogenetic relationships among mammals; they restructure students' frameworks on the basis of significant underlying dimensions including reproductive strategies and dietary patterns. Subsequent work using concept maps and sorting techniques showed that the emergence of these new concepts is correlated with qualitative superiority in the use of inferential reasoning and the ability to recognize and use large, meaningful patterns in the assignment of class membership.

This contribution to our understanding of knowledge restructuring is based on the work of a former graduate student, Kimberly Markham (JJM). Kim received the M.S. degree in 1992 and reported her findings at the Third International Seminar on Misconceptions and Educational Strategies in Science and Mathematics at Cornell University in 1993. Her work provides further evidence that conceptual change of the type that distinguishes

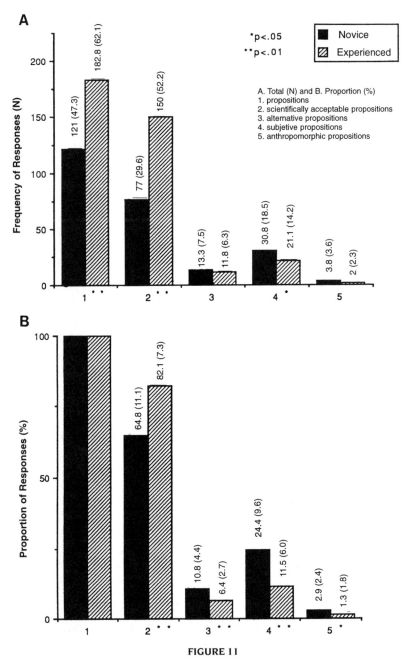

**FIGURE 11**

Propositions about mammals by novice and experienced students.

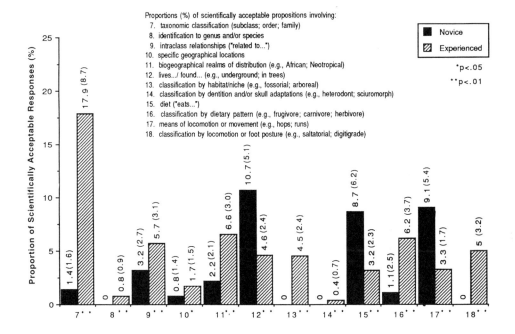

Proportions (%) of scientifically acceptable propositions involving:
7. taxonomic classification (subclass; order; family)
8. identification to genus and/or species
9. intraclass relationships ("related to...")
10. specific geographical locations
11. biogeographical realms of distribution (e.g., African; Neotropical)
12. lives.../ found... (e.g., underground; in trees)
13. classification by habitat/niche (e.g., fossorial; arboreal)
14. classification by dentition and/or skull adaptations (e.g., heterodont; sciuromorph)
15. diet ("eats...")
16. classification by dietary pattern (e.g., frugivore; carnivore; herbivore)
17. means of locomotion or movement (e.g., hops; runs)
18. classification by locomotion or foot posture (e.g., saltatorial; digitigrade)

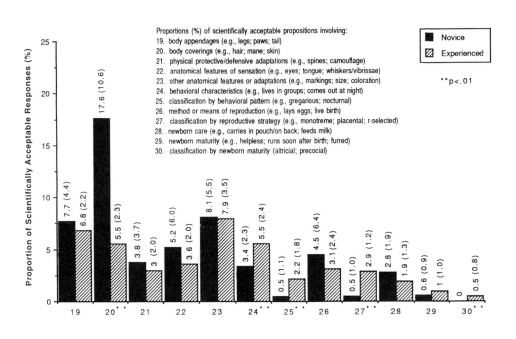

Proportions (%) of scientifically acceptable propositions involving:
19. body appendages (e.g., legs; paws; tail)
20. body coverings (e.g., hair; mane; skin)
21. physical protective/defensive adaptations (e.g., spines; camouflage)
22. anatomical features of sensation (e.g., eyes; tongue; whiskers/vibrissae)
23. other anatomical features or adaptations (e.g., markings; size; coloration)
24. behavioral characteristics (e.g., lives in groups; comes out at night)
25. classification by behavioral pattern (e.g., gregarious; nocturnal)
26. method or means of reproduction (e.g., lays eggs; live birth)
27. classification by reproductive strategy (e.g., monotreme; placental; r-selected)
28. newborn care (e.g., carries in pouch/on back; feeds milk)
29. newborn maturity (e.g., helpless; runs soon after birth; furred)
30. classification by newborn maturity (altricial; precocial)

knowledgeable individuals in scientific domains is a result in part of super-ordinate learning, a process which restructures students' frameworks on the basis of new and more powerful higher-order concepts. In our view studies of this type provide the fundamental knowledge we need to rethink present-day teaching strategies.

## Knowing and Feeling

Studies that examine relationships between knowing and feeling are sorely needed. The writings of D. B. Gowin (1981) provide a strong theoretical framework for exploring how prior knowledge influences our belief systems, our attitudes, and our value claims. Although science educators have de-voted considerable time to the study of "affective outcomes" of instruction, few have taken a systematic and sustained look at how cognitive structure influences and is influenced by the structure of our beliefs and attitudes. The prevailing view seems to be that the development of a complex framework of knowledge is strongly correlated with positive attitudes and these in turn enhance self esteem. The work of Gilligan (1982), Kohlberg (1964), and Perry (1970) provide useful insights into issues of "moral development" and might provide additional direction to those interested in this area. How are our attitudes about controversial social issues (e.g., abortion, euthanasia, nuclear energy, environmental pollution) affected by the structure of our knowledge in related disciplines (e.g., reproductive biology, atomic physics, population and community ecology)? This is certainly an area worth exploring and could have substantial payoff in classroom effectiveness.

## Metacognition

As suggested earlier, one of the characteristic attributes of successful science students that has enormous implications for the future of science education is their well-honed ability to monitor, regulate, and control their own learn-ing. The importance of metacognitive strategies becomes clear as we begin to recognize that efforts to improve science teaching are rapidly approaching a point of diminishing return and that substantial breakthroughs will need to focus more on the "learning side" of the equation. Metacognitive strate-gies such as those described in Chapters 4 and 5 offer ways to empower learners; that is, they promise to help students "learn how to learn" (Novak & Gowin, 1984). At this point, however, the evidence suggests that short-term efforts to introduce these techniques are likely to have limited effects (Edmondson and Novak, 1993). What we need are long-term commitments aimed at introducing age-appropriate metacognitive strategies across the entire spectrum of the elementary, secondary, and college years. Clearly, this is not an undertaking that can be successfully accomplished by a degree candidate working in isolation, but rather it requires a collaborative effort by teams of researchers, teachers, administrators, and parents. However, once such a team has been assembled the avenues for productive research are almost limitless. Can metacognitive strategies be taught successfully to large numbers of students? Will students use these strategies when given the opportunity? If the strategies are regularly employed, will they substantially impact understanding and conceptual change? Who stands to benefit most by these strategies? These are just a few of the questions that quickly come to mind.

## Intervention

To many beginning graduate students, the raison d'etre for research in science education is to explore the efficacy of newly proposed teaching methods and curriculum designs. The next section of this book (Chapters 4–12) offers a handful of promising new approaches that deserve careful scrutiny, extended trials in a variety of classroom settings, and well-designed, sustained assessment efforts. They are offered not as panaceas and certainly not as "foolproof" answers to the difficult questions of understanding and conceptual change. Rather, these strategies grow out of a commitment to the view that science classrooms are best seen as laboratories for meaningful learning; that science teachers and science education researchers are engaged in an ongoing experiment to enhance this kind of learning; and that applied research is the only reasonable route for adjudicating the knowledge claims of those who offer new proposals. Encumbent upon researchers in turn is the obligation to examine newly proposed interventions within the context in which they are offered and to attempt to replicate findings of previous studies. One of the lasting and unfortunate legacies of previous generations of researchers was the tendency to adopt inappropriate assessment measures in evaluating the efficacy of new proposals in science teaching and learning.

A recent dissertation study by Ph.D. candidate Jo Wallace reveals how critical the choice of assessment measures can be. Jo was interested in evaluating the efficacy of a widely used third-generation computer-based program for teaching concepts in marine biology. Students were assigned to an "instruction" group and a "placebo" group and were tested before and after instruction. The assessment measures included a commercially prepared multiple-choice test developed by the publishers and a set of concept maps. An analysis of the multiple-choice tests revealed negligible growth in understanding as measured by student achievement. The concept maps however showed substantial and significant change in the structural complexity and propositional validity of knowledge held by the instructed group, and the findings were confirmed in follow-up interviews (Wallace & Mintzes, 1990).

With this brief introduction to theory and research we invite you now to explore nine new proposals designed to encourage understanding and conceptual change in science classrooms. We further invite your comments and criticisms which we promise to faithfully convey to the authors (e-mail addresses: mintzes@uncwil.edu; ciwand@lsuvm.sncc.lsu.edu; jdn2@cornell.edu).

## References

Atran, S. (1990). *Cognitive foundations of natural history*. Cambridge: Cambridge University Press.
Arnaudin, M. (1983). Students' alternative conceptions of the human circulatory system: A cross-age study. M.S. thesis. University of North Carolina at Wilmington.
Arnaudin, M., & Mintzes, J. (1985). Students' alternative conceptions of the human circulatory system: A cross-age study. *Science Education*, 69, 721–733.
Arnaudin, M., & Mintzes, J. (1986). The cardiovascular system: Children's conceptions and misconceptions. *Science and Children*, 23, 48–51.
Arnaudin, M., Mintzes, J., Dunn, C., & Shafer, T. (1984). Concept mapping in college science teaching. *Journal of College Science Teaching*, 14, 117–121.
Ausubel, D. P. (1963). *The psychology of meaningful verbal learning*. New York: Grune and Stratton.
Ausubel, D., Novak, J., & Hanesian, H. (1978). *Educational psychology: A cognitive view*. New York: Holt, Rinehart and Winston.
Barnard, J. D. (1942). The lecture-demonstration method versus the problem-solving method of teaching a college science course. *Science Education*, 26, 121–132.
Bloom, B. (1971). Learning for mastery. In B. Bloom, J. Hastings, & G. Madaus (eds.), *Handbook or formative and summative evaluation*. New York: McGraw–Hill.
Boenig, R. (1969). *Research in science education: 1938 through 1947*. New York: Teachers College Press.
Bond, A. (1940). An experiment in the teaching of genetics with special referrence to the objectives of general education. *Teachers College Contributions to Education*, No. 796. New York: Bureau of Publications, Teachers College, Columbia University.
Burnett, R. W. (1941). The opinions of science teachers and their implications for teacher education. *Teachers College Record*, 42, 709–719.
Carey, S. (1987). *Conceptual development in childhood*. Cambridge, MA: MIT Press.
Chi, M., Glaser, R., & Farr, M. (1988). *The nature of expertise*. Hillsdale, NJ: Lawrence Erlbaum.
Clement, J. (1983). A conceptual model discussed by Galileo and used intuitively by physics students. In D. Gentner & A. Stevens (eds.), *Mental Models* (pp. 325–339). Hillsdale, NJ: Lawrence Erlbaum.
Cole, S. (1992). *Making science: Between nature and society*. Cambridge, MA: Harvard University Press.
Conant, J. (1957). *Harvard case studies in experimental science*, Vols. 1 & 2. Cambridge, MA: Harvard University Press.
Curtis, F. D. (1926). A *digest of investigations in the teaching of science*. Philadelphia: P. Blakiston's Son & Co., Inc.
Driver, R., & Easley, J. (1978). Pupils and paradigms: A review of the literature related to concept development in adolescent science students. *Studies in Science Education*, 5, 61–84.
Driver, R., Guesne, E., & Tiberghien, A. (1992). *Childrens' ideas in science*. London: Milton Keynes.
Edmondson, K., & Novak, J. (1993). The interplay of scientific epistemological views, learning strategies, and attitudes of college students. *Journal of Research in Science Teaching*, 30, 547–559.
Gardner, H. (1985). *The mind's new science: A history of the cognitive revolution*. New York: Basic Books.
Gilbert, A. (1943). Science content in the elementary school. *School Science and Math*, 43, 769–773.
Gilligan, C. (1982). *In a different voice: Psychological theory and human development*. Cambridge, MA: Harvard University Press.
Good, R., Trowbridge, J., Demastes, S., Wandersee, J., Hafner, M., & Cummins, C. (1994). *Proceedings of the 1992 Evolution Education Research Conference*. Baton Rouge: Louisiana State University.
Gowin, D. B. (1981). *Educating*. Ithaca, NY: Cornell University Press.
Hall, C. (1939). Trends in the organization of high school chemistry since 1920. *Journal of Chemical Education*, 16, 116–120.

Howard, F. T. (1943). Complexity of mental processes in science testing. New York: Bureau of Publications, Teachers College, Columbia University.

Hunter, G., & Spohr, L. (1941). Science sequence and enrollments in the secondary schools of the United States. *Statistics of Public High Schools.* Washington, DC: U.S. Office of Education, Bulletin No. 2, Chapter 5.

Johnson, P. O. (1940). The measurement of the effectiveness of laboratory procedures upon the achievement of students in zoology with particular reference to the use and value of detailed drawings. *Proc. Minnesota Academy of Science*, 8, 70–72.

Kohlberg, L. (1964). Development of moral character and moral ideology. *Review of Child Development Research*, 1, 383–431.

Kuhn, T. (1962). *The structure of scientific revolutions.* Chicago: University of Chicago Press.

Lythcott, J. (1985). "Aristotelian" was given as the answer, but what was the question? *American Journal of Physics*, 53, 428–432.

Markham, K., Mintzes, J., & Jones, G. (1994). The concept map as a research and evaluation tool: Further evidence of validity. *Journal of Research in Science Teaching*, 31, 91–101.

Matteson, H., & Kambley, P. (1940). Knowledge of science possessed by pupils entering the seventh grade. *School Science and Math*, 40, 244–247.

Minstrell, J. (1982). Explaining the "at rest" condition of an object. *Physics Teacher*, 20, 10–14.

Mintzes, J. (1975). The A-T approach 14 years later: A review of recent research. *Journal of College Science Teaching*, 4, 247–252.

Mintzes, J. (1984). Naive theories in biology: Children's concepts of the human body. *School Science and Math*, 84, 548–555.

Mintzes, J., & Arnaudin, M. (1986). The cardiovascular system: Children's conceptions and misconceptions. *Science and Children*, 23, 48–51.

Mintzes, J., Littlefield, D., Shaub, D., Crockett, R., Rakitan, R., & Crockett, R. (1976). Studies on individualized instruction in biology. *School Science and Math*, 76, 675–686.

Mintzes, J., Markham, K., & Jones, G. (1993). The structure and use of biological knowledge in novice and experienced students. Paper presented at the 66th annual meeting of the National Association for Research in Science Teaching, April 15–19, Atlanta, GA.

Mintzes, J., Trowbridge, J., Arnaudin, M., & Wandersee, J. (1991). Children's biology: Studies on conceptual development in the life sciences. In S. M. Glynn, R. H. Yeany, & B. K. Britton (eds.), *The psychology of learning science.* Hillsdale, NJ: Lawrence Erlbaum Associates, 179–204.

Mintzes, J., Wandersee, J., & Novak, J. (1997). Meaningful learning in science: The Human Constructivist perspective. In G. D. Phye (ed.), *Handbook of Academic Learning.* Orlando, FL: Academic Press.

National Education Association. (1893). *Report of the committee on secondary school studies.* Washington, DC: U.S. Government Printing Office.

National Education Association. (1918). *Cardinal principles of secondary education: A Report of the commission on the reorganization of secondary education.* (U.S. Bureau of Education, Bulletin No. 35). Washington, DC: U.S. Government Printing Office.

Novak, J. (1973). *A summary of research in science education* 1972. Columbus, OH: ERIC Clearinghouse for Science and Mathematics Education.

Novak, J. (1977). *A theory of education.* Ithaca, NY: Cornell University Press.

Novak, J. (1980). Learning theory applied to the biology classroom. *The American Biology Teacher*, 42, 280–285.

Novak, J., & Gowin, D. B. (1984). *Learning how to learn.* Cambridge: Cambridge University Press.

Novak, J., & Musonda, D. (1991). A twelve-year longitudinal study of science concept learning. *American educational research journal*, 28, 117–153.

Novick, S., & Nussbaum, J. (1978). Junior high school pupil's understanding of the particulate nature of matter: An interview study. *Science Education*, 62, 273–281.

Novick, S., & Nussbaum, J. (1981). Pupils' understanding of the particulate nature of matter: A cross-age study. *Science Education*, 65, 187–196.

Nussbaum, J., & Novak, J. (1976). An assessment of children's concepts of the Earth utilizing structured interviews. *Science Education*, 60, 535–550.

Pearsall, N. R., Skipper, J., & Mintzes, J. (1997). Knowledge restructuring in the life sciences: A longitudinal study of conceptual change in biology. *Science Education*, 81, 193–215.

Perry, W. (1970). *Forms of intellectual and ethical development in the college years*. New York: Holt, Rinehart and Winston.

Pfundt, H., & Duit, R. (1994). *Students' alternative frameworks and science education*. Kiel, Germany: Institute for Science Education.

Shulman, L., & Tamir, P. (1973). Research on teaching in the natural sciences. In R. Travers (Ed.), *Second handbook of research on teaching* (pp. 1098–1148). Chicago: Rand McNally.

Smith, M. (1990). Knowledge structures and the nature of expertise in classical genetics. *Cognition and Instruction*, 7, 287–302.

Songer, C., & Mintzes, J. (1994). Understanding cellular respiration: An analysis of conceptual change in college biology. *Journal of Research in Science Teaching*, 31, 621–637.

Taylor, L. (1940). Science in general education at the college level. Paper presented at the American Science Teachers' Association, June 14, Columbus, OH.

Toulmin, S. (1972). *Human understanding, Vol. I: The collective use and evolution of concepts*. Princeton, NJ: Princeton University Press.

Trowbridge, J., & Wandersee, J. (1994). Identifying critical junctures in learning in a college course on evolution. *Journal of Research in Science Teaching*, 31, 459–473.

von Glasersfeld, E. (1989). Cognition, construction of knowledge, and teaching. *Synthese*, 80, 121–140.

Vygotsky, L. (1962). *Thought and language*. Cambridge, MA: MIT Press.

Wallace, J., & Mintzes, J. (1990). The concept map as a research tool: Exploring conceptual change in biology. *Journal of Research in Science Teaching*, 27, 1033–1052.

Wandersee, J. (1983). Students' misconceptions about photosynthesis: A cross-age study. In H. Helm & J. Novak (eds.), *Proceedings of the international seminar on misconceptions in science and mathematics* (pp. 441–466). Ithaca, NY: Dept. of Education, Cornell University.

Wandersee, J., Mintzes, J., & Arnaudin, M. (1989). Biology from the learner's viewpoint: A content analysis of the research literature. *School Science and Math*, 89, 654–668.

Wandersee, J., Mintzes, J., & Novak, J. (1994). Research on alternative conceptions in science. In D. Gabel (ed.), *Handbook of research on science teaching and learning*. New York: MacMillan and Company, 177–210.

Watson, F. (1963). Research on teaching science. In N. Gage (ed.), *Handbook of research on teaching* (pp. 1031–1059). Chicago: Rand, McNally.

Wise, H. (1947). The measurement of ability to apply principles of physics in practical situations. *Science Education*, 31, 130–144.

Zapf, R. (1938). Superstitions of junior high school pupils. *The Journal of Educational Research*, 31, 435–446.

# Theory-Driven Intervention Strategies

# Theory-Driven Graphic Organizers

JOHN E. TROWBRIDGE
*Southeastern Louisiana University*

JAMES H. WANDERSEE
*Louisiana State University*

## WHAT ARE GRAPHIC ORGANIZERS?

Imagine the biggest metropolitan center in the world, home to 40 million people, and yet, virtually none of its streets have names. This place is Tokyo, Japan—where the organization of streets has been compared to a bowl of slippery noodles (WuDunn, 1996). Home visits, deliveries, and emergency services all require extra time to circle the area—seeking an address, getting further directions from a local policeman or merchant, and knocking on many doors until the correct building is finally located. To circumvent this problem, Japanese citizens who live in Tokyo frequently fax a hand-drawn, landmark-based map to someone when inviting them for a business or social visit. Could such a system and culture that prides itself on efficiency benefit from the use of a well-developed and comprehensive graphic organizer, one with consistently labeled nodes and links? We think so. But social custom and tradition currently work against introducing such a mapping and labeling system there.

Contrast this with a similar situation in London, England. Prior to 1936, the best map of the city was 17 years out of date. London's 3000-mile labyrinth of streets and roads was a virtual nightmare to traverse. Many places weren't even shown, much less identified, on the old city map. Phyllis

Pearsall, who is now well-known for creating the famous "A to Z" maps of London, decided to rectify the situation. To make sure the first edition of her London map was correct, she walked the city from dawn to dusk, day after day, covering some 23,000 streets and roads (Lyall, 1996). Cartographers call this process obtaining "ground truth." Later editions continued this practice. To this day, Londoners still purchase her A-Z maps and they ought to give thanks for the time and effort she has saved them. Cognitive psychology has corroborated that the better organized our knowledge is, the easier it is for us to access and use it. Can cartography teach us something about school science learning? Our answer is "yes."

Maps have a long and noble intellectual history (Wandersee, 1990). While a map is, admittedly, not equivalent to the territory, it is certainly a working representation of it—a thinking tool that condenses a host of prior experiences and opens up alternative pathways to a destination. A product of metacognition (the process of conscious and intentional mental reflection upon and restructuring of one's experiences), the map was one of the first recorded graphic organizers humans invented—and we think it is still one of the best.

Graphic organizers came to science education by way of reading research (Earle & Barron, 1973) and can be defined as visual representations that are added to instructional materials to communicate the logical structure of the instructional material (Jonassen, Beissner, & Yacci, 1993, p. 166). It is important to note two things about graphic organizers: (1) they were not originally intended to be constructed by the learner, but by the specialist, in order to aid the learner; and (2) they originally consisted of a hierarchy of boxed concepts connected by *unlabeled* lines, so that the exact nature of the relationship between them remained unspecified for the learner. Figure 1 shows a traditional type of graphic organizer which we have prepared to depict a recent research finding: The earth has a solid core that rotates faster than the rest of the planet (Cromie, 1996). While you may think you understand the gist of the text being represented in Figure 1, you really can't be sure, can you?

In contrast to that kind of graphic organizer, Novak and Gowin's (1984) research led them to develop what he called a *concept map*. Figure 2 presents a concept map of the same geoscience text. Try reading our concept map from the top concept downward. Isn't its meaning clearer than that of the traditional graphic organizer? The concept map is actually a type of graphic organizer which was first constructed by Novak in 1977 and his science education research group to summarize clinical interview data. Gradually, these researchers came to understand that a concept map was equally valuable as a metacognitive device when constructed by science learners themselves. The finished product was shown to reflect the understanding the learner had (for the science concepts that were mapped) better than traditional forms of testing did.

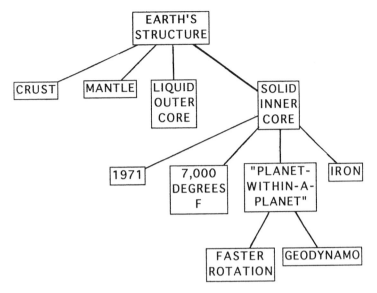

**FIGURE 1**

A graphic organizer for a geoscience text.

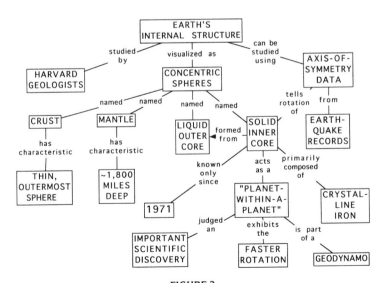

**FIGURE 2**

A concept map for a geoscience course.

Novak's research and development of concept mapping revealed the importance of specifying the links between concepts, including cross-links across branches of the hierarchy and adding examples to anchor concepts to the real world (Wandersee, 1990).

It was through our reading of Novak's publications on concept mapping almost two decades ago that we first became aware of the power of graphic metacognitive tools for improving science learning. At that time both of us were teaching the life sciences. Not only did we begin using concept mapping ourselves, we shared it with our students and watched them benefit as well.

As a result, we began to use and/or study not only concept mapping, but also other graphic tools consistent with Ausubel, Novak, and Gowin's constructivist theories in our own science education research programs. In this chapter, we will focus on theory-based graphic organizers, with particular emphasis on those that correspond to the theoretical frameworks of psychologist David Ausubel, science educator Joseph Novak, and philosopher D. Bob Gowin.

## A BASIC TAXONOMY OF GRAPHIC ORGANIZERS

Readence, Bean, & Baldwin (1985, p. 129) proposed five principal types of graphic organizers and classified graphic organizers according to their functions. We have found their basic taxonomy of visual organizational patterns to be useful for our purposes in this chapter, and we present it here, with our own modifications:

1. *Cause/Effect*: The graphic organizer connects reasons with results.
2. *Comparison/Contrast*: The graphic organizer highlights apparent likenesses and differences between objects or events.
3. *Time Order*: The graphic organizer depicts chronological sequences of objects or events.
4. *Simple Listing*: The graphic organizer groups related items.
5. *Problem/Solution*: The graphic organizer shows how a question can be answered.

We think all of the graphic organizers presented in this chapter fit this taxonomy and can be better understood by using it.

In an attempt to help learners organize, abstract, and reflect upon expository information, graphic organizers have emerged as the basis of some successful learning strategies. There is a great variety of graphic organizers in use in teaching today. See Table 1 for some typical examples in each of the five taxonomic categories presented previously. However, few have been studied to ascertain their effectiveness and even fewer are learning theory driven. An interesting property of such graphic organizers is that eventually

TABLE I
Examples of Graphic Organizers by Function Categories

| Function category | Example 1 | Example 2 |
| --- | --- | --- |
| Cause/effect | Fishbone diagram | Vector diagram |
| Comparison/contrast | Concept map | KWL chart |
| Time order | Flow chart | Cycle diagram |
| Simple listing | Concept circle diagram | Spectrum |
| Problem/solution | Vee diagram | Frame |

they become unnecessary. Yelon (1996, pp. 144–145) points out that para-medics who used a decision tree graphic organizer to guide their interventions in treating drug victims said they eventually internalized it and had no more need to actually look at it. We see graphic organizers as analogous to a "crutch for the mind," a temporary yet essential prosthetic device useful for initial understanding.

Some of the above examples from Table 1 as well as other graphics we have found frequently used in science education are presented below:

## Fishbone or Skeletal Illustrations

A frequently used graphic is the skeletal illustration. These may take the form of a branching tree or of a fish skeleton aptly named Herber's Herringbone Technique (Manzo & Manzo, 1990). The central or backbone part of the graph represents a major idea or landmarks related to the major idea or event sequence. The branching rays can be any number of supporting ideas, facts, or landmarks along the graphic (see Figure 3).

## K-W-L Charts

The K-W-L-plus strategy was developed by Carr and Ogle (1987). It involves probing what the student *knows*, what the student *wants* to know, and what the student *learned*. The resulting product most often is a three-column chart labeled with each category. The important, added feature in Carr and Ogle's strategy is its visual stimulation of the learner to restructure and organize the learned component into a summary or concept map (see Figure 4). This graphic organizer is used extensively in elementary school teaching. We find it appealing that a student actually gets a chance to state what they *want* to learn. We think this tool is appropriate for all levels of science instruction, not just for the lower grades.

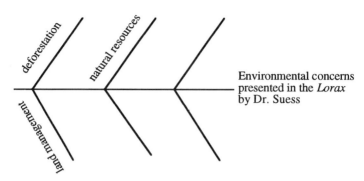

**FIGURE 3**
Sample skeletal graphic of partially completed student exercise
on the *Lorax*.

## Flowcharts

Flowcharts were developed by logicians and early computer programmers. Their purpose is to visually depict procedural knowledge. Briscoe (1990) discusses that flowcharts are useful to illustrate pathways, hypotheses, techniques, procedures, and schema. Flowcharts typically start with an oval labeled "enter" and end with a similar oval labeled "exit" or "end." Lines with arrows connect boxes (or rectangles) and diamonds. The boxes (or rectangles) enclose statements of procedural information. The diamond shapes enclose binary decision-point questions and provide two pathlines out, de-

| K<br>(Know) | W<br>(Want to Know) | L<br>(Learned) |
|---|---|---|
| Some are parks. | Where does the sand come from? | Parks allow everyone a chance to visit the beach. |
| Some are very crowded. | Where do the shells come from? | When an island looses its sand, its called erosion. |
| They have lots of sand. | Are there sharks in the water? | People living or visiting on these islands must watch for hurricanes. |
| There are shells on the beach. | Why aren't there many trees? | There is all kinds of ocean life in the waters around these barrier islands. |
|  |  | Salt spray and poor soil keeps trees from growing there. |

**FIGURE 4**
Example of K-W-L chart for the topic "barrier islands."

pending upon how the question is answered. Sometimes one of the pathlines loops the user back to previous procedures. At other times, both
pathlines lead to distinctly different subprocesses. We have found flowcharts
to be especially helpful in teaching students how to plan and conduct laboratory experiments and in teaching science teachers how to plan and execute
instructional procedures. The student can make use of a visual instead of
trying to decode and follow written directions. A flowchart showing the process of constructing roundhouse diagrams has been constructed below
(see Figure 5).

## Frames

A frame is a grid where a concept is examined in rows and columns. The first
row and column are the frames with labeled relationships (West, Farmer, &
Wolf, 1991; Grugel, 1996). The students then fill in the remaining boxes of
the grid with information they know and proceed to find out what they currently lack in order to complete the frame (see Figure 6).

## Thematic Maps

Thematic maps feature superimposition and provide opportunities for students to link science concepts to appropriate positions on geographic maps
(e.g., plotting variables such as ocean currents, butterfly migration paths,
hurricane tracks, red tide occurrences). An example of a thematic map showing the general flow of the Gulf Loop current is illustrated below (see Figure 7).

## Semantic Networking

Semantic networks were first proposed by Quillian (1967) as a hierarchical
model of human semantic memory. Quillian's Spreading Activation model
contends that at every level, general concepts offer access to more specific
ones. The semantic networks produced by Fisher and the SemNet Research
Group at San Diego State University are defined as multidimensional networks of concepts linked by named relations with associated text and images
(Fisher, 1992).

The SemNet Research Group has developed a widely used semantic networking application for the Macintosh computer which they call SemNet.
The semantic networks created by this program are $n$-dimensional, but can
only be viewed and printed out one node at a time. There are similarities
between printed excerpts from these networks and concept maps; however,
dimensionally and window-of-view are important distinctions.

Concept maps are two-dimensional, hierarchical representations that can
be viewed in their entirety. SemNet products can capture a larger number of
concepts and relationships. The computer can display or print out visually

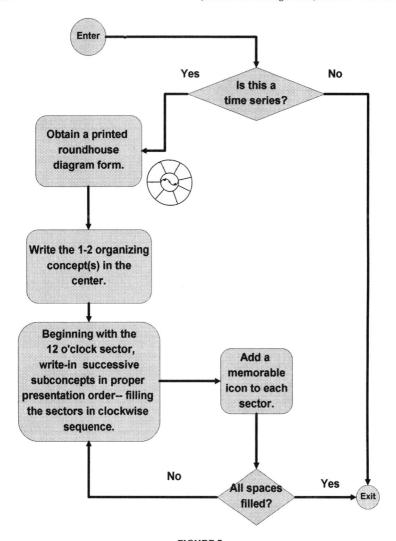

**FIGURE 5**

A flowchart showing the process of constructing roundhouse diagrams.

appealing network components. However, SemNets *in toto* are computer bound; whereas concept mapping, while also computerized, can also be done with pencil and paper in computer-less instructional settings and displayed in full. SemNet networks can capture enormous amounts of detail and may encompass thousands of concepts. In addition, they can be computer analyzed to reveal the most embedded concepts and important

| Diving history | Typical equipment | Commercial uses/discoveries | Scientific uses/discoveries | Military uses |
| --- | --- | --- | --- | --- |
| Pre 1800s | | | | |
| 1800s | | | | |
| 1900 -1920 | | | | |
| 1921 - 1940 | | | | |
| 1941 - 1960 | | | | |
| 1961 - 1980 | | | | |
| 1981 - present | | | | |

**FIGURE 6**

An example of a frame organizer for the topic "history of diving."

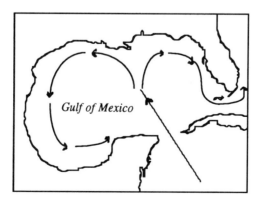

**FIGURE 7**

A thematic map showing loop current in the Gulf of Mexico.

relations. However, they may also lead to a representation that is too overwhelming to be useful for learning purposes.

From the work of Ausubel, Novak, and Gowin on how pupils learn, we hypothesize that the lack of distinct hierarchy is a further disadvantage for learners who want to incorporate ideas into long-term memory (LTM). However, we think that these disadvantages might be mitigated if students were taught how to morph the network and extract concept maps (smaller, more useable hierarchical node-link sets) from a large SemNet network that they have constructed.

The development of semantic networking and concept mapping have interesting parallels and important distinctions. They both have a substantial research base demonstrating their effectiveness as research and metacognitive tools. We think teachers and students will benefit from using both of these techniques in a complementary fashion. For example, science students can build concept maps around smaller, more manageable science topics, combine those "*micromaps*" into a larger concept map (map unit) at the end of instruction, then use concepts drawn from the upper levels of all the micromaps to construct a *macromap* (a map of maps). That way both detailed and big-picture views of the subject are available. In addition, building a SemNet network seems ideal for science education researchers investigating the nature of a large science content knowledge base for pairs of students who coconstruct a SemNet for a unit while discussing and debating the science content and connections during the construction process and for curriculum designers intent on making many connections to a single concept (see Figure 8).

## Grid Systems

While grid systems for drawing structures may be familiar to the engineer and the artist, they have also been demonstrated to be useful in biology education. Moncada and Wandersee (1993) reported that the use of a grid system to teach about the structure and function of fish, frog, and mammalian hearts was successful in enhancing student understanding of these structures. Despite the current use of multicolored plates in modern texts, we have found that a simple black-line drawings assembled within a grid is easily constructed and more likely to be understood and remembered by students (see Figure 9). Furthermore, students with limited drawing ability are able to work within the grid system with success. Again, the linking of labeled visual concepts to self-constructed graphic organizers is the key.

## Roundhouse Diagrams

Roundhouse diagrams are named after the circular buildings with central turntables that are used by railroads for housing and switching locomotives.

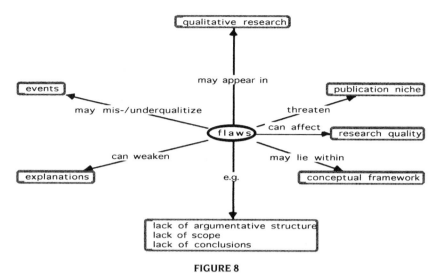

**FIGURE 8**
An example of a SemNet node.

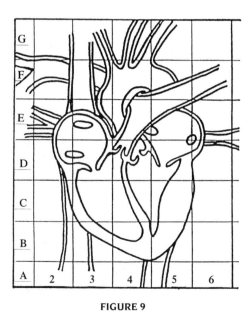

**FIGURE 9**
An example of a grid graphic constructed of the heart.

This science curriculum diagramming technique was named, standardized, and introduced to the science education community by a Louisiana State University professor, James Wandersee. He introduces it to teachers by asking them to imagine that the center of the diagram is a *conceptual turntable*. It is initially at the 12 o'clock position and it rotates clockwise—applying the central concept(s) to successive subconcept sectors (exit/entry tracks) of the outer circle. The order of the stops represents a sequence of events. Since the term *curriculum* originally meant *the path one traveled*, one complete rotation of such a conceptual turntable can, at different resolutions, represent a lesson, a unit, or a whole curriculum—all represented from a conceptual-event perspective.

The diagram's basic configuration was adapted from a course syllabus diagram prepared by a Michigan State University professor, Dr. Edwin Kashy, for ISP 209 *Physics of the World Around Us*. Based on constructivist principles, we have hypothesized that when we ask *students* to construct these diagrams, as opposed to giving them ready-made ones that we have constructed, it can serve admirably as a metacognitive tool. The flowchart introduced earlier in this chapter details the steps of the technique, as standardized by Wandersee. Wandersee's "15 Degree Laboratory" has shown that the iconic features of self-constructed roundhouse diagrams significantly improve science content recall, in comparison to similar diagrams containing only text. After introducing it to hundreds of teachers and science students since late 1994, Wandersee conducted a small-scale study in late 1995 which revealed that elementary and high school science teachers who learned the technique were able to remember the science content contained in these self-constructed diagrams better than they could remember the science content contained in journal descriptions that they wrote. Recently, we have found that students also appear to benefit from this technique when they use it to represent the "Procedure" section of their science laboratory reports. Not only do they prefer this to writing textual accounts, they report they can remember their procedures without interference from previously learned procedures after they construct roundhouse diagrams of them. Finally, we have found that it is important to limit the number of outer sectors in such a diagram to seven or less, in line with psychological research on short-term memory capacity (see Figure 10).

## Lab-o-Gram

The *Lab-o-gram* was first introduced to science teachers by Wandersee (1992) at a session for biology teachers at the national convention of the National Biology Teachers Association held in Boston. It is a compound metacognive tool that integrates declarative and procedural knowledge with the elements of knowledge construction needed to conduct a scientific procedure with understanding. We recommend it to be the culminating activity of a week-

**FIGURE 10**
An example of a roundhouse diagram.

long laboratory investigation conducted during the second half of a course, after students are already proficient at the component techniques of concept mapping, flow charting, and vee diagramming. We consider these three techniques and their fusion in the Lab-o-gram to be comprise the first comprehensive system of metacognive graphics to be used in science education (see Figure 11).

## THE EYE–BRAIN SYSTEM AND GRAPHIC ORGANIZERS: I CAME, I SAW, I UNDERSTOOD

Seeing has two meanings in our culture: (1) sensing something by the light it gives off or reflects and (2) interpreting those visual sensations. These meanings are sometimes confounded. In ordinary conversation, we often say

**Labogram**

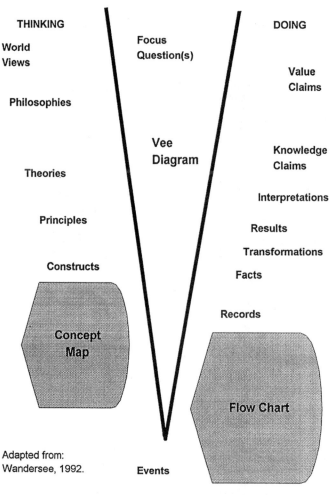

Adapted from:
Wandersee, 1992.

**FIGURE 11**
An example of a labogram graphic.

"Oh, I see!" when we mean we understand something. We also say "I see it!" when we sense something; for example, a parade finally coming into view after a long curbside wait. That confluence can perhaps be explained by the following information.

Scientists tell us that vision evolved to enhance survival of the organism. Three important survival questions (Solso, 1994, p. 49) to which vision provides answers are:

1. Just what is that object?
2. Where is that object?
3. What is that object doing?

Perhaps this explains why such a large proportion of the human brain is dedicated to visual processing.

The visual processing of information involves the eye–brain system. Much of what we call vision occurs, not just in the eye, but in the cerebral cortex of the human brain. All visual processing appears to follow quite similar neurological routines. The visual primitives, which include such characteristics of the visual image as lines, edges, and shapes, are later analyzed in terms of basic contours such as vertical and horizontal lines, angles, and curved lines. (This suggests why simple line art illustrations are often as effective for learning as detailed color photographs.) Ultimately such features are compared with associations to prior knowledge and the cerebral cortex interprets what our eyes detect.

We assert that if graphic organizers are constructed according to the graphic design principles set forth by Tufte (1983, 1990), we see a relatively good fit between those diagrams and what neuroscience has learned about visual cognition. We think that the parameters of the visual sensory apparatus and the neural network that processes and interprets those raw sensory signals must be considered when we discuss graphic organizers.

A few of these principles to consider include extra material, vibrations, and grids. It is tempting to embellish graphic organizers with extraneous artwork or artistic touches. While at times this may be suitable and we are certainly not trying to stifle creativity, but when extra material near, on, or overlapping a graphic organizer interferes with its intentional use by distracting or misleading the reader of the graphic, then extra art is not suitable. Another graphic principle to consider is a vibration effect or moiré effect (Tufte, 1983). Having lines too close together produce an appearance of vibration and movement. This can be very distracting and is comparable to having distracting noise when listening to a piece of music. The grids used in graphic organizers should not distract from the information being presented. Using heavy lines may box in information and not allow intentional comparisons to be made.

In graphic construction one must consider the viewer. Studies have shown that the human visual system fatigues rather rapidly (Solso, 1994). Strong contrasting lines that may create a grating effect result in quick fatigue and the viewer does not continue his/her gaze. In creating graphic organizers consideration should be given to mute heavy dark lines, boxes, or frames. Likewise, the constructor of graphic organizers should not crowd the field of vision. Careful construction of graphic organizers in terms of human vision and perception will enhance the cognitive gain.

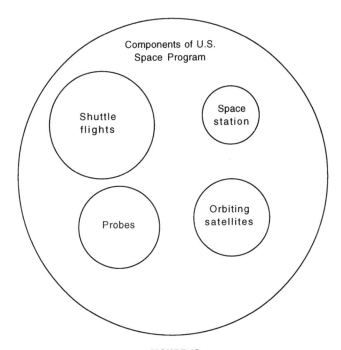

**FIGURE 12**
An example of concept circle diagram showing major components of the
U.S. Space Program.

## THREE AUSUBELIAN TOOLS
## FOR SCIENCE TEACHING

### Concept Circles

Graphic metacognitive tools, such as the concept circle diagramming strategy developed by Wandersee (1987), focus on the use of self-constructed diagrams to aid the process of reflection on constructed knowledge and to restructure personal knowledge. Using physiological and psychological parameters of visual learning and visual perception (for example, the field of human vision is approximately circular) a set of labeled isomorphic circles can be constructed that demonstrate the structure of a particular piece of knowledge. These diagrams are not to be confused with Venn diagrams, but are more like Euler's Circles—showing a representation of judgment and of relationships such as class exclusion, class inclusion, class equality, class product, and class sum. A suggested five-circle limit for each circle diagram is based upon the unit capacity (7 plus or minus 2) of short-term memory. The design of concept circles is based on Ausubelian learning theory and the

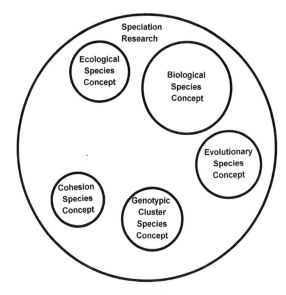

**FIGURE 13**
A concept circle diagram of major components of research on speciation.

diagrams allow the learner to visually interrelate a small set of concepts (see Figures 12–14 and Table 2).

Nobles (1993) research with a fifth-grade science class showed that the concept circle diagrams (CCDs) were useful as a diagnostic tool for assessing prior knowledge. Thus, allowing the research to assess students' background with regard to a conceptual framework necessary to understand the lesson. Further, the circle diagrams revealed alternative conceptions allowing the teacher to adjust her instruction in a timely manner. Nobles also found that the construction of concept circle diagrams facilitate individual knowledge construction and that the learner has the ultimate responsibility for the construction of knowledge—a basic component of constructivism.

Going beyond individual knowledge construction, Nobels and Konopak (1995) used concept circles for peer evaluation strategies and as a vehicle for social construction of meaning about concepts related to radioactivity. In the milieu of social negotiation of peer assessment, peer review, and one-on-one as well as group negotiations, individuals' conceptual frameworks of understanding went through a consensus process and thus social construction of knowledge related to radioactivity.

Nichols (1993) used concept circle diagramming as a research technique in an entomology education study involving students in grades 5, 7, 9, and 11. She found CCDs to be especially useful in characterizing students' understanding of complete and incomplete insect metamorphosis. They revealed

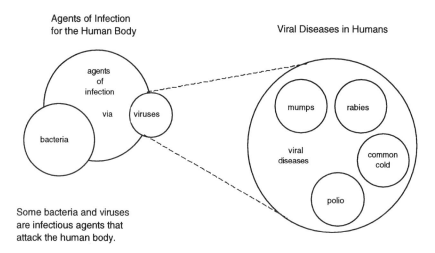

Agents of Infection
for the Human Body

Viral Diseases in Humans

Some bacteria and viruses
are infectious agents that
attack the human body.

Examples of viral diseases found in
humans include the common cold,
mumps, polio, and rabies.

**FIGURE 14**
A telescoped concept circle diagram showing diseases.

the lack of integration of concepts of insect metamorphosis and insect evolution (Nichols & Wandersee, 1996).

## Gowin's Vee

Another graphic metacognitive tool is Gowin's epistemological vee. Otherwise
known as a vee diagram, this graphic allows one to view the actual activities
of science as it moves from the events to data collection to data transformations to knowledge claims to values claims as a research project is being
planned or completed. This "doing" or "methodological" side is mirrored with
the "epistemological" side of the vee diagram. This theoretical side includes:
relevant concepts, principles, theories, philosophy, and world view driving the
research. In the middle, forming a motive wedge between these two sides is a
focus question with associated subquestions. The questions direct the selection of the objects and events being studied (see Figure 15).

Novices to vee diagramming can start off by making a vee diagram of a
simple research study reported in a journal. The emerging vee diagram can
be analyzed to see if all the standard elements of a vee diagram can be
extracted from the research report as written. Further, such analysis may
reveal several things such as (1) lack of a clear question to focus the research,
(2) possible mismatches between data collection and data transformation,

**TABLE 2**
**Procedures for Developing Concept Circles (Modified after Wandersee, 1987)**

Suggested rules and procedures for concept circle diagrams

1. A circle can represent only one concept.

2. Label the name of that concept (e.g., vertebrates) inside the circle using lowercase letters.

3. To show inclusive relationships (e.g., all fish are vertebrates) draw a smaller circle within the larger circle. Label each circle with the name within the appropriate circle.

4. When you want to show common characteristics between concepts (e.g., some water contains minerals), draw partially overlapping circles and label appropriately.

5. Concepts that are mutually exclusive should be separate circles.

6. Limit drawings to five circles in a separate diagram, no more. This is due to limitations of the working capacity of human memory. Circles can be separate, overlapping, included, or superimposed. All circles must be labeled.

7. The relative sizes of the circles used in a diagram can show the level of specificity for each concept or relative amounts of instances. Larger circles stand for more general concepts.

8. A psychologically sized template with openings that appear to be 2, 3, 4, or 5 times larger than a standard circle can easily be constructed. If you wish to show that quantity is being represented, place a lower case "n" near each concept label and enclose it with parentheses (n).

Note: Sizes of circles in a standard template designed to represent circles that appear to be 2, 3, 4, and 5 times larger than a standard circle are found below:

| 1" | 1 7/8" | 2 1/8" | 2 1/2" | 3 1/8" |
|---|---|---|---|---|
| $x$ | $2x$ | $3x$ | $4x$ | $5x$ |

9. Time relationships (such as those found in the history of biology) can be represented by drawing nested (or concentric) circles with the oldest concepts being the center one. If chronological relationships are shown, a "t" should be enclosed by parentheses (t).

10. Diagrams can be telescoped to connect each other. Telescoped diagrams should be made to read from left to right. Several stages of telescoping can be used if a large, scrolllike piece of paper is available.

11. Most circle diagrams can be improved if redrawn to leave sufficient space around the labels to give the diagram an uncluttered look.

12. Making the relationships between concepts easier to visualize, understand and recall can be accomplished with different color pens, markers, pencils, or highlighters.

13. Empty space (white space) around included concepts is used to imply that there are other concepts that are not shown. A shaded or colored area surrounding concepts is used to indicate that no important concepts have been omitted.

14. The title that describes what the diagram is about should be written in the upper lefthand quadrant of the page and an explanatory sentence should be written in the area directly beneath the diagram.

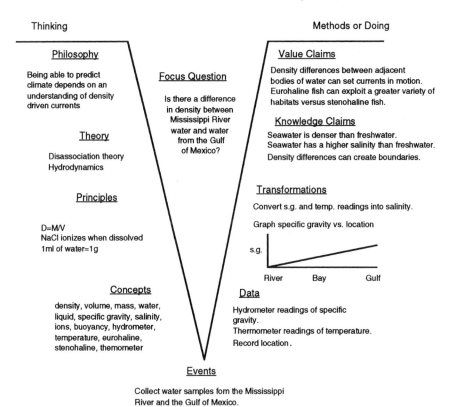

**FIGURE 15**

A vee diagram of a water density laboratory.

(3) lack of data to support the researcher's knowledge and value claims, (4) a lack of connection between theory and research, and (5) failure to acknowledge the limitations of the research. Such an analysis allows one to see the theoretical flaws or missing pieces of a research study, resulting in a biased results. Kuhn (1970) offers the analogy of "conceptual goggles" to describe this "limited worldview" phenomenon.

The vee diagram has been found to be useful in guiding and reporting laboratory work; it does go much deeper than the average laboratory report. Figure 14 is an example of a vee diagram about the relationship between fresh and salt water. Note that other graphics such as flow diagrams, concept maps, and the picture graphics may be embedded within the vee diagram. Science education graduate students at Cornell University and Louisiana State University now make use of vee diagrams to explain their own proposed or completed research to their university's examining committee.

Many admit it was the first time they had an overview and a clear vision of their entire study. Vee diagrams may at first be tedious to construct because of the need to identify all the elements of an investigation. Many times these elements are implicit or missing. However, the basic steps to construct a vee diagram are surprisingly simple and easily taught. When constructing a vee diagram start with the focus question and then decide upon the events you must study, elaborate the methodological or "doing side" of your study. Next, develop the theoretical side and you will be able to see how theory affects and modifies practice. However, once the research is done you will be able to see even more how doing or practice affects theory and vice versa. Many more hours sitting around the academic campfire ought to be devoted to discussing the agreement between theory and practice in research.

Ideally, once constructed and analyzed, vee diagrams naturally lead to further research questions and further the advance of scientific knowledge and a line of investigation.

## Concept Mapping

As theories of metalearning and metacognition developed, the use of concept maps as a heuristic was proposed by Novak and Gowin (1984) in their handbook *Learning How to Learn*. The National Association for Research in Science Teaching (NARST) recognized the emerging utility of concept mapping and published a special issue of its official journal on *Perspectives of Concept Mapping* (Novak & Wandersee, 1990). Articles in this issue elaborate on the many uses of concept maps for teaching and learning as well as for research. As part of this special issue, Al-Kunifed and Wandersee provided 100 references related to concept mapping.

Among its many uses, concept maps allow for evaluation of prior knowledge and diagnosis of alternative conceptions. Further, the concept map serves as a device to illustrate the hierarchical, conceptual, and propositional nature of knowledge. It also serves as a metacognitive tool to help learners reorganize their cognitive frameworks into more powerful integrated patterns.

As a graphic metacognitive tool, the concept map is the research product of Novak and his colleagues at Cornell (Novak & Gowin, 1984). It is the result of almost 20 years of research and development focusing on helping students learn how to learn. Concept mapping seems to fit well with constructivist learning perspectives. Mappers, on their own, must hierarchically order concepts and connect concepts using linking words and thus whether completed individually or socially, an ordered framework of knowledge results.

In addition, as a metacognitive tool, concept mapping promotes meaningful learning. Building on Ausubel's (1963) theory of meaningful learning, concept mapping is useful for evoking prior knowledge, progressive differentiation, the sequencing of concepts into a distinct hierarchy, and integrative reconciliation, where interrelationships of concepts can be demonstrated (cross-links). Chapter 2 of this book gives an overview of Ausubel's theory of meaningful learning.

Concept maps are two-dimensional representations of a set of concepts. The concepts are arranged in a hierarchy with a superordinate concept at the top. The concepts are linked by lines labeled with connecting words that form the propositions uniting the concepts. There are cross-links connected by dotted lines (by convention) that bridge branches of the map to create new and insightful propositions. A concept map should be anchored with examples—ideally, novel, mapper-supplied examples.

A useful metaphor was extended by Wandersee (1990) in his comparison of knowledge construction and cartography, "to map is to know." Wandersee claims that cartography informs the concept mapping process and draws out similarities between the two processes. Both traditional map construction and concept mapping explore the world of experience and hence are meaningful if there is relevant previous experience or prior knowledge. Both mapping processes have generative capabilities since the interaction with experience and exploring new territory or concepts allow further exploration of the existing map. Both the traditional map and the concept map suggest further exploration. A historical series of maps, as well as a set of successive concept maps, reflects changes in understanding. Both types of mapping are part of a complex communications process complete with coding and conventions.

Concept mapping requires an understanding of what a concept entails and promotes the ability to use concepts as the basis of scientific language. Concept mapping requires the mapper to prioritize and make judicious use of selected concepts when mapping. This may well serve proponents of science education reform who advocate the "less is more" approach to reform (AAAS, 1989). Science courses and texts are overloaded with information and, predictably, science information will continue to increase. It will be necessary for educators at all levels to decide which concepts are the most important to learn and use. What are the important concepts that constitute the "big picture" or pervasive principles at the core of scientific disciplines? Concept mapping may help science educators make these selections. The extraction, selection, and prioritizing of concepts from information-dense material are often-overlooked skills vital to culling out extraneous material.

## The Process of Concept Mapping

We propose a standard format for constructing concept maps for many reasons. Many people are calling all semantic networks "brainstorming webs," and hub-and-spoke diagrams "concept maps." We are not trying to be over-restrictive or impose our will onto the mapper, but the structure of Novakian "concept maps" is based upon sound practices derived from learning theory and research. Cognitive science indicates that knowledge is stored hierarchically. Any attempt to create a hierarchy before a learning commitment takes place seems to be advantageous. Plus, the use of this mapping convention allows us to make comparisons among mappers over time. A standard format also contains a self-selected superordinate concept and self-supplied examples. These will be discussed later as being powerful aspects of a concept map.

Constructing a concept map can be accomplished using the following steps and review process (see Table 3 and the flowchart of Figure 16).

The last step ("Review and reflect") is an extremely powerful one. Here is where the mapper must reflect upon the construction of the map analyzing the map's scientific validity in terms of conceptual linkages, the suggested propositions between concepts, the hierarchy or prioritization of the concepts, and the grounding of the map in reality by selection of relevant (and hopefully, novel) examples. It must be recognized that this process takes time. This means the mapper is spending more time working with selected concepts and is not reviewing pages of notes or text material that often times have been over highlighted with a fluorescent maker. Research conducted in a university zoology classroom by Trowbridge and Wandersee (1994) found students spent an average of 45 minutes beyond their normal study time developing a concept maps of zoology class lectures.

Computer software is available to assist in the construction of concept maps. One program designated C*map* 2.0 is designed specifically for concept mapping (Stahl & Hunter, 1990). Various graphics programs, drafting programs, flowcharting programs, and computer-assisted design programs (CAD) can also be adapted to produce high-quality concept maps.

## Coconstruction of Concept Maps

Coconstruction of a concept map (Wandersee & Abrams, 1993) is a technique first employed by Abrams (1993). In her study, students' answers to clinical interview questions were mapped on a ceramic-coated, erasable, white board using colored markers. Thus, the map was created in real-time, as opposed to constructing a concept map at a later time based upon the interview transcripts. This allowed for additional probing and clarification. Students retained veto power over their maps and were allowed to suggest whatever corrections and additional connections they thought necessary to accurately portray their conceptual framework related to the hierarchical concept. The interviewer is thus merely the graphic assistant and the student is the one directing construction of the map. We find this adds to the validity of using a concept map as a representation of the student's own knowledge about a particular topic.

In another study done by Trowbridge (1995), students were given a term that would serve as the superordinate term of their concept map and asked to generate concepts about the topic. Their responses were placed on a

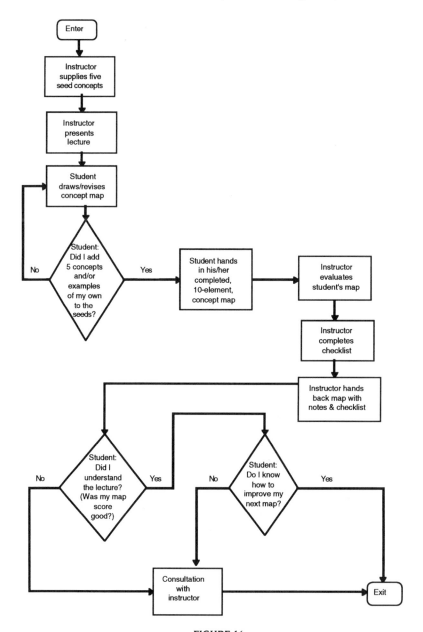

**FIGURE 16**
A flowchart for constructing a concept map.

**TABLE 3**
**Steps in Concept Map Construction**

Concept mapping procedure

1. Select $\approx$ 1–12 concepts from the science content material being considered (e.g., lecture notes, videotape, journal aritcle, textbook).

2. Write each concept on a separate note card. Lay these cards down on a large sheet of paper.

3. Select a superordinate concept to be placed at the top of your map. This is the organizing concept for your map.

4. Arrange the other concepts in a distinct hierarchy under the superordinate concept. The concepts should be arranged from general to specific, in levels from top to bottom of the map.

5. Once the concepts have been arranged, draw lines between related concepts and label each linking line with words that characterize the relationship between those concepts.

6. If you wish to cross-link two concepts in different branches of your map, use a dashed line and label their relationship by writing on the linking line.

7. If you wish to provide examples of certain concepts, enclose these in broken ovals.

8. Examples should be connected to their source concepts by an "e.g."-labeled linking line.

9. Review and reflect. Once you are satisfied with your concept map's revised arrangement, redraw the map in final form.

Post-It note and set aside. Once a student had generated a number of concepts, he or she was asked to create the spatial array of the map. Using the student-generated array, the researcher constructed a map on the white board and asked the students to verify that this represented their intentions. If the map had only a few elements or no examples, the student was asked to add to the map. At the same time, the student was asked to write-in the propositional linkages between the concepts. Once the student was satisfied with the map construction, it was immediately photographed using a Polaroid Camera. The researcher now had a permanent copy of the coconstructed map for later analysis. The students were always impressed by the photograph of their map and proud that they were able to recall, reflect on, and order information that they had previously learned (sometimes as long as 2 weeks after the unit of instruction). The benefits of an instant hard copy include the following: (1) the student can receive a copy of his/her own concept map; (2) the researcher can verify that the photograph was properly exposed and he/she has a clear record of the map; and (3) the resulting records are compact and easy to scan. More expensive "white board" technologies are available that transform drawn maps directly to computer files or displays at remote locations.

## Concept Map Formats

The particular format for concept mapping may vary depending on the instructor's or learner's need and type of assessment or evaluation required.

Ruiz-Primo and Shavelson (1996) examined format in terms of response mode (here, paper and pencil and oral generation), characteristics of response format (here, skeletal map and seed terms), and the mapper (student, teacher, expert). We suggest beginning with the use of micromaps and discuss the possibilities of other formats such as a macromap and progressive map.

## Micromap

A micromap is a concept map that limits the number of elements, including examples on a concept map (Trowbridge & Wandersee, 1994). As a rule 10–15 elements comprise a micromap. The advantages of micromaps are: (1) the map does not become too large and cluttered, (2) the mapper must prioritize elements, (3) it takes less time, and (4) it is easier to evaluate. Since these maps are easier to evaluate, there is a quicker turnaround time, advantageous to both the instructor and the student. We heartily recommend a micromapping approach to introduce the process of concept mapping to students. While concept mapping is not a difficult strategy to learn, students experience some initial frustration constructing their first concept maps. It takes constructing at least 10 maps to become proficient. Since it is something new, remember that many students are already locked into other study strategies, be it a formal process or informal process, and are reluctant to change their strategies, especially if they have been successful for multiple-choice tests. Students of low- to mid-range ability frequently comment they wish they had known about this process years ago. Successful or high-ability students may be even more resistant at first, but usually warm up to the concept mapping process when they see that it can enhance their success. In fact, many realize the eventual economy in concept mapping, because their previous strategy, though successful, was centered on hours of rote memorization, rereading, recalling lengthy outlines, using mnemonic devices, or some other laborious method. Most of the aforementioned strategies do not promote integration of knowledge, provide an opportunity to construct knowledge, or enhance the generation of novel examples—hallmarks of meaningful learning.

Two research studies (Trowbridge & Wandersee, 1994; Trowbridge, 1995) used student generated micromaps to assess conceptual knowledge on topics related to biological evolution and topics related to marine science. In both studies, the students were impressed with their own ability to create such overview graphics and seemed to experience a profound sense of accomplishment.

Another variation in the student construction of microconcept maps is to seed the mapping process with instructor-provided terms (concepts, propositions, examples). In a study of college biology students (Trowbridge & Wandersee, 1995) the instructor provided 5 seed concepts that he determined to be important as a basis for constructing an understanding of that particular lecture. These terms were to be incorporated in the students' concept maps. The student had to provide the other 7–10 elements for a particular micromap. This process is also recommended to initiate students into the concept mapping process. The seed concepts help overcome the "activation barrier" of the mapping process (the perceived difficult first steps of construction a concept map).

## Macromap

As the name implies a macromap is larger than a micromap. It may be a composite of many maps. A micromap may summarize a course, text, a series of videos, or a whole curriculum. It is much more of an overview and more encompassing than a micromap. Ideally, a macromap is constructed from a set of micromaps. The mapper selects key elements from the upper levels of hierarchy of his/her previously constructed micromaps and constructs the macromap.

## Progressive Map

Similar to the macromap just described, we see the use of time series (progressive) concept maps as useful in documenting changing student knowledge over time. In a longitudinal study of conceptual change within a biological knowledge domain conducted by Pearsall, Skipper, and Mintzes (1996), students were given a periodic opportunity to add to or restructure their maps on cells or living things. At 4-week intervals throughout a semester-long college biology course, the students reworked their previous maps. At the end of the semester, these researchers had a set of four maps from each student, allowing them to reconstruct the process of conceptual change and document trends.

## Scoring or Grading Concept Maps

Several attempts have been made to quantify concept maps for scoring purposes. Despite attempts at authentic and alternative assessment many teachers, parents, and administrators want to see a score that falls within a traditional, 100-point scale system. Wandersee (1992) proposed a Standard Concept Map Checklist as seen (modified) in Table 4 below:

The above checklist could also serve as the basis of a scoring rubric developed by the instructor.

A scoring key was developed by Novak and Gowin (1984) and was modified by the authors. It is shown in Table 5 below.

**TABLE 4**
**A Standard Concept Map Checklist**

Items to consider when evaluating a concept map (micromap)

1. Does the map contain five seed concepts provided by the instructor?
2. Are all the links between the concepts precisely linked?
3. Does the map have any labeled cross-links?
4. Does the map also contain examples (preferably novel examples)?
5. Is the map treelike (dendritic) instead of stringy (linear)?
6. Is the superordinate concept the best choice, given the way the rest of the concepts arranged?
7. Are the examples included appropriate?
8. Is the map of acceptable scientific quality?
9. Has the mapper used the proper map symbols and followed standard mapping conventions?
10. Is the map limited to approximately 12 elements?

Another modified version of this scoring strategy was used by Wallace and Mintzes (1990) in their study on conceptual change in college biology students for the topic of ocean life zones.

A variant method of assessing concept maps is to compare student concept maps to a criterion map, such as one developed by an expert. We see that as funneling thinking into conformity. In addition, we recommend that that criterion maps developed by experts, teachers, or scientists not be given to students initially. We have found that students will simply mimic the

**TABLE 5**
**Scoring Rubric For Concept Maps**

1. Score 1 or 2 points for each meaningful and relevant proposition of concept–linking word(s)–concept. More precise propositions are to receive 2 points.

2. Score 5 points for each valid level of hierarchy shown on the map, provided the map is treelike and not linear.

3. Score 10 points for each cross-link that is both valid and significant. Score 2 points for a valid cross-link that does not indicate a synthesis between sets of related concepts or propositions.

Note: cross-links may indicate creative thinking and care should be given to identify and reward those when present. A cross-link always bridges two distinct branches of a map.

4. Examples (specific events or objects that are valid instances of a concept) should be scored 1 point each. (By themselves, these do not count as a level of hierarchy.)

given map and resort to rote memorization, thus failing to construct a knowledge base of their own.

## RESEARCH PERSPECTIVES ON CONCEPT MAPS

### Research Findings of Concept Maps and Mapping

#### Reveal Alternative Conceptions

Concept maps have also been useful in identifying alternative conceptions, often referred to as misconceptions. Various aspects of a student constructed map may reveal alternative conceptions. The presence of incorrect linkages forming invalid propositions is one indicator. The incorporation of concepts not related to the superordinate concept or concepts that seem trite or irrelevant is another indicator. Furthermore, the student's choice of both the superordinate concept and anchoring examples gives insight into his or her understanding of the material. For example, in a concept map about amphibians, a student incorporated turtles into his map (Abrams & Wandersee, 1992).

Missing concepts further indicate a student's lack of understanding. Likewise, it can be assumed that a concept map that is poorly constructed, missing many standard map elements such as hierarchy, lacking linking words, missing cross-linkages, and devoid of novel examples signals that the student may not have sufficient depth of knowledge about a particular concept to construct a meaningful map.

#### Examining Changes in Cognitive Structure

Not only is concept mapping an activity which fosters active engagement in every student, but it is also a "highly sensitive tool for measuring changes in knowledge structure" (Novak & Wandersee, 1990, p. 946). Carey (1986) recommended the comparing of successive concept maps in determining knowledge acquisition. Concept maps were also used to explore conceptual change in college biology classes by Wallace and Mintzes (1990). They found that maps are a useful mechanism to look at changes in cognitive structure. Novak and Musonda (1991) performed a 12-year longitudinal study which demonstrated that concept maps can be used effectively in analyzing conceptual change, even across large time intervals.

#### Critical Junctures

Trowbridge and Wandersee (1994) state that a critical juncture is a conceptual watershed which divides students into two groups on the basis of their prior understanding of foundational concepts relevant to those currently being taught. Where these prior concepts are essential to future learning, students may or may not be able to demonstrate holistic, unified understanding of course content beyond such a juncture. The use of concept mapping in a college course on evolution was explored by Trowbridge and Wandersee (1994). A key finding was that critical junctures in learning evolution can be identified by monitoring the degree of concordance of the superordinate concepts appearing on the class set of concept maps submitted after each course lecture.

Particular attention should be paid to the student's selection of the superordinate concepts. The superordinate concept is the key to a whole array of information and has a powerful organizing effect (Mintzes, Markham, & Jones 1993). Generally, there is no preferred superordinate concept for a particular lecture or reading, but a moderate degree of consistency in choices across the class (while allowing for individual interpretations) indicates advancing class understanding (as opposed to a diverse range of interpretations).

## Student Success

The process of concept mapping can enhance students' self-esteem through the sense of accomplishment of constructing a map and the subsequent realization that they can extract concepts to construct their own meaning. In three studies (Trowbridge & Wandersee, 1994, 1995, 1996) clinical interviews revealed that students were impressed with their emerging ability to construct concept maps. Several students stated they would pursue concept mapping on their own as a study tool in other classes. In a study involving high school students, learners reflected on their completed concept maps with pride and became very animated in verbalizing that they could accomplish such a task successfully. This is certainly something to consider when attempting to build self-esteem in students. We think some of the pride comes from the uncommon intellectual ownership of the concept map. This may be further evidence for the need to avoid teacher-prepared or fill-in-the-blank-type concept maps. Such maps can not have the learning benefit of true student construction.

## Curriculum Design

Novak and Gowin (1984) urge that concept mapping be used in the curriculum-planning process. In fact, Starr & Krajcik (1990) believe the use of the concept mapping can improve curriculum development as both a product and as a process. As a process, teams of planners can construct and revise concept maps to reach consensus about the important concepts to be taught. Furthermore, this process allows planners to integrate the curriculum elements and to tie the curriculum to the learner's meaningful personal experiences.

A new national environmental education curriculum entitled Project WET (Water Education for Teachers) was developed using the concept mapping process (Watercourse and Council for Environmental Education, 1995). *Benchmarks For Scientific Literacy,* one of the standard-type reform documents in science education, was developed through the use of "back maps," a variant form of graphic organizer resembling concept maps and semantic webs.

## Teacher Education

Preservice teachers, just like many other college students, often resort to rote memorization as their primary learning strategy (Novak, 1990). The use of concept mapping as a metacognitive tool allows future teachers to "conceptualize" discipline's content, integrate concepts across disciplines, plan for instruction, and develop assessment strategies. While the whole range of applications of concept mapping should be part of teacher preparation, another important outcome is the development of constructivist practices.

## Theory Models

Concept maps have been useful in representing scientific models conceptually. For example, Trowbridge (1995) proposed a model of "Gulf literacy" as a subset or working model of scientific literacy. The model was based upon interviews of experts and content analysis of newspapers from major coastal cities along the Gulf of Mexico. A series of concept maps were drawn to present a concrete representation of what "Gulf literacy" means in conceptual terms. Teaching materials and activities were then developed using the model as represented by the concept maps as a guide. Wandersee, Wissing, and Lange (1996) used concept maps as chapter organizers in a recent "content update" book on bioinstrumentation.

## Integrated Graphics

Spiegel and Barufaldi (1994) tested the use of a student-constructed postgraphic organizer on student recall of science text information. The graphic organizer they used was a hybrid of concept mapping, semantic mapping, networking, and knowledge maps. They concluded that training in the use of graphic postreading organizers can increase retention and recall of science textbook information.

Embedding other graphics into a concept map may also be useful. In a study on how graphics presented during college biology lessons affect students learning, a concept map analysis (Trowbridge & Wandersee, 1996) by the researchers found that some students iconically embed the instructor's graphics in their concept map. This is a form of knowledge integration that we heartily endorse.

Integrating flowcharts and concept maps into vee diagrams was proposed by Wandersee (1992). This seems somewhat intuitive, if you consider that the right side of the vee is the doing side and procedural, thus lending itself to the use of flowcharts. Next, consider the left side as the thinking side, thus lending itself to concept maps.

## Context

In an attempt to theorize about concept mapping, Ruiz-Primo and Shavelson (1996) examined the task of concept mapping, the type of response format, and the development of a scoring system. Their first approach was to characterize the task of concept mapping. They found that there is a great deal of variety in the literature of what the actual task of concept mapping entails. They propose that these tasks be viewed in light of the demands (e.g., fill-in-the-blank map, raw generation of a map), constraints (standard format or free-form which may yield wagon wheel or linear train-type maps), and content structure. Some consideration must be given to the question, is the content hierarchical in nature?

We would further add to Ruiz-Primo and Shavelson's taxonomy by including context as a referent in analyzing concept maps. The results of a meta-analysis of learning skills interventions by Hattie, Biggs, and Nola (1996) support notions of situated cognition in some learning situations and suggest that study skill intervention be done in context.

## LIMITATIONS OF GRAPHIC ORGANIZERS

Graphic organizers such as concept maps do have certain limitations. One limitation is when the graphic becomes the reality. There is a tendency to overgeneralize that a map or graphic is the manifestation of that particular topic or concept. While philosophers will argue about what is object reality and its existence, a map is only a snap shot. Straus (1996) considers how students get confused trying to interpret the semantics of chemical symbolism. He uses the example of the many representations of water that may be used; $H_2O$, H-O-H, H:O:H. Domin (1996) adds that the researcher may erroneously infer representational systems when water is written as $H_2O$. Plus, the analogies such as a water molecule looks like Mickey Mouse ears and other visual models such as the Dalton model, Orbital bonding, and gas cloud. It can be very easy to mistake the map for the territory.

## THE FUTURE OF GRAPHIC ORGANIZERS

### Research and Development

A potential topic of research to explore is the *resolution* or *scale* the graphic organizer employs. By this we mean does a graphic show too much detail perhaps and thus obscures the big picture. Likewise, can a graphic be too general and supporting material never realized. Along the East and Gulf Coasts of the U.S., hurricane tracking maps are distributed widely and many teachers make use of them to teach latitude and longitude, as well as about hurricanes. However, as a storm approaches the coast the scale of the typical tracking chart is not fine enough to track the nearby storm. So it is, at the most critical time to track a storm, the graphic fails. Is it possible to develop a sense of cognitive scale or resolution in terms of graphic organizers?

The research-based development of new graphic organizers or tools for learning should continue. A research and development laboratory founded by Wandersee, the 15-degree laboratory, is doing just that. This R&D laboratory focuses on improving science learning and science literacy via Visual Probes, Templates, and Filters. The Laboratory coined these terms to encapsulate the various roles that the graphic devices it designs and tests can serve in understanding science and in science learning.

Hyerle (1996) believes that visual model building may one day surpass other forms of assessment of content learning. He reasons that there is a greater degree of authenticity in using graphic visual models then current "test" methods. He contends it is easy to learn to construct concept maps and other graphic forms. Such graphics represent independent demonstration of mental models, holistic knowledge, and nonlinear representations of student knowledge.

### Use of Technology

It is obvious to anyone involved with schools and university instruction that there is a push for the use of technology in the classroom. Certainly, computers with current and future software will allow students to construct graphics. Hopefully, these programs will allow students to construct their own graphics and not just be a hypercard text of flash cards for students to memorize.

While "high tech" is nice, and we sincerely hope all teachers and students have direct access to such equipment, we admit that it may take some time for even and equitable distribution of technological resources. Therefore, we recommend that "low-tech" approaches also be explored. For instance, when we made use of the white ceramic marker boards with students for coconstruction of concept maps, we went "low tech" with good results. Perhaps tables could be built with tops of the same material and thus students could be allowed to draw on these tables with dry-erase markers and participate in social construction of science graphics.

## Interventions

In an attempt to assess conceptual change interventions, it is recognized that achievement test items alone are inadequate and that graphics such as concept maps, vee diagrams, and concept circle diagrams are more sensitive to subtle changes in student's understanding (Wandersee, Mintzes, & Novak, 1993). A metaanalysis of the effects of learning skills interventions on student learning found metacognitive interventions to be highly effective (Hattie, Biggs, & Nola, 1996).

# CONCLUSION

James R. Flynn, a New Zealand political scientist based at the University of Otago, has discovered the average IQ-test scores in the U.S. have risen steadily and dramatically from 1918 on, but that this has been masked by the score-scaling system. While his best evidence comes from mandatory IQ tests given to Belgian, Israeli, Norwegian, and Dutch soldiers, data from the U.S. and other countries confirm this. The so-called "Flynn effect" suggest that the environment has a strong influence on whatever IQ tests measure. Since the biggest improvements have come on the sections of the tests that make use of pattern-completion maze items, psychologist Patricia M. Greenfield hypothesizes that, increasingly, we live in a culture that rewards visual-spatial thinking and that people in contemporary societies need to, and do, develop intelligence in those areas. She claims that our new visually intense world is our ecocultural niche and, more and more, we thrive in visually stimulating environments. In this visual-cognitive milieu, we forecast that graphic organizers consistent with the research on visual cognition will continue to increase in appeal, credibility, and utility for today's science students and their teachers.

# References

Abrams, E. (1993). A comparison of the effects of multiple visual examples and nonexamples versus prototypical examples on science concept learning: An exploratory study based upon the concept of photosynthesis. Unpublished doctoral dissertation, Louisiana State University, Baton Rouge.

Abrams, E., & Wandersee, J. H. (1992). How to use a concept map to identify students' biological misconceptions. *Adaptation*, XIV(1), 1, 4–6, 1–16.

American Association for the Advancement of Science (AAAS) (1989). *Project 2061: Science for all Americans*. Washington, DC: Author.

Ausubel, D. P. (1963). *The psychology of meaningful learning*. New York: Grune and Stratton.

Briscoe, M. H. (1990). A researcher's guide to scientific and medical illustrations. New York: Springer-Verlag.

Carey, S. (1985). Conceptual change in childhood. Cambridge, MA: MIT Press.

Carr, E., & Ogle, D. (1987). K-W-L Plus: A strategy for comprehension and summarization. Journal of Reading, 30, 626–631.

Cromie, W. J. (1996). Putting a new spin on earth's core. Harvard University Gazette, August 15, pp. 1, 5.

Domin, D. S. (1996). Comment: Concept mapping and representational systems. Journal of Research in Science Teaching, 33(8), 935–936.

Earle, R. A., & Barron, R. F. (1973). An approach for teaching vocabulary in content subjects. In H. L. Heber and R. F. Barron (eds.), Research in reading in the content areas: Second year report (pp. 84–110). Syracuse, NY: Reading and Language Arts Center, Syracuse University.

Fisher, K. (1990). Semantic networking: The new kid on the block. In J. Novak & J. Wandersee (eds.), Special issue: Perspectives on concept mapping. Journal of Research in Science Teaching, 27, 1001–1018.

Fisher, K. (1992). SemNet: A tool for personal knowledge construction. In P. Kommers, D. Jonassen, & J. Mayes (eds.), Cognitive tools for learning (pp. 63–75). New York: Springer-Verlag.

Grugel, B. (1996). Using graphic organizers to teach reading. The Visual Literacy review, 26(2), 1–3.

Hattie, J., Biggs, J., & Nola, P. (1996). Effects of learning skills interventions on student learning: A meta-analysis. Review of Educational Research Summer 1996, 66,(2), 99–136.

Hyerle, D. (1996). Visual tools for constructing knowledge. Alexandria, VA: Association for Supervision and Curriculum Development.

Jonassen, D. H., Beissner, K., & Yacci, M. (1993). Structural knowledge: Techniques for representing, conveying, and acquiring structural knowledge. Hillsdale, NJ: Lawrence Earlbaum Associates.

Kuhn, T. S. (1970). The structure of scientific revolutions. Chicago: University of Chicago Press.

Lyall, S. (1996). Phyllis Pearsall, 89, dies; creator of "A to Z" London maps. The New York Times, August 30, p. C16.

Manzo, A., & Manzo, U. (1990). Content area reading: A heuristic approach. Columbus, OH: Merrill Publishing.

Mintzes, J. J., Markham, K. M., & Jones, G. M. (1993). The structure and use of biological knowledge in novice and experienced students: Mammals II. Paper presented at the Annual Meeting of the National Association for Research in Science Teaching, April, Atlanta, GA.

Moncada, G. J., & Wandersee, J. H., (1993). Graphics and learning. Adaptation, XVI(1), 3–4, 17.

Nichols, M. S. (1993). A cross-age study of students' knowledge of insect metamorphosis: Insights into their understanding of evolution. Unpublished doctoral dissertation, Louisiana State University, Baton Rouge.

Nichols, M. S., & Wandersee, J. H. (1996). Why can't they integrate the biological concepts we teach them? A cross-age study of pupils' understanding of insect metamorphosis. Adaptation, 17(4), 8–13, 16–19.

Nobles, C. (1993). Concept circle diagrams: A metacognitive learning strategy to enhance meaningful learning in the elementary science classroom. Unpublished doctoral dissertation, Louisiana State University, Baton Rouge.

Nobles, C. H., & Konopak, B. C. (1995). Eighth-Grade Students' Use of Concept Circle Diagrams for Meaningful Learning from Science Text. Yearbook of the College Reading Association.

Novak, J. D. (1972). A theory of education. Ithaca, NY: Cornell University Press.

Novak, J. D. (1990). Concept mapping: A useful tool for science education. Journal of Research in Science Teaching, 27(10), 937–949.

Novak, J. D., & Gowin, D. B. (1984). Learning how to learn. New York: Cambridge University Press.

Novak, J. D., & Musonda, D. (1991). A twelve-year longitudinal study of science concept learning. American Educational Research Journal, 28(1), 117–153.

Novak, J. D., & Wandersee, J. H. (eds.). (1990). Perspectives on concept mapping. Journal of Research in Science Teaching, 27(10). [special issue].

Pearsall, N. R., Skipper, J. E. J., & Mintzes, J. J. (1996). Knowledge restructuring in the life sciences: A longitudinal study of conceptual change in biology. Paper presented at the annual meeting of the National Association for Research in Science Teaching; St. Louis, Missouri, 1–4 April.

Quillian, M. R. (1967). Word concepts: A theory and simulation of some basic semantic capabilities. *Behavioral Sciences*, 12, 41–430.

Readence, J. E., Bean, T. W., & Baldwin, R. S. (1985). *Content area reading: An integrated approach*. Dubuque, IA: Kendall/Hunt Publishing.

Ruiz-Primo, M. A., & Shavelson, R. J. (1996). Problems and issues in the use of concept maps in science assessment. *Journal of Research in Science Teaching*, 33(6), 569–600.

Shea, C. (1996, September 27). Researchers try to understand why people are doing better on IQ tests. *The Chronicle of Higher Education*, p. A18.

Solso, R. L. (1994). *Cognition and the visual arts*. Cambridge, MA: MIT Press.

Spiegel, G. F., & Barufaldi, J. P. (1994). The effects of a combination of text structure awareness and graphic postorganizers on recall and retention of science knowledge. *Journal of Research in Science Teaching*, 31(9), 913–932.

Stahl, H., & Hunter, S. (1990). *Cmap 2.0* [Computer program for concept mapping]. Ithaca, New York: HSSH (Exceller Software).

Starr, M. L., & Krajcik, J. S. (1990). Concept maps as a heuristic for science curriculum development: Toward improvement in process and product. *Journal of Research in Science Teaching*, 27(10), 987–1000.

Straus, M. (1996). Mistaking the map for the territory. *Journal of College Science Teaching*, 25(6), 408–412.

Trowbridge, J. E. (1995). Gulf literacy: A marine science-based model of scientific literacy. Unpublished doctoral dissertation, Louisiana State University, Baton Rouge.

Trowbridge, J. E., & Wandersee, J. H. (1994). Using concept mapping in a college course on evolution: Identifying critical junctures in learning. *Journal of Research in Science Teaching*, 31, 459–475.

Trowbridge, J. E., & Wandersee, J. H. (1995). Concept mapping in a college course on evolution: Identifying critical junctures in learning. In A. Hofestein, Bat-Sheva Eylon, & G. Giddings *Science education: From theory to practice*. Weizmann Institute of Science: Israel.

Trowbridge, J. E., & Wandersee, J. H. (1996). How do graphics presented during college biology lessons affect student's learning?: A concept map analysis. *Journal of College Science Teaching*, 26(1), 54–57.

Tufte, E. R. (1983). *The visual display of qualitative information*. Cheshire, Connecticut: Graphics Press

Tufte, E. R. (1990). *Envisioning information*. Cheshire, Connecticut: Graphics Press

Wallace, J. P., & Mintzes, J. J. (1990). The concept map as a research tool: Exploring conceptual change in biology. *Journal of Research in Science Teaching*, 27(10), 1033–1052.

Wandersee, J. H. (1987). Drawing concept circles: A new way to teach and test students. *Science Activities*, 27(10), 923–936.

Wandersee, J. H. (1990). Concept mapping and the cartography of cognition. *Journal of Research in Science Teaching*, 27(10), 923–936.

Wandersee, J. H. (1992). A standard format for concept maps. Invited NARST section paper presented at the 1992 national convention of the National Science Teachers Association, March, Boston, MA.

Wandersee, J. H. (1992). The lab-o-gram: Using student-constructed graphics to improve learning. Paper presented at the 1992 national convention of the National Association of biology Teachers, November, Boston, MA.

Wandersee, J. H., & Abrams, E. (1993). Coconstruction of a concept map in a clinical interview setting. AERA *Subject Matter Knowledge and Conceptual Change Newsletter* 20, December, 4–5.

Wandersee, J. H., Mintzes, J. J., & Novak, J. D. (1993). Research on alternative conceptions in science. In D. L. Gabel (ed.). *Handbook of research on science teaching and learning* (pp. 177–211). New York: MacMillian.

Wandersee, J. H., Wissing, D. R., & Lange, C. T. (1996). *Bioinstrumentation: Tools for understanding life.* Reston, VA: National Association of Biology Teachers.

Watercourse & Council for Environmental Education. (1995). *Project WET: Curriculum and activity guide.* Bozeman, MT: Author.

West, C. K., Farmer, J. A., & Wolff, P. M. (1991). *Instructional design: Implications from cognitive science.* Englewood Cliffs, NJ: Prentice Hall.

WuDunn, S. (1996). Tokyo, where streets are noodles. *New York Times,* July 16, A4.

Yelon, S. L. (1996). *Powerful principles of instruction.* White Plains, NY: Longman.

# Metacognition and Conceptual Change

RICHARD F. GUNSTONE

*Monash University*

IAN J. MITCHELL

*Monash University and Eumemmering Secondary College*

In Chapter 2 of this volume Novak's conception of Human Constructivism is outlined. Included in that description are three assertions fundamental to his conception:

1. Human beings are meaning makers.
2. The goal of education is the construction of shared meanings.
3. Shared meanings may be facilitated by the active intervention of well-prepared teachers.

These assertions are central to this chapter and can be taken as the beginning points of our arguments about conceptual change and metacognition.

We begin by elaborating some detail of our meanings for conceptual change and metacognition and then show why we see these two constructs to be necessarily intertwined. This provides the basis for the description we then give of approaches to sequencing, teaching, and assessment of Grade 10 mechanics. The chapter then concludes with some more general issues about teaching from the perspectives of metacognition and conceptual change.

*Teaching Science for Understanding: A Human Constructivist View*

## OUR MEANINGS FOR CONCEPTUAL CHANGE
## AND METACOGNITION

Some general research influences underpinning the growth of concern with conceptual change have been described in Chapter 3 of this volume (Section 3: "Understanding and Conceptual Change in Science: The Current Research Agenda"). These influences have been of fundamental importance to the evolution of our own ideas. Our work in this area over the past 15 years has been largely in physics (e.g., Gunstone & White, 1981) and chemistry (e.g., Mitchell & Gunstone, 1984). Much of this work has been located in, and therefore intertwined with, the dailiness of our normal teaching in high school science (e.g., Baird & Mitchell, 1986; Baird & Northfield, 1992; Mitchell, 1993; White & Mitchell, 1994) and teacher education (e.g., Champagne, Gunstone, & Klopfer, 1985; Gunstone, 1994; Gunstone & Northfield, 1994). Our concerns throughout this work have been to develop our understanding of conceptual change and metacognition in the context of normal school and university classrooms.

### Conceptual Change

One significant aspect of our current conception of conceptual change is that the content to be learned is a major variable in terms of the process of conceptual change (Mitchell & Baird, 1986; White, 1994). We return to this point in the concluding section of the chapter and, for the moment, consider conceptual change in more general terms.

When considered in terms of an individual learner, the essence of a constructivist view of conceptual change is that it is the learner who must recognize his/her conceptions, evaluate these conceptions, decide whether to reconstruct the conceptions, and, if they decide to reconstruct, to review and restructure other relevant aspects of their understanding in ways that lead to consistency. While ultimately these processes of recognize, evaluate, decide whether to reconstruct, review other aspects of understanding are individual, each is profoundly influenced (positively or negatively) by the ways in which the teacher, and other class members, structure classroom practice.

These processes of recognize, evaluate, reconstruct, and review do not often lead to dramatic conceptual change. Conceptual change is rarely a sharp replacement of conception X by conception Y. Rather, conceptual change is more often "an accretion of information that the learner uses to sort out contexts in which it is profitable to use one form of explanation or another" (Fensham, Gunstone, & White, 1994, p. 6).

Mitchell (1993) studied the learning of all students in four Grade 10 science classes during a 6-week unit on mechanics, a unit very similar to the sequence we describe below. He began this research looking for, and expecting to find, numerous examples of "ahha" experiences/incidents—that is, experiences/incidents that were crucial to the conceptual change of individual students. Although almost all students could on completion of the unit identify lessons and specific experiences that they had *not* found personally useful, there was only a very small number of "ahha" experiences. Most students found that most lessons made some useful contribution to their learning. Their conceptual change was evolutionary rather than revolutionary. This can be explained by the view of Hewson and Hewson (1992) that conceptual change involves a change in the status of competing ideas. The new ideas (Newtonian in this mechanics case) appeared to need a number of successful classroom episodes in order to gain the status of unquestioned superiority.

It is often appropriate to consider the process as "conceptual addition" rather than "conceptual change."

> The example of drinking through a straw illustrates the point about shifts as well as additions in meaning. When learners come to understand the notion of pressure difference, they do not drop the word "suck," though their conceptions of sucking change. Knowledge about pressure has been added, but old knowledge is revised rather than abandoned. A conceptual addition has occurred. Central to this formulation of what is often described as "conceptual change" is that *the individual also has informed approaches to deciding which of a number of meanings is appropriate in a particular context.*
> (Fensham, Gunstone, & White, 1995, p 7; emphasis added)

A further significant aspect of conceptual change, a term we continue to use in this chapter because it is so widespread as a general description for the development of understanding, is also related to contexts. Often learners will accept the scientific concept in one context, but then revert to using their prior conception in another context that we as science teachers would see as essentially the same as the first context. That is, conceptual change can often be seen to first take place in a particular context. Then the student may vacillate between scientific and prior conceptions from one context to another; the conceptual change is then context dependant and unstable. Long-term and stable conceptual change is achieved when the learner recognizes relevant commonalities across contexts and the generality of the scientific conception across these contexts (Tao, 1996; Tao & Gunstone, 1997).

## Metacognition

Our conception of metacognition has been formed through research in classrooms (ours and others). It is a multifaceted conception, described in a number of sources (e.g., Baird & Mitchell, 1986; Baird & Northfield, 1992; Gunstone & Northfield, 1994; Mitchell, 1993; White & Mitchell, 1994). We now give a brief summary (based on Gunstone, 1994, pp. 134–136) of the various and complementary aspects of our meaning for metacognition.

1. "Metacognition refers to the knowledge, awareness and control of one's own learning" (Baird, 1990, p. 184). Metacognitive knowledge refers to

knowledge of the nature and processes of learning, of personal learning characteristics, and of effective learning strategies and where to use these. Metacognitive awareness includes perceptions of the purpose of the current activity and of personal progress through the activity. Metacognitive control refers to the nature of learner decisions and actions during the activity. Inadequate knowledge restricts the extent to which awareness and control are possible.

2. Metacognitive knowledge, awareness, and control are all learning outcomes (as well as fundamental influences on the nature of more usual learning outcomes). Hence metacognitive knowledge, awareness, and control can be developed with appropriate learning experiences. (This is well illustrated by extensive work in the Project for Enhancing Effective Learning (the PEEL project); see Baird & Mitchell, 1986; Baird & Northfield, 1992).

3. Often the learning which gives rise to a learner's metacognitive ideas and beliefs has been unconscious learning, and the learner finds it difficult to articulate his/her metacognitive views.

4. All learners have metacognitive views of some form. That is, all learners have some form of metacognitive knowledge. This can be of a form that is in conflict with the goals of conceptual change teaching (e.g., "it is the teacher's job to tell me so I understand"; "we have discussions in science when the teacher can't be bothered teaching"). There are many examples of such conflict (see, for example, Baird & Mitchell, 1986; Baird & Northfield, 1992).

5. There can be tensions between metacognitive knowledge, awareness, and control. Most obvious are contexts where the assessment of learning is via rote recall—here learners with enhanced metacognitive knowledge and awareness will see that they should not invest time and effort in developing their understanding and controlling their learning if they wish high grades. Teaching concerned with conceptual change and enhanced metacognition must have assessment approaches consistent with these learning goals.

6. One helpful description of an appropriately metacognitive learner is a learner who undertakes the tasks of linking and monitoring their own learning.

7. There are a number of commonly occurring poor learning tendencies exhibited by many learners (Baird, 1986). Examples are superficial or impulsive attention, premature closure (where "closure" is used here and at other points in this chapter to mean bringing together in a conclusion; "premature closure" is then concluding or deciding that the task is complete before this is appropriate), lack of reflective thinking, and staying stuck (i.e., one problem or error stops all progress). These represent inadequate metacognition and are major barriers to learning.

8. On the other hand, there are good learning behaviors which illustrate more appropriate metacognition in classrooms (Baird & Northfield, 1992, p. 63); these good learning behaviors can be fostered by appropriate teaching.

These behaviors are many. Examples include telling teacher *what* they don't understand, planning a general strategy before starting a task, seeking links with other activities or topics, and justifying opinions.

## The Intertwined Nature
## of Conceptual Change and Metacognition

The links between conceptual change and metacognition seem to us an obvious consequence of our description of conceptual change. The processes of recognizing existing conceptions, evaluating these, deciding whether to reconstruct, and reviewing are all metacognitive processes; they require appropriate metacognitive knowledge, awareness, and control.

We now give an outline of a teaching sequence that is derived from these conceptual change/metacognition perspectives, beginning with some aspects of the broad intent of the sequence. After the outline we discuss some more general aspects of classrooms that are relevant to the sequence.

## AN EXAMPLE OF TEACHING
## FROM THESE PERSPECTIVES

The sequence we describe below is about introductory mechanics. The sequence has been shaped by research on students' alternative conceptions in mechanics and by the views of conceptual change and metacognition outlined above. We have taught the sequence on a number of occasions, and reflections on these experiences have contributed to the form given here. Our own uses of the approaches in this content area have largely been with Grade 10 high school students in the state of Victoria (where science in Grades 7–10 of the 6-year high school is a General Science taken by all students) and with science graduates who are Biology majors undertaking a 1-year postgraduate course to qualify as high school science teachers (and who may therefore be required to teach introductory mechanics in the General Science program). We describe the sequence in terms of a Grade 10 class. We do not give fine detail in our description—class, school, and curriculum contexts vary; so then will the fine detail of the sequence.

The sequence begins with the probing of students' existing ideas, then seeks to promote the reconstruction of ideas about particular content, then explicitly considers the exploration of the consistency ideas across a variety of contexts, and finally concludes with some ideas for the assessment of learning from the sequence. It uses a range of experiences to foster students' intellectual engagement with the ideas to be learned. We assume throughout that much of the language that students use will be tentative, exploratory, and hypothetical as they grapple with the ideas of mechanics—this assumption is a consequence of our recognition that students need time to consider and discuss these ideas if they are to develop understanding. We also assume that there will commonly need to be risk taking on the part of both learners and teachers.

Throughout the sequence there should be an emphasis on the creation of links between lessons and with experiences students bring to the classroom and on the central issue of the consistency of students' views across situations. It is intended that students will learn from the questions and ideas and exploratory language of other students and that the rate of progress through the sequence (and some of the detail of the sequence per se) will be influenced by students and their ideas.

The sequence includes three teaching approaches that may be unfamiliar: predict-observe-explain (POE); concept maps; relational diagrams (or Venn diagrams). We give a very brief description of the nature and intent of each of these here. Space prevents our giving a comprehensive account of the range of ways each of these approaches can be used, and of the linkages between these approaches and student learning. Such an account is in White and Gunstone (1992).

## Predict-Observe-Explain (POE)

Students are shown a real situation, asked to give their prediction about the consequences of a particular change to the situation and the reasons they have for their prediction, then when the change is made they give their observation, and finally predictions and observations are reconciled if necessary. POEs can be used to explore students' ideas at the beginning of a topic, or to develop ideas during a topic, or to enhance understanding at the end of a topic by having them attempt to apply their learning to a real situation. In all of these uses, the reasons students have for a prediction are crucial; predictions, reasons and observations are usually best written, not verbal.

An example of a POE for the content area of heat capacity of materials: The situation is a beaker of water and a beaker of cooking oil (equal volumes of liquids) placed on a hotplate and with thermometers (0–200°C.). Students are asked to predict how the temperatures of the two liquids will compare when the hot plate has been turned on long enough for the water to be boiling (it is helpful to give alternatives for students to choose—"Is the temperature of the cooking oil less than, the same as, greater than the boiling water?"), and to write their reasons. The observation is the readings of the thermometers. Reconciliation commonly involves addressing their prediction that the cooking oil temperature is less than the boiling water because the oil is not burning.

## Concept Maps

Students have a set of words representing concepts, and perhaps other relevant things, and put these on a sheet of paper. They draw lines between those words that they see to be linked, and write the nature of the links on the lines. (This last point is crucial; it is the nature of the links students perceive that is the essence of the concept map.) Usually the teacher provides the students with the terms to be mapped, although there are a number of reasons for students themselves to sometimes generate some or all of the terms. Concept maps are highly effective for exploring the links students perceive between ideas, and for fostering further linking. (See Chapter 3 of this volume for description and examples of concept maps.)

## Relational (or Venn) Diagrams

Students are given a small number of terms and asked to draw a circle or rectangle for each term, arranged so that the shapes represent the relationships between the terms. An example is "trees, grasses, flowering plants." The appropriate response has the shape for grasses totally within flowering plants, and that for trees partially within and partially without flowering plants.

There are two important issues to recognize in using each of these three approaches, particularly concept maps and relational diagrams.

1. Students need to be taught how to approach each of these if the students have not experienced them before. It is rather like having a class who have never seen multiple choice questions—before you give multiple choice to such a class you would need to help them understand the structure and intent of the questions, and how to respond. Failure to do this would mean that students would be unable to respond in the ways you intend. This is less of an issue for POEs—these are sufficiently similar to conventional science demonstrations that students will not have great difficulty in seeing what they are required to do, but it is a very important aspect of introducing concept maps or relational diagrams to a class who have not previously experienced these.

2. It really is important to try any particular examples of the three approaches yourself before you use these with a class. With concept maps and relational diagrams in particular, this "trialling" is a necessary step in considering what terms should be given to the students. For example, we have been using concept maps in our science teaching for over a decade. Yet we still find that our first list of terms to give to students as a concept mapping task is frequently changed when we try the task ourselves. That is, often when we do the concept map ourselves we see that one (or more) terms should be replaced by others for the task to achieve what we intend.

The outline of the sequence is now presented as a series of points. Comments on the sequence and its intent are given in italics.

Name: ...................

### FORCE SURVEY

1.    Which of these words give the best idea of force?
      (You may choose more than one)
      (a) push                    (b) pressure              (c) pull ·
      (d) energy                  (e) momentum              (f) motion.


2.    A ball is rolling along a flat table.  It slows down and stops.
      Which of the following could explain this? (Choose one).
      (a) The ball ran out of force
      (b) The ball just stopped naturally
      (c) Friction caused the ball to stop
      (d) Gravity caused the ball to stop.

3.    A skate board rider is moving down a gently sloping path.
      The person is going at the same speed all the time.  She is not
      getting faster or slower.

      moving at a steady speed
      not speeding up or slowing down

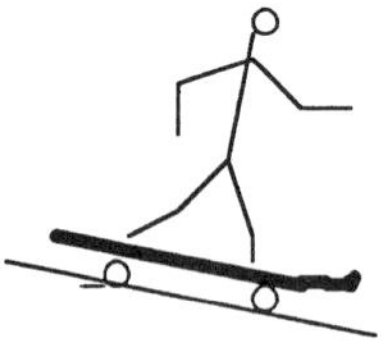

Which of these sentences about the total force on the rider is correct?

(a)    There is no total force on the rider because her speed is steady.
(b)    There must be a total force on the rider because she is moving.

4.    A person is learning against a brick wall.
        Is the person putting a force on the wall?

       (a) Yes

       (b) No

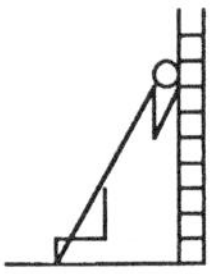

**FIGURE 1**
Survey of students' ideas about force.

5.   A car is parked on a hill.  It is not moving and the brakes are on.
     Which of the following is correct?
               *(Sketch of car on hill with label "Not moving*
                                              *Brakes are on!")*

     (a) There are many forces on the car but the total force is zero.
     (b) There are many forces on the car and the total force is downwards
     (c) There are no forces on the car at all

6.   A football has been kicked toward the goalpost.
               *(Sketch of appropriate form of footballer and goalpost)*
     As it moves through the goalpost what are the forces on it?
     (You can choose more than one.)

     (a) The force of gravity
     (b) The force of friction
     (c) The force of the kick

7 - 9.  (from Osborne & Freyberg, 1985)
        A person throws a tennis
        ball straight up into the
        air just a small way.

        The questions are about
        the total force on the ball.

7.   If the ball is on the way up, then the force on the ball is shown by which
     arrow?

     *(Diagram above repeated three times, labelled (a), (b), (c), with (a)*
     *including a downwards arrow on the ball, (b) an upwards arrow on the*
     *ball, (c) the statement "no force" beside the ball.)*

8.   If the ball is just at the top of its flight, then the force on the ball is shown
     by which arrow?

     *(Diagrams for Qn 7 repeated.)*

9.   If the ball is on the way down, then the force on the ball is shown by
     which arrow?

     *(Diagrams for Qn 7 repeated.)*

**FIGURE 1—*Continued***

## A. Probing Students' Ideas

1. Clarify the meaning of the term "total force" (is "net" force).

*We see this as a matter of terminology.*

2. Give a written survey of students' existing ideas. Our survey is given in Figure 1. The range of alternative conceptions the survey is probing are shown in Figure 2.

*If this was the first experience of the class with questions with this intent—to show to teacher and students the range of existing ideas—we would make the survey anonymous.*

3. Collate results from survey (e.g., for Q3 x students chose (a), y students chose (b)) and report the data to the class.

*This serves to show the class the range of ideas and to reassure students that others share their ideas and raises through the disagreements that are shown a set of issues to be resolved. Where there is uniform agreement with a non-scientific idea, such as all students choosing (b) for Q3, then at an appropriate point in the sequence the teacher will need to provide experiences or arguments to challenge the idea.*

4. Assert the resolution of Q1: a force is a push or a pull; forces are described by indicating what object is exerting the force and what object is experiencing the force; the direction of the force is important so the direction is always included in describing the force.

*The first of the above assertions, a force is a push or pull, assumes that the issues embraced by Q1 are properly seen as just terminological. The remaining two assertions will need constant revisiting and reinforcement through the sequence, although we do want to point out that the importance of directionality of force is intuitively accepted by even very young children—try asking them to help you push something stationary in a particular direction; they will always push in that direction. This intuitive understanding is rarely recognized in teaching mechanics and is often subsumed under technical and initially unnecessary vocabulary such as "vector."*

*continued*

Qn 1    (Terminology rather than an alternative conception; a reinforcement of the first point in the sequence.)

Qn 2    A moving object has a net force in the direction of movement. If the object is slowing then this force is decreasing (friction may wear the force down). When there is no net force the object stops.

Qn 3    Steady speed means constant net forward force.

Qn 4    The wall is not moving so there is no force on the wall.

Qn 5    Brakes (or friction) just "stop" the car. (Not many students choose (c) no forces, but many students say there are no uphill forces.)

Qn 6    There is a forward force on the ball from the kick.

Qn 7-9    As the ball rises there is a decreasing upwards force on it (usually the "force of the throw" which gradually reduces). At the top the "force of the throw" and gravity are in balance (although some students still choose "upwards" at the top of the flight).

**FIGURE 2**

Alternative conceptions being probed by the questions in Figure 1.

## B. Promoting Reconstruction of Ideas About:

5. Force and stationary objects

*We begin with static situations in order to develop an acceptance of zero net force for a stationary object. This then leads to considering the consequences of a net force; see item 6 below.*

5.1 Debate on Qs 4 and 5 from the survey (with that debate and other subsequent class discussions being very much in the form of "interpretative discussions" (Barnes, 1976); that is, the teacher has students elaborate reasons for survey answers and debate these reasons, the teacher withholds judgement on the reasons).

Then similar discussions about whether there are forces on a book on a table and a book on a student's outstretched hand. As appropriate in the development of class thinking a number of phenomena are introduced to direct the debate:

- a book suspended from a string
- the book suspended from a spring
- the book on a foam rubber pillow
- books on meter rule held up by bricks at either end (the meter rule is intended as a model of a table, with movement of the supporting bricks showing how the ruler distorts less as the supports come closer).
- showing the distortion in a table supporting an object by shining a beam of light onto a mirror on the table.
- considering how a chair is able to push up with greater force when heavier people sit on it (the "magic" chair).

*Here we use a book on a table as an example of static situations. Commonly students hold the view that the table cannot push up, it just "stops" the book. In this section we initially focus on exploring situations where the upwards force on the book may be more plausible to students (although some students argue that with only one book on his/ her hand a student is not pushing up either or that a string cannot pull— although a spring is seen to be pulling up on the book, or that while the meter rule does push up it is not as "hard" as the gravity pull down, or that while the meter rule does push up, real tables do not). The meter rule as "model table" is intended to lead to the position of accepting an upwards force when there is distortion in the supporting surface. Then, by using mirror and light beam to magnify the distortion it is possible to show this distortion in many tables. This also links to the "magic chair"—a heavier person causes greater distortion in the chair.*

*continued*

From this is established

- reaction forces exist because objects deform
- the more an object is pushed or pulled the more it deforms (hence chairs adjust to the weights of different people)
- less flexible objects do not need to deform very much to exert reaction forces, hence the deformation is not noticed
- Newton's Third Law

*The provision of student notes on these points can take a number of forms, for example, fill in gaps or students in small groups to write explanations for Q4 and Q5 from the survey for "someone who was away" for the relevant classes. Details of this part of the sequence as used with intending high school science teachers are given in Gunstone (1994, p. 138). Details of the use with Grade 10 students, including some class transcripts and student reflections via journal and interview, are given in Baird & Northfield, (1992, pp. 70–74); a section of transcript is given at the end of this chapter.*

5.2 Further exploration/consolidation of Newton's Third Law through experiences such as Predict-Observe-Explain (POE) for two students (of very similar mass) on skateboards. First the prediction required is for the motions of the two when they both push each other (most will predict correctly), then predict the motions of the two when only one skateboarder pushes (here many will predict that one will move further than the other).

*Giving reasons for predictions means that students are explicitly giving aspects of their current conceptions; observations will often then challenge these conceptions.*

*The common alternative conception here is that, for the second POE, the student being pushed will go further because the student pushing does not have a force on them.*

5.3 Discussion of and closure on the above situations involving Newton's Third Law allows the assertion of an aspect of Newton's First Law: "If an object is remaining stationary then the net force on that object must be zero." This is followed with a set of drawings of different stationary objects (e.g., a boy sitting on a trampoline, a hanging basket, a girl pushing against a wall). Students draw and label the forces on one object in each draw-

*In the case of the girl pushing against the wall, classwork to this point should result in three forces acting on the girl: gravity down, reaction of the floor up, and the reaction of the wall pushing against the girl. Consideration of an opposing force to the reaction of the wall is the next instructional step.*

continued

ing. The teacher states to the student that their classwork thus far should result in them being able to explain forces that show the part of Newton's First Law given above being satisfied. However, in a few cases this will not be so—there will be some "missing forces."

Discussion and debate lead to students generating at least some aspects of the concept of friction as a force. During the discussion have a student push against a wall and then pour concentrated soap solution under his or her feet.

*At some point during the content on which this sequence focuses, the concepts of friction and gravity need to be introduced. We introduce friction at the point noted above and gravity below, because they are needed at these points to enable a consistent explanation to be applied to the particular new contexts. That is, we seek to create a reason for the introduction of the concept.*

5.4 Continue the discussion of friction. First develop the idea of friction seen as, for example, for the above case of the girl pushing on a wall, reaction forces from little bumps on the floor which distort under the (sideways) force from her feet. Then consider the direction of friction in other situations (including situations where friction acts in the direction of motion): on a block sliding on a table, on a man walking, on the rear (i.e., powered) wheel of a bicycle, on the same bicycle wheel as it skids to a halt, on the (unpowered) wheel of a skateboard rolling on a level surface. In each case the direction of friction is developed from a consideration of the distortion of the bumps on the road or table.

*Throughout 5.1–5.4 it is important to continually reinforce that in all contexts the reaction force acts on a different object, that forces do not "cancel out."*

*A common alternative conception is that friction is not a force, it is just something that tends to stop things moving.*

5.5 Gravity situations such as the book on the table necessarily embrace gravitational forces. At

*continued*

this point we consider gravitational forces specifically.

5.5.1 Give a survey of existing ideas. This comprises asking students to compare, on a scale of: a lot more/a tiny bit more/the same/ a tiny bit less/a lot less/zero, the "strength of the force of gravity on you in this classroom" with the strength: in this room with all the air pumped out; on top of Mt. Everest; on top of (tallest building in Melbourne); on the moon (described as one-sixth the size of the earth); on an asteroid 10 km across; on Jupiter (1000 times the size of earth); in this room if the earth stopped spinning; on you if you were swimming underwater; on you if you were in free fall after jumping from a plane; on you if you were an astronaut alone in deep space.

5.5.2 Report back and debate (as in item 3 above). Some views can be challenged with "indirect" data such as photographs of astronauts on the surface of the moon.

5.5.3 POE involving a spring balance and weight inside a bell jar connected to an air pump. Predict whether the spring balance reading will change when air is pumped out of the bell jar. (A diagram of this apparatus is shown in Figure 3.)

5.5.4 Use the force on the earth underneath an occupied chair as another "find the situations with a missing force" task. (All the forces on the earth seem to be downwards.) Use the situations in 5.5.1 to bring out the upwards force of gravity on the earth by the occupied chair.

*The alternative conceptions that have shaped the survey are*

- *gravity is caused by air or air pressure (and thus there is no gravity on the moon)*
- *gravity is caused by the earth's spin*
- *gravity is greater on high mountains*
- *gravity is noticeably less on high mountains.*

*The association of gravity with atmosphere is a very common view. It can be valuable to show the consequences for the spring balance reading of placing the weight in water before setting up the POE so as to show the balance will register a reduction in net downwards force.*

*continued*

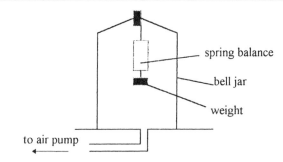

**FIGURE 3**
Apparatus for a POE to probe student conceptions regarding air and gravity.

5.6 Student notes about friction and gravity (in a form to demand some intellectual engagement, such as writing explanations for observations such as a weight sliding across a desk slows down and stops, or the POE in 5.5.3, or a parachutist falls at a steady speed. These then are student notes of the same form as those described at the end of 5.1 above.)

5.7 At appropriate points throughout 5 students are asked to write thinking questions (e.g. "Write a question that is puzzling you about today's lesson"). These questions will often influence the sequence and content of the teaching.

5.8 Throughout Section 5 qualitative force diagrams are consistently used, that is diagrams showing forces acting but not relative magnitudes of the forces. An example is shown in Figure 4.

6. Forces and moving objects

*Relevant alternative conceptions are given in Figure 2.*

6.1 Begin with relevant questions from the initial survey of existing ideas (2 above; Qs 2–3, 6–9).

*continued*

A student sits on a swing. Show the forces on the student.

reaction force
from seat on student

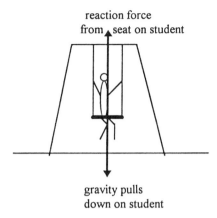

gravity pulls
down on student

**FIGURE 4**

A task requiring a qualitative force diagram and a correct response.

Open debate on the relationship between force and motion (including the nature of the motion).

6.2 Use some or all of the following (with judgement about this to be made as the class thinking develops).

6.2.1 POE with glider on air track (or puck on air table or air puck): what will you need to do with a ruler to get the glider to start and keep moving at a steady speed?

*In this case the observation should be the trying of the suggestions contained in the predictions. The common alternative conception is that the ruler will need to keep pushing on the puck for steady speed.*

A second POE is then appropriate, provided it can be managed without damage to the equipment: predict how the motion will be changed, if at all, if the air is turned off from the air track.

*Each of the predictions/observations needs analysis via class discussion to establish the significant features involved in those cases where steady speed motion was achieved and to explore how other motions related to the nature of the applied force.*

*continued*

6.2.2 A number of valuable POEs use a bicycle wheel mounted as a large pulley with a block of wood and bucket of sand hanging from either side (a photograph of this apparatus is in White & Gunstone, 1992, p. 50; a pulley serves as an adequate but much less dramatic alternative to the bicycle wheel). Not all of the following might be used, depending on the class and their ideas. Figure 5 shows the apparatus.

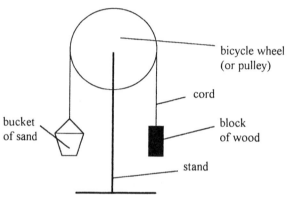

**FIGURE 5**

Apparatus for a series of POEs concerning force and motion.

(a) Place the wood and sand on the wheel so that the wood is higher than the sand. Explore students' opinions of the relative weights of the sand and wood. Then pull the wood down until it is level with the sand, and "hold" it in this position. Ask for prediction of motion when the wood is released.

*In the ensuing debate it is important to move to the weights of the wood and sand being equal before leaving this situation and undertaking (b). The common alternative conception is that the wood and sand will return to their initial position, sometimes because this is seen as the equilibrium position.*

(b) Reposition the sand so that it is higher than the wood. Ask for prediction of motion when a heavier weight (which will result in motion) is added to the sand and observe.

*Considerable debate about the explanation of the motion is appropriate at this point. It will very likely be helpful at some point in the debate to repeat the POE and ask for predic-*

*continued*

tion of the relative speeds of the sand at two well-separated points along its motion in order to reinforce the accelerating nature of the motion. The common alternative conception is that the sand will move just a small distance and then stop.

(c) Repeat (b), but ask for a prediction of the effect on the motion of the sand of removing the added weight after the sand has moved a short distance.

The common alternative conception is that the sand will stop again because the force is removed.

(d) Repeat (c), but this time add twice the weight added to the sand to the wood when the system is moving.

Some students predict an immediate reversal of the motion. This is useful in building the conceptions that motion in one direction is possible even though the net force is in the opposite direction and that such motion will result in deceleration. The earlier situations with this apparatus mean that students do regard the net force on the block as downward.

(e) Repeat (d), but add weight to the wood only equal to the weight already added to the sand.

After (c) has been done, instead of proceeding on to (d) and (e), the teacher can instead call for suggestions of other POEs to do with the apparatus. Situations (d) and (e), and other variations, are often suggested by students. These sorts of interactive situations with a piece of apparatus can be used in a number of ways and are an effective way of stimulating changes in students' conceptions concerning who has the intellectual control of the classroom (from teacher to shared), as well as reinforcing to them the importance of their ideas and suggestions. These changes in conceptions are essential for changes in learning behaviors such as offering and defending new

continued

*ideas. These changes occur gradually and should be promoted and supported at every opportunity.*

6.2.3 A number of short, qualitative laboratory exercises are of value. Each can be done as a POE with the observation being undertaken in small groups each with their own apparatus.

(a) Use a spring balance to find the minimum force needed start a laboratory trolley moving, then predict the motion that would result from maintaining that force— steady speed or acceleration?

(b) Predict the direction of the net force on a weight on an oscillating spring at various points during the oscillation. Observation of this direction can be achieved by stopping the weight at the various positions and feeling the direction of the force.

*It is worth spending time in whole-class discussion to reach common observations of direction of net force and direction of motion. This is an important and complex example.*

(c) Use magnets to provide constant force on an airtrack glider (with varying loads) and consider the effects of constant force "with and against" motion.

6.2.4 Throughout 6.2.1–6.2.3 there needs to be a continuing emphasis on net force leading to changing speed (and/or changing direction of motion). There will also be many opportunities to gradually develop a qualitative understanding of $F = ma$.

6.2.5 Return to the POE in 5.2, but this time use two students of very different mass.

*The earlier work established that the forces on the two students are equal, now the forces is on the effect of these identical forces on different masses. Students generally predict correctly here, so the key issue is to use the fact of equal forces on the*

*continued*

*students to lead to Newton's second law.*

As part of the tying together of these common features of 6.2.1–6.2.3 that is the focus of 6.2.4 and 6.2.5, students can now be asked to complete some formal tasks

(a) A sheet of explanations (e.g., for the POEs with the bicycle wheel "The bucket of sand started moving when we added the weights because . . . . . . ," "The bucket continued to speed up all the way to the floor because . . . . . . ," "If we *removed* the weight the bucket kept moving because . . . . . . and gradually slowed down because . . . . . ."; for the air track glider "The glider kept 'running away' from anyone who tried to keep pushing it because . . . . . . ," and so on.)

(b) Give examples of objects moving in the same direction as the net force on them and objects moving in a different direction from the net force on them.

(c) Notes are given about Newton's First and Second Laws.

6.3 Throughout 6.1 and 6.2, as for 5., qualitative force diagrams are consistently used and written thinking questions are called for at appropriate points.

## C. Exploring Consistency of Ideas across a Variety of Contexts

7.1 For particular events (such as a golf ball on a tee, golf ball in contact with a golf club, golf ball in flight) draw the forces on (the ball), describe the net force and therefore justify the motion.

*The teacher should predict to the students that many of them will draw initially on non-Newtonian ideas, and stress to the students the sequence of asking themselves "What is my first reaction"? "Is this*

*continued*

*consistent with Newton?" "If not, how do I make it consistent"? It is very easy for this to be done in a way that belittles or demeans the student. It is essential that this is not the case.*

7.2 As a further and crucial integrating and consolidating exercise, students complete a written reflection on their ideas as shown in the initial survey, the explanation advanced by science, and their current opinion. This is done via the worksheet shown in Figure 6.

*Note that this approach presumes that students' names are on the survey responses so that these can be returned and students thus given the data about their initial views. We have described the science explanations as "Isaac Newton's opinion" in order to decrease—but not totally remove—the possibility that students will repeat the science explanation in the last column without seriously thinking about their understanding of the situation.*

| Situation | My original opinion | Issac Newton's opinion | My present explanation |
|---|---|---|---|
| Q2. Ball rolling on a flat table; slowing down | | | |
| Q3. Skateboard rider on a gentle slope; steady speed | | | |
| Q7. Football going through the goal-posts. | | | |
| Q8. Ball tossed straight up; ball moving up (and slowing down) | | | |
| Q9. Ball at top of its flight | | | |
| Q10. Ball coming down again; speeding up. | | | |

**FIGURE 6**
A worksheet to encourage reflection on learning.

*continued*

8. If a quantitative dimension is seen to be needed, work with ticker timers and sketch graphs can now be introduced.

*We do not use ticker timers in our teaching as, given the strong conceptual focus in our purposes, we see it as much more appropriate to aim to develop understandings of relationships. Quantitative approaches in such introductory contexts often distract students from the thinking required for these relationships to be developed.*

9. Further integrating activities and possible assessment tasks:

*Given the strong conceptual focus we see a test as appropriate assessment. We now give some examples of tasks appropriate for a test or for further class work.*

9.1 Force diagrams and explanations of motion for, for example: a high jumper going over the bar; a bottle empty and floating in water, having filled with water and sinking through the water at a steady speed, having come to rest on the ocean floor; a parachutist falling at a steady speed; a trampolinist in the air rising up, in contact with the trampoline and still moving down, lying still on the trampoline; a basketball thrown toward the basket while still rising, at its highest point, on the way down again.

9.2 A concept map for "force," "motion," "change of motion," "gravity," and "acceleration."

9.3 A relational diagram (or Venn diagram) for "objects which are moving," "objects which are stationary," "objects which have a net force on them," and "objects with no net force on them." Figure 7 shows the correct response to this task.

*continued*

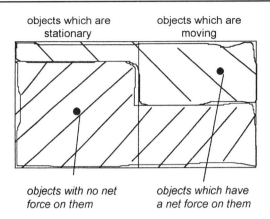

objects which are
stationary

objects which are
moving

*objects with no net
force on them*

*objects which have
a net force on them*

**FIGURE 7**

Correct response for relational diagram task given in Section 9.3.

9.4 Statements from science textbooks and other such sources which are correctly described to students as misleading. The task is to explain how the statement has got the physics wrong. Examples include

- (In discussing a lead ball and a rubber ball sitting on the floor) "the lead ball will need a harder push (more net force) than the rubber ball to change its state of rest because of its greater mass."
- "When a stone falls to earth, not only does the earth exert a force on the stone, the stone exerts a force on the earth. But because the force exerted by the earth is very much greater than the force exerted by the stone, then the stone moves much faster."

(Note: Throughout the whole sequence worksheets are constantly used to create written student responses to tasks.)

## SOME ASPECTS OF THE NATURE
## OF THE CLASSROOM IN WHICH THIS
## TEACHING CAN BE SUCCESSFUL

In this section we outline some issues that are discussed much more fully in Baird and Northfield (1992) and Mitchell (1993).

Classrooms in which the above sequence is used differ sharply from didactic contexts. Central to many of the differences is the utterly central focus on student learning as opposed to a focus on teacher completion of a curriculum. The pace of "coverage" of the curriculum appears much slower. However, this is usually misleading. If this pace is judged in terms of the quality of student understanding it is usually more rapid than in a didactic environment. The pace of student learning is also not "linear" in these classrooms. Rather, apparently slow early progress leads to much more rapid learning later in the sequence. There is, we assert, a rough form of parabolic curve for progress. This contrasts sharply with the usual linear progress of didactic teaching where no more time is spent on the fundamental ideas underpinning a topic than is spent on later applications of those fundamental ideas.

Our assertion of a "parabolic" learning curve has some support, although there has been very little research on the matter. One relevant study (Mitchell & Gunstone, 1984) is a classroom-based study of the learning of stoichiometry, a topic widely described in the literature as difficult for students to learn. One class was taught the topic in a way consistent with the approach we have described here for mechanics: apparently slow progress early as probing of student ideas and student debate was used to develop understanding of underlying concepts; delaying the introduction of the concept of mole; then considerably less time spent on drill and practice with standard stoichiometry problems. Two other classes covered the same content in exactly the same class time, but were taught in the much more usual linear approach. All three classes undertook the same examination. The "experimental" class achieved much better results.

There is considerable teaching experience consistent with our assertion of a form of parabolic learning curve. We give two examples. After one occasion of the use of this sequence with a Grade 10 science class, some of these students took a specialist physics class in Grade 11. This physics class was taken by a teacher whose approach focused on the mathematics of mechanics—an element that is not central to our approach. The physics teacher consistently asked the Grade 10 science teacher (IM) what these students had experienced in Grade 10 as he claimed that every new concept introduced in Grade 11 was already understood "better than any class I have ever had." Because these students already had a substantial conceptual understanding, the mathematics the physics teacher was intent on teaching became relatively trivial. Our second example is within the teaching sequence we have described above. Friction is considered quite late in the sequence. This is usually a difficult concept at the Grade 10 level. Even so, this section of the sequence takes only one class lesson to start from the "missing force" (Section 5.3 above), consider the idea of friction as a reaction force from little bumps and then decide the direction of friction in the situations described in Section 5.4 above. Note that some of these situations are very difficult (e.g., a person walking, comparing powered and unpowered wheels).

Another central characteristic of classrooms in which this approach has been successful is trust. For the approach to have value, students need to have a belief that they will learn from the approach. This requires that they trust the teacher in a number of ways: that she/he will show serious interest in and support for students' ideas and questions; that she/he will eventually address these questions; that the confusion that students will sometimes experience will be resolved (and not necessarily in today's class). Students need also to trust other students to be supportive.

It is the teacher who is central to the creation of such trust (although, clearly, this trust cannot be developed without the acceptance of students). Other significant teacher attributes that are central to teaching with the intents we describe are the appropriate delaying of judgement about ideas and substantial wait times (Rowe, 1974). The issue of delaying judgement is a particularly complex area, and approaches to this are necessarily influenced by context (the nature of the class, including the extent to which they have experienced the approach; the topic; the time of day; etc). It is important to attempt to balance the issues of coming too quickly to conclusions about questions with the potential problems arising from student confusion. Another way of describing this is in terms of creating some sense among students of progress and coherence in classes which are so loosely structured.

Also important for the approach we have outlined is that the teacher understands the nature, purpose, limitations, and likely student reactions for a range of classroom teaching procedures (e.g., POE, interpretive discussion, concept map).

One frequent problem is that the resolution of some of these big ideas takes more than one lesson. It is common to have a lesson in approaches such as our mechanics sequence that involves vigorous debate which clarifies for students the competing views and associated arguments and perhaps begins a process of testing these views. However, such a lesson often will not resolve the competing views because of the time required for this. The teacher may be delighted with this, but some of the students (or most of the students if the class is not used to such sequences) may leave such a class feeling confused or depressed (or disengaged) because they must have "missed the right answer." One way of overcoming this is for the teacher to provide clear closure, not on the right view, but on where the class is (or is not) at the end of the lesson; for example "There are three competing views about _____, Ward's, Katie's, and Danielle's. If you can summarize these by three diagrams you have an excellent understanding of this lesson."

## CONTENT AND APPROACHES
## TO CONCEPTUAL CHANGE

We indicated early in this chapter our belief that the processes of conceptual change had some linkage with the content to be learned. The content to be learned will also have some influence on approaches used in teaching for conceptual change. We now illustrate these issues by reference to the mechanics sequence we have outlined.

There are three significant characteristics of the content of introductory mechanics for these issues. The first two are that it is a highly conceptual content area; and that almost all students have had a rich array of personal experiences that have relevance. The combination of these two characteristics means that the oscillating between existing and scientific conceptions as the context changes, described earlier in the chapter, is more likely than for content areas that do not possess one (or both) of the characteristics. Hence concern for exploring concepts and conceptual relationships across a range of related contexts becomes more central in this content area, a point of significance for both teaching and for relevant research on learning and classrooms.

The third significant characteristic of the content of introductory mechanics for considering conceptual change is that it is rich in what Mitchell and Baird (1986) called "compelling situations." These are situations where the competing views lead to very different and directly testable predictions about what will occur. (The situations involving a pair of students on skateboards in the sequence above is a good example.) However, there are other important areas of science where there are far fewer compelling situations. This is true, for example, for much of chemistry where the accepted scientific view, such as a particulate view of matter, offers greater explanatory power than the competing and common student view of matter as continuous through being more consistent, more coherent, more parsimonious, and more detailed. But a continuous view does not predict many different outcomes than a particulate view. The characteristics of a better explanation—more consistent, coherent, parsimonious, detailed—are valued by scientists and teachers, but not necessarily by students who can also assert "more abstract, more complex, and more boring." Certainly as one studies more chemistry the cohesive ideas of atoms and molecules do acquire very significant predictive power, but, in the general science high school contexts we are considering, compelling situations cannot be used in many content areas. In these cases the second stage of the broad structure of our mechanics sequence ("promoting reconstruction of ideas") is done in very different ways, although these ways are still based on our ideas of conceptual change and metacognition. (Further detail is given in Mitchell & Baird, 1986; Mitchell, 1993.)

In considering a variety of contexts in our sequence we have deliberately made relatively little use of conventional qualitative laboratory work such as "verifying" Newton's laws. Because of the highly conceptual nature of this content area our central concern has been with creating intellectual engagement among students—our use of discussion stimuli such as written questions and POEs is for this purpose. Our approaches generate substantially more student thinking about concepts and the relationships between them, and consequently much greater student understanding, than is the case with conventional laboratory work. Content areas that are not so strongly conceptual will require a different approach. We note that "conventional" laboratory can often result in passive learning associated with a lack of monitoring by students of what they are doing and why they are doing it (e.g., Newman, 1985; Tasker, 1981).

## A CONCLUDING COMMENT
## ON INTRODUCING THESE APPROACHES

The approaches we suggest assume major changes for students and teachers, by comparison with a traditional, didactic classroom. We offer now some thoughts, derived from research and practice, on the nature of student change required. This is a crucial issue for action, for both those wishing to introduce these approaches to their classrooms and for those who wish to research the consequences of these approaches. Note that the points we now briefly make are elaborated, with data, in many aspects of the PEEL project (Baird & Mitchell, 1986; Baird & Northfield, 1992; Mitchell, 1993).

Moving from didactic classrooms to the classrooms involved in our mechanics sequence involves changes in students' metacognitive knowledge, awareness, and control. Put another way, changes are involved in students' ideas about learning (e.g., discussion can be "real work," considering mistakes can contribute to learning), attitudes toward learning (e.g., there is benefit to my learning in investing the effort needed to engage with tasks and in taking risks by publicly expressing a point of view), and learning behaviors (e.g., asking questions about issues that are puzzling). One substantial difficulty in fostering these changes is that it is often quite impossible to meaningfully describe to students what the benefits of the changes will be before starting to teach in this manner. It is necessary to slowly build towards the changes through successive classroom experiences and to reward (via the nature of assessment) the consequences of students engaging intellectually in the ways we describe. Regular, short debriefing of successful experiences in terms of the nature of the learning behaviors (e.g., pointing out the value to the development of ideas by the class of a "wrong" answer that raised an important issue) is one important component of strategies for achieving this student change. Another was referred to in 6.2.2 of our mechanics sequence.

It is common for teachers who are first hearing about or reading about these ideas to be sceptical. We frequently experience such reactions in our professional development work with other teachers, with comments about classroom management and content coverage often being made. The issue of content coverage has already been discussed; classroom management is not an ongoing issue when students are genuinely engaged. Our approaches have been used by many teachers, and the PEEL project (already frequently referred to in this chapter; Baird & Mitchell, 1986; Baird & Northfield, 1992) provides many classroom examples of these approaches. We reinforce this assertion of the feasibility of our approaches by concluding with an extract from a class disscussion in one of our classes. The class is a Grade 10 in an average government high school.

Two views of whether or not a table pushes up on a book placed on it have already been advanced: the table does not push up, initially advanced by Katie ("The table does not push up on the book, it just stops it falling; a table can't push"); the table does push up with a force equal and opposite to gravity, initially advanced by Ward. Other students have advanced arguments to support one of these views. The teacher has set up a meter ruler supported at either end and with weights placed at the middle of the ruler as an example of a much more flexible "table." (This is in 5.1 of the above sequence.) The extract begins with Ward commenting on the meter ruler demonstration. Comments in italics were inserted by the teacher to provide explanation of his thinking and decisions.

| | |
|---|---|
| Ward: | The ruler is pushing up, it's like a spring, because when you put it [the weight] on it, it's like you've loaded a spring. If you took it off it's going to spring back up. |

[This comment could lead to the class working out how a table can push up. I want it noted, but I don't want to reveal my views yet.]

| | |
|---|---|
| Teacher: | So you reckon because it's bent it's pushing back up? |

[I am extracting neutrally what I see as the key new point Ward is making.]

| | |
|---|---|
| Ward: | Yes. |
| Brad: | If it was pushing up, wouldn't it be straight? |

[Brad is reacting to Ward's views. His argument is a common one. Brad cannot (yet) picture the ruler pushing up and not moving up. This issue is central and I want it thought through. I respond to Brad similarly to how I responded to Ward.]

| | |
|---|---|
| Teacher: | If it's pushing up wouldn't it be straight . . . so you're saying it's not pushing up at the moment because it's bent? |
| Brad and Kay: | Yeah. |
| Ward: | [interrupts] It must be pushing down with the same power as it's pushing up. |

| Teacher: | So you're saying gravity is pulling down and the ruler's pushing up . . . |
| Danielle: | [interrupts] If it was pushing down the same as it was pushing up the ruler would be straight. |

[Danielle now introduces a new possibility. I want everyone to be clear on what it is so I draw a diagram of her view beside the summary of the views of Ward and Katie that I drew earlier. Danielle's view, that there must be some upwards force, may be very useful in moving toward Newton's Third Law.]

| Teacher: | All right. So Danielle's argument is . . . they can't be equal and opposite because the ruler would not be bent. |
| Danielle: | It could be a force going up and bigger force going down. |
| Teacher: | OK. So you're prepared to accept some upward force, but it must be less than gravity down, so your drawing of this one, Danielle, would be [Teacher draws diagram]. You're prepared to accept that (points to an upward force) but because the ruler's bent, this one (the downwards force) must be bigger. |
| Ward: | If there was more force pointing down, then why isn't it going down? |
| Kay and Danielle: | [interrupting] But it has—it has gone down. |

[This is the start of a sequence of student-to-student debate where I don't even need to maintain a chairperson role. The students are very involved and interested.]

| Ward: | But it's not—it's not moving down, what I mean is it's not moving now. So if there's still more force pushing down, then it's not still going down. |
| Danielle: | But it can't be equal. |
| Brad: | But it's like adding more weight on the floor. It can't go down any further. |
| Ward: | Why not? |
| James: | Because he hasn't got any more weights. [Not a very useful comment.] |
| Ward: | If there's still more force pushing down, why can't it bend? |
| Brad: | Because this is the base—you know—I mean if you stick the books on the table they're not going to push the table under the ground. |

[Brad believes that the rigid floor does not need to exert an upwards force to prevent weights placed on it from moving downwards.]

| Ward: | The table would just push back up again. |
| Kay: | Anyway if you put those weights on this table [points to a classroom table] they're not going to go down. |
| Danielle: | No, but if you put heavier things on it, it might. |

[Kay may be getting convinced by Ward. She raises the important point that we have achieved little by showing a ruler table bends under a weight unless we can also show that "real" tables bend. I intend to show this later by standing students on tables. I don't want to discourage Kay, but I do want to stop the discussion becoming too complex by dealing with two sorts of tables at once—Danielle has made a good point. I decide to intervene, to promise Kay we will address her query but to try and resolve one issue at a time.]

| Teacher: | OK so we will have to go back and check on this [classroom] table later, won't we. You're saying on this [ruler] table, I've rigged the situation a bit, Kay, because I got a bendy ruler. OK. We'll come back to that . . . probably today . . . but let's just stay with this situation . . . [the ruler table] may not be identical to that, but it's a situation in its own right. |
| Kay: | Yeah. |

[I think that Kay trusts me to remember to return to her point.]

# References

Baird, J. R. (1986). Improving learning through enhanced metacognition: A classroom study. *European Journal of Science Education, 8*, 263–282.

Baird, J. R. (1990). Metacognition, purposeful enquiry and conceptual change. In E. Hegarty-Hazel (ed.), *The student laboratory and the science curriculum*. London: Routledge.

Baird, J. R. & Mitchell, I. J. (eds.) (1986). *Improving the quality of teaching and learning: An Australian case study—The PEEL project*. Faculty of Education, Monash University.

Baird, J. R., & Northfield, J. R. (eds.) (1992). *Learning from the PEEL experience*. Faculty of Education, Monash University.

Barnes, D. R. (1976). *From communication to curriculum*. Harmonsworth, U.K.: Penguin.

Champagne, A. B., Gunstone, R. F., & Klopfer, L. E. (1985). Effecting changes in cognitive structures among physics students. In L. H. T. West & A. L. Pines (eds.), *Cognitive structure and conceptual change*. Orlando, FL: Academic Press.

Fensham, P. J., Gunstone, R. F., & White, R. T. (eds.) (1994). *The content of science: A constructivist approach to its teaching and learning*. London: Falmer Press.

Gunstone, R. F. (1994). The importance of specific science content in the enhancement of metacognition. In P. J. Fensham, R. F. Gunstone & R. T. White (eds.), *The content of science: A constructivist approach to its teaching and learning*. London: Falmer Press.

Gunstone, R. F., & Northfield, J. R. (1994). Metacognition and learning to teach. *International Journal of Science Education, 16*, 523–537.

Gunstone, R. F., & White, R. T. (1981). Understanding of gravity. *Science Education, 65*, 291–299.

Hewson, P. W., & Hewson, G.A.B. (1992). The status of students' conceptions. In R. Duit, F. Goldberg, & H. Neidderer (eds.), *Research in physics learning: Theoretical issues and empirical studies*. Keil, Germany: IPN.

Mitchell, I. J. (1993). Teaching for quality learning. Unpublished Ph.D. thesis, Monash University.

Mitchell, I. J., & Baird, J. R. (1986). Teaching, learning and the curriculum—1: The influence of content in science. *Research in Science Education, 16*, 141–149.

Mitchell, I. J., & Gunstone, R. F. (1984). Some student misconceptions brought to the study of stoichiometry. *Research in Science Education, 14*, 78–88.

Newman, B. (1985). Realistic expectations for traditional laboratory work. *Research in Science Education, 15*, 8–12.

Osborne, R., & Freyberg, P. (1985). *Learning in science: the implications of children's science*. Auckland: Heinemann.

Rowe, M. B. (1974). Wait time and rewards as instructional variables, their influence on language, logic, and fate control: Part I. Wait time. *Journal of Research in Science Teaching, 11*, 81–94.

Tao, P. K. (1996). Conceptual change, collaboration and the computer: Learning introductory mechanics. Unpublished Ph.D. thesis, Monash University.

Tao, P. K., & Gunstone, R. F. (1997). The process of conceptual change in force and motion. Paper given at the meeting of the American Educational Research Association, March, Chicago.

Tasker, R. (1981). Children's views and classroom experiences. *Australian Science Teachers Journal, 27*(3), 33–37.

White, R. T. (1994). Dimensions of content. In P. Fensham, R. Gunstone, & R. White (eds.), *The content of science: A constructivist approach to its teaching and learning*. London: Falmer Press.

White, R. T., & Gunstone, R. F. (1992). *Probing understanding*. London: Falmer.

White, R. T., & Mitchell, I. J. (1994). Metacognition and the quality of learning. *Studies in Science Education, 23*, 21–37.

# History and Philosophy of Science and the Preparation for Constructivist Teaching: The Case of Particle Theory

JOSEPH NUSSBAUM

*Michlalah-Jerusalem College and Weizmann Institute of Science*

It is Democritus' atom, not your chemistry teacher's atom, that is the key to matter.
Lederman (1993, p. 3)[1]

## INTRODUCTION

The introductory chapters of this book elaborated on the basic rationale for the constructivist approach in science education and on the history of its development over the past 25 years. Nonetheless, it will be necessary to briefly revisit some foundations of this approach in order to better understand the ideas and arguments of the present chapter.

Three academic areas have nurtured the evolution of the constructivist approach in science education: (1) *Research on students' misconceptions* (which showed that students construct their own variations or alternatives to science concepts which were taught); (2) *new developments in cognitive psychology* (which elaborated on some aspects of Gestalt psychology and which

[1]Nobel Prize laureate, 1988.

demonstrated the role of general schemata in organizing and constructing the meaning of information); and (3) *new developments in the history and philosophy of science* (which changed the classic image of science. According to the new image, science is always engaged in constructing and reconstructing models aimed at enhancing our understanding of nature, but which can never be claimed to represent an absolute truth).

Novak (1977) proposed that the teaching of science could benefit by combining ideas and findings from these three areas. However, Novak (1987) and other contemporaries, such as Driver and Oldham (1986), did not use the present term "constructivism" until the Eighties.

Essentially, the constructivist approach in the teaching of science stipulates that teachers should apply certain strategies and methods which involve students *in constructing the desired meaning* of scientific concepts and which help the students *undergo the desired conceptual changes*.

This approach is also recommended in order to achieve a higher-level objective, namely, the development of a recognition that science is an ongoing project in which alternative models continue to be constructed and examined in a critical manner. Accordingly, even though a powerful model may enhance our understanding of the world, it should always be considered "tentative."

The first objective level relates to the subject matter per se, while the second, higher one relates to its epistemological[2] aspects. Both levels had already been advocated by some proponents of the reform movement in high school science curricula in the Sixties (such as Schwab, 1962). The achievements of those curricula never reached the initial aspirations. The argument today could be that those new curricular materials could indeed have been improved a great deal, (1) had the authors related to our current understanding of constructivist learning, and (2) had the teachers been trained to teach for *meaningful learning* and to deal with epistemological ideas.

Only a minority of the present-day science educators who claim a certain commitment to "constructivism" show a clear interest in both of these levels of learning. Many educators who present their rationale and objectives relate only to the first level. The avoidance of epistemological aspects may have resulted from the view that students cannot comprehend them or that they are irrelevant to the majority of the student population. By the fact that epistemological aspects are disregarded, students and teachers might receive a subliminal message; that is, that scientific concepts and theories indeed represent some objectively verified "truth" and that constructivist teaching methods were selected only in order to teach these truths more effectively.

Those who restrict the application of constructivism in this way would probably not turn to the sources of history and philosophy of science in

---

[2]Epistemology: The study of the nature of knowledge with reference to its limits and validity.

order to gain new ideas and insights for improving their teaching strategies. It is more likely that they would restrict their interest to *misconception research*, to their knowledge of *psychodidactic principles*, and to their *pedagogical intuitions*.

Clearly, the study of relevant areas of the history and philosophy of science is a prerequisite to the preparation for teaching the second level mentioned above, the epistemological aspects of science. Our focus in this chapter is to demonstrate to the reader that this study can also contribute significantly to achieving the first level—namely, meaningful learning of currently accepted science concepts.

Since research and development in science education within the constructivist context is still emerging, many have naively looked for schematic prescriptions of strategies for achieving meaningful learning of concepts and desired conceptual changes. This chapter supports the view that each of the various science subjects taught in school presents unique cognitive demands and difficulties. Therefore, any proposed general teaching scheme or strategy should be adapted to and intertwined with the specific demands of the given subject matter. This view also supports Driver's suggestion (1989) that ". . . strategies for promoting conceptual change need to be investigated in the context of particular domains of knowledge." Therefore, the various arguments presented in this chapter will be illustrated by an immediate application to a specific teaching subject; namely, the introduction to the particulate nature of matter. This subject was selected because (1) it is the most fundamental conceptual framework in science and (2) it has been shown that it presents various substantial conceptual difficulties to learners of all ages (Novick & Nussbaum, 1981; Nussbaum & Novick, 1982; Brook, Briggs, & Driver, 1984; Nussbaum, 1985; Ben-Zvi, Eylon, & Silberstein, 1986; Andersson, 1990; Benson, Wittrock, & Baur, 1993; de Vos, 1996). Thus, this fundamental teaching subject is a paradigm for applying the constructivist approach.

The purpose of this chapter is to demonstrate how the relevant study of the history and philosophy of science can contribute to the thorough preparation which is required for constructivistic teaching of the particle theory at the seventh-grade level. Such preparation is needed from the stage of constructing the general rationale through the selection of appropriate teaching strategies and the sequencing the main concepts and down to the designing of specific learning activities.

In order to make this concept clear, we will begin with an examination of various approaches represented by four alternative programs for teaching particle theory, to be followed by a demonstration of the way in which *our* (Nussbaum, 1996) preparation for teaching this theory had been nurtured from cognitive analyses of the content and especially from the history and philosophy of science.

## FOUR APPROACHES TO TEACHING
## PARTICLE THEORY—A REVIEW OF
## ALTERNATIVE RATIONALES

An international seminar in science education on Relating Macroscopic Phenomena to Microscopic Particles (Lijnse, Licht, de Voss, & Waalo, 1990)[3] included a number of lectures which reported on unique attempts to improve the teaching of particle theory. Each project presented had been initiated in the Eighties as a result of a growing awareness of the difficulties of teaching this subject.

These lectures did not provide definitive, comparable descriptions of the learning achievement of each project. However, the *rationales* behind the studies and the general report of the nature and processes of each program were presented quite explicitly by the lecturers. This made it possible to compare them. The summary reflections on that seminar (Millar, ibid p. 328) indicated a general agreement among the participants regarding the importance of *constructivism* in science teaching. This reported general agreement might have led the reader to expect to find similarities in the assumptions, considerations, and conclusions constituting the various rationales. This was not the case, as we will illustrate.

The rationales of four projects which we will review were based upon considerations drawn from various areas, including psychology, the history and philosophy of science, and from didactic principles and practice. Each rationale was based upon differing combinations and emphases of those considerations.

In general, it is important to realize that although two people may claim that their considerations were drawn from the same area, their conclusions may not necessarily be identical, and may even contradict each other.

This review is not meant to suggest any value judgment regarding these projects, but rather to illustrate the complexity of identifying and selecting the most appropriate considerations which can lead to a successful curriculum. More specifically, it is meant to illustrate the fact that these programs had benefited only minimally from the study of the relevant history and philosophy of science.

A brief review of the four reports[4] is given below.

Johnstone (1990)[5] described an experiment in teaching the particulate model to children ages 13–14. She claimed that the project which she rep-

---

[3]Held in Utrecht, The Netherlands, 1990.

[4]The seminar took place in 1990. It is naturally possible that the reporters' positions may have changed by the present time and that their project, if it is still in progress, may have taken a new direction.

[5]Children Learning in Science Project—CLIS, University of Leeds, UK (then directed by R. Driver). More detailed reports of this project may be found in Wightman et al. (1986) and Wightman et al. (1991).

resented was based upon the constructivist perspectives on learning. Their experimental unit was based upon a general scheme for constructivist teaching which was proposed by Driver and Oldham (1986) and which included the following general phases of instruction:

1. An *elicitation phase*. Students were provided with opportunities to put forward their own ideas and to consider the ideas of their peers;
2. A *restructuring phase*. The teacher introduced activities which interacted with students' prior ideas, and which encouraged students to move their thinking towards school science; and
3. A *review phase*. Students were asked to reflect upon the ways in which their ideas have changed.

They began the first phase of their project by asking the students to compare the properties of *gases*, *liquids*, and *solids*, observed in various phenomena (and presented in "a circus of activities"). The students were then asked to propose a theory which would explain the differences. This task actually required that students construct an inclusive theory or model which would encompass all of the basic ideas, including *particles*, *vacuum*, *kinetics*, *variable density*, and *mutual attraction of particles*.

Johnstone indicated that in the first phase many students showed that concepts such as *atoms* and *molecules* are familiar to them from elementary school or from television programs. However, very soon the students demonstrated all of the familiar relevant misconceptions shown in the research literature. These misconceptions related to the concepts of vacuum, particle motion, particle forces, and the connection of the "macro" to the "micro."

One phase of the teaching scheme was a lesson in epistemology. Through "theory-making games" in a nonscientific context, the students learned about the characteristics of scientific theories in general. The activities during this phase were related more to a general philosophy of knowledge than to the particle model. According to the report, many students had difficulty creating links between the games and the scientific activities.

Indeed, Johnstone mentioned Driver's proposal (1989) that a strategy for promoting conceptual change in science classrooms "needs to be investigated in the context of particular domains of knowledge." However, it seems from her report that their effort focused more on creating and testing the impact of a *general* constructivist teaching scheme than on considering unique and specific problematic points relevant to particle theory. There is no sequencing and/or graded emphases of concepts. The description gives no evidence that the program benefited from an analysis of the history of particle theory or its epistemological foundations.

Millar (1990)[6] presented an elaborate and well-organized rationale which was based primarily on psychodidactic and practical considerations.

---

[6]His project resulted in a textbook. See *Salter's Science* (1989).

According to Millar, science should be taught by carefully designed sequences which would lead the learner "from everyday contexts to scientific concepts." He argued that the manner by which particle theory is normally taught "is of almost *no use* to children" and that they reject it because they consider it is as "a piece of inert knowledge." Thus, particle theory should *not* be taught as a single instructional unit. Rather, various elements of particle theory should be introduced to 14- to 16-year-olds across the general science program. In any event, these elements would only be taught in those parts of the curriculum in which they contribute to an understanding of everyday phenomena being taught at that point.

Millar referred to research findings on students' alternative conceptions which demonstrated that children have difficulty understanding that *gas* is "a real stuff," and that it is composed of constantly moving, invisible particles within a vacuum. Based upon this research, he recommended that the study of the particulate nature of gases be postponed and that the concept of particles be studied only when necessary in order to explain the behavior of solids. Similarly, Millar recommended postponing the study of kinetic aspects of particles and the notion of vacuum until a very late stage of the curriculum.

From a psychodidactic point of view, he argued that students need to be convinced of the existence of substructures which are so tiny that they are imperceptible. To accomplish this task, he proposed using a method which he called ostentation—"showing"—rather than by abstract discussions regarding the behavior of imperceptible particles. For example, their curriculum brought the student from the macroscopic to the microscopic world in stages. First they studied fabric thread using a hand-held magnifying glass. Then they used a microscope to study the microstructure of fibrils. At the last stage, they were introduced to the ultramicroscopic level of "macromolecules."

Millar referred to the history of science very briefly by indicating that the evidence which finally persuaded the scientific community in the nineteenth century to adopt the particulate view of matter came largely from the work on chemical reactions by Dalton and others. Similarly, he concluded that the teaching of gas as a subject should be based upon gas-producing chemical reactions and from a discovery that matter is conserved in these reactions. Later in this chapter, we will illustrate that a more complete historical analysis may point to other developments which in turn could lead to entirely different conclusions.

In a previous article (1989), Millar held that a constructivist view of *learning* (namely, that learning is a reconstruction of meanings rather than the accretion of new ideas) does *not* imply the necessity of "constructivist methods of *instruction*" (such as elicitation of student preconceptions, exposure to conflict situations, and the construction of new ideas).

He maintained that "science should be taught in whatever way is most likely to engage the active involvement of learners, as this is most likely to make them feel willing to take on the serious intellectual work of reconstructing meaning." (*ibid*, p. 589). This may explain why Millar's students were not required or encouraged to construct the elements of the particle theory by themselves. Rather, they were presented with these ideas "in a quite matter-of-fact way" (Millar, 1990, p. 286) as an explanation for what they already observed in hands-on activities.

In his 1989 article, Millar admitted that it might be argued that the constructivistic method of teaching could be used "sparely" when the restructuring of ideas is likely to be a particularly central feature of the learning. From the description of his own approach to the teaching of the particle theory, it seems that he did not feel that the students would have to restructure their own ideas to a significant degree when learning this topic. We, on the other hand, have indicated *supra* that the learning of the particle theory is rather a paradigmatic case of a major conceptual change.

Meheut and Chomat (1990)[7] presented their analysis of the essential aspects of atomistic theory as follows: (1) particles are to be conceptualized as *invariable* constituents of matter, while (2) the empty spaces between the particles and the motion of the particles are the *variable* factors of matter which appear in different magnitudes. Meheut and Chomat indicated that these essentials had already existed in the models of the first Greek atomists. Their historical and content analysis did not extend much beyond this, and the historical problems and misgivings of the atomist school were not used for identifying or responding to cognitive difficulties.

Their instruction differed from Millar's recommendations. The experiments dealt entirely with air and with other gasses. Changes in pressure and volume and the diffusion of two gases into each other were demonstrated. The decision to begin with gases, rather than with liquids or solids, resulted from their explicit assumption that a study of gases could be the best means for identifying the variables of *empty space* and *particle motion*.

They argued that Piaget's definition of an "atomistic view" is rather superficial since it does not include the essential "unvarying" attributes of particles. In other words, even if a child would think about particles in the Piagetian manner, he would have no reason or need to see those small pieces of matter as *unvarying*.

Their experiment presented children with phenomena and expected them to construct an explanation which would account for their observations. However, the very idea of the existence of unvarying particles was not elicited from the students but was rather presented to them from the outset.

Although they did show an awareness of the existence of misconceptions in their reported findings, they did not show that the former were anticipated or that this anticipation had been taken into account when planning the instruction.

---

[7]From Institut National de Recherche Pédagogique LIRESPT, Universite Paris 7.

De Vos (1990)[8] integrated a psychological and content-oriented analysis in a relatively highly developed manner. He also integrated knowledge of and lessons from the history of atomistic theory. In content-oriented analysis, he showed how textbook definitions were sometimes imprecise and how they contributed to the formation of misconceptions. He emphasized how important it was to identify which qualities that are well known at the *macroscopic* level may also be attributed to *microscopic* particles and which ones should be avoided. He identified certain misconceptions from the history of science and described the intuitive processes which apparently influenced those scientists. He proposed that it would be quite natural for the intuition of the modern student to operate in the same way.

De Vos' analysis restricted the study of particle theory to five unique qualities of the macroscopic world: *mass, space, time, mechanical energy,* and *electric charge.*

Why was this list of qualities so limited? In order to answer this, de Vos refers to a very important epistemological principle, known as Ockham's razor, which says that "one should try to explain a maximum number of phenomena by making a minimum number of assumptions." De Vos raises the following insightful questions: "Do students spontaneously and intuitively accept and apply Ockham's rule"? After expressing his heavy doubts about students' relevant abilities, he connected the problematics of this general epistemological rule to those of the specific notions of particle theory. De Vos indicated that these five elements were usually considered to be a very clear and simple matter for instruction, yet he asked ". . . would it be obvious to students why the elements from which a corpuscular model is to be built should be *mass, space, time, energy* and *electric charge*? Or would students prefer to choose, say, *color, taste, toxicity, temperature,* or *malleability*?" (*ibid,* 173)

De Vos' comments and analyses as presented in the report do not yet hint how they influenced the sequence and the specific methods of his teaching unit. The last section of his article, describing his general strategy, which has a clearly epistemological orientation, is worthy of note:

> In science lessons at lower secondary school level, it is not very important which corpuscular model a child learns. *It is much more important to preserve something of the uncertainty and the tentativeness which are characteristic of models* . . . It means that children should experience how it feels to work with ideas without being sure whether they are correct or not. *Working with models is not just an intellectual affair, but also an emotional one. It requires creativity as much as discipline, and it may lead to frustration as well as to satisfaction.* This way of learning to work with models is encouraged if the teacher does not present corpuscular models as facts discovered by a famous scientist, but instead asks students about their own ideas, stimulating them to discuss these and to test their consequences in suitable experiments. |*italics mine*|

[8]His project resulted in a textbook—*Chemistry in a thousand questions*, De Vos (1989).

## Contrasting the Rationales: Summary

We suggested that educators may gain insight for practical classroom teaching by studying the history of particle theory and its specific epistemological assumptions. To what extent do these four approaches agree with this suggestion?

Aside from the fact that Johnstone shows an awareness of relevant student misconceptions, she does not mention how an analysis of historical or epistemological aspects, which are specific to particle theory, may enhance teaching for conceptual change.

In general, Millar presents psychological considerations. He mentions but one point from the history of particle theory, using it to propose that the subject of gas be taught in the context of chemical reactions and the conservation of matter.

Meheut and Chomat mention the important historical distinction between variant factors in particles (movement, empty space, and density) as compared to the invariant factors (particles). We did not find that this distinction led to an identification of the problematic aspects of learning.

De Vos does relate to specific points in the history of particle theory, and he draws conclusions regarding some of the problematics of learning the subject. Similarly, he anticipates some difficulties, based upon an epistemological analysis.

# PREPARATIONS FOR THE CONSTRUCTIVISTIC TEACHING OF PARTICLE THEORY

This section will elaborate on our view of the potential contributions of cognitive analysis of content, an analysis of relevant history of science, and an analysis of relevant epistemological aspects, to the preparation for teaching our selected subject.

## Cognitive Analysis of Content

For some educators, the common usage of "content analysis" may merely represent an initial process which results in a list of terms, concepts, principles, or theories. It is the format in which syllabi are usually submitted. For others, it may refer to the "concept mapping" process of an area of knowledge. Concept mapping is indeed a significant step forward when compared to a linear-style list, since it visually emphasizes which ideas are more central or inclusive than others. Content analysis maps the subject from a disciplinary perspective (through an expert's eye).

Cognitive analysis of content, on the other hand, examines the product of the former analysis from the student's cognitive perspective (the novice's eye). It identifies genuine cognitive demands which are presented to the learner by the various components of a concept list or map. It also attempts to identify the potential sources for the cognitive (and/or emotional) difficulties presented by the various content elements, especially by the most central ideas and concepts.

Hawkins (1992) expressed the need for cognitive analysis of content and argues that

> . . . a still-dominant style of science teaching . . . has been set for us by the intellectual habits of some professional scientists who often cannot retraverse the sometimes crooked pathways by which they themselves, as beginners, have come to their present understanding and competence. What many of them, and their textbooks, consider to be elementary is therefore often inaccessible to students who have not yet traversed some part of those same or equivalent pathways. They forget the double meaning of the word "elementary." Sometimes it means just where one begins, where one *enters* a discipline. Sometimes it refers to the elements, the essential abstractions—and these may be the deepest of all, not where one begins, but hard won along the way.

Despite 20 years of research on "students' alternative frameworks," several conferences on "misconceptions," and about 10 years of explicit discussion of "constructivism," we still need more demonstrations of a thorough analysis of this kind in various subject areas.

The following three examples from the teaching of particle theory are ordered according to the level of difficulty which they represent.

1. It is quite trivial to list the following ideas as components of particle theory: *invisible tiny particles, empty space (vacuum), variable density of particles, particle motion* and *mutual forces of attraction*. However, it is not at all trivial to recognize that a comprehension and adoption of the notion of "vacuum" demands much greater conceptual change than is required by the notion that matter consists of tiny invisible particles (Engel & Driver, 1981; Nussbaum, 1985). The failure of educators to recognize this point is likely to cause them to think that if they will but declare that a vacuum exists between the particles of matter, then it will be understood and accepted by the students.

2. Instructional units typically assert that particles have *mass, kinetics,* and *electrical charges*, which are also physical characteristics of macroscopic bodies. However, not as many textbooks and teachers recognize that students remain perplexed when they try to understand why these macroscopic characteristics are "legitimately" assigned to the ultramicroscopic particles while some other characteristics (such as color, taste, temperature, malleability, etc.) may not be assigned to the particles at all (De Vos, 1990). Students have difficulty distinguishing between genuine primary characteristics of particles and secondary characteristics which are not at all pertinent to the individual particles. These secondary characteristics represent our subjective psycho-

logical impressions of the behavior of great masses of particles. They are rarely treated explicitly in student textbooks. However, they are the essential notion of particle theory, without which any treatment would remain technical and superficial.

3.  As we will discuss later in this chapter, the particle theory approach to an explanation of reality is both *reductionistic* and *mechanistic*. Although the mechanistic approach is essential to all sciences, it is counterintuitive for children and even for adults.

Many children and adolescents may believe that nonliving objects behave purposefully. For example, air *wants* to escape from a hot container, or opposing electrical charges *want* to stay together. This is certainly the case regarding animals, which are perceived to be driven by wishes and intentions and which are believed to have some true freedom of will (a notion which is antimechanistic). These basic views conflict with modern biology, which attempts to reduce every biological phenomenon to the mechanical interaction of particles.

Thus, particle theory may naturally conflict with these students' preconceptions. This may be the root of many student misconceptions involving *teleological* and *anthropomorphic* thinking in physics, chemistry, and especially in biology.

### Who is Expected to Carry out Cognitive Analysis of Content?

Essentially, every teacher is faced with this challenge when approaching the task of translating the written sources of knowledge to a specific sequence of teaching activities which are adapted to the specific students of his/her class. Indeed, many teachers do not do it, and they assume that the authors of the student textbook have already carried out all of the requisite analysis.

### Are Student Textbook Authors Really Influenced by the Kind of Analysis Described Above?

All too many of the textbooks which we have seen are based on content analysis and on the attempt to sequence the materials *logically*. We have not found many textbooks which reflect an awareness of the various levels of cognitive demands presented by the material and/or of the cognitive difficulties faced by the students.[9]

[9]This argument was already presented by Ausubel, Novak, & Hanesian (1978, pp. 48–50) who called for the need to implement a *psychological* structure to students' textbooks rather than a *logical* structure as is conventionally applied.

## What Competencies Are Required for this Project?

Cognitive analysis of content can be carried out by anyone who has a good understanding of the subject matter and a natural tendency to delve into the subject and to expose its deeper basic assumptions and conceptual implications. It is also necessary to have some psychodidactic knowledge and intuition as well as a familiarity with relevant research on student misconceptions.

Cognitive analysis of content does not immediately lead to the identification of proper instructional strategies or activity sequences. Good instruction requires additional preparation.

# Analysis of the Relevant History of Science

In order to illustrate the potential contribution of the history of science to the development of curricular materials and teaching methods in the area of particle theory, it is necessary to briefly review several points along the 2000-year-old historical debate of *atomism vs antiatomism*. The review will be highly selective, and will utilize the fewest figures and facts necessary in order to make the points clear.

The selected sources for this survey were a historical review and analysis by Toulmin and Goodfield (1962) and an anthology by Sambursky (1975).

We do not know how the first Greek atomists arrived at their brilliant ideas and we are amazed that Leucippus (450 BCE) and Democritus (410 BCE), the first scholars to formulate the theoretical bases of atomism, propounded nearly all of the essentials of the atomistic theory: that (1) matter is constructed of separate particles, which are invisible and indivisible corpuscles[10] and that when they are combined they comprise the mass known as matter; (2) particles exist within an absolute empty space—a vacuum; (3) particles move freely, randomly, and continuously within that vacuum and interact with each other; and (4) the interaction of the particles creates visible macroscopic changes. These interactions include situations of *association* (condensation, solidification, and the creation of new compounds) as well as *disassociation* (breaking down of the existing compounds by attack from outside) and the *creation of gas pressure*.

The concept of atomism according to Democritus postulates the existence of "vacuum" as a necessary element for allowing movement of particles, and thus it also allows interaction and changes. This concept of vacuum was at least as significant as the concept of the atom itself.

As we noted in the previous section, the atomistic view is a *reductionistic* and *mechanistic* model for understanding reality. The model is reductionistic because it reduces the number of components and factors affecting all com-

---

[10]Even today, when we know about subatomic particles, the basic idea remains that our research always arrives at particles which in this stage of the research are for us indivisible.

plex phenomena to an interaction among the simplest microscopic particles. The model is mechanistic because it assumes that these basic particles move, bump into each other, and rebound according to mechanistic laws. This model is therefore *causal* rather than *teleological.*

This mechanistic model was applied by atomists such as Epicurus (350 BCE) to all areas of existence, including cosmology, physiology, and even to human mental processes. Reductionism combined with mechanism is a substantial characteristic of all of our natural sciences.[11] We feel that the acquisition of this approach should be a metagoal of science education.

Apparently, just after the generation of Democritus and Leucippus a hot debate burst out between those who agreed with and those who opposed atomism. The prime figure in the opposing faction was Aristotle (350 BCE). The main aspect of Aristotle's debate was not the actual possibility of the existence of minuscule, imperceptible particles, but rather the plausibility of the existence of a vacuum.

The very concept of vacuum created the major philosophical obstacle and therefore it faced most of the effort of refutation. Aristotle gave a long series of philosophical and physical arguments explaining why the existence of a vacuum is substantially impossible.

Greek atomism remained strong among its supporters for about 500 years. In the first century BCE it was described in vivid detail in the great poem of the Roman poet Lucretius, "On the Nature of Things" (see Toulmin and Goodfield, 1962, p. 88), and it was also the basis for scientific and technological experiments in the behavior of the air performed about 60 CE by Hero of Alexandria (*ibid*, p. 222).

However, in the Middle Ages atomism was clearly rejected, and Aristotle's position of antiatomism apparently took hold. His philosophy was adopted in nearly all areas of thought and science, both by the Catholic Church and by many Arab philosophers. Regarding the notion of vacuum, most scholars accepted Aristotle's principle that vacuum is implausible and that "Nature abhors a vacuum."

It should be noted that the power assigned by Aristotle's followers to a vacuum, which enables it to "pull" stuff to fill a "void," indicates that such a view is *nonmechanistic.* In a mechanistic view, only matter can exert a force. "Vacuum," which is nothingness, cannot exert a force.

The beginning of the seventeenth century saw a clear return to atomism. It was based to some degree upon experiments, but was rooted in speculative philosophical considerations. Toulmin and Goodfield (1962) in their historical survey argued that Galileo (1564–1642)

---

[11]We are aware that the present argument is restricted to the state of science at the end of the nineteenth century and that quantum physics in the twentieth century introduced an opposing concept, indeterminism. In school science we generally teach nineteenth century physics, and we still have difficulty carrying out this task in a meaningful way.

> . . . was happy to follow Democritus in most respects, differing from him only in the central importance he attached to mathematics . . . |He| and his pupils began to experiment on the physical properties of elastic (i.e., compressible or gaseous) fluids–notably, on the air of the atmosphere. (*ibid*, p. 196)

Toulmin and Goodfield emphasize here that the starting point of the experiment with *gases* in order to return to atomism was "no accident."

> *Atomism had always appeared most plausible when applied to the physics of gases*, and Hero of Alexandria's treatise on the subject was familiar both to Galileo in Italy and, a generation later, to Robert Boyle in England. |emphasis mine, J.N.| (*ibid*, p. 196)

The experiments carried out by Toricelli (1608–1655), a student of Galileo, on atmospheric air brought about the invention of the first barometer, which demonstrated the natural formation of a vacuum at the top of a barometer. Toricelli's demonstration, as well as his subsequent explanation of air pressure, created a wave of excitement which spread among European scientists. It was clear that Toricelli's experiments challenged Aristotle's claim that "Nature abhors a vacuum."

Pascal (1623–1662) continued Toricelli's experiments and showed that the column of mercury in a barometer is shorter and "left" more vacuum at the top of a glass tube when measured on the top of a hill than in a valley. These breakthrough experiments with air pressure acting on a barometer (as well as subsequent experiments with pumps which could create partial states of vacuum) resulted in a situation whereby atomism became more acceptable and therefore could be brought to the center of scientific thinking after 2000 years of opposition.

Pascal's original writing is quite interesting here:

> It is not difficult to demonstrate . . . that nature does not abhor a vacuum at all. This manner of speaking is improper, since created nature . . . is not animated, and can have no passions. . . . |Nature| is supremely indifferent to a vacuum, since it never does anything either to seek or to avoid it. (quoted in Sambursky, 1975, p. 261)

This article of Pascal concludes with a pathos emphasizing the stormy historic argument about the plausibility of vacuum.

> . . . Does Nature abhor a vacuum more in the highlands than in the lowlands? In damp weather more than in fine? Is not its abhorrence the same on a steeple, in an attic, and in the yard? Let all the disciples of Aristotle collect the profoundest writing of their master and of his commentators in order to account for these things |the barometer's changes| by abhorrence of vacuum if they can . . . (*ibid*, p. 263)

Boyle (1627–1691) continued the line of research of Toricelli and Pascal and carried out experiments on the *elasticity of air*. In his summary, Boyle writes (in 1660):

> . . . the notion I speak of is that there is a spring or elastic power in the air we live in (*ibid*, p. 281) . . . this notion may perhaps be somewhat further explained, by conceiving the air near the earth to be . . . resembled to a *fleece of wool* |which| . . . consists of

many slender and flexible hairs; each of which may indeed, like a little spring, be easily bent or rolled up; but will also, like a spring, be still endeavoring to stretch itself out again. (*ibid*, p. 282)

Thus, we see that at this stage of his research, Boyle's particles were not necessarily ball-shaped, as we usually envision them, but rather they were hairlike. Boyle did not explain the springiness of air by a kinetic model with invisible corpuscles bumping into each other and into the walls, but by the elasticity of each hair. Boyle's particles were basically static (and elastic) rather than dynamic.

## Why, If Such Is the Case, Is Boyle's Model Worthy of Being Considered Atomistic?

It is indeed atomistic, because he assumed that air is composed of matter which is not continuous but rather is composed of *discrete* particles, surrounded by empty space—a vacuum.[12]

Boyle's model did not include kinetic aspects at this stage, but he later arrived (or returned) to a full kinetic model, as seen from his writings in 1666 (Toulmin and Goodfield, 1962, p. 201).

Toulmin and Goodfield summarize these historical stages as follows:

The basic appeal of atomism to seventeenth-century corpuscular philosophers remained general and philosophical: their experimental work on air did not, by itself, provide compelling evidence of the truth of the atomic doctrines. It carried conviction only to the convinced. (*ibid*, p. 199)

Newton (1642–1727), who preceded the modern chemical period by a full century, significantly promoted the physical view of atomism. As an analogy to his universal gravitational force which acts from a distance, he proposed similar forces between microscopic particles. In so doing, Newton explained physical and chemical phenomena such as *cohesion and adhesion, capillary attraction, absorption of water vapor by hygroscopic materials, the warming of a base when it reacts with water,* and *the warming of acids when they react with different materials.*

Newton's contribution to atomic theory was very significant. However, the very transfer of his concept from the macroworld of magnetism and gravitation to the microworld of atomic interaction caused the great Newton to propose a misconception which remained in force during much of the 19th century. Drawing from the phenomenon of magnetism, Newton assumed the existence of *repulsion* among gaseous atoms (acting from a relatively large

---

[12]It may be assumed that Boyle, who considered himself to be an empiricist, adopted the atomistic model in this article (1660) only insofar as experiments "compelled" him to do so. The compressibility of air compelled him to believe that air consists of discrete particles scattered in empty space. He did not see the need to relate to the kinetic aspect of Democritus' model. The speculation regarding moving particles in that model seemed to be too bold. He thus proposed a simpler explanation which assumed static and elastic particles.

distance). He believed that this repulsion created the elasticity of air which Boyle had described (*ibid*, pp. 213–214).[13]

Dalton (1766–1844) retained this misconception and argued that the forces of repulsion exist only between atoms of the same gas and do not exist between atoms of different gases. In this way, he explained the homogenic diffusion of two gases within each other. His model assumed that gas particles remained *static* after they repelled each other enough to become evenly scattered. This misconception did not interfere with his other major contributions to chemistry.

It was not until the beginning of the twentieth century that the kinetic model of particles was universally accepted—following Einstein's explanation of Brownian motion. Because of space limitations, our brief review has omitted many of the relevant outstanding figures and facts.[14]

This review illustrates that science returned to Democritus' model in the seventeenth century, during which time the existence of *vacuum* became generally accepted, although another century was required to suggest the existence of *forces between particles*. It took yet another century in order to achieve universal acceptance of *particle motion*.

We will now propose some major implications for teaching, based upon the preceding historical review.

1. *Learning by debating essential ideas.* Our historical analysis demonstrates that experiments in and of themselves cannot convince everybody of the correctness of a particular theoretical explanation. Furthermore, the fact that a person knows or understands a theory does not guarantee that he will accept it. Aristotelian scholars would have received high marks had they been tested on the arguments of the atomists, despite the fact that they absolutely rejected atomic theory.

Indeed, it seems that throughout history conceptual change occurred only as a result of debates. Classical experiments became significant and critical only when they were an element of a debate.

---

[13]Another misconception held by Newton through his many years of research was that space is not an absolute void, but rather is continuously filled with ether (a hypothetical elastic type of gas which has no mass, "a subtle spirit." See Toulmin & Goodfield, 1962, pp. 217–220). This brought him to regress to one of the components of Aristotle's concepts. Newton needed ether in order to explain the impact of magnetism and gravity over distances. When Newton's mechanics is taught today, this misconception is disregarded and the theory is presented as if the assumption about absolute empty space was always self-evident. The concept of ether was finally discarded following the famous experiment of Michelson and Morely in 1887 and the publication of Einstein's Theory of Relativity of 1905.

[14]No review would have been complete without mentioning Descartes (1596–1650), who argued against the notion of vacuum; Gassendi (1592–1655), who revived and elaborated upon ancient atomism; Bernoulli (1700–1782), who contributed to a refinement of the kinetic theory of gases; Maxwell (1831–1879), who was fully convinced that the void between particles of matter is filled with even smaller particles of ether; Boltzmann (1844–1906), who developed statistical mechanics, and others too numerous to mention here.

In the classroom, the strategy of open debate allows students to clarify their preconceptions to themselves, while understanding how they differ from others' opinions. Such debate helps classroom experiments become more significant and illuminating. A detailed illustration of the classroom debate about particle theory may be found in Nussbaum and Novick (1982).

Our discussion of the significance of classroom debates related to the achievement of meaningful learning of the essential ideas of particle theory per se. An important by-product of this learning, which is beyond the purview of this chapter, is likely to be the development of an epistemological view of the way in which science works.

2. *Initiating instruction with a discussion of the concept of vacuum.* The main inno-vative idea of particle theory is the fact that vacuum is a significant immanent component of physical existence or even the primary one:

> Particle physics is not the right starting point for particle physics. Vacuum physics is. (Wheeler, 1973)[15]

Only if there is a vacuum could matter be noncontinuous and thus partic-ulate. Only if there is a vacuum could there be a possibility of particle move-ment which could be described by the laws of mechanics. The specific form of the particles and their kinetic quality are secondary.

Unlike many textbooks, we hold that telling "the facts"—that matter is composed of particles separated by empty space—is not likely to lead to a genuine understanding of the meaning of vacuum and of its essential prob-lematics.[16] We propose that the quality of instruction be tested by its ability to create a genuine philosophical discussion of the concept of a vacuum.

3. *Initiating the study of the particle model by investigating the behavior of air and other gases.* It was demonstrated historically that the gaseous state was the right starting point for establishing the idea of the existence of vacuum, which in turn made the concept of particulate matter more acceptable. We therefore recommend initiating the study of particle theory in the classroom by examining air qualities and behavior.[17]

4. *Utilizing analogies and key experiments which have been found to be effective in the history of science.* An important element of scientific thinking has always been the use of *analogies*. A review of historical studies which led to the develop-

---

[15]Quoted by Popper and Eccles, (1990).

[16]The reader is reminded that in modern physics (from the time of the development of the concept of fields and electromagnetic waves through the development of the inner atomic structure and up to the mathematical representation of elementary particles in quantum me-chanics), the physical meaning of empty space (vacuum) still remains vague and perplexing. Indeed, these aspects of modern physics are beyond the grasp of our students. However, they should be given the opportunity to cognitively experience some of these essential concepts, which still perplex today's physicists.

[17]Although some research studies argue that it is difficult for children to accept that air is "real stuff," our experience has shown that if proper methods are used, then even younger children can internalize this concept (Nussbaum, 1995; research report in Hebrew).

ment of particle theory may indicate specific analogies which had been effective in the past and which could also promote classroom discussions.[18]

In addition, we can use key experiments in class in order to promote students' imagination, with the proviso that these experiments are carried out subject to point (1) above.

Indeed, without the benefit of good instruction, students have difficulty understanding the simple physics of air. Hawkins (1992) described it as follows:

> . . . My own teaching experience with college freshmen, with ten-year olds and with their teachers as well, has indeed seemed to confirm that we live mostly in that pre-Torricellian world . . .

However, he does stipulate that

> . . . we can, in our own time and place, be confronted by the same questions that confronted Galileo or Torricelli or Stahl. We can quite literally repeat their investigations as they described them.

5.  *A study of the particle model is a lengthy process of conceptual change.* The history of science has shown that conceptual change is a lengthy process accompanied by a struggle with different types of misconceptions and that it includes alternating stages of advance and retreat. It is not reasonable to expect our students to internalize the model in a meaningful manner after it is presented by several statements of knowledge over the course of one or two class sessions. The educational process which applies to points (1) through (3) above has to be given time and it must be gradually developed in a spiral fashion over the course of several months or even years of study.

6.  *Misconceptions may have a positive role.* Historical research has shown that even great scientists who broke new ground in any given area still held misconceptions in other areas or aspects. These misconceptions may be viewed as essential steps in the evolution of innovative ideas. Prior misconceptions are the raw materials for critical research which then leads us to higher levels of understanding.

It is also necessary to apply this view to the classroom. Despite the fact that teachers want to help their students reach the desired conceptions, it is necessary to be tolerant and relate positively to their misconceptions. These misconceptions may be analogous to *childhood illnesses* or *problems of adolescence.* True, they are not welcomed and we may wish that they would not exist, but we know that ultimately they have a positive function in human development. The development of the history of science can be perceived as an incomplete dialectic process (thesis–antithesis–synthesis; today's concep-

---

[18]For example, Pascal's and Boyle's comparison of air to wool or to a spring in order to explain its compressibility or Torricelli's comparison of the atmosphere to an ocean in order to explain differences of pressure at different altitudes.

tion is tomorrow's misconception). We should understand the function of misconceptions in student intellectual development in a similar manner.

For this reason, educators should not try to ignore or to declare war on misconceptions, but should rather focus the class on them. Only in this way can they initiate the desired process of conceptual change.

## Analysis of Relevant Epistemological Ideas

It was argued elsewhere that the philosophy of science can contribute to the development of teaching strategies for meaningful science learning.[19]

The broad trend predominating today in the philosophy of science is *constructivism*, which replaced the two rival classical trends, *empiricism* and *rationalism*. Empiricism emphasizes the primacy of sensory experience as the source of knowledge, while rationalism argues that reason alone is the source, since the senses are elusive.

Democritus' "atomism" was founded on his "rationalistic" view, which implied that his speculation about vacuum and particles represented the truth, while continuity of matter was a sensual illusion. On the other hand, Aristotle's' "antiatomism" resulted from his "empiricistic" view, which implied that matter was to be defined as that which is perceived by the senses. Thus, the disagreement between those who believed that matter is particulate and those who maintained that matter is continuous evolves from a deeper philosophical dispute.

Each of these major trends served as a philosophical root for a unique approach to instruction.[20] Empiricism is the basis for the behavioristic approach, while the Kantian version of rationalism is the basis for the Piagetian approach.

Does constructivism offer us any practical implications for education and instruction? It could be shown that each of the main variations within the constructivist stream might lead to differing instructional implications.[21] We will breifly present some of these implications here.

The main issue on which constructivist philosophers differ is whether there is (and whether it is proper that there be) clear criteria for abandoning an older theory and adopting another one. From Popper (1959) it is clear that scientists should abandon a theory when a critical experiment "falsifies" it. A simplistic belief in the power of a "critical experiment" which either "proves" a theory or "falsifies" it, still influences some textbook authors. Many educators feel that critical experiments in and of themselves can prove a theory while others feel that they can convince students of the fallacy of

---

[19]Nussbaum (1989). That article elaborated on these matters, while this paper presents only a brief summary of the main arguments.

[20]*ibid.*

[21]*ibid.*

their misconceptions. Kuhn (1970) argues that inclusive theories ("para-digms") are not necessarily replaced merely by falsifying critical experiments, but to a great extent because of social and psychological factors, outside the scientific realm, which affect the individual scientist and the community of scientists. Kuhn views also conceptual changes in the history of science mainly as "revolutions" or "paradigm shifts" which occur over relatively short periods of time.

Kuhn's notions influenced science educators during the Seventies. It was at that time that educators began to realize the wide prevalence of the phe-nomenon of student misconceptions. Therefore, science educators naively looked for strategies which would yield a paradigm shift in the classroom.

Lakatos (1970) and Toulmin (1972) take intermediate stands between Popper and Kuhn and emphasize that it is not the critical experiments them-selves which create conceptual change. Lakatos argues that the abandon-ment of a theory does not result from "a conflict between the theory and a new experiment," but rather from *an open debate between alternative theories*. A theory is abandoned only when its proponents gradually realize the advan-tages of an alternative theory and the disadvantages of continuing to adhere to their own theory. Toulmin emphasizes the gradual and *evolutionary* (as opposed to *revolutionary*) nature of historical conceptual changes. These two philosophers emphasize that the conceptual change occurring in scientists is not a purely intellectual process but also includes a process of social negotiation.

A very valuable analysis of factors influencing conceptual change in the scientific community as well as in the classroom was carried out by Posner, Strike, Hewson, & Gertzog (1982) and Strike & Posner (1992).

Of the various philosophical concepts which have been presented, we would tend to accept the approaches proposed separately by Lakatos and by Toulmin. Accordingly, we feel that when the objective of instruction is the achievement of a major conceptual change, then the instructional strategy must include debates and negotiations among proponents of alternative models.

Furthermore, we believe that these debates and negotiations should focus on more than relevant details: they should also analyze the philosophical foundations of the given theory together with the alternative theories pre-sented by the students.

On the basis of our teaching experience we have found that philosophical arguments can be conducted at almost any grade level, including classes with students of lower than average ability. This can be achieved without referring to philosophical terms or to names of historical figures. However, in order for this process to succeed, we believe that the instructor must serve the essential and active function of *moderator*.

This process will expose many of the hidden assumptions which influence student thinking. Teachers should make students aware of these assumptions. They should also find appropriate methods to challenge them and to encourage and support conceptual change. Table 1 shows the complexity of the confrontation between various levels of assumptions underlying the particle model and those of its alternative.

## SUMMARY

When preparing for constructivist teaching which is aimed at achieving conceptual change in students, it is important to identify and clarify the unique problems of the specific teaching subject.

This chapter has argued that an important element in such preparation should be a study of the relevant aspects of the history and philosophy of science.

This summary relates primarily to the case of teaching particle theory. However, the reader is invited to consider the transfer of these general ideas and principles to the teaching of other scientific subjects.

Following is a brief review of our recommendations for teaching particle theory, based upon our previous analysis:

1. A main teaching strategy should be to provoke and promote open debates of the essential ideas and assumptions which are pertinent to alternative theories raised in the class. The debates should lead to intellectual give and take among the students about ideas and meanings.[22]

2. A primary, important idea to be debated is the meaning and plausibility of *vacuum* as an immanent part of physical reality.[23]

3. An investigation of the physical properties of air and other gases should serve as the introduction and the basis for speculating and debating about the structure of matter.[24]

4. Analogies and key experiments which have been proven to be helpful in the historical development of particle theory should be considered for use in the present instruction of the subject.[25]

5. Curricular materials should be designed in anticipation and acceptance of the fact that conceptual change will require an extended period of time and that this evolutionary process will not occur simultaneously among all students. It must be recognized that each concept such as *vacuum* and *particles*, *particle motion*, and *interparticle forces* constitutes in and of itself a chal-

---

[22]In order to understand this item fully, it is strongly recommended to refer to Nussbaum and Novick, 1982.

[23]*ibid.*

[24]See Appendix A.

[25]See Appendix A.

**TABLE I**
**Alternative Beliefs about Matter—Ideas and Assumptions**

| Characteristics | Theories | |
| --- | --- | --- |
| | The essence of the particle theory | The essence of alternative matter theory |
| Ideas and concepts Exist in the teacher's awareness. They are generally conveyed to students as informative items which are clearly evident. | Matter is a group of tiny unvarying and invisible particles. The spatial state between and surrounding particles is a "vacuum." Vacuum is a genuine component of nature. Particles are constantly in motion. Particles attract each other. | Matter is essentially continuous. Space is filled with matter. Vacuum may appear only as an artificial and temporary state. "Nature abhors a vacuum." Rest/statics is the natural state of every material body while motion is a temporary and artificial state.[a] |
| The typical focus of instruction in classrooms. | | |
| Domain-related presumptions Do not exist in many teachers' awareness in a clear and organized manner. Unquestionably, these are not part of students' awareness. | Changes in matter occur only by physical causality. Thus, in every phenomenon there is essentially some mechanism.[b] | Changes in matter may result alternatively either by "blind" physical causality or by purpose-oriented moves (teleology) or by some combinations of both. |

*continues*

lenge for conceptual change. This implies that those concepts should be taught as separate issues which develop sequentially.[26]

6. An open discussion of various epistemological assumptions of particle theory is of central importance to achieving the desired conceptual change and meaningful learning.[27]

7. Misconceptions should be regarded positively. They provide the raw materials for intellectual interaction from which a desired conception will evolve and be constructed.[28]

We believe that a wider and deeper study of the sources mentioned above will be required in order to realize the significance of these recommenda-

[26]See Appendix B.
[27]See Appendixes C and D.
[28]See Appendix E.

**TABLE I**—*Continued*

| | | |
|---|---|---|
| General epistemological assumptions Generally do not exist in teachers' awareness in a clear and organized manner. Unquestionably these are not part of students' awareness. | A valid explanation is only that which proposes the hidden mechanism of the phenomenon.[c] The rue reality is invisible. The micro accounts for the macro. Senses are misleadingand illusive. Thus, *speculation* and *deep thought* are the prime means of cognition and knowledge | Valid explanations may be either causal, teleological, or simply the very designation of material characteristics.[d] The true reality is that which is perceptible. Senses are the most valid means by which we discover reality. Thus, *sensual experience* is the prime means of cognition and knowledge. |
| Assumptions of differing world views Do not always exist in teachers' awareness in a clear and organized manner. Certainly these are not part of the students' awareness. | Physical phenomena result merely from a complicated combination of random *chance* (resulting from particle motion) and *mechanisms* (resulting from particle structures and forces). The physical world does not represent an overall design and is thus purposeless.[e] | Physical phenomena occur partly according to laws of nature and partly by an influence of nonmaterial entities or factors. The physical world represents a preexisting overall design and thus it is purposeful.[e] |

[a]This certainly applies to the inner state of matter in bodies.

[b]The indeterminism of quantum theory is beyond the school level and therefore is disregarded here.

[c]Air is compressible because there is a vacuum between its particles. Hot air rises, because cold air (of higher specific density) has pushed it upward.

[d]Air is compressible because it is flexible! Juice goes up the straw in order to fill the vacuum! Hot air rises because that is the nature of hot air.

[e]It should be noted that the comparison of these two world views leads to the antinomy regarding the materialistic–mechanistic view implied by science and the humanistic view emphasizing ethics and freedom of will. This is a large topic which is beyond the scope of this chapter, but which is discussed in Nussbaum (1987).

tions and to become convinced of their potential contributions. This is indeed a task for curricular experts. However, we believe that in order to achieve an implementation of constructivist teaching, a simplified version of this analysis should be an integral part of the teacher-training program.

The adoption of this approach to the teaching of particle theory, as well as to other paradigmatic subjects, requires two very difficult changes on the part of teachers. The first change is *conceptual* while the second is *behavioral*. We believe that an acceptance of the concepts of the constructivist theory is not sufficient. Adopting an innovative cognitive view rarely yields, as a natural consequence, the implied new behavior. In order to achieve a genuine lasting change in teaching style of most teachers we must provide them with curricular materials especially designed to support the desired behavioral changes both in teachers and students.

Our program (Nussbaum, 1996), currently in its 3rd experimental year, has applied the above recommendations. Our experience working with 60 teachers and over 3000 students leads us to certain general and preliminary conclusions. The classroom interactions, including the debates over essential issues (such as particulate matter vs continuous matter; mechanistic explanations vs animalistic or teleological explanations), have created an outstanding intellectual tension and extremely high motivation in students of all levels. As a result, they have been able to construct a viable model for the structure of matter.

We have found that the high investment of time and effort involved in such interactions during the first half of the course pays off in achieving genuinely meaningful learning, which in turn permits faster and more efficient learning during the second half of the course and in the following year.


## APPENDIXES

The sample pages presented in the following appendixes were translated from the Hebrew original (Nussbaum, 1996). The reader may learn more about the nature of the program, the teaching style and the classroom atmosphere from a detailed description of one unique lesson, out of which the whole program grew (Nussbaum & Novick, 1981, 1982).


## Appendix A

In page 43 the students classify a group of metal and rubber objects (a solid cube, a steel spring, steel wool, a sponge, and a rubber stopper), as *compressible* or *noncompressible*. The students conclude that some metal objects and some rubber objects are compressible while others are not. The determining factor is the *internal structure* of the object rather than of the material itself. If the internal structure includes *spaces*, then the material objects will be compressible. If the internal structure is compact (no internal spaces) then the object is not compressible.

This macroscopic phenomenon can serve later as an *analogy* for modeling the microscopic structure of air. An analogy to a *sponge* or *wool* was proposed by both Pascal and Boyle.

The compressibility of air is the prime feature which can lead to a hypothesis that gaseous air includes empty spaces.

In pages 45–47 (Figure 1), students learn to distinguish between *elasticity* and *compressibility* and recognize that **spiral springs** and **sponges** include both of these features.

---

**We compress air**
- Put an eraser in the opening of the syringe in order to close it off) when it is full of air.
- Force the top part into the syringe and compress the air in the syringe as much as you can.
- Now let go of the top part of the syringe.

Q: What did you feel when you pushed on the top part of the syringe?
Q: What happened to the top part when you stopped pushing?
Q: Does the behavior of air which is compressed and then released remind you of anything?.............................................

- Air in a closed syringe behaves like ........................ (a spiral spring)
- Air a closed syringe also behaves like ...........................(a sponge)

---

**FIGURE 1**

## Appendix B

A sequence of activities (on pages 49–71; Figure 2) helps students gradually answer Sharon's question about the *compressibility* of air. The accompanying student discussions gradually lead to a model of *vacuum* and *particles*. This sequence of activities takes about 15–17 lessons (45 min each).

Similarly, another sequence of activities (on pages 72–95) helps students gradually answer Dan's question regarding the *elasticity* of air. They develop a view of continual and random movement of air particles which explains phenomena of air pressure and the diffusion of gases. This sequence also takes about 15–17 lessons.

Gradually, the students replace their misconceived intuition that vacuum exerts force (suction) with a mechanical conception of the differential pressure exerted by moving particles.

## Appendix C

This staged discussion can trigger or reinforce a similar one in the class. Students distinguish between *curiosity* and *indifference*. Stating *"It just happens to be that way"* blocks creative thinking. Asking *"what makes air compressible?"* or *"why is water wet"* may lead to important scientific inquiries (Figure 3).

## Appendix D

After pouring sugar from a cup and pouring milk from a cup, students realize that the term "to pour" is valid only in order to describe the behavior of many grains of sugar (an individual grain falls but it does not pour). They are encouraged to wonder whether an individual liquid particle behaves as a fluid (does it pour, leak, or flow?) or whether an individual gas particle

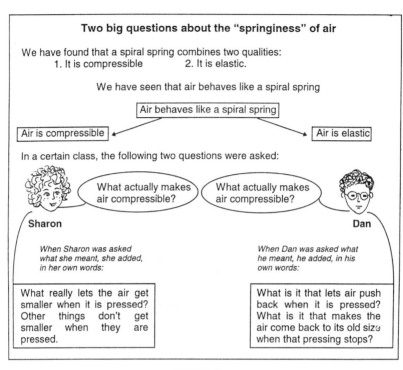

**FIGURE 2**

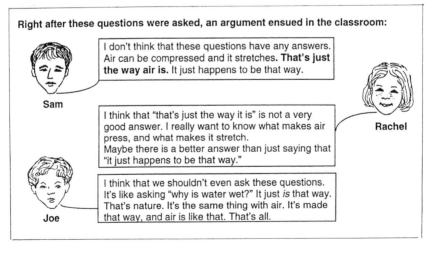

**FIGURE 3**

Let us imagine a very small dwarf which is even more tiny than the smallest particle of matter. He is holding a needle which is also more tiny than these particles of matter.

1. If the little dwarf sticks his tiny needle into one particle of water, will water leak out? Will it make ?  a tiny, invisible puddle near the particle of water?
2. If the little dwarf sticks his tiny needle into a one particle of gas, will a tiny bit of gas burst out? Will ?  the dwarf hear a "pssss...sss...ss..." sound when that happens?

**FIGURE 4**

The liquid acetone particles spread around, because they were warm, crowded, and stuffy, and they felt uncomfortable. They tried not to get close to each other. They tried to move apart. Then they pushed against the sides of the bottle, in order to give themselves more room and so that it would be less crowded and stuffy inside.

Rafi

I disagree with Rafi. How can you say that particles feel warm? Do they have feelings? That would be like saying that a frying pan on the stove feels hot and that it wants to run away.

Efrat

I agree with Efrat that particles of acetone don't have feelings or desires or opinions! Particles of matter are not alive!

Shlomit

Let us assume that particles of liquid acetone (which are very crowded, like any other liquid) move around all the time, in straight lines. But since they are so crowded, they bump into each other all of the time. They push each other and finally they also push the bottle's wall outside.

Shilo

Then how, according to Shilo, does the liquid acetone disappear when we warm it up? How does warming it up turn it from a liquid to a gas? I still think that the acetone particles attempt to escape from the heat and they want to burst out of the bottle.

Tirtza

**FIGURE 5**

behaves as a gas (does it fill all of the available space (Figure 4). Is it compressible?)

## Appendix E

The class carried out an experiment. They took a plastic soda pop bottle, flattened it, put in a few ml of pure acetone, and then put on the cover. The flattened bottle was put into boiling water. The liquid acetone disappeared, and the bottle was inflated.

The class was asked to think about the following questions:

1. What happened to the particles of liquid acetone that were in the plastic bottle when the bottle was heated?
2. How does heating cause the crowded acetone particles (liquid phase) to be distributed (gaseous phase)?
3. How do the particles of the gaseous acetone cause the bottle to expand?

The following staged discussion encourages the students to express their (mis)conceptions in an open and legitimate manner (Figure 5).

## Acknowledgment

I express my thanks to Dr. David Grossman from Michlalah-Jerusalem College for his assistance in the preparation of this chapter and to Dr. Sherman Rosenfeld from Weizmann Institute of Science for his insightful comment on the manuscript.

## References

Andersson, B. (1990). Pupils' conceptions of matter and its transformations (age 12–16). *Studies in Science Education*, 18, 53–85.

Ausubel, D. P., Novak, J. D., & Hanesian, H. (1978). *Educational Psychology: A Cognitive View*, 2nd edition. New York: Holt Rinehart and Winston.

Benson, D. L., Wittrock, M. C., & Baur, M. E. (1993). Students' preconceptions of the nature of gases. *Journal of Research in Science Teaching*, 30, 587–597.

Ben-Zvi, R., Eylon, B., & Silberstein, J. (1986). Is an atom of copper malleable? *Journal of Chemical Education*, 63, 64–66.

Brook, A., Briggs, M., & Driver, R. (1984). *Aspects of secondary students' understanding of the particulate nature of matter*. Leeds, UK: Centre for Studies in Science and Mathematics Education.

De Vos, W. (1989). *Chemie in Duizend Vragen (Chemistry in a thousand questions)*. Utrecht: The University of Utrecht.

De Vos, W. (1990). Seven thoughts on teaching molecules. In P. L. Lijnse, P. Licht, W. de Vos, & A. J. Waarlo, (Eds.), *Relating macroscopic phenomena to microscopic particles*. Utrecht, The Netherlands: University of Utrecht.

De Vos, W., & Verdouk, A. H. (1996). The particulate nature of matter in science education and in science. *Journal of Research in Science Teaching*, 33, 657–664.

Driver, R. (1989). Theory into practice II: A constructive approach to curriculum development. In P. Fensham, (ed.). *Developments and dilemmas in science education*. London: Falmer Press.

Driver, R., & Oldham, U. (1986). A constructionist approach to curriculum development. *Studies in Science Education*, 13, 105–122.

Engel, E., & Driver, R. (1981). Investigating pupils' understanding of aspects of pressure. In *Proceedings of the international workshop on problems concerning students' representation of physics and chemistry knowledge*. Ludwigsburg, Germany.

Hawkins, D. (1992). Investigative arts: science and teaching. An opening chairman's address to the 2nd International Conference on the history and philosophy of Science and Science Teaching held at Kingston, Ontario, Canada.

Johnstone, K. (1990). Students' responses to an active learning approach to teaching the particulate nature of matter. In P. L. Lijnse, P. Licht, W. de Voss, & A. J. Waarlo, (eds.), *Relating macroscopic phenomena to microscopic particles*. Utrecht, The Netherlands: University of Utrecht.

Johnstone, K., & Driver, R. (1991). *A case study of teaching and learning about particle theory*. Leeds, UK: Centre for Studies in Science and Mathematics Education.

Kuhn, T. S. (1970). *The structure of scientific revolutions*, 2nd edition. University of Chicago Press.

Lakatos, I. (1970). Falsification and the methodology of scientific research programmes. In I. Lakatos & A. Musgrave (eds.) *Criticism and the Growth of Knowledge*. Cambridge: Cambridge University Press.

Lederman, L. (1993). *The god particle*. London and New York: Bantam Press.

Lijnse, P. L., Licht, P., de Vos, W., & Waarlo, A. J. (1990). *Relating macroscopic phenomena to microscopic particles*. Utrecht, The Netherlands: University of Utrecht.

Meheut, M., & Chomat, A. (1990). The bounds of children's atomism: an attempt to make children build up a particulate model of matter. In P. L. Lijnse, P. Licht, W. de Vos, & A. J. Waarlo, (eds.), *Relating macroscopic phenomena to microscopic particles*. Utrecht, The Netherlands: University of Utrecht.

Millar, R. (1989). Constructive criticism. *International Journal of Science Education*, 11, 587–596.

Millar, R. (1990). Making sense: What use are particle ideas to children? In P. L. Lijnse, P. Licht, W. de Voss, & A. J. Waarlo, (eds.), *Relating macroscopic phenomena to microscopic particles*. Utrecht, The Netherlands: University of Utrecht.

Novak, J. D. (1977). *A theory of education*. Ithaca, NY: Cornell University Press.

Novak, J. D. (1987). Human constructivism: Toward a unity of psychological and epistemological meaning making. In J. Novak, (ed.) *Proceedings of the 2nd international seminar on misconceptions and educational strategies in science and mathematics*, Vol. I–II. Ithaca, NY: Cornell University Press.

Novick, S., & Nussbaum, J. (1981). Pupils' understanding of the particulate nature of matter: A cross age study. *Science Education*, 65, 187–196.

Nussbaum, J. (1985). The particulate nature of matter in the gaseous phase. In R. Driver, E. Guesne, & A. Tiberghien, (eds.) *Children's ideas in science*. Milton Keynes, UK: Open University Press.

Nussbaum, J. (1989). Classroom conceptual change: Philosophical perspectives. *International Journal of Science Education*, 11, 530–540.

Nussbaum, J. (1996). *The structure of matter: Vacuum and particles*. Israel, Rehovot: Weizmann Institute of Science. [A 7th-grade program; in Hebrew. A translated version of the final product is currently being planned]

Nussbaum, J., & Giami, S. (1987). The physico-chemical reduction of life: paradigm, biologists and human values. In J. Novak (ed.) *Proceedings of the 2nd international seminar on misconceptions and educational strategies in science and mathematics*. Vol. I–II. Ithaca, NY: Cornell University Press.

Nussbaum, J., & Novick, S. (1981). Brainstorming in the classroom to invent a model: A case study. *School Science Review*, 62, 771–778.

Nussbaum, J., & Novick, S. (1982). Alternative frameworks, conceptual conflict and accommodation: Toward a principled teaching strategy. *Instructional Science*, 11, 183–200.

Popper, K. (1959). *The logic of scientific discovery*. London: Hutchinson.

Popper, K., & Eccles, J. C. (1977). *The self and its mind*, 1st edition. London and New York: Routledge.

Posner, G. J., Strike, K. A., Hewson, P. W., & Gertzog, W. A. (1982). Accommodation of a scientific conception: Toward a theory of conceptual change. *Science Education*, 66, 211–227.

*Salter's science* (1989). York: University of York, Science Education Group.

Samburski, S. (1975). *The evolution of physical thought—From the presocratics to the quantum physicists: An anthology.* New York: Pica Press.

Strike, K. A., & Posner, G. J. (1992). A revisionist theory of conceptional change. In R. A. Duschl & R. J. Hamilton (eds.), *Philosophy of science, cognitive psychology, educational theory and practice.* Albany: State University of New York Press, 147–176.

Schwab, J. (1962). *The teaching of science as enquiry.* Cambridge, MA: Harvard University Press.

Toulmin, S. (1972). *Human understanding.* Princeton: Princeton University Press.

Toulmin, S., & Goodfield, J. (1962). *The architecture of matter.* Harmondsworth: Penguin.

Wheeler, J. A. (1973). From relativity to mutability. In J. Mehra (ed.), *The physicist conception of nature.* Dordrecht, Holland: D. Reidel.

Wightman, T., Green, P., & Scott, P. (1986). *The construction of meaning and conceptual change in classroom setting: Case studies on the particulate theory of matter.* Leeds, UK: Centre for Studies in Science and Mathematics Education.

# The Case for Analogies in Teaching Science for Understanding

ZOUBEIDA R. DAGHER

*University of Delaware*

## INTRODUCTION

Known as ancient tools of communication, analogies are commonly used in political rhetoric, scriptural documents, religious interpretations, philosophical arguments, and scientific discourse. Teachers use analogies to simplify difficult concepts and render abstract notions concrete by comparing less familiar systems, concepts, or even objects to more familiar ones.

In addition to their popular role in communication and learning, analogies are mechanisms for creating and advancing scientific knowledge (Dreistadt, 1968, 1969). Campbell (1957, p. 129) believes that "analogies are an utterly essential part of theories, without which theories would be completely valueless and unworthy of the name." More recently, Nersessian (1992) has recognized analogical reasoning as one of several critical heuristic procedures usually employed in the process of scientific discovery. Newton's theory of universal gravitation, Darwin's theory of natural selection, and Rutherford-Bohr's theory of the configuration of subatomic particles exemplify the central role of analogy in the construction of new knowledge. Nercessian (1992, p. 20) concludes that "analogies are not 'merely' guides to thinking, with logical inferencing actually solving the problem, but *analogies themselves do the inferential work and generate the problem solution.*"

Researchers usually distinguish between two different purposes of using analogy, namely the expository/communicative versus the inferential/generative function. In addressing this distinction, Indurrkhya (1992) refers to the simple and predictive senses of analogy. A simple or proportional analogy "has to do with similarities between the two situations—whether noticing the existing similarities or creating new ones"; for example, an instructor's appeal to the solar system to describe the structure of the atom (Bohr model). Predictive analogy, on the other hand, "has to do with predicting further similarities between the two situations based on the existing ones" (p. 28). For example, if a person who has no experience steering boats but has driven automobiles predicts, based on their experience, that the steering wheel in the boat will behave in the same way as in the car—this inference resembles a predictive analogy. So while the purpose of simple analogy is to map the features/relations from one known domain to an unknown domain, the purpose of predictive analogy is to go beyond the limits of given relations between two domains to generate new problem solutions. Consequently, predictive analogies cannot be deduced from the existing relations but could only be *justified* by them (Indurrkhya, 1992, p. 315). This type of analogies have been the focus of study of cognitive psychologists (for example, Goswami, 1992; Piaget, Montangero, & Billeter, 1977; Vosniadou & Ortony, 1989) and science educators (for example, Clement, 1988; 1989).

The generative function of analogies is well illustrated by Clement's (1989) studies on expert problem solving. His work demonstrates how experts use analogs that bear structural similarities to a target domain to predict how its components behave under certain conditions. The analogical reasoning evident in these predictions provides a noninductive source for generating hypothetical models that are further elaborated, evaluated, and modified. Clement's descriptive account of model development provides insights for understanding both the predictive and explanatory function of analogies in historical cases of scientists, expert problem solving, and student's spontaneous analogies (such as those described by Wong, 1993).

Recognizing learning as a process of personal construction of knowledge, science educators generally view analogies as useful tools for the restructuring of student knowledge frameworks. Reservations concerning the use of simple analogies derive from the very fact that only partial resemblances exist between target and analog domains. Consequently, the potential focus on the nonrelevant features or relations between the two domains may lead to false predictions or generalizations. Also it is possible that too much emphasis on the valid mappings between analog and target constrains the ability of the learner to develop more sophisticated conceptions of the target concept.

This chapter focuses on instructional analogies which involve comparisons of attributes or relationships between the target domain (to be explained) and the analog or source domain (that is familiar). The instructional strategies described will not be limited to the use of "simple" analogies (Indurrkhya's term), but will include strategies of how predictive analogies (analogical reasoning) can be used in instruction to generate inferences for problem solving [for example, Wong's (1993) student-generated analogies and Kolodner's (1997) Case-Based Reasoning].

In the following sections, approaches to teaching with analogies will be described, a synthesis will be presented, and practical considerations for instruction will be discussed.

## APPROACHES TO INSTRUCTIONAL ANALOGIES

Constructivist learning strategies endorse analogies as tools for rendering counterintuitive ideas more intelligible and plausible (Cosgrove & Osborne, 1985). Science educators have developed several approaches to instructional analogies to aid students' learning. Although some approaches or teaching models bear resemblance to others, each carries a different emphasis. The advocates of these models view learning as an active process of knowledge construction. They are cognizant of the role of students' prior knowledge in facilitating or hindering learning and the teacher's role in mediating expert knowledge. In the rest of this section seven models for teaching with analogies will be described.

### The General Model of Analogy Teaching (GMAT)

One of the earliest models for teaching scientific analogies was proposed by Zeitoun (1984). The development of the General Model of Analogy Teaching was prompted by the realization that if analogies are to be used effectively and their shortcomings are to be minimized, a guiding model was needed for teachers and researchers. It is one of the most comprehensive models in terms of incorporating many contextual details within its nine steps. Because the details capture many of the instructional concerns shared by other authors, these details are preserved for the purpose of clarity and brevity (in the description of the other models). The nine steps consist of:

1. Measuring student characteristics related to analogical reasoning ability, ability to handle visual imagery, or tasks demanding cognitive complexity. This stage is optional.

2. Assessing prior knowledge possessed by the students to determine whether analogies are helpful or not. Class discussions, clinical interviews, or written questionnaires can serve that purpose.

3. Analyzing the learning materials of the topic to determine whether they already contain analogies. If none exist teachers could construct new analogies or look for appropriate ones.

4. Judging the appropriateness of the analogy by considering the extent to which the analogies are (a) familiar and/or (b) highly complex, having many attributes that correspond to the target domain. Zeitoun recommends piloting those analogies with few students while experimenting with different strategies of teaching and different mediums of presentation.

5. Determining the characteristics of the analogy in relation to the characteristics of the students. This would help the teacher decide on the level of the concreteness of the analogy and the necessity for using a physical model.

6. Selecting the strategy of teaching and medium of presentation. This involves choosing between three strategies: student self-developed, guided teaching, or expository teaching. Additional choices have to be made concerning the medium of presentation—this involves considering the appropriateness of the following mediums: written, oral by teacher, audiocassette, television, slide presentations (other multimedia approaches certainly apply under this title), demonstrations, games, manipulatory models, pictures, and graphs.

7. Presenting the analogy includes several steps: Introducing the target concept, introducing the analog (if it is not familiar to students it will need to be explained), connecting the analogy to the target, presenting the analogous attributes one by one starting with the most salient first, using transfer statements to present the irrelevant attributes, and finally discussing those irrelevant attributes.

8. Evaluating the outcomes by determining students' knowledge of the attributes of the topic and identifying misconceptions they might have acquired from using the analogy.

9. Revising the stages after evaluating every stage of the model in order to determine whether additional discussion, an alternative analog, or a different strategy is needed.

While the thoroughness of this model constitutes one of its many advantages, it suffers from one disadvantage. Its many steps make it more cumbersome to implement despite its theoretical rigor. Some of the teaching models described later capture the spirit of this model in fewer and more manageable steps.

## Teaching With Analogies Model (TWA)

The Teaching With Analogies model (Glynn, 1991; Glynn, Britton, Semrud-Clikeman, & Muth, 1989) is based on an extensive study of high school physics, chemistry, and biology textbooks. The model could serve as a guide for textbook writers and for science teachers alike. There are six components to this model: (1) introducing the target concept, (2) recalling the analog concept, (3) identifying similar features of concepts between target and analog, (4) mapping similar features, (5) drawing conclusions about concepts, and (6) indicating where the analogy breaks down.

The authors recommend using this model as a tool to: (1) help teachers explain steps that had been ignored by textbook writers, (2) teach students how to analyze textbook analogies and reflect critically on teacher–student and student–student discussions, and (3) guide teacher and student construction of new analogies. The model encourages students to look at the same idea from different perspectives to achieve a deeper understanding of the given concepts and how they relate to other concepts. A modified version of the TWA model in which the sequence of the last two steps was reversed has been used with reasonable success in two studies (Harrison & Treagust, 1993; Treagust, Harrison, Venville, & Dagher, 1996).

---

### TWA Model: Excerpt from a Physics Text (Hewitt, 1989, p. 393) Suggested by Glynn et al.

The last step of the model (where the analogy breaks down) is missing in this excerpt.

*To attain a sustained flow of charge in a conductor, some arrangement must be provided to maintain a difference in potential while charge flows from one end to the other. The situation is analogous to the flow of water from a higher reservoir to a lower one* [reader is referred to a drawing]. *Water will flow in a pipe that connects the reservoirs only as long as a difference in water level exists. The flow of water in the pipe, like the flow of charge in the wire that connects the Van de Graaff generator to the ground, will cease when the pressures at each end are equal (we employ this when we say that water seeks its own level). A continuous flow is possible if the difference in water levels—hence water pressures—is maintained with the use of a suitable pump* [reader is referred to a drawing].

---

### Bridging Analogies Model

Bridging analogies were first described in the context of tutorial interviews (for example, Brown & Clement, 1989). The approach capitalizes on students' intuitions to help guide their thinking through a carefully chosen series of intermediate analogies, each building on the earlier one and refining it until students arrive at the scientific view. The goal of this strategy is to "increase the range of application of the useful intuitions and decrease the range of application of the detrimental intuitions" (p. 239).

While such interventions are helpful, sometimes students fail to see the connections. Brown and Clement (1989) hypothesize that two factors could account for possible failure of this approach: "difficulty with the necessary spatial image manipulation skills (as in explaining the phases of the moon); or competition with a prior conception (e.g., seeing tables as rigid barriers rather than elastic sources of force)." The ability of students to see the plausibility of the proposed model in the target is deemed critical for effecting conceptual change.

The authors present four important conditions for successful use of this strategy. First, students must possess a useable anchoring conception. Second, if students fail to see the anchor and the target as analogous, connections must be developed explicitly through the use of bridging analogies. Third, connections between analog and target are best accomplished in an interactive teaching environment. Fourth, students must be helped to see the target concept in a new way so as to make the scientific concept plausible and acceptable to them.

Clement (1993) applied this tutorial model to whole classroom instruction and found significant quantitative and qualitative gains in student understanding. Students in the experimental group tended to understand the anchoring cases readily though some did not initially see the anchor and the target as analogous. Students engaged in more arguments and generated more bridging analogies of their own as well as new scientific questions pertaining to the lesson.

---

### Bridging Analogies Model: An Example Based on Brown & Clement (1989) Paper

Taking the domain of forces in physics as an example, students typically have difficulty accepting that in the case of a book on the table, the table exerts an upward force on the book. In order to make the claim more plausible, the teacher asks the student to imagine the book on a spring (the anchor). This enables the student to note that the spring indeed exerts a force against the book, however, the student may still reject the analogy between the spring and the table. At this point the tutor introduces the case of a book resting on a flexible table as an intermediary step (the bridging case). The student then is able to see this situation as analogous to the book on the spring and eventually that it is equivalent to the book on the table (the target).

---

## Multiple Analogies Model

The case for multiple analogies is developed by Spiro, Feltovish, Coulson, & Anderson (1989) out of concern for the limitations posed by using analogies that employ one mapping between the target and the source domain. Because analogies have the tendency to lead to oversimplification of complex concepts or "reductive bias," the authors attempted to restrict such bias when dealing with complex target concepts. Their alternative approach consists of deliberate and systematic use of successive analogies whereby each builds on the previous one and dismantles potentially limiting misconceptions. The process of continuous refinement provides a self-correcting mechanism that minimizes the possibility of creating unintended misconceptions.

Perhaps one of the most important steps in this model is selecting the set of multiple analogies that are *"interlocking*, because each new analogy is chosen to correct the negative aspects of the preceding analogies" (Spiro et al. 1989, p. 520). Typically each modified analogy uses aspects of the old analogy, but in some cases a new analogy is introduced (see the third analogy in the sequence presented in the boxed example).

Both the multiple analogy and the bridging analogy approaches utilize a series of analogs with each successive analogy improving on the one that preceded it. The main difference between the two approaches is one of reference point in selecting the intermediate analogs. In Spiro's approach, the selection of the successive analogs is determined by the extent to which the new analog corrects the negative aspects of the preceding one. In Brown and Clement's, the selection of the intermediate analogs (choice of anchors and bridging cases) is dependent on the extent to which they build on student intuitions.

---

### Multiple Analogies Model: An Example
### Based on Spiro et al. (1989)

Spiro et al. (1989) provide a detailed description of a set of five analogies, with diagrams, used to explain muscle fiber function, specifying the concepts that each analogy captures and those it misses. The first analogy employed to explain this mechanism is a rowing crew analogy. The features this analogy shares with the target domain are: (1) *anatomy of force producers: the little arms*; (2) *nature of the movement of the force producers: back and forth, hitting a resistance*; and (3) the presence of *many individual force producers.* However, this analogy could be misleading because it (1) *conveys synchronicity*, (2) *conveys notion that oars can get tangled*, (3) *misses actual nature of gross movement*, and (4) *misses things related to* **width.** The second analogy included rowing crews facing each other in the same boat. This analogy captures *the notion that action tends to pull something to the middle* (the water), but it misses *attachment to some* **structure** *that gets pulled toward middle (problem is that oars slip through water).* Then a third analogy is offered, the turnbuckle analogy, which reinforces the (1) *notion that action pulls something toward middle, with no change in length of puller*; and (2) *notion that there are limits to shortening.* But the analogy misses the notion of (1) *cross-bridges*, (2) *individual force producers*, and is (3) *weak on limits to lengthening.*

*continued*

This analogy is followed by a Chinese finger cuffs analogy followed by a galley ship analogy. In a similar manner to the analogies already described, each of these analogies help demonstrate some relationships and mechanisms but misrepresent others. By the time the fifth analogy is explored in this sequence, the authors believe that enough of the essential aspects of the topic will have been discussed leading to a much more substantial understanding of a complex target domain than would have been possible if one analogy was used.

## Student-Generated Analogies Model

Student-generated analogies were presented by Zeitoun (1984) as one of three strategies to teach analogies. The following description, however, is inspired by Wong's (1993a,b) study on self-generated analogies in which he noted significant improvement in the quality of explanations of teacher education students. Teaching by this method consists of presenting students with a new topic or an event that illustrates a number of science concepts and asking them to produce and modify explanations about that particular phenomenon. With the teacher as facilitator, students engage in three parts to the task which are to be repeated before they engage in the fourth: (1) explain the phenomenon, (2) create their own analogies to achieve a better understanding of the phenomenon, (3) apply the analogy to the phenomenon by identifying similarities and differences, and (4) participate in a class discussion to discuss the degree of adequacy of the suggested analogies in explaining phenomena. The process leads to a continuously evolving set of explanations and analogies. Although step 1 could be skipped in this model, I believe it is a valuable starting point to prepare for step 2.

Wong (1993a) notes that "moving through a series of analogies helped participants to clarify, evaluate, and, ultimately, modify their initial explanations of the air pressure phenomena" (p. 372). Furthermore, creating analogies demands that students draw on their prior knowledge and connect it with the new situation. By continuously cycling through the process, the students are engaged in developing their own set of "bridging analogies" which may simulate the learning outcome described by Clement (1993). The difference is that the bridges are being constructed by the students themselves and not by the teacher. The advantage of student-developed analogies is that students are actively involved in identifying and developing their knowledge and taking ownership of their ideas. There are less risks involved in missing students' intuitions, but there are additional demands on the teacher for coordinating open-ended discussions and critical assessment of a diverse range of mental models.

---

### Student-Generated Analogies: An Example Based on Wong (1993b) Study

While this example is adopted from a research study, the instructional uses of this model would be somewhat similar. The teacher presents the students with a piston/cylinder device that demonstrated three air pressure phenomena (pp. 1262–1263): *As the plunger is pushed into the syringe with the nozzle covered by a finger, the amount of force required to move the plunger increases (compression); as the plunger is pulled out of the syringe with the nozzle still covered, the amount of the force required to move the plunger increases (decompression); when the plunger is released after being pushed or pulled, it returns toward its initial position (return).*

The teacher asks the students to explain the three phenomena they had just observed. Later the teacher asks the students to develop their own analogies as a way of improving their understanding of the phenomena. After they create their analogies, students are asked to specify how their analogy is similar to the phenomenon they were attempting to describe. Then they are asked to specify how it was different from the phenomenon. The process is to be repeated several times resulting in a rich set of evolving explanations and analogies that make a fertile ground for discussion and refinement of proposed analogs/explanatory models.

---

### Narrative Analogies Model

Narrative analogies are derived from an instructional analogy reported in a descriptive study on teacher analogies (Dagher, 1995a). The teacher uses a dynamic source domain to explain several concepts in the target domain, but unlike bridging or multiple analogies, the anology proceeds in a story-like fashion.

Embedded in this approach are key ingredients that were present in the formal approaches described earlier: choosing a familiar domain, developing multiple mappings, exploring connections, building on students' intuitions, and prior knowledge. What is noteworthy about this approach, and therefore the reason for highlighting it, is the appeal of story telling to students, and Bruner's (1990, p. 80) conviction "that logical propositions are most easily comprehended by the child when they are imbedded in an ongoing story." If it is well-chosen, a good narrative analogy keeps the students tuned to the details and engaged in the active coconstruction of the connections between the two domains. The narrative analogy is not added on to the lesson, but constitutes the backbone of the lesson.

The construction of narrative analogies is itself a highly creative act and is worth more attention in instruction and research. While it is difficult to establish a mechanism for identifying appropriate analogs for building narrative analogies, it may be helpful to locate areas of contact between these two powerful means of meaning-making (story and analogy). Taking Egan's (1988) set of guiding questions for developing instruction around storytelling, I have constructed additional questions that would guide the selection and use of an analog domain that would be embedded in the story (since not all stories are not necessarily analogs). Egan situates his guiding questions within the scope of the following five actions (pp. 232–233):

1. *Identifying the importance: What is most important about this topic? Why does it matter? What is affectively engaging about it?* Are there difficult concepts about this topic that demand further explication through more familiar experiences?

2. *Finding binary opposites: What binary opposites best express and articulate the importance of the topic?* What events can be constructed about students or their world that make appropriate analogical connections with this topic? Are those parallel events flexible enough to accommodate the development of the target concepts?

3. *Organizing content in story form: What content most dramatically articulates the binary opposites, in order to provide access to the topic? What content best articulates the topic into a developing story form?* How should the analog domain be sequenced and developed to articulate the mechanism in question?

4. *Conclusions: What is the best way of resolving the dramatic conflict inherent in the binary opposites? What degree of mediation of those opposites is it appropriate to seek?* What is the best scenario for moving between the featured "players" in the story and the target concepts?

5. *Evaluation: How can one know whether the topic has been understood, its importance grasped, and the content learned?* To what extent did the analog story enhance or complicate the understanding of concepts?

The most difficult step is identifying a rich analog domain that lends itself to sequential development. From there on, the analog and source are intertwined in the story from the beginning of the story to the end. In an extended story coupled with an extended analog, interactive discussions of similarities and differences, highlighted in the other approaches, may be conducted at appropriate breaks in the plot or at the end of the story depending on the extensiveness of the analogical connections, length of story, and ability of students to retain details.

---

**Narrative Analogies:
An Example from Dagher's (1995) Study**

In the eighth-grade classroom where this analogy was observed, the teacher constructed a story about a hypothetical journey that a few students in the class undertook on the nearby lake. As the plot of the story

---

*continued*

unfolds, the teacher shifted back and forth between the target concepts (movement of crust and mantle; topographical changes in terrain) and the events in the story (students' boat trip) pointing out the similarities and differences using drawings and key questions to maintain student involvement. The following excerpt from a classroom transcript (Dagher, 1995, p. 264) gives a flavor of the model:

... *Let's assume Jenny was out on Lake Darling, and she was sitting here* [illustrated by drawing] *in a boat.* [comments] ... *So Jenny is down here at Lake Darling, and she's got herself a boat and she's out in the water, and the boat is floating fairly high in the water, and we could use this as an analogy for the—section of the earth' crust floating on the mantle. The crust would be ... the counterpart of the boat; the water would be the counterpart of the mantle ... And we just suppose that as Jenny was there paddling around Lake Darling that she ran into some people she knew; say she ran into, say, Katy and Mike and Dany down there, and being the swell person Jenny is, she invited them to go along with her. What do we notice when these three other people get into the boat?* [It'll sink.] *The boat is gonna sink* [to the bottom] *to the bottom. You think so? We'll assume that the boat Jenny is in is big enough that it will hold four people; what we're gonna notice different about the boat with four people in it compared to the boat with one ... The boat is gonna set lower in the water* [adjusts drawing on the board]. ...

## Case-Based Reasoning Model

This model, described by Kolodner (1997), puts decades of analogy research in cognitive science in the service of teaching. It provides students with opportunities for learning and problem solving by giving them problems for which they have to devise solutions by building on their experiences and those of others (peers and experts). By providing students with useful cases and examples, students are encouraged to "make useful analogical inferences: to identify issues to pay attention to, to form ideas about how to move forward, and to project the effects of the solutions they have come up with" (p. 57).

This approach is motivating and interesting for students especially because of the design component that enables them to move back and forth between the concrete and the abstract, testing and refining their ideas as they propose new solutions. Their personal experience in learning is valued in terms of determining what previous idea to use and which one to avoid. The purpose of case-based reasoning is to help students encode and later access their experiences and improve their perception of functional (not only feature) similarities between components of systems. Inferential/analogical reasoning is at the heart of these processes. The usefulness of the cases in science teaching is very much dependent on their content and the availability of adequate resources that could support the exploration of this content.

---

**Case-Based Reasoning: Two Brief Examples from Kolodner's (1997, p. 57) Paper**

Sixth-grade students learn about the respiratory system by designing artificial lungs. Seventh-grade students learn about arthropods by designing useful arthropod-like robots.

---

## Are Analogies Effective Teaching Strategies?

Few studies specifically examine these approaches to analogy teaching in comparison to others that examine the "unstructured" use of analogies. Fewer yet are empirical studies that compare different models to one another. Various methods have been used to determine the effectiveness of using analogies in science texts or instruction (for a review of those studies refer to Dagher, 1995b). Because many research reports lack adequate detail, it is difficult to make the needed connections between the findings and the instructional approach that is followed. The reading of these studies suggests that it is not the existence of analogy in instruction/textbook that makes a difference in the outcome, but rather the contextual factors that surround the presentation of the analogy. Dagher (1995b) explained the negative findings of some studies by suggesting that the research designs failed to meet one or more essential conditions for successful analogy use; namely, that the analogy be simpler than the target concept, that it be accessible and relevant to students' background knowledge, and that similarities and differences be part of the discussion.

From a cognitive science perspective Holyoak and Thagard's (1997, p. 35) multiconstraint theory "assumes that people's use of analogy is guided by a number of general constraints that jointly encourage coherence in analogical thinking." The constraint of similarity suggests that "the analogy is guided to some extent by direct similarity of the elements involved." The second constraint of structure acknowledges that "the analogy is guided by the pressure to identify consistent structural parallels between the roles in the source and target domains." The third constraint of purpose "implies that analogical thinking is guided by the reasoner's goals—what is the analogy intended to achieve."

From an instructional perspective these three constraints operate at two levels simultaneously, that of the producer and that of the interpreter of the analogy. If the analogy producer is interested in communicating with the interpreter, he/she will have to take into consideration the ability of the latter to perceive the similarity, the structure, and goal of the producer and ideally that should feed back into alternating or modifying what could have been the original analogy.

Teacher awareness of how these three constraints operate at the receiver end of the analogy should be helpful in guiding their selection of, explication of, and purpose for using a given analogy. First, it is not enough that the teacher be aware of the similarity of key relations, if the students cannot access that similarity. Thus the used analogy should be easily accessible to students. Familiarity alone may not be adequate. Students may have superficial familiarity with water pumps but fail to understand how they work. Gentner and Gentner (1983) point out that students who do not know enough about water pumps may not benefit from using this analogy when explaining currents in electric circuits. Second, teachers' understanding of the correspondence relationships between the target and analog enables them to explicate those relationships to students. Intricate knowledge of structural parallels should affect choices of analogy presentation in order to increase students' understanding of the structural similarities and differences. Three descriptive studies on teacher use of analogies (Dagher, 1995a; Jarman, 1996; Treagust, Duit, Joslin, & Lindauer, 1992) reveal that teachers in general do not use extended analogs or map the relations between them and the target adequately, thus neglecting key elements for limiting the likelihood of developing false conceptions and understanding the target concepts (Duit, 1991; Webb, 1985). Third, broadly conceived purposes and goals could be used effectively to access relevant analogs and to explore pertinent content and values.

A word of caution on textbook analogies is in order. Stocklmayer and Treagust (1996) examined the mental models of electricity and found that those used by high school, postsecondary students, and school teachers are different from those used by university lecturers and electrical engineers. The first group adheres to mechanistic models whereas the latter group subscribes to a field model. As a case in point, despite the century's advances in understanding electricity, textbooks and teaching practices still adhere to mechanical analogies that have been found to constrain students' ability to understand more advanced concepts. Despite its cited limitations and the difficulties students experience with understanding it to begin with, the water currents analogy remains popular in physics texts. Stocklmayer and Treagust rightly call for a reexamination of the usefulness of this analogy.

The historical legacy of some scientific analogies and their long shelf life in textbooks do not necessarily speak to their pedagogical appropriateness. Therefore, teachers are advised to examine textbook analogies very carefully and contemplate alternatives before they present them to students. Selection of the instructional analogy should be based on its critical evaluation with respect to the following factors: (1) cognitive accessability, as in the flowing water analogy commonly used to explain electrical circuits (Gentner & Gentner, 1983; Stocklmayer & Treagust, 1994); (2) adequacy of mappings between the two domains; and (3) cultural accessibility and relevance, such as using the Russian doll analogy to describe earth layers when students have no past experience with the doll (Dagher, 1995c).

## PRACTICAL CONSIDERATIONS FOR INSTRUCTION

Analogies, like other conceptual tools, do not possess inherent virtues that are independent of the purpose to which they are put. In the same way a certain type of fertilizer may not be needed when working with rich soil, an analogy may not be needed when working with concepts that are well within students' reach. If using fertilizers is contingent on certain factors such as the type of fertilizer and the type of plant and soil condition, so is using analogies subject to the teacher's assessment of student background knowledge in relation to the target concept. Some students may benefit from a given analogy, others may benefit more from using a different analogy, while some others may simply reason better with other abstraction techniques or experimental work. The choice of analogs is subject to constant assessment of the difficulty of the target concept and the meaningfulness of the intermediary analogies relative to students' background knowledge. An understanding of student learning styles (Sternberg, 1994) might guide teachers' use of analogies in combination with other instructional techniques to motivate students and maximize their interest and participation.

The usefulness of analogies derives from their being personally and culturally pertinent to students. A good knowledge of students and their cultures plays a key role in judging the familiarity and merit of proposed analogies. Regardless of the source of the analogy (teacher, student, textbook, or media), the teacher assumes prime responsibility for helping students distinguish between valid and invalid mappings to reduce the potential for misconstruing explanations. While the "rigor" of an analogy might be predetermined by examining the soundness of mappings between the analog and target (á la Gentner, 1983), the instructional worth of the analogy may not be, for it is constrained by the range of knowledge and experience of a given group of students. It is for this reason that it is almost impossible to make a list of successful analogies that are guaranteed to work with all students.

One of the research gaps noted in studies on analogies relates to matters other than the attainment of specific concepts in science. Very few studies in science education, for instance, examine the effect of analogies on attitudes toward science (Gilbert, 1989; Tsaparlis & Sarantopoulos, 1993) and understanding the nature, conduct, and language of science (Clement, 1998; Dagher, 1995a; Wong, 1993). As pointed out elsewhere (Dagher, 1994, 1995b), studying the effects of analogy on cognitive gains must be supplemented with studying more broadly defined cognitive and affective outcomes so that conclusions concerning their effectiveness is not limited to a narrow set of worthwhile goals.

Emphasis on using analogies to enhance conceptual understanding is a serious undertaking in teaching science. Using one of the surveyed approaches to guide analogy use should assist teachers in minimizing the formation of distorted conceptions or constraining more advanced understanding. As teachers contemplate the role of analogies in furthering student understanding of target science concepts, they might consider using analogies to promote additional educational goals. Those include, among other things, understanding the nature of science and technology (considered content goals in the "National Science Standards" and "Science For All Americans"). Analogies can convey to students more concrete images of how scientists work and explicit messages on how scientific knowledge is constructed and validated (see example in Dagher, 1995a). In addition to enriching knowledge frameworks in and about science, analogies can trigger metacognitive thinking (documented in Clement, 1993; Wong, 1993) and innovative problem solving (Brown & Clement, 1989; Kolodner, 1997). More specifically, analogies could be used in science teaching to promote some of the following learning goals:

1. Demonstrate the thought processes scientists use to arrive at major breakthroughs and how continuous elaboration of models enables them to refine their theories (as in the case of Faraday and Maxwell described by Nercessian, 1992).
2. Engage students in talking science by humanizing the language of science and enabling them to appropriate that language and make it their own. (Gallas, 1994; Lemke, 1990) (see Chapter 12).
3. Engage students in the doing of science by way of model construction, evaluation, and modification.

Teachers are encouraged to experiment with the various approaches described in this chapter and to develop their own style taking into consideration their instructional goals and students' needs and interests. Since each of the approaches discussed may lead to different learning outcomes (for example, different degrees of problem solving), the selection of the approach should be guided by the teacher's comfort level with its format and the educational goals they have adopted for their students. Ultimately, analogies are only tools to achieve those goals and not ends in themselves. Whether teachers select and sequence analogies strategically in their instruction or give students opportunities to develop and refine their own, their skill in eliciting valid mappings and discussing invalid ones is critical for maximizing meaningful learning.

## References

Brown, D., & Clement, J. (1989). Overcoming misconceptions via analogical reasoning: Abstract transfer versus explanatory model construction. *Instructional Science*, 18, 237–261.

Bruner, J. (1990). *Acts of meaning*. Cambridge, MA: Harvard University Press.

Campbell, N. (1957). *Foundations of science*. New York, NY: Dover.

Clement, J. (1988). Observed methods for generating analogies in scientific problem solving. *Cognitive Science*, 12, 562–586.

Clement, J. (1989). Learning via model construction and criticism: Protocol evidence on sources of creativity in science. In J. A. Glover, R. R. Ronning, & C. R. Reynolds (eds.), *Handbook of creativity* (pp. 341–381). New York: Plenum Press.

Clement, J. (1993). Using bridging analogies and anchoring intuitions to deal with students' preconceptions in physics. *Journal of Research in Science Teaching*, 30, 1241–1257.

Cosgrove, M., & Osborne, R. (1985). Lesson frameworks for changing children's ideas. In R. Osborne & P. Freyberg, (eds.) *Learning in science: The implications of school science* (pp. 101–111). Auckland, New Zealand: Heinemann.

Curtis, R. V. (1985). *The analogy as an instructional and motivational design strategy in text*. Unpublished dissertation, Syracuse University, Syracuse, NY.

Dagher, Z. R. (1994). Does the use of analogies contribute to conceptual change? *Science Education*, 78(6), 601–614.

Dagher, Z. R. (1995a). Analysis of analogies used by science teachers. *Journal of Research in Science Teaching*, 32(3), 259–270.

Dagher, Z. R. (1995b). Review of studies on the effectiveness of instructional analogies in science education. *Science Education*, 79(3), 295–312.

Dagher, Z. R. (1995c). What makes an analogy successful? *SMEC Newsletter*, 1, 13–14.

Dreistadt, R. (1968). An analysis of the use of analogies and metaphors in science. *The Journal of Psychology*, 68, 97–116.

Dreistadt, R. (1969). The use of analogies and incubation in obtaining insights in creative problem solving. *The Journal of Psychology*, 71, 159–175.

Duit, R. (1991). On the role of analogies and metaphors in learning science. *Science Education*, 75(6), 649–672.

Egan, K. (1988). *Primary understanding: Education in early childhood*. New York, NY: Routledge.

Gallas, K. (1994). *The languages of learning: How children talk, write, dance, draw, and sing their understanding of the world*. New York, NY: Teachers College Press.

Gentner, D. (1983). Structure-Mapping: A theoretical framework for analogy. *Cognitive Science*, 7, 155–170.

Gentner, D., & Gentner, D. R. (1983). Flowing waters or teeming crowds: Mental models of electricity. In D. Gentner & A. L. Stevens (eds.), *Mental models* (pp. 99–129). Hillsdale, NJ: Lawrence Erlbaum Associates.

Gilbert, S. (1989). An evaluation of the use of analogy, simile, and metaphor in science texts. *Journal of Research in Science Teaching*, 26(4), 315–327.

Glynn, S. M. (1991). Explaining science concepts: A teaching-with-analogies model. In S. M. Glynn, R. H. Yeany, & B. K. Britton (eds.), *The psychology of learning science* (pp. 219–240). Hillsdale, NJ: Lawrence Erlbaum.

Glynn, S. M., Britton, B. K., Semrud-Clikeman, M., & Muth, K. D. (1989). Analogical reasoning and problem solving in science textbooks. In J. A. Glover, R. R. Ronning, & C. R. Reynolds (eds.), *Handbook of creativity* (pp. 383–398). New York: Plenum Press.

Goswami, U. (1992). *Analogical reasoning in children*. Hove, UK: Lawrence Erlbaum Associates.

Harrison, A. G., & Treagust, D. F. (1993). Teaching with Analogies: A case study in Grade-10 optics. *Journal of Research in Science Teaching*, 30, 1291–1307.

Hewitt, P. (1989). *Conceptual physics*. Harper Collins.

Holyoak, K., & Thagard, P. (1997). The analogical mind. *American Psychologist*, 52, 35–44.

Indurrkhya, B. (1992). *Metaphor and cognition*. Dordrecht: Kluwer.

Jarman, R. (1996). Student teachers' use of analogies in science instruction. *International Journal of Science Education*, 18, 869–880.

Kaufman, D., Patel, V., & Magder, S. (1996). The explanatory role of spontaneously generated analogies in reasoning about physiological concepts. *International Journal of Science Education*, 18, 369–386.

Kolodner, J. L. (1997). Educational implications of analogy: A view from Case-Based Reasoning. *American Psychologist*, 52, 35–44.

Lemke, J. (1990). *Talking science: Language, learning, and values*. Norwood, NJ: Ablex.

Nersessian, N. (1992). How do scientists think? Capturing the dynamics of conceptual change in science. In R. Giere (ed.), *Cognitive models of science* (pp. 3–44). Minnesota Studies in the Philosophy of Science, Vol. XV. Minneapolis, MN: University of Minnesota Press.

Piaget, J., Montangero, J., & Billeter, J. (1977). Les correlats. In J. Piaget (ed.), L'*Abstraction reflechissante*. Paris: Presses Universitaires de France.

Spiro, R. J., Feltovich, P. J., Coulson, R. L., & Anderson, D. K. (1989). Multiple analogies for complex concepts: Antidotes for analogy-induced misconception in advanced knowledge acquisition. In S. Vosniadou & A. Ortony (eds.), *Similarity and analogical reasoning* (pp. 498–531). Cambridge: Cambridge University Press.

Sternberg, R. J. (1994). Allowing for thinking styles. *Educational Leadership*, 52(3), 36–40.

Stocklmayer, S., & Treagust, D. (1994). A historical analysis of electric currents in textbooks: A century of influence on physics education. *Science & Education*, 3, 131–154.

Stocklmayer, S., & Treagust, D. (1996). Images of electricity: How do novices and experts model electric current. *International Journal of Science Education*, 18, 163–178.

Taber, K., & Watts, M. (1996). The secret life of the chemical bond: Students' anthropomorphic and animistic references to bonding. *International Journal of Science Education*, 18, 557–567.

Thagard, P. (1992). *Conceptual revolutions*. Princeton, NJ: Princeton University Press.

Treagust, D. F., Duit, R., Joslin, P., & Lindauer, I. (1992). Science teachers' use of analogies: Observations from classroom practice. *International Journal of Science Education*, 14(4), 413–422.

Treagust, D., Harrison, A., Venville, G., & Dagher, Z. (1996). Using an analogical teaching approach to engender conceptual change. *International Journal of Science Education*, 18, 213–229.

Tsaparlis, G., & Sarantopoulos, P. (1993). Using analogies with a strong social content in chemistry teaching: Effects on learning and on the attitude of students. In A. Bargellini & P. E. Todesco (eds.), *Proceedings of the second* ERICE (pp. 339–344). Pisa, Italy: Università Degli Studi di Pisa.

Vosniadou, S., & Ortony, A. (eds.). (1989). *Similarity and analogical reasoning*. Cambridge: Cambridge University Press.

Webb, M. J. (1985). Analogies and their limitations. *School Science and Mathematics*, 85(8), 645–650.

Wong, E. D. (1993a). Self-generated analogies as a tool for construction and evaluating explanations of scientific phenomena. *Journal of Research in Science Teaching*, 30(4), 367–380.

Wong, E. D. (1993b). Understanding the generative capacity of analogies as a tool for explanation. *Journal of Research in Science Teaching*, 30, 1259–1272.

Zeitoun, H. H. (1984). Teaching scientific analogies: A proposed model. *Research in Science and Technological Education*, 2, 107–125.

# The Computer as Powerful Tool for Understanding Science

RON GOOD
*Louisiana State University*

CARL BERGER
*University of Michigan*

## INTRODUCTION: OVERVIEW OF THE CHAPTER

In this chapter we focus on three uses of the computer that merit particular attention: microcomputer-based laboratories (MBLs), simulations, and Internet/World Wide Web applications. Of the many ways the computer has been used in education, MBLs and simulations are powerful tools when used appropriately and the Internet offers the promise of equal access to educational and scientific resources around the world.

The optimism of scientific literacy for all citizens proposed in *Science for All Americans* (1989) is tempered by the misconceptions-in-science research that shows convincingly that most people do not understand most science concepts. Can the most powerful tool of the 20th century, the computer, be used effectively to help achieve the goal of science literacy for most people? We are optimistic that MBLs, simulations, and the Internet, in the hands of competent science teachers, can help to make the egalitarian goal of science for all (or at least *most*) citizens a reality before the return of Halley's comet in the year 2061.

Following this introduction, we: (1) review some of the history of the development of computers and microcomputers as tools for doing and teaching science, (2) consider research on the effectiveness of using computers in science education, (3) describe the nature and use of MBLs in science teaching and learning, (4) consider the power of the computer to simulate real and imaginary complex systems, (5) define and discuss intelligent computer-assisted instruction (ICAI), and (6) explore current uses of the Internet for science teaching.

Teaching science for understanding to all citizens, rather than to only a select few, is a significant challenge, one that requires the wise use of our best resources. The computer is clearly one of these critical resources that has the potential to help students understand what Wolpert (1993) has called the "unnatural" nature of science. This unnatural or counterintuitive nature of many scientific concepts is the source of a great many of the common "misconceptions" reported widely in the science education research literature. Helping students of science build better scientific models of nature is a highly promising role for the computer, especially for simulations and MBLs. Visualizing science can take on a whole new meaning with the computer as a powerful teaching tool.

## DEVELOPMENT OF COMPUTERS AS TOOLS
## FOR UNDERSTANDING SCHOOL SCIENCE:
## A BRIEF HISTORY

Our main goal here is to provide a concise history of the more recent advances in using computers as tools for understanding school science and to provide an argument for going beyond word processing, spreadsheet, and CD-ROM exploration in the use of computers in science teaching. More detailed accounts of the general history and nature of computers and cognitive science can be found in Collis et al. (1996), Lawler and Yazdani (1987), and Vosniadou et al. (1996). In a later section we describe some characteristics of intelligent computer-assisted instruction and consider the future of ICAI in school science.

Although the use of computers to study intelligence began in the 1950s, their use in public schools for instruction did not begin in earnest until the 1970s. Based on a national survey, Becker (1986) reported that the number of computers used for instruction in schools increased from 1000–2000 in Spring 1980 to more than 1 million by Spring 1985. Since 1985 computer use in school instruction has increased steadily. Today most science teachers report some use of computers for instruction (often the use of word processing for writing and presenting reports, some use of spreadsheets for analysis of data, and some use of specialized science exploration CD-ROMs), but the systematic use of microcomputer-based laboratories and simulations is not widespread.

The advances in instructional computer hardware and software since the mid-1980s are impressive. Microcomputer memory capacity has increased by a factor of about 1000 and operating speed has increased proportionately, allowing software programs to operate much faster with more and better options for the user. Simulations, in particular, have come into their own. Students can now see and control realistic, dynamic simulations of physical phenomena on one part of the video screen, while another part shows real-time line graphs of the event(s), and still another part shows the actual values of relevant parameters (e.g., temperature, velocity, voltage, pH, and so on).

The 1986–1987 edition of *The Educational Software Selector* (EPIE Institute and Teachers College Press) listed about 700 entries for biology (213), chemistry (237), and physics (249), with many of marginal quality by today's standards. The large increases in microcomputer memory capacity and operating speed mean that today's instructional software for school science is more realistic in modeling physical phenomena.

With much more instructional software available now, compared to only a decade ago, there is an increased need to help science teachers learn what is on the market and what experienced science educators think of it. For science computer software there are a number of organizations that review and recommend software for use in science teaching. For example, The Physics Courseware Evaluation Project is operated within the Physics Department of North Carolina State University, publishing a quarterly 16-page newsletter that contains reviews of physics instructional software/courseware, plus other news of interest to physics teachers who use computers in their classes.

The most recent, and some think the most exciting, tool of computer users is the Internet. Direct access to the Internet allows the user to explore/browse a great many sites that are open and free. The concept of networking, with the Internet as the ultimate example, is explored more fully in the last section in this chapter.

As science and society become more dependent on the computer it seems inevitable that science teachers and their students will do the same. The question seems to be how, not if, education will adapt to the computer age. How will science teachers use this marvelously powerful tool to help all citizens become more scientifically literate?

## RESEARCH IN COMPUTER-BASED EDUCATION (CBE)

In the 1994 *Handbook of Research on Science Teaching and Learning*, Berger et al. review research on the uses of computers in education. Eight metaanalyses ($N = 123$) published during the 1980s showed overall effect sizes of CBE on science achievement of about 0.38 standard deviations. Of course the main problem of combining studies in metaanalysis work is the loss of information about individual studies, so knowing that 123 studies show an average effect size of about 0.38 standard deviations does not allow one to make conclusions about specific studies. Because we are interested mostly in MBLs and simulations, our review will focus primarily on research that uses these tools.

## A Review of Reviews

In their review of 26 reviews (from 1972 to 1987) of CBE, Roblyer, Castine, and King (1988) reported that nearly all reviews (total number of studies = 357) found that CBE provided advantages over other instructional methods and that simulations were more effective at higher grade levels; however, only one review (4 studies) involved science instruction. Three hundred and fifty-seven is a large number so we should keep these generally positive results in mind, but it is important to factor science into the picture. For MBLs and simulations of the physical world, what do we know about their use in science teaching and learning?

## Relevant Research in Science Education: Simulations

In their review of various kinds of simulations used in pre-1980s science education, Lunetta and Hofstein (1981) included a small number of computer-based simulations (e.g., Bork & Robson, 1972; Caven & Logowski, 1978). They concluded that relatively little was known about the effects of simulations on science learning and recommended more careful research.

During the next decade-and-a-half more research has been done on the effects of simulations on science learning, but less than might be expected considering their potential to help students explore complex systems. Rather than present a comprehensive summary of the existing research on simulations, we have selected just a few studies that represent important features of the research base.

The first study, by Rivers and Vockell (1987), is reported in a special issue on technology of the *Journal of Research in Science Teaching*, edited by Marcia Linn. They reported on results of three studies of high school biology students using seven biology simulations: (1) BALANCE: A Predator-Prey simulation; (2) PLANT: A Plant Growth Simulation; (3) OSMO: Osmosis in Red Blood Cells; (4) MOTHS: Peppered Moth Evolution; (5) MONOCROSS: Monohybrid Crosses; (6) DICROSS: Dihybrid Crosses; and (7) POLLUTE: Impact of Water Pollutants. The studies were experimental in design, involving many biology classes that included a wide range of students in both urban and suburban schools. Students were pretested and posttested using the BSCS Process of Science Test, the Test of Integrated Process Skills, and the Watson-Glaser Critical Thinking Appraisal. Rivers and Vockell reported that students who received guidance while using the simulations did considerably better than those who received little or no guidance and, when compared to students who did not use the simulations, the guided simulation students were better at making inferences and interpretations from data.

A second study, this time in the science content area of chemistry, is reported by Williamson and Abraham (1995). Two groups of college students used simulations of atomic and molecular behavior while a third group (control) received no computer animation treatment. One of the simulation treatment groups viewed the animations during lectures only, while the other simulation treatment group viewed the animations both during lectures and scheduled discussion sessions. Each of the simulation treatment groups achieved higher scores on tests designed to measure their understanding of the dynamic, particulate nature of chemical reactions and underlying concepts such as pressure, phase transitions, and intermolecular forces. Treatment with animations gave the students about a one-half standard deviation advantage over the students who received no simulation treatment. Williamson and Abraham conclude that "treatment with animations may increase conceptual understanding by promoting the formation of dynamic mental models of the phenomena" (p. 532).

A third study using computer simulations of natural phenomena and related science concepts with high school physics students is reported by Roth (1995). Using the well-known *Interactive Physics* microworld, Roth studied students' ways of seeing and talking science. He did not compare the effectiveness of computer simulation with other instructional strategies as did Rivers and Vockell (1987) and Williamson and Abraham (1995), but focused instead on the potential of a computer simulation microworld to engage students in "science talk." An underlying assumption of Roth, the classroom teacher as well as researcher, was "teacher use of the microworld and discourse contribution allows an evolutionary adaptation of students' descriptive science talk so that it may become compatible with the scientific canon" (p. 343).

These three studies offer different perspectives on the use of computer simulations of physical phenomena as tools in science teaching and learning. As the computer hardware and software become more sophisitcated at the close of the 20th century, simulations are becoming more realistic, with many more options for the user to control the dynamics of the phenomena depicted on the screen. It seems inevitable that well-designed simulations will become a more important and pervasive science teaching and learning tool in the twenty-first century.

## Relevant Research in Science Education: MBLs

Whereas the simulation of physical phenomena can be used apart from the science laboratory, MBLs are tied directly to the laboratory setting. In her review of the role of the laboratory in science learning, Linn (1995) notes:

> Students do not learn what makes science exciting for scientists by following cook-book laboratory procedures. MBLs can provide opportunities for more autonomous, independent, and exciting scientific investigation. (p. 4)

Like the research on the use of simulations in science education, the research on MBL use is thin. It is curious that so many "experts" think MBLs and simulations offer such high potential for improving science education, while relatively little research on their effectiveness has been conducted.

Some of the more interesting research on MBLs and their use to help students interpret line graphs of moving objects and heat and motion has been conducted at the Technical Education Research Centers (TERC) in Cambridge, MA. As part of a 5-year effort to develop and study MBL applications in science education Mokros and Tinker (1987) and their colleagues focused on students' abilities to interpret graphs. Most observers agree that understanding scientific representations of our physical world is essential to achieving higher levels of scientific literacy. Clement (1985), McDermott et al. (1983), and others have shown that even college students have difficulty interpreting graphs of physical phenomena.

Mokros and Tinker found that many students misunderstand graphs as pictures and they confuse slope with height. These researchers found MBLs to be effective in helping students correct their misunderstandings about heat and temperature, sound, and motion during 3 months of classroom investigations. Mokros and Tinker (1987) conclude their paper with these observations:

> It is very likely the combination of these four factors (multi-modal reinforcement, real-time linking of concrete and abstract, meaningful context, and elimination of drudgery) that contributes to the power of learning via MBL. When students are in control of a learning experience that they design, are given real-time feedback about that experience, and are freed from the painstaking task of producing a graph, they are in an ideal position to learn what a graph says and means. (p. 382)

In another interesting study of the effectiveness of the use of MBLs to promote scientific reasoning skills, particularly observation and prediction, Friedler, Nachmias, and Linn (1990) studied 110 students in four eighth-grade classes for an entire semester. In lab activities during 29 class periods the students used MBLs to measure the temperature of various objects while observing and making predictions and outcomes. The researchers found that students in the MBL environment could develop their observation and pre-diction skills and that the prediction activities seemed to facilitate more integration of domain-specific knowledge. In support of the importance of prediction as a science literacy skill, Lavoie and Good (1988) found that successful predictors engaged in more expert-like behavior during explora-tion of computer-simulated ecology investigations. The potential of MBLs for science education is summed up nicely by Linn (1995):

> MBLs have provided a new impetus for resolving the discovery-learning/constructivist dilemma in the laboratory. These new tools make learning in the science laboratory

far more powerful and potentially abstract. By judicious use of MBLs, a dramatic improvement in the science curriculum can be made. (p. 46)

We share Linn's optimism on the potential of MBLs as powerful tools to help students better understand and appreciate the often abstract ideas of the natural sciences. However, much more research is needed to see more clearly and fully the implications of widespread use of CBE.

## MICROCOMPUTER-BASED LABS

Collecting and analyzing data in laboratory settings can be a very lengthy, tedious process and yet the laboratory experience is considered by most scientists and science educators to be central to effective science teaching and learning. The MBL couples sensors to measure properties such as temperature, light intensity, and pH to digital analyzers that can display immediate representations in tabular, graphic, and other forms. Thus, the MBL allows the student to collect very large amounts of data that are then quickly transformed into graphic representations (e.g., line graphs) more compatible to pattern analysis by human inspection. The length of time for data collection can vary widely from fractions of a second to days or even weeks, depending on the target of the scientific investigation. More importantly, MBLs can facilitate a more visceral understanding of the scientific representation of natural phenomena, enabling students to learn science in ways not possible otherwise.

### The MBL and Cognition

Models of human cognition describe a short-term, (working) memory system with certain characteristics that can determine how and whether information is stored in long-term memory. The amount of information (often referred to as "bits") encoded and how it is interpreted all contribute to whether and how the information is stored in long-term memory. From the pioneering memory work by Miller (1956) to more recent ecological and evolutionary approaches by Neisser (1982), Sherry and Schacter (1987), and Rumelhart and McClelland (1986), working or short-term memory is seen as a key to understanding human cognition.

The MBL is a tool for science teaching and learning and it can be used to study memory-related issues as well. Collecting, analyzing, and interpreting data from scientific investigations are critical components of science laboratories, but if they are not well planned and coordinated they may be seen by students as tedious, meaningless exercises. Translating data points into meaningful patterns that students can use to build more accurate conceptions of nature is one of the strengths of the MBL and it may fit nicely with the nature of short-term memory. Brassell (1987) reported MBL research with high school physics students that showed, among other things, a short (about 20 seconds) delay between data collection and graphing of the data can cause a reduction in the learning of kinematics. Apparently, even a brief delay between the laboratory experience and seeing a representation of that experience can cause a degradation in the information in short-term memory and how that information gets into long-term memory. The MBL may be a valuable, even critical tool in aiding students to translate the everyday "sensible" world of nature into the more abstract, quantified world of the scientist.

Unlike simulations, MBLs do not replace the real world with computer-generated imitations. To the extent that "real-world" laboratory experiences are needed by students to understand scientific explanations of nature, the MBL is a powerful tool in the science educator's toolbox.

## Simulations and Microworlds

The best-known example of a microworld is Logo. In Logo a "turtle" is programmed by simple commands (e.g., FORWARD 50, LEFT 90) that can be combined to form complex turtle maneuvers. The resulting line drawing can be made to repeat itself, with endless possible variations. Procedures that are developed can be stored and used in conjunction with other procedures to make complex designs and solve problems invented by the Logo user. The Logo microworld is described by its "father," Seymour Papert, in *Mindstorms: Children, Computers, and Powerful Ideas* (1980). "Mindstorms" is still the best description of the early concept of a microworld as conceived by Papert and his colleagues.

Papert was influenced by Jean Piaget's work on the development of children's ideas of number and by Piaget's more general ideas on the nature of knowledge and how it develops in humans (i.e., genetic epistemology). The need to allow children to explore environments rich with possibilities for learning was paramount in Piaget's ideas on learning and development and Papert developed Logo with this feature in mind.

## Other Microworlds and Simulations

Logo, Sprite-Logo, Lego-Logo, and similar microworlds allow students to creatively and actively construct objects and ideas, especially in geometrical mathematics and computer programming. Lawler (1987) describes some examples and characteristics of microworlds and considers their potential for education now and in the future:

> Miniworlds and microworlds may have once been perceived as a "technical fix" for problems in education. They are not. They are, however, a better way to approach education when it is seen as the self-construction of mind, guided by our shared knowledge of the world and our perceived social needs. (p. 23)

The dynamic simulation of physical phenomena is an extremely promising use of the computer environment for science education. User-controlled simulations such as "Graphs and Tracks" by David Trowbridge (published by Physics Academic Software) and "Electric Field Hockey" by Ruth Chabay (Physics Academic Software) allow students to set initial conditions and make multiple runs to compare outcomes. In Graphs and Tracks, for example, the student constructs a linear track that has column support at various sites. Each support can be raised or lowered to make that part of the track level or inclined. A ball is rolled down the track and as it moves across each segment of the track, the ball accelerates, decelerates, or moves with constant velocity. The user can vary the ball's initial velocity and its starting position, both of which affect the nature of its motion and resulting graph. Graphs of position-time, velocity-time, and acceleration-time are plotted as the student adjusts the track and initial conditions in order to replicate various line graphs that are presented as "challenges." After working with Graphs and Tracks for a while, the user begins to see the relationship between the shape of the track and the resulting ball motion and corresponding graphs. For labs that are difficult, dangerous, or expensive to do in the typical science classroom, simulations offer an attractive alternative for teachers and their students. In genetics experiments, for example, students can select species and individuals for crosses that might take weeks, months, or even many years to achieve in real settings. In astronomy the student can travel to different planets or even different galaxies, controlling the spaceship and learning physics in the process. Students' models of their world are confronted with scientists' models via simulations of objects and events in nature.

It is important to emphasize that simulations should not be used to replace effective lab work in schools that has stood the test of time; rather, they should be used where, for one reason or another, lab work cannot be done. The laboratory in science instruction, especially with the computer as "lab partner," (see Linn, 1992; Linn, 1995) is considered by most informed observers to be a crucial part of school science. Although the goals of school science have changed somewhat during the 20th century, the role of the laboratory continues to be central to the curriculum. With increasingly good simulations of physical phenomena becoming available, the concept of "laboratory" is changing. The computer as MBL or as simulator of nature will surely become more central to school science laboratories of the 21st century.

## INTELLIGENT COMPUTER-ASSISTED INSTRUCTION (ICAI)

Reif (1987) identifies four essential characteristics of scientific knowledge:

1. The knowledge must be sufficiently explicit so that it can be readily examined and modified.

2. "Declarative knowledge" consisting of factual assertions must be accompanied by procedural knowledge that specifies what one must actually do to decide whether statements are true or false.
3. Knowledge must be highly coherent so as to ensure ease of remembering and retrieving, consistency, and the ability to make inferences.
4. Reliable, flexible performance requires quality-control processes for preventing, detecting, diagnosing, and correcting errors and other deficiencies. (p. 311)

These characteristics of scientific knowledge are consistent with the domain knowledge of scientists and they suggest an educational system compatible with ICAI. Expert systems in medicine, for example, have large knowledge bases that are structured along the lines suggested by Reif's essential characteristics. These computer systems (e.g., MYCIN or INTERNIST) are as good as experienced physicians in diagnosing patients' illnesses.

Although high levels of expertise have been achieved in medical expert systems, ICAI achievements have been much more modest. Good (1987) suggests three reasons for the modest achievements of ICAI: (1) a soft knowledge base, (2) difficulty of machine processing of natural language, and (3) machine learning problems. Compared to science knowledge, knowledge of science teaching and learning is "soft" or "fuzzy." Also, the discipline of science education has existed for only a few decades compared to a few centuries for the natural sciences so we should not expect to see a science of science education anytime soon.

The feat of achieving understanding of natural language is much more difficult than was expected by AI researchers in the 1950s and 1960s. The metaphorical nature of language, the necessity of having many experiences associated with words, and the complex relationship between sentence structure and meaning all contribute to the difficulty of working to get computers to understand natural language. Until effective natural language interfaces can be developed, ICAI must rely on predetermined user-friendly menus that allow computer users to interact within microworlds with reasonable efficiency.

## ICAI Research and Development

R&D on ICAI systems during the 1980s (Anderson, Boyle, & Reiser, 1982; Clancey, 1987; Kearsley, 1987; Lawler & Yazdani, 1987) led to a number of attempts to develop intelligent tutoring systems in science education. One of them, MENDEL, is briefly described here as an example of ICAI techniques applied to science.

Stewart et al. (1989) describe the primary objectives of MENDEL as helping students conduct genetics experiments and giving them problem-solving advice. The components of MENDEL include: (1) a problem generator, (2) a tutor, (3) a student modeler, (4) an advisor, and (5) a hypothesis checker. The tutoring philosophy of MENDEL builds on the concept of "post-Socratic" tutoring (Jungck & Calley, 1985), where students learn by trial-and-error while receiving problem-solving advice. Like other computer tutors, MENDEL tries to simulate human teachers who tutor individual students.

## ICAI's Future

Just how intelligent will ICAI systems of the twenty-first century become? If sufficient R&D efforts are invested in science tutors, is it reasonable to expect that they will be effective in helping students achieve higher levels of science literacy?

For restricted, well-defined knowledge domains such as classical genetics problem solving, it seems likely that effective ICAI systems will be developed and used selectively in schools of the future. Knowledge that falls outside the "essential characteristics of science" domain identified by Reif (1987) is not likely to be taught intelligently by computer tutors. The less coherent, less reliable knowledge that is characteristic of domains outside mathematics and the natural sciences is less conducive to effective instruction by ICAI systems. Even within mathematics and natural science domains, human teachers with their human intelligence (i.e., affective as well as cognitive) will be required to coordinate and guide the overall educational process, adding the fundamental human qualities of compassion, discipline, and the many other factors that contribute to socialization and human growth.

## INTERNET AND THE FUTURE

Networking is seen by some observers as the most powerful way to use computers in education and the Internet is the ultimate network, linking computer users worldwide. The common language of the Internet (TCP/IP) allows all computers to share information. With a proper address any Internet user can send and receive information from any other user. This "email" system makes it possible to communicate instantaneously with millions of people throughout the world. Also, entire computer files can be transferred from one site to another, allowing users to work on common projects. The decade of the 1990s is the age of the Internet as far as computer use is concerned.

How might the Internet be used to improve science education? This is the question we consider throughout the remainder of this section, following a brief introduction to the Internet.

## The Internet (Briefly)

The Internet is a worldwide network of thousands of smaller networks, all using a common language that computers use to transfer information to one another. Sometimes called the Information Superhighway, the Internet uses phone lines and modems, digital datalines, and communication satellite systems to link computers together. During the mid- to -late 1980s the National Science Foundation funded five supercomputer centers and regional networks around them, leading to the Internet today. In the early 1990s various tools such as Gopher and the World Wide Web (WWW) were developed to help Internet users sort out the huge amount of information that was becoming available. In 1993, under the urging of U.S. Vice-President Al Gore, federal funds were made available to get schools and libraries connected to the Internet to take advantage of the vast array of resources available.

Email is probably the most basic of the Internet tools, allowing the user to send and receive information throughout the world. Addresses consist of a user ID, the computer address, and the type of organization (domain). A typical address might be jsmith@mit.edu. The various kinds of domains include commercial organization (com), government organization (gov), education institution (edu), military (mil), and so on.

Discussion groups consisting of any number of people who have email addresses are known as *listservs*. When you subscribe to a listserv you can send the same information to all members on the list and you receive all messages sent out on the listserv. Unfortunately, just as much "junk" mail can accumulate in your email box as in your regular mailbox, so it is important to be judicious in adding your name to a lot of listservs. The openness of the Internet can be a weakness as well as a strength!

The latest implementation of use of the Internet has been the introduction of the World Wide Web (WWW). The WWW was formed to allow images and text to be easily transferred using a standard called Hypertext Markup Language (HML). Not only has this standard and its implementation, called a Web Browser enabled the transmission of text and images, but extensions to WWW have encouraged interaction, animation, and simulation. Perhaps the greatest benefit for the science education community is the ability to find and contact others for excellent information, programs, or interaction. Interesting locations include (1) Exploratorium Science & Nature Museum (http://www.exploratorium.edu/); (2) NASA (http://www.nasa.gov); (3) Science Daily (http://www.sciencedaily.com/); (4) Science in the Headlines (http://www2.nas.edu/new/newshead.htm); (5) National Science Teachers Association (http://www.nsta.org/conv/); Yellowstone Journal (http://www.wyoming.com/yellowstonejournal/); and (6) Earth Times (http://www.earthtimes.org).

More information on the nature and many uses of the Internet can be found in guides such as *The Internet Tool Kit* (Cedeno, 1995), *The Internet Yellow Pages* (Hahn & Stout, 1994), and K–12 *Resources on the Internet* (Junion-Metz, 1996).

## Science Education and the Internet

All the resources of the Internet are available to science teachers; the challenge is to find ways to use them wisely. Communication with other science teachers and their students is one obvious way to use the Internet; another is to communicate with scientists. During the late 1980s the Technical Education Research Center in Cambridge, MA started the Kids Network, a project funded by the National Science Foundation, National Geographic, and Apple Computer to improve elementary science education. Network-based projects dealing with environmental science involve science teachers and their students in collecting and analyzing data in conjunction with the Environmental Protection Agency. Students can experience the peer-review process and publish their papers on electronic media. TERC's LabNet Project brings microcomputer-based labs into network science, allowing science teachers and their students to transfer data files from MBL-assisted investigations to other network locations. Science curriculum units such as "*Radon*," "*Solar House*," and "*Weather*" have been designed around the network science concept with related efforts to provide science teachers with the skills needed to use network science tools effectively.

Being connected to the Internet in the mid-1990s means having access to a huge number of resources to improve science education. It remains to be seen how network science will change science education across the U.S. and beyond, but it seems inevitable that important changes will occur. The science literacy discussed in *Science for All Americans* (AAAS, 1989) just might be realized before the year 2061 with the help of network science education. Of course the many problems facing education and society at large, such as poverty, overpopulation, and apathy toward child health and welfare, will have to be solved before science literacy for *all* citizens can become a reality.

A word of caution as we close this chapter on the computer as powerful tool in learning science. Pepi and Scheurman (1996) use the tale of *The Emperor's New Clothes* by Hans Christian Andersen to raise questions about the implications of increased use of computers in education. Will increased use of CBE lead to the kinds of schools and students that are envisioned and described in *Science for All Americans*, *National Science Education Standards*, and other efforts to redefine contemporary education as we enter the twenty-first century? Can this powerful tool be used in ways that will ensure higher levels of literacy for all and reduce the apparent flight from reason described in recent books by Gross, Levitt, and Lewis (1997), Holton (1996), and other critics of New Age relativism? Or will CBE one day be viewed much the same way television is seen today by critics of the mindless "boob tube"? Internet surfing and unguided use of CBE, like supermarket shopping, in no way ensures a nutritious diet for the unwary, uninformed consumer. The uncommon sense of science requires expert guidance by well-informed teachers to help students construct concepts compatible with scientists' ideas about our natural world. We need to be very careful that the "new clothes" of technology in education fit the goals of education described in *Science for All Americans* and similar well-reasoned, realistic guides to reform.

## Acknowledgment

Thanks to Marcia Linn, John Risely, and Herman Weller for providing information that was helpful during completion of this chapter.

## References

AAAS—Project 2061 (1989). *Science for all Americans.* Washington, DC: AAAS Press.

Anderson, J., Boyle, C., & Reiser, B. (1982). Intelligent tutoring systems. *Science*, 228, 456–462.

Becker, H. (1986). *Instructional uses of school computers: Reports from the 1985 national survey.* Baltimore, MD: Johns Hopkins University.

Berger, C., Belzer, S., and Voss, B. (1994). Research on the uses technology in science education. In D. Gabel (ed.), *Handbook of research in science teaching and learning.* New York, NY: Macmillan.

Berger, C., Jones, T., & Skov, N. (1996). Students' use of concept maps to guide multimedia science instruction. Paper presented at the annual meeting of the National Association for Research in Science Teaching, St. Louis, MO.

Bork, A., & Robson, J. (1972). A computer simulation for the study of waves. *American Journal of Physics*, 40, 1288–1294.

Brassell, H. (1987). The effect of real-time laboratory graphing on learning graphic representation of distance and velocity. *Journal of Research in Science Teaching*, 24, 385–395.

Caven, C., & Logowski, J. (1978). Effects of computer simulated or laboratory experiments and student aptitude on achievement and time in a college general chemistry laboratory course. *Journal of Research in Science Teaching*, 15, 455–463.

Cedeno, N. (1995). *The internet tool kit.* Alameda, CA: SYBEX.

Clancey, W. (1987). *Knowledge-based tutoring: The GUIDON program.* Cambridge, MA: MIT press.

Clement, J. (1985). Misconceptions in graphing. Paper presented at the Ninth Conference of the International Group for the Psychology of Mathematics Education, Noordwijkerhout, The Netherlands, July.

Collis, B., Knezek, G., Lai, K., Migashita, K., Pelgrum, W., Plomp, T., & Sakamoto, T. (1996). *Children and computers in school.* Mahwah, NJ: Lawrence Erlbaum.

Friedler, Y., Nachmias, R., & Linn, M. (1990). Learning scientific reasoning skills in microcomputer-based laboratories. *Journal of Research in Science Teaching*, 27, 173–191.

Good, R. (1987). Artificial intelligence and science education. *Journal of Research in Science Teaching*, 24, 325–342.

Gross, P., Levitt, N., & Lewis, M. (Eds.) (1997). *The flight from science and reason.* Baltimore, MD: Johns Hopkins University.

Hahn, H., & Stout, R. (1994). *The Internet yellow pages.* Berkeley, CA: Osborne.

Holton, G. (1996). *Einstein, history, and other passions.* New York, NY: Addison Wesley.

Jungck, J., & Calley, J. (1985). Strategic simulations and post-Socratic pedagogy: Constructing computer software to develop long-term inference through experimental inquiry. *The American Biology Teacher*, 47(1), 11–15.

Junion-Metz, G. (1996). *K–12 resources on the Internet.* Berkeley, CA: Library Solutions.

Kearsley, (1987). *Artificial intelligence and instruction: Applications and methods.* Reading, MA: Addison Wesley.

Lavoie, D., & Good, R. (1988). The nature and use of prediction skills in a biological computer simulation. *Journal of Research in Science Teaching*, 25, 333–360.

Lawler, R. (1987). Learning environments: Now, then, and someday. In R. Lawler & M. Yazdani (eds.), *Artificial intelligence and education: Volume One*. Norwood, NJ: Ablex.

Lawler, R., & Yazdani, M. (eds.) (1987). *Artificial intelligence and education: Learning environments and tutoring systems*. Norwood, NJ: Ablex.

Linn, M. (1992). The computer as learning partner: Can computer tools teach science? In K. Sheingold, L. Roberts, & S. Malcom (eds.), *Technology for teaching and learning*. Washington, DC: AAAS Press.

Linn, M. (1995). Science learning: The role of laboratory. Graduate School of Education, University of California, Berkeley.

Lunetta, V., & Hofstein, A. (1981). Simulations in science education. *Science Education*, 65, 243–252.

McDermott, L., Rosenquist, M., Popp, B., and van Zee, E. (1983). Student difficulties in connecting graphs, concepts, and physical phenomena. Paper presented at the American Educational Research Association meeting, Montreal, Canada.

Miller, G. (1956). The magical number seven plus or minus two: Some limits on your capacity for processing information. *Psychological Review*, 63, 81–96.

Mokros, J., & Tinker, R. (1987). The impact of microcomputer-based labs on children's ability to interpret graphs. *Journal of Research in Science Teaching*, 24, 369–383.

Neisser, U. (1982). Memory: What are the important questions? In U. Neisser (ed.), *Memory Observed*. San Francisco: W.H. Freeman.

Papert, S. (1987). Microworlds: Transforming education. In R. Lawler & M. Yazdani (eds.), *Artificial intelligence and education: Volume One*. Norwood, NJ: Ablex.

Papert, S. (1980). *Mindstorms: Children, computers, and powerful ideas*. New York: Basic Books.

Pepi, D., & Scheurman, G. (1996). The emperor's new computer: A critical look at our appetite for computer technology. *Journal of Teacher Education*, 47, 229–236.

Reif, F. (1987). Instructional design, cognition, and technology: Applications to the teaching of scientific concepts. *Journal of Research in Science Teaching*, 24, 309–324.

Rivers, R., & Vockell E. (1987). Computer simulations to stimulate scientific problem solving. *Journal of Research in Science Teaching*, 24, 403–415.

Roblyer, M., Castine, W., & King, F. (1988). Assessing the impact of computer-based instruction. *Computers in the Schools*, 5, 1–149.

Roth, W. M. (1995). Affordances of computers in teacher–student interactions: The case of Interactive Physics. *Journal of Research in Science Teaching*, 32, 329–347.

Rumelhart, D., & McClelland, J. (1986). *Parallel distributed processing: Volume 1*. Cambridge, MA: MIT Press.

Sherry, D., & Schacter, D. (1987). The evolution of multiple memory systems. *Psychological Review*, 94, 439–454.

Skov, N. (1996). Investigation of hypermedia use and effect on grade in general college chemistry. Submitted for publication.

Stewart, J., Striebel, M., Collins, A., & Jungck, J. (1989). Computers as tutors: MENDEL as an example. *Science Education*, 73, 225–242.

Vosniadou, S., DeCorte, E., Glaser, R., & Mandl, H. (1996). *International perspectives on the design of technology-supported learning environments*. Mahwah, NJ: Lawrence Erlbaum.

Weller, H. (1996). Assessing the impact of computer-based learning in science. *Journal of Research on Computing in Education*, 28, 461–485.

Williamson, V., & Abraham, M. (1995). The effects of computer animation on the particulate mental models of college chemistry students. *Journal of Research in Science Teaching*, 32, 521–534.

Wolpert, L. (1993). *The unnatural nature of science: Why science does not make (common) sense*. Cambridge, MA: Harvard University Press.

# CHAPTER 9

# Using Hypermedia to Represent Emerging Student Understanding: Science Learners and Preservice Teachers

MICHELE WISNUDEL SPITULNIK
University of Michigan

CARLA ZEMBAL-SAUL
Pennsylvania State University

JOSEPH S. KRAJCIK
University of Michigan

## INTRODUCTION

Many possibilities for student-produced artifacts exist. In this chapter, one type of technological artifact is emphasized—hypermedia documents. Growing evidence suggests that artifacts in general assist students in constructing understanding and serve as external representations of that emerging understanding. For the purpose of the research presented here, artifacts are considered to be products students construct collaboratively over an extended period of time (Papert, 1991). The construction of artifacts provides students with the opportunity to represent, share, and defend ideas. Moreover, recent research indicates that the use of technological tools, such as hypermedia authoring applications, can facilitate the development of students' ideas, promoting understanding of content (Lehrer, Erickson & Connell, 1993;

Spitulnik, 1995; Spitulnik, Stratford, Krajcik, & Soloway, in press). This chapter includes a rationale for engaging students in the construction of hypermedia artifacts. The chapter also examines the influence hypermedia artifact construction has on students' conceptual understanding by presenting two cases of students building hypermedia artifacts. The first case highlights high school chemistry students as they create artifacts to represent their emerging understanding of concepts associated with kinetic molecular theory. The second case presents preservice elementary teachers as they construct artifacts to represent their developing understanding of how to teach science to children. In each case, the structure of the artifacts and the representations students use as a means to illustrate their developing understanding of science and science teaching are analyzed.

## THEORETICAL FRAMEWORK

The rationale for engaging students in constructing hypermedia artifacts is grounded in recent research on learning that emphasizes the active role of the learner, the importance of collaboration, and the need for authentic, or meaningful, contexts for problem-solving. In general, educational researchers have come to view learners as active constructors of knowledge rather than passive recipients of information. Students build complex understanding as they purposefully integrate their prior knowledge and new experiences. Novak and Gowin (1984) describe a rich conceptual understanding as one that has many interconnections and relationships between concepts. Students can build this rich conceptual understanding by working with and synthesizing ideas. (Cognition and Technology Group at Vanderbilt, 1992; Papert, 1980; Perkins, 1986). In light of this perspective on learning, several approaches are potentially powerful in terms of facilitating the development of meaningful understanding. First, providing opportunities for students to collaborate within the context of communities of learners is believed to foster the development of deep understandings more so than learning in isolation (Brown & Campione, 1990). Another approach advocated by Blumenfeld (Blumenfeld, Soloway, Marx, Krajcik, Guzdial, & Palincsar, 1991) and others (Brown, Collins & Duguid, 1989; Cognition and Technology Group at Vanderbilt, 1992) suggests that teachers should provide engaging and motivating learning opportunities for students—opportunities fostered by personally meaningful activities situated in real-world contexts.

### Artifact Construction

Building artifacts is one possible means for helping students develop conceptual understanding. Students engage in many elements of design when building artifacts. For example, when students construct artifacts they (1) organize and synthesize information from many sources, (2) structure the artifact, and (3) represent the information. By designing and creating appropriate representations of concepts, students develop understanding (Daiute, 1992). As students design and construct artifacts, they integrate new information into their existing conceptual framework, developing relationships among ideas. The degree to which students illustrate relationships among ideas within their artifacts provides insights regarding their level of understanding (Spitulnik, 1995). As students work collaboratively on building artifacts they have opportunities to share and debate ideas, providing rich interactions for creating these connections among concepts. The public nature of these products provides an opportunity for students to give and receive feedback from other students regarding their artifacts, so that students may not only learn through the construction of their own artifact, but may also develop understanding by critiquing another group's artifact. Therefore, providing opportunities for students to design, construct, critique, and revise their artifacts engages them in the learning process (Blumenfeld et al., 1991).

Constructing artifacts provides the aforementioned learning opportunities both for science learners and preservice science teachers. Artifact-building engages students in selecting and organizing concepts, representing those concepts, and developing connections among them. For example, within chemistry-related artifacts, science learners can construct and link representations of microscopic phenomena with other analogies and examples of those phenomena. With regard to preservice elementary teachers, artifact construction encourages learners to engage in critical reflection by selecting representations that illustrate their emerging understanding of how to teach science to children. More specifically, preservice teachers can reflect on their philosophy of education within their artifacts by writing about the influences that shaped their beliefs about science teaching. In addition, preservice teachers can represent various aspects of their philosophy with exemplar lessons from actual teaching experiences. The artifacts created by both science learners and prospective teachers not only incorporate a variety of representations of the builder's choice (e.g., text, drawings, movie clips), but also illustrate the state of students' understandings in terms of the artifact as a whole. For science learners artifacts are a representation of their degree of science learning and for preservice teachers artifacts are a representation of their thinking about science teaching and learning.

## Technological Tools

Technological tools and software offer new opportunities for creating artifacts. Technology enhances the value of student-constructed artifacts by allowing easy incorporation and linking of multiple representations, interactive testing, and document revision. These affordances may better facilitate the development of understanding among learners.

Technological tools, like hypermedia authoring systems (HyperCard and HyperStudio are two examples), aid learners in representing phenomena and concepts in a variety of ways and making connections between concepts. The term multimedia is used to describe the usually computer-controlled, coordinated use of several types of media, like text, video, animation, and sound. Hypermedia is an extension of multimedia, in that a hypermedia environment also incorporates many types of media, but it also contains an inherent structure with connections, or links, between chunks of information. This type of environment is called *hyper*media, because a user can access information through many different, often nonlinear, paths, depending on how the information is organized. Hypermedia authoring systems, or tools designed to facilitate the construction of hypermedia artifacts, allow learners to incorporate diagrams, drawings, graphs, animations, and video into their productions. Daiute (1992) observed that as students create and incorporate multiple representations—like images, text, and sounds—their cultures, values, and interests are expressed in their artifacts. Hypermedia authoring systems also allow learners to make connections between chunks of information or different representations of concepts. Learners can develop richer understandings by building connections between representations that may be familiar and representations that may be more abstract, like those used by scientists. This is supported by the literature which suggests that students form more integrated understandings as they create thoughtful connections and construct meaningful relationships among various representations (Novak & Gowin, 1984; Linn, in press). Science learners, for example, can generate more thorough explanations of the melting process by linking a graphical representation of melting to a microscopic or particulate drawing of an object melting. Similarly, preservice teachers may develop an understanding of the importance of connecting science learning to students' daily lives by linking video clips of themselves trying to foster these practices during interactive teaching to the underlying pedagogical principles explored through university coursework.

Technological tools also have the potential to promote students' interactive testing and monitoring of conceptual development. Interactive testing can facilitate the process of making connections between students' existing ideas and the new understandings gleaned from building and evaluating their artifacts. Such immediate ability to visualize abstract ideas and test representations can challenge science learners to develop understandings of scientific phenomena and encourage preservice teachers to generate connections between beliefs, theory, and practice. For example, within artifacts constructed by science learners, technological tools allow students to create and revise animations or drawings to explain phenomena. For preservice teachers, technological tools allow the pairing of video clips of interactive teaching episodes to related lesson plans and written reflections.

Finally, technological tools allow students to more readily revise their work. The revision process may contribute greatly to the longitudinal development of understanding (Harel, 1991; Spitulnik, 1995). More specifically, technology permits students to rework their ideas and build new versions of their product, while providing the option to save older versions of artifacts. By comparing versions, students and teachers have a record of how ideas change over time. In this way, the revision process can be used by teachers for evaluation purposes. For example, science learners can keep various versions of their attempts to represent and explain kinetic molecular theory—these versions allow both the students and their teachers to track conceptual development. Likewise, preservice teachers can keep versions of their artifacts to monitor the changes in their knowledge and beliefs about science teaching over the course of their professional development.

In summary, there are many indications that artifact construction can contribute to both science learners' and preservice teachers' conceptual development. Creating artifacts allows students to (1) participate with others to construct understanding and (2) become actively engaged in their own learning. Furthermore, technologically based artifacts have advantages that include the incorporation of various media (multiple representations), the visualization and immediate testing of ideas, and the ease of revision.

## TWO CASES OF HYPERMEDIA ARTIFACT BUILDING

The following cases provide examples of students constructing hypermedia artifacts as part of their coursework. In the first case, high school chemistry students developed class projects that involved building hypermedia artifacts. These artifacts focus on phenomena related to kinetic molecular theory. The second case examines hypermedia artifacts developed by preservice elementary teachers as part of their science methods course. These artifacts emphasize preservice teachers' developing understanding of how to teach science to children. In both cases a variety of issues are discussed, including the nature of the hypermedia projects, analysis of the artifacts and emergent trends, and the ways in which the artifacts represent student understanding.

In the two cases presented the hypermedia authoring tool HyperStudio was used to create the artifacts. HyperStudio allows students to create *cards* (computer screens containing text, video, drawings, etc.). Several cards together form what is called a *stack* (of cards). Students create links, or connections, between cards with a HyperStudio tool called a *button*. To create a link students must decide which two cards are to be linked and they create a button that when pressed "moves" the user from the first card to the next card. HyperStudio also comes with a number of other tools, like drawing and animation tools that students use to represent their ideas.

## Case One: Integrating Hypermedia Artifact
## Construction into a High School Chemistry Class

### Introduction

Kinetic molecular theory provides the foundation for many chemistry concepts including chemical changes and equilibrium. However, many students have difficulty understanding concepts associated with this theory (Linn & Songer, 1991; Lee, Eichinger & Blakeslee, 1993). Students often hold intuitive ideas or misconceptions about the particulate nature of matter (Novik & Nussbaum, 1978, 1981; Benson, Wittrock & Baur, 1993), the properties and dynamic explanation of states of matter (Osborne & Cosgrove, 1983; Stavy, 1990; Bar & Travis, 1991), and the properties and thermodynamics of changing states of matter (Linn & Songer, 1991). A number of strategies have been used to assist students in developing more expert-like conceptions of kinetic molecular theory. Nussbaum (Chapter 6 in this volume), for instance, offers a strong argument for a critical analysis of cognitive demand, historical antecedents, and philosophical underpinnings in preparing to teach students about the particle theory of matter. For more complete reviews of student conceptions and related research see Gabel and Bunce (1994) and Nakhleh (1992).

This case focuses on how students develop understanding of kinetic molecular theory by constructing and revising hypermedia artifacts. It was hypothesized that the process of building artifacts provides students with opportunities to generate models of kinetic molecular theory, thereby contributing to their developing conceptual understanding. The research presented here seeks to address the following questions: (1) how do students model (i.e., represent and explain) the phenomena and concepts associated with kinetic molecular theory with their artifacts; (2) how do these representations reflect students' understanding of concepts; and (3) how do students' artifacts and understandings change over time? Below we describe how hypermedia artifact development was integrated into a high school chemistry course. This description is followed by an analysis of a subset of student-produced artifacts, focusing on how these artifacts reflect students' developing understanding. Finally, this case closes with a discussion that summarizes the findings and explores the implications of using hypermedia artifact development as a means of promoting conceptual understanding in science.

### Method

Eighty-five sophomore chemistry students enrolled in a specialized math and science magnet program in mid-Michigan studied a unit on the kinetic molecular theory as part of their chemistry course. Two experienced high school science teachers cotaught the course. The unit of study was centered around pairs of students constructing hypermedia artifacts of kinetic molecular theory based on both empirical evidence (i.e., laboratory work) and various scientific models of the theory. Students were asked to construct models that would explain and represent the phenomena observed in the laboratory and interpret other descriptions or models of the theory.

Construction of the hypermedia documents was integrated with laboratory work, demonstrations, class discussions, and textbook assignments. Before beginning the hypermedia project students conducted two laboratories. During the first lab, students observed and graphed the melting of $p$-dichlorobenzene. The second lab engaged students in hypothesizing about the forces that hold molecules together and designing experiments to determine which type of force is stronger—the forces which hold molecules to other molecules (intermolecular forces) or the forces which hold atoms together within a molecule (intramolecular forces). Typical student experiments involved measuring the energy (as a predictor of the amount of force) needed to initiate a state of matter change (an indicator of a molecule to molecule force) and the energy of a chemical change, like the burning of a substance (an indicator of the forces between atoms within a molecule).

Once students completed these two laboratories they began constructing their hypermedia artifacts on kinetic molecular theory. Students worked on their artifacts for approximately nine class hours. During this time students provided written and oral feedback to each other and the instructors provided written feedback to students at least twice.

Students incorporated the following concepts in their artifacts: states of matter, state or phase changes, boiling point, melting point, heat, temperature, kinetic energy, evaporation, equilibrium, vapor pressure, heat of vaporization, condensation, pressure, volume, and gas laws. The project guidelines specified that students should (1) describe and represent states of matter; (2) describe and represent changes in states of matter; (3) describe factors that influence changes in states of matter (e.g., changes in temperature and pressure); and (4) describe how kinetic molecular theory explains 1–3. Students were encouraged to create multiple representations of concepts and to model kinetic molecular theory with animations.

### Description of Hypermedia Artifacts

An in-depth analysis of the hypermedia artifacts is presented for two pairs of students: (1) Jason and Tim and (2) Wendy and Kelly. These two pairs were purposefully selected to demonstrate a contrast among artifacts constructed by the group as a whole (i.e., less developed and more thoroughly developed). The artifact analysis focused on three versions (over time) of the students' artifacts. Analysis identified the representations students used to explain phenomena associated with kinetic molecular theory, how these depictions of concepts developed and changed over time, and how they reflected students' understanding of the concepts. Specifically, the appropriateness

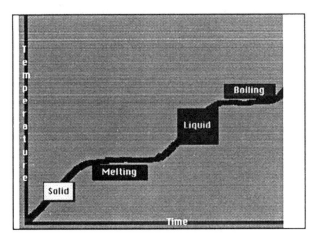

**FIGURE 1**
Jason and Tim represent states of matter.

of the representations was characterized by identifying whether the students exhibited particulate, continuous, or observable properties of matter. The connections students constructed were characterized by identifying whether students used multiple representations for a particular concept, as well as whether and how they linked representations. The coherence between concepts was characterized by identifying any conflicting representations associated with a given concept. Finally, any connections students made between concepts associated with kinetic molecular theory and real-world examples or applications of the theory were noted.

### Jason and Tim

**Early Version.**  Jason and Tim began construction of their artifact with an introduction card that directs the user to three different sections of their stack. Labeled buttons guide the user to the different sections—Phases, Kinetic Theory, and Krypton. When the "Phases" button is pressed, a temperature vs time graph is presented (Figure 1). This graph appeared in all versions of the artifact and served as the *interface*, or organizer, to the rest of their artifact. Each section on their graph has a button which, when pressed, opens a card and continues with a model for that section. As their versions progressed, the models for the different sections were completed.

The section on the graph that was completed in the earliest version of the artifact was the "solid" section. When the "solid" button on the temperature vs time graph is pressed, a particulate representation appears (Figure 2). In Figure 2a, Jason and Tim constructed an analogy between people dancing

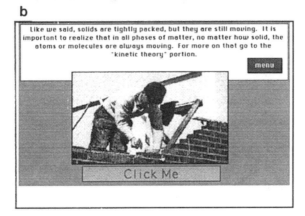

**FIGURE 2**

Jason and Tim represent a solid. (a) Use of image and movie to represent solid. (b) Use of image to represent solid.

and particles moving in the solid state. On this card they explained, "The first stage of matter is the solid phase. When matter is in the solid stage its atoms are very similar to a mosh pit in that the atoms are like people—they are very tightly packed and the distance they move is very small." Through this explanation, Jason and Tim demonstrated an understanding of the particulate nature of matter, as well as the dynamic nature of matter explained by the kinetic molecular theory. Jason and Tim continued, however, with another representation for solid—a scanned image of a brick layer laying bricks (Figure 2b). Here, they included a conflicting representation by presenting a more static analogy, that of solid particles as closely packed and unmoving. Their textual explanation continues, "Like we said, solids are tightly packed, but they are still moving. It is important to realize that in all

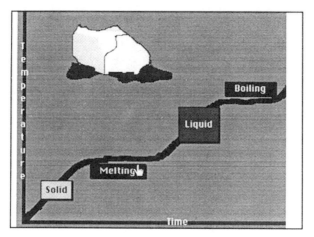

**FIGURE 3**
Jason and Tim represent melting.

phases of matter, no matter how solid, the atoms or molecules are always moving." Although it appears Jason and Tim have a particulate and dynamic understanding of solid matter, they continued to use the static, or brick wall, representation in all versions of their artifact.

**Middle Version.**    Even though Jason and Tim illustrated the individual states of matter with particulate representations, they show the changing stages of matter with observable or continuous qualities and not with particulate representations (Figure 3). In a middle version of their artifact, Jason and Tim represented changing states of matter with animations of the observable changes in that matter. For example, when the "melting" button is pressed on the temperature vs time graph, an animation begins with a solid (represented as a pale blue and white cube) changing to a liquid (represented as darker blue dripping "liquid") (Figure 3). Here, matter is depicted with a continuous representation. Jason and Tim's representation of boiling is very similar. As the "boiling" button is pressed an animation begins. A pool of water is seen changing to string-like gas (a continuous representation of gaseous particles) and then droplets (gas particles).

**Final Version.**    In the final version of their artifact, a separate section was constructed and devoted to illustrating and explaining kinetic molecular theory. As a button labeled "kinetic molecular theory" is pressed, a card opens with a representation of evaporation and condensation (Figure 4). Jason and Tim model evaporation and condensation with an animation that includes both particulate as well as more observable or continuous properties. More

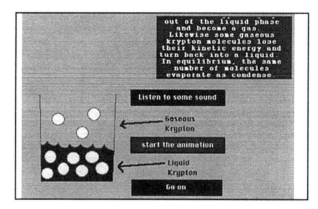

**FIGURE 4**
Jason and Tim represent evaporation.

specifically, the representation includes a container that holds both liquid and gas. The liquid is illustrated with light blue particles and a dark blue wavy "liquid." The gas is depicted with the same blue particles spread further apart. Accompanying this representation is a scrolling textual explanation. The scrolling text reads, "When you have some liquid krypton, some of the molecules have enough kinetic energy to 'jump' out of the liquid phase and become a gas. Likewise some gaseous krypton molecules lose their kinetic energy and turn back into a liquid. In equilibrium, the same number of molecules evaporate as condense."

Jason and Tim applied their understanding of the kinetic molecular theory to explain and represent the phenomenon of evaporation. Their model exhibits both an understanding of the particulate nature of matter as well as a more continuous understanding of the nature of matter. It seems that Jason and Tim were attempting to reconcile their understanding of the particulate nature of matter with the more observable properties displayed above in their representation of changing states of matter. As learners, they seemed to be challenged with how to represent changing states of matter with microscopic properties. It is interesting to note, however, that this section of the model is labeled kinetic molecular theory and is separate from the temperature vs time graph section of the artifact. The representation of evaporation is not connected to, nor does it reference, the other representations of changes in state (i.e., the temperature vs time graph). In other words, Jason and Tim failed to construct explicit links among their various representations of kinetic molecular theory.

### Wendy and Kelly

*Early Version.* The early version of Wendy and Kelly's artifact contains primarily textual explanations. After an introduction, Wendy and Kelly proceeded in their artifact development by explaining the gas state. Wendy and Kelly described the gas state as "the phase where the molecules are moving around the fastest. They are moving with space around them too. The gas phase is like a normal highway, because you are moving really fast and have space around you."

**Middle Version.**    In a middle version of their artifact, Wendy and Kelly incorporated more types of representations, including interactive "experiments," data, drawings, and animations (Figure 5). They continued modeling the gas phase by demonstrating how the pressure and volume of a contained gas are related (Figure 5a). They also modeled vapor pressure by constructing and explaining an animation that represents the movement of gas particles at two different temperatures (Figure 5b).

Also in their middle version, Wendy and Kelly attempted to explain temperature. They described temperature as a measure of molecules' kinetic energy and they used a qualitative graph to represent temperature as being directly related to kinetic energy (Figure 6). In the same version, this "temperature" card connects to a card about melting point (with a "next card" button). Wendy and Kelly did not make any connections among the concepts presented on the temperature card and the concepts presented on the melting point card (other than the button as "link"). Wendy and Kelly represented melting point in a number of different ways. They described melting point with text—"Melting point is when a solid turns into a liquid or changes from a solid to a liquid. This happens when the heat of vaporization is high enough to have the molecules change phase. We normally find a water changing from ice to liquid water at about 25°C." They included a graphical representation, a temperature vs time graph, with the melting point circled on the graph. They also included an animation that shows an ice cube melting and a thermometer. As the "actions" button is pressed, the ice cube melts and the thermometer gauge rises. These students represented solid matter with observable or continuous properties.

Wendy and Kelly included three representations of seemingly the same concept—melting point. However, these representations do not coincide. The temperature–time graph shows that temperature does not change during melting; however, during the melting animation, the temperature gauge rises. Aside from these discrepancies between representations, the students' textual explanations showed indications of potential misconceptions. For example, the pair uses the phrase "heat of vaporization" to explain melting and they describe ice melting at 25°C. Given this evidence, it is apparent that the students did not have a deep understanding of melting at this time. Although they recognized the importance of kinetic energy in the explanation of temperature (i.e., they linked the description of temperature to melting), Wendy and Kelly did not make the connection between phase changes and kinetic molecular theory. In other words, they did not use the theory, or

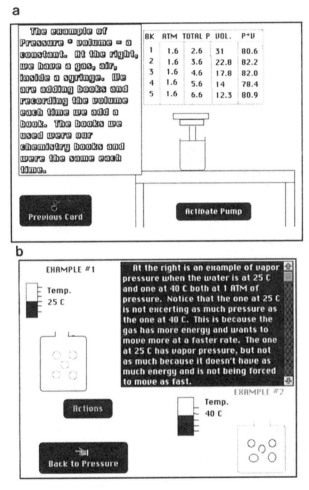

**FIGURE 5**

Wendy and Kelly represent the gas state. (a) A pressure-volume experiment.
(b) A vapor pressure animation.

representations of the theory, to explain the physical phenomenon of melting.

**Final Version.** In a final version of their artifact, Wendy and Kelly introduced a new card that attempted to relate temperature to the movement of molecules in the solid state. They presented three scenarios (Figure 7). The first scenario has text which reads, "Molecules moving slow and close together." A drawn representation shows four particles close together. Below

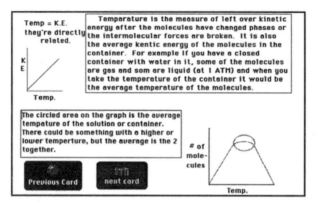

**FIGURE 6**
Wendy and Kelly explain temperature and melting.

this representation is a heading which states, "Ice cube/solid stage temperature is −10°C." Another representation depicts the observable properties of a solid and a temperature gauge. This scenario reads, "Molecules moving a little bit faster and further apart . . . ice & water/solid stage. Temperature has increased." Particles are drawn a bit further apart. The representation below

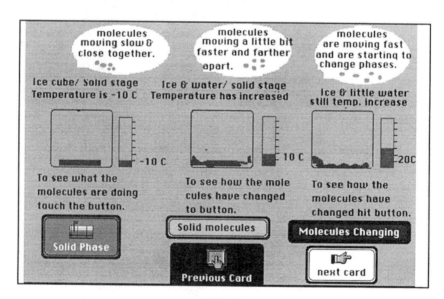

**FIGURE 7**
Wendy and Kelly represent solid and solid changing to liquid.

the heading has a container of what appears to be some melted solid (observable properties). Finally the third scenario reads, "Molecules are moving fast and are starting to change phase . . . ice and & little water still temp. increase." Particles are drawn even further apart. The representation below has a container with what appears to be some solid and liquid (observable properties).

Wendy and Kelly were trying to use the kinetic molecular theory to explain both the solid stage and the change between the solid state and the liquid state. They represented matter with both observable and particulate properties and tried to explain the relative positions and velocities of the particles as the temperature increases. It appears they were making the connection between kinetic energy, velocity, and temperature with increases in temperature during the solid state. However, on this card they did not appear to understand the connections between position and velocities of particles and temperature during a phase change (i.e., they still were not linking their representations to the temperature vs time graph).

Nevertheless, in their final version, Wendy and Kelly linked their third scenario (in Figure 7) to another card with the button, "Molecules Changing." This card presents multiple representations of a solid changing to a liquid, including the temperature vs time graph. The area on the graph were solid changes to liquid is circled. The textual explanation reads, "Here is where the temperature is staying the same, but time is still going by. This is because the kinetic energy is being used to change the molecules and to break apart the intermolecular forces . . . The molecules are all changing to liquid molecules. Like from ice to water you drink. The temperature is not increasing because the energy is changing the molecules." It appears that for this scenario, Wendy and Kelly were building coherence among the many representations by linking the temperature vs time graph to the particulate representations and by making a distinction between temperature and (heat) energy. These students explained that during the phase change energy is used to separate the molecules (break the intermolecular forces). They did not explicitly state that the molecules are not increasing in velocity and that is why there is not an increase in temperature. They did, however, appear to develop a deeper understanding of the kinetic molecular theory and how the theory explains states of matter and changes in states of matter.

## Discussion

The construction of hypermedia models provided students with a context to manipulate symbol systems scientists routinely use (e.g., graphs and molecular level drawings). It also allowed students to construct meaningful understanding of challenging concepts by providing a context for relating and connecting many different types of representations.

In early versions of their artifacts, both pairs of students represented concepts associated with kinetic molecular theory primarily with text or with temperature vs time graphs. For example, Wendy and Kelly initially represented the gas state primarily with text. As they continued constructing their artifact, the pair used more media, including drawings, animations, and graphs, to construct representations of various concepts, such as states of matter. Jason and Tim began in a similar way; however, they started with the temperature vs time graph and incorporated drawings, animation, and text as they continued constructing their artifact.

Both pairs of students represented distinct states of matter (i.e., not in the context of changing states of matter) with drawings and animations that usually depicted a particulate view of matter. However, when the states of matter were represented in the context of changing states of matter, both pairs used drawings and animations which illustrated the more observable properties of changing matter (or with drawings that used both observable properties, as well as particulate properties). Jason and Tim expressed a particulate understanding of matter when they represented the solid state; yet their animations of melting, boiling, and evaporation all suggest a more continuous understanding of the nature of matter. Wendy and Kelly also used more observable properties initially when they represented a solid changing to a liquid. However, as their artifact developed they incorporated a particulate representation of matter. Wendy and Kelly kept their particulate and observable representations separate; however, Jason and Tim exhibited a conflict as they represented evaporation with both particulate and observable properties.

It is apparent that during the process of incorporating and integrating multiple representations, students were challenged in their own conceptions and often presented their understanding as nonlinked or conflicting representations. It seems that more well-developed understanding occurred as students crafted connections among the representations they used to explain the phenomena. Jason and Tim modeled the states of matter, melting, boiling, and evaporation, but did so with conflicting representations (by incorporating both observable and particulate representations within the same drawing) and did not build connections among the various representations. The final version of their artifact contains a section that focuses on states of matter and changing states of matter, with a separate section for kinetic molecular theory. Their understanding seemed to be less integrated and developed. As Wendy and Kelly incorporated many representations, particularly of the melting phenomenon, they first built conflicting representations and did not develop connections between representations, like the temperature vs time graph and the melting drawings. As time progressed, Wendy and Kelly seemed better able to integrate these representations to build deeper explanations of the phenomena and kinetic molecular theory. For both pairs of students, however, the process of building these artifacts provided opportunities for students to represent and explain phenomena as a way to build conceptual understanding.

## Case Two:
## Integrating Hypermedia Artifact Construction
## into an Elementary Science Methods Course

### Introduction

A common finding of many studies is that prospective teachers have difficulty learning to teach subject matter in ways that are meaningful to students (Ball, 1989; Borko & Livingston, 1989; McDiarmid, 1990). Several explanations have been advanced for preservice teachers' difficulties in this area. They include the fact that preservice teachers often have inadequate subject matter knowledge (Ball, 1990; McDiarmid, Ball, & Anderson, 1989), limited understanding of and experiences with learners (Civil, 1992; Grossman, 1989), and limited practical knowledge of classrooms (Borko & Livingston, 1989; Kagan, 1992). In light of these explanations, teacher educators have used several approaches to assist preservice teachers with learning to teach content. Some attempts emphasize subject matter coursework (Grossman, Wilson, & Shulman, 1989; Smith & Neale, 1989). Others focus on innovative subject-specific methods courses (Ball, 1989; Civil, 1992; McDiarmid, 1990). Still other approaches rely on field experience (Kagan, 1992) and promoting reflective practices (Calderhead, 1989; Weinstein, 1990; Zulich, Bean, & Herrick, 1992). Some benefits of each approach have been demonstrated. In this case, however, the integration of hypermedia artifact construction into a year-long methods course for preservice elementary teachers enrolled in a special elementary science teacher preparation program is described. This is followed by an analysis of a subset of student-produced artifacts, focusing on how they reflect prospective teachers' developing conceptions of how to teach science. Finally, this section culminates with a discussion that synthesizes the findings and explores the implications of using hypermedia artifact development as part of preservice science teacher preparation.

### Elementary Science Methods

The preservice elementary teachers who participated in this project were enrolled in a year-long science methods course. This course was one component of a 2-year teacher preparation program that was designed to enhance the teaching of science at the elementary level (Krajcik, Blumenfeld, Starr, Palincsar, Coppola, & Soloway, 1993; Starr, Zembal & Krajcik, in press). The elementary science teacher preparation program was organized around several key features—(1) integrated coursework and field experiences—

chemistry/physics content, science methods, educational foundations, and extended practicum; (2) assignments and experiences designed to integrate key concepts from coursework; and (3) multiple opportunities to teach prior to student teaching. Most of the 19 students in the cohort program were nonscience majors.

The hypermedia artifact project was assigned at the beginning of the second semester of the science methods course. Preservice teachers were asked to select video clips, graphics, photographs, student work, lesson plans, and written reflections from their first and second semester teaching experiences for inclusion in their documents, which became known as "Personal Case Histories." In addition, the preservice teachers generated science autobiographies in which they reflected on their knowledge and beliefs about science and science teaching and how they had changed over time, especially in terms of their involvement in the program.

The science methods instructor developed a nine-card HyperStudio template. The template was basically a "shell" that included premade titles, buttons, text and image boxes, etc. To a large extent, personalization was easily accomplished by importing documents and graphics from other sources. The template included a title card, a Personal Case History main menu, and additional cards with space for personal information, a science autobiography, a description of classroom context, Semester 1 and 2 highlights of interactive teaching, analysis of questioning, and analysis of management. The template was designed to serve two basic purposes. First, it provided the preservice teachers with specific guidelines regarding the kinds of artificats that were to be included in the project (e.g., autobiography and semester highlights). Second, the template was intended to shift the emphasis of the project from mastering the technological application to developing a hypermedia artifact that reflected a developing understanding of how to teach science. In other words, providing a template with premade borders, titles, and buttons was intended to allow the preservice teachers to focus on selecting and integrating meaningful representations into their artifacts rather than becoming overburdened with the design features of the stack.

The preservice teachers were provided with a hard copy of the template early in the methods course to guide their selection of materials. During the last 4 weeks of the semester, a series of hypermedia computer lab sessions were scheduled outside of regular class meetings. At this time, preservice teachers were introduced to basic features of HyperStudio and they began personalizing their templates. The students worked independently to insert text and clip art. In addition, they learned how to scan and import their own photographs and pictures. However, the instructor provided assistance with more technical procedures, such as capturing and digitizing selected video clips. Finally, when each student was satisfied with their document, it was transferred to CD-ROM for long-term storage and future use by the preservice teachers.

## Description of Hypermedia Artifacts

In this section, analyses of two preservice elementary teachers' hypermedia artifacts are presented. These portfolios were purposefully selected because they represent the range of artifacts produced by class members in terms of their level of development. The analysis focused on three major issues— (1) the representations selected by the preservice teachers to illustrate their understanding of various aspects of science teaching, (2) the modifications that the preservice teachers made to the template as they personalized it, and (3) how the representations included in the artifact reflected the preservice teachers' emerging understanding of how to teach science. More specifically, the hypermedia stacks were examined to determine whether the selected representations appropriately reflected various course and program themes, such as accurate and multiple representations of science content, as well as active cognitive and physical student engagement. In addition, we were interested in how the preservice teachers reflected on and synthesized their early science teaching experiences.

### Megan

Megan's hypermedia portfolio is typical of those constructed by many of the preservice teachers in that she stayed primarily within the guidelines of the template with regard to content and organization. Megan used the "All About Me" portion of her stack to explain why she decided to become a teacher. In addition, she noted her participation in the elementary science teacher preparation program and her experience with project-based science. Most of the preservice teachers included similar content on this introductory card.

The Science Autobiography proved to be a key component of the hypermedia artifacts in terms of representing the preservice teachers' emerging understanding of how to teach science. Megan organized her autobiography by constrasting her images of science before her involvement in the program with her present views of teaching science. Her prior ideas about science mirror those of many prospective elementary teachers (Raizen & Michelsohn, 1994). She writes:

> Before the science cohort, science to me meant a bunch of test tubes bubbling with solutions, a white beard scientist in a white lab coat with safety goggles, dissecting a frog, equations, and black lab desks. I never "saw" or experienced science outside of science class.

Megan included a scanned picture that represents this "image" of science with her autobiography (Figure 8). She proceeded by elaborating on her experiences as a learner of science.

> The format of the science education I received before the cohort was basically taught through a textbook and lecture approach. My teachers would lecture during class, and assign chapters to be read and questions to be answered. Then I would be given a formal paper and pencil exam to test my "understanding" of these concepts. I

**FIGURE 8**
Megan's science autobiography.

realized then that I never really learned the material. I read the information, memorized it for the test, and then forgot it all.

Megan's description of her present views of science teaching stands in stark
contrast to her own experience as a learner of science. In her discussion of
her current philosophy, she elaborated on the importance of students as
active participants in the learning process and making science relevant to
students' daily lives. She concluded her autobiography by writing:

The difficult part of teaching is representing content in many different ways through
analogies, examples, demonstrations, experiments, student investigations, discussions, and whatever else seems to work for students. As a teacher, I need to become
aware of how each of my students learns, what my students already know about a
topic, and how I can tell when they have mastered a concept. Because of my experiences in the science cohort, I feel much more comfortable about teaching science. I
want my students to enjoy learning, succeed at learning, and truly understand
science.

These kinds of comments were overwhelmingly characteristic of the other
preservice teachers' views on science and science teaching. Moreover, they
demonstrate the preservice teachers' struggle to depart from the way they
were taught science and adopt course and program philosophies.

The standard template format for semester highlights and the analysis of
questioning and management was a text box for narrative (i.e., description
of highlight and reflections) and space reserved for a corresponding digitized
video clip. Megan, and many of the other students in the class, maintained

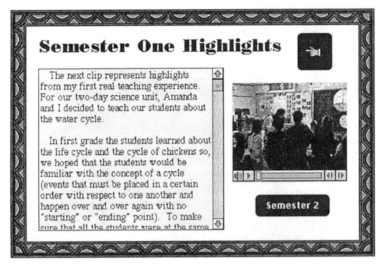

**FIGURE 9**
Megan's highlights of water cycle demonstration.

this structure (Figure 9). In the first semester, Megan and her partner taught two consecutive lessons on the water cycle to a class of 26 second graders. The video clip she included was actually from the second day of instruction when she and her partner demonstrated the water cycle by placing a metal tray filled with ice above a container of boiling water. The emphasis was on the class discussion associated with the demonstration. However, Megan's narrative contextualized the clip by providing an overview of the previous lesson, particularly how cycles were introduced through a small group activity that addressed students' prior knowledge of cycles. Her reflections on the demonstration illustrate her developing understanding of the pivotal role of students' prior knowledge in new learning. She writes:

> This part of the lesson reminded me that students may have prior knowledge and/or prior misconceptions about a topic. Teachers need to be aware that students come into the classroom with a whole suitcase of previous experiences and knowledge, some of which may be inaccurate.

During the second semester, Megan and her partner taught three consecutive lessons about color and light to the same group of second-grade students. To represent this aspect of her artifact, Megan included a brief overview of the content of each of the lessons; however, her in-depth narrative focused on key concepts (i.e., reflection and absorption of light; relationship between light and color) and how they were represented. The video clip Megan selected for this semester was from a class review that took place near the end of the final lesson. The clip shows Megan and her partner conducting a class discussion in which they chose a student from the class and used the example of his sweatshirt to prompt other children to explain why we see the color blue.

Megan's reflections on her second semester teaching experiences emphasized the use of K-W-L. This strategy, which was adopted from reading methods, allows students to begin instruction on a new topic by identifying what they already *know* about the topic (i.e., prior knowledge) and what they *want* to learn about it (i.e., student interest). Instruction on the topic culminates with a discussion about what students have *learned* (i.e., assessment). Megan and her partner had experimented with this approach and found it effective for introducing new content, guiding instruction, and assessing student understanding at the end of their mini-unit. This attempt demonstrates their developing understanding of how to tailor various strategies appropriately for use during science instruction. See Chapter 4 (this volume) where Trowbridge and Wandersee discuss K-W-L as an important theory-driven graphic organizer.

In her analysis of questioning, Megan provided a very thoughtful narrative that addressed how a variety of questions were used to engage all students in thinking about the content. She addressed issues of wait time and open-ended versus dichotomous questions. In particular, she discussed questions that encourage students to make predictions.

> Before we discussed both reflection and absorption [of light], we asked the students: What do you think will happen if we shine a flashlight into a mirror? We wanted to encourage the students to use scientific processes and predict what might happen rather than tell the students what is going to happen.

Megan's discussion of questioning also illustrates that she was interested in listening to students' questions as a way to monitor their learning and encourage participation.

> For clarification, one of the students asked, "If light travels in a straight path, why does it light up the whole room?" I thought this was an excellent question because it showed me that the student was really thinking about the concept and how light travels by trying to apply it to a real life situation.

The video clip that corresponded to the section on questioning captured Megan asking her second-grade students a series of application-type questions associated with light and color. This reflected her attempts to monitor for understanding before proceeding with the lesson.

The final component of the hypermedia artifacts was the section on analysis of management. In her narrative for this segment, Megan discussed much of what she had learned from her interactive teaching experiences and from her cooperating teacher about orchestrating classroom activities. She also pointed out several problems that arose as a result of poorly managed materials and discussed ways to avoid similar issues in the future. In addition, Megan devoted a great deal of attention to management of cooperative groups. She writes:

> Although many teachers have apprehensions about small groups, I have learned that they can be very valuable if they are used properly. Cooperative learning is very important for the development of social skills and communication skills in young children. Many teachers feel that in small groups one person usually pulls the work load for the whole group. To avoid this situation, Amanda and I gave each student a specific role or job in the group. All of the students had to cooperate and collaborate in order to complete the assignment.

Megan illustrated her point about cooperative groups through the use of a video clip taken from her first-semester teaching experience. See Jones and Carter (Chapter 10 in this volume) for a more in-depth discussion of small groups and shared constructions.

## Wayne

In contrast to Megan, Wayne developed a hypermedia artifact that included a number of modifications and additions to the initial framework of the template. While many of the preservice teachers made minor alterations to the original format, Wayne and several other students made major modifications to the template in order to include hypermedia materials that they viewed as relevant to learning to teach science. Some of these changes included the addition of a thematic unit design, links to other science-related experiences (e.g., chemistry project), and a portfolio assessment design. In what follows, Wayne's hypermedia artifact will be reviewed with particular emphasis on how his modifications to the template illustrate his developing understanding of how to teach science.

To the extent that Wayne used the cards included in the initial template, his hypermedia artifact closely resembles Megan's. For example, his Science Autobiography reflects the differences between the way science was portrayed in school and how he has come to view science through his experiences in the elementary science teacher preparation program. Like Megan, Wayne selected the image of the "mad scientist" to represent his early views of science. Interestingly, his image is a personal photograph (Figure 10).

Also similar to Megan's artifact, Wayne described video clips of highlights from his teaching experiences within the context of providing an overview of the entire mini-unit that he and his partner taught each semester. His reflections demonstrate his emerging understanding of many of the same issues mentioned previously, such as the role of prior knowledge in learning new concepts and the importance of hands-on experimentation. Wayne began modifying the template here by building additional links to semester highlight cards in which he displayed photographs of interactive bulletin boards that he and his partner constructed for use during their teaching (Figures 11a and 11b).

**FIGURE 10**
Wayne's science autobiography.

Wayne further modified his hypermedia document by changing the main navigation card for the Personal Case History. In the original template, this card provided the user with the following options: content highlights (from both semesters), analysis of questioning, analysis of management, and home card. Wayne combined his analysis of questioning and management with his semester highlights, eliminating them as separate cards, and added a link to Apprenticeship Teaching. Apprenticeship Teaching is a peer teaching experience conducted in the early phases of the program (Zembal, Blumenfeld, Krajcik, & Palincsar, 1994). It is used to introduce many of the key concepts associated with teaching science, such as how to represent concepts, attend to the needs of learners, and manage organization structures, resources, and time in the interest of effective content representation. Wayne's narrative for this section was as much about the process of preparing for his first experience teaching science content as it was about what he and his partner actually taught. He writes:

> My partner and I, feeling quite confident, requested to present the first lesson. Sure, I had seen plenty of lessons in my 16 plus years of formal schooling, but now the shoe was on the other foot. Just how does one go about teaching? And our lesson was on watersheds!! A what-er-shed?? Research needed to be done . . .
>
> After my partner and I discovered the nature of watersheds (no, it isn't where one keeps the pool supplies . . .), we needed to determine what we wanted the students to learn through the lesson. We identified the general and specific goals and went about searching for ways to represent the content for the learner. Our representations needed to be simple. They needed to be ideas and materials our audience could

a

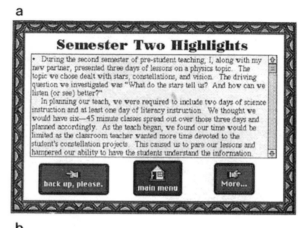

b

**FIGURE 11**

Wayne's second semester highlights. (a) Highlights with template
modifications. (b) Additional card connected to Semester 2.

relate to. The learner needs to be engaged and if he or she had existing schema, we
needed to find a way to exploit that and have the learner connect to it.

The video clip that Wayne selected to represent his Apprenticeship Teaching
experience was drawn from the initial moments of the lesson during which
he introduced the concept of watershed using an analogy that students could
relate to their everyday lives.

Wayne made an even more drastic modification to the original template
with the addition of a section he referred to as "Stretching Out: Examples of
How the Classroom Will Operate." He incorporated this piece by developing
another main navigation card (Figure 12) that was linked back to the main
menu on the title card. This menu allows the user to explore a number of

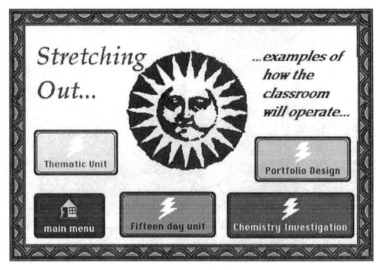

**FIGURE 12**
Wayne's addition to template.

other cards associated with his experiences learning to teach science. Analysis of the additional cards and connections revealed two main themes associated with Wayne's emerging conceptions of how to teach elementary school science. First, Wayne's interest in promoting a question-driven, student-centered approach to science teaching is evident in his selection of an interdisciplinary thematic unit (Figures 13a and 13b), a 15-day project-based science unit design, and a chemistry investigation as representations that he included in his hypermedia document. For instance, the chemistry investigation was adapted from an assignment that Wayne completed in the chemistry content course he took as part of the elementary science teacher preparation program. The final project for this course required students to ask original questions and conduct their own investigations. Wayne was so intrigued with this process that he adapted the investigation for use in an elementary classroom. He writes:

> I feel that this type of assignment is an important educational tool. We all have questions about the world around us, but rarely do we take the time to investigate what fascinates us. This type of assignment also pushes students past a simple textbook understanding of concepts. Natural phenomena move into the classroom and can be investigated in a manner that could teach students to take their own learning a little more seriously. Students can construct their own knowledge, which is much better than a teacher simply telling a student something.

The second theme that emerged from Wayne's additions to his artifact emphasizes his developing interest in authentic forms of assessment. Wayne

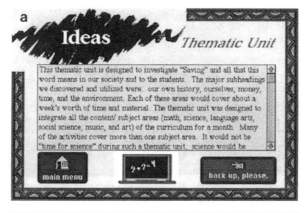

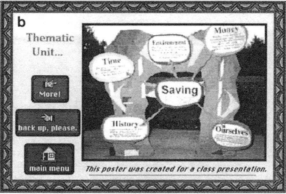

**FIGURE 13**

Examples from Wayne's thematic units. (a) Example from Wayne's "Stretching Out" section. (b) Poster associated with Wayne's thematic unit on "Saving."

devoted an entire section of his hypermedia document to portfolio assessment design ideas in which he addressed the purpose, major educational goals, instructional strategies, methods for collecting information about students, specific artifacts, and assignment criteria associated with the portfolio. In addition, his thematic unit and 15-day project-based science unit included a culminating assessment.

## Discussion

Engaging preservice teachers in the construction of hypermedia artifacts provided them with an opportunity to reflect critically on the key concepts associated with the science methods course and teacher preparation program in which they were enrolled. In addition, they were able to build connections between their developing understanding of these concepts and representations of their initial attempts to teach science to children. This process allowed preservice teachers to become more metacognitive about their own learning.

Although a number of students, like Megan, who merely filled in the existing template with representations, did not build physical connections among representation, they were still challenged to consider the coherence between their emerging beliefs about elementary science teaching and their interactive teaching practices. For example, in the narrative associated with her first-semester highlights, Megan addressed the importance of connecting representations of science content to students' prior knowledge. The video clip that corresponded to this section closely matched this explanation. Such a match suggests that Megan was thoughtful in the selection of her video clip representation of this aspect of science teaching, making the connection between her beliefs and classroom practices.

Preservice teachers, such as Wayne, who made major modifications and additions to the content and organization of the template, were able to engage in the process of building original connections among the representations they selected and included in their hypermedia documents. This offered an even richer and more integrated picture of their developing understanding of how to teach science—one that often demonstrated how experiences outside of science methods were interpreted and integrated. For example, although he addressed the importance of inquiry-based science in the representations he included in the template cards, the depth of Wayne's commitment to this approach was most evident in the "Stretching Out" section he incorporated into his document. He used this section to build connections to relevant experiences outside of the science methods course, like the chemistry investigation, to inform his developing understanding of how student investigations can be a powerful tool in science teaching.

As mentioned previously, the Science Autobiography provided preservice teachers with an important opportunity to reflect on conflicts between their personal experiences as learners of science and their emerging framework for effective elementary science teaching. In both of the examples presented here, as well as the majority of other projects, this section reflected a dramatic shift in emphasis from a view of science that is fact-driven, textbook-based, and often intimidating to a more question-driven, collaborative, and dynamic view of science. The Science Autobiography also allowed preservice teachers to synthesize their experiences and consider how their personal understandings had changed over time as they attempted to articulate their current philosophies of science teaching.

The multiple representations included throughout the preservice teachers' hypermedia artifacts reflect their attempts to adopt various aspects of the framework of the science methods course and the teacher preparation program. In particular, this is demonstrated in their attention to an inquiry-based approach to science, interest in students' prior knowledge, and attempts to make science relevant to students' daily lives. However, it is important to consider that the preservice teachers are still at a relatively early phase of their professional development. Their struggles to put the aforementioned ideas into practice are clearly evident in the video clips they selected to represent their classroom teaching, as well as their written reflections. Nevertheless, engaging in hypermedia artifact construction appears to be a useful tool in assisting preservice teachers in becoming more metacognitive about their own learning experiences, reflecting their emerging understanding of how to teach science.

## CONCLUSIONS

The process of designing, constructing, and revising hypermedia artifacts provides students with the opportunity to represent and explain both scientific phenomena and beliefs about science teaching. In both of the cases presented in this chapter, students decided on what representations to include in their artifacts to best characterize their understandings. The process of building these representations and artifacts provided students with a context to work with and build meaning for the concepts highlighted in their respective courses. The technological affordances provided by the hypermedia software facilitated the construction of multidimensional representations; students in each case used many types of media, including scanned images, drawings, video, text, and graphs, to develop and link ideas. The use of technology, in this way, sets these types of student constructed artifacts apart from other types of artifacts. The use of multiple forms of media allowed students to express their understandings in a number of different ways. The findings from both cases suggest that students build deeper understandings of both scientific phenomena and science teaching by building links, or connections, between these different representations.

The implications of this research for teaching and learning suggest that student construction of hypermedia artifacts appears to be an effective method for encouraging students to build meaningful understanding. Hypermedia artifacts also appear to be an effective form of alternative assessment, where students' understandings can be documented within their artifacts. Teachers and educational researchers can use these student constructed artifacts as a way to identify concepts that are difficult for learners to understand. The concrete products can serve as a medium of exchange between students and teachers or researchers when working to build deeper understandings. Finally, it is apparent that students' understandings develop as they engage in artifact construction and that they need more opportunities to construct meaning in this way.

# References

Ball, D. L. (1989). *Breaking with experience in learning to teach mathematics: The role of a preservice methods course.* Paper presented at the annual meeting of the American Educational Research Association, March, San Francisco, CA.

Ball, D. L. (1990). The mathematical understandings that prospective teachers bring to education. *Elementary School Journal, 90,* 449–466.

Bar, V., & Travis, A. (1991). Children's views concerning phase changes. *Journal of Research in Science Teaching,* 28(4), 363–382.

Benson, D., Wittrock, M., & Baur, M. (1993). Students' preconceptions of the nature of gases. *Journal of Research in Science Teaching,* 30(6), 587–597.

Blumenfeld, P. C., Soloway, E., Marx, R. W., Krajcik, J. S., Guzdial, M., & Palincsar, A. (1991). Motivating project-based learning: Sustaining the doing, supporting the learning. *Educational Psychologist,* 26(3&4), 369–398.

Borko, H., & Livingston, C. (1989). Cognition and improvisation: Differences in mathematics instruction by expert and novice teachers. *American Educational Research Journal, 26,* 473–498.

Brown, A., & Campione, J. (1990). Communities of learning and thinking, or a context by any other name. In D. Kuhn (ed.). *Developmental Perspectives on Teaching and Learning Thinking Skills,* 21, 108–126.

Brown, J. S., Collins, A., & Duguid, P. (1989). Situated cognition and the culture of learning. *Educational Researcher,* 18(1), 32–42.

Calderhead, J. (1989). Reflective teaching in teacher education. *Teaching & Teacher Education,* 5(1), 43–51.

Civil, M. (1992). *Prospective elementary teachers' thinking about mathematics.* Paper presented at the annual meeting of the American Educational Research Association, April, San Francisco.

Cognition and Technology Group at Vanderbilt (1992). Jasper Series as an example of anchored instruction: Theory, program, description and assessment data. *Educational Psychologist,* 27(3), 291–315.

Daiute, C. (1992). Multimedia composing: Extending the resources of kindergarten to writers across the grades. *Language Arts, 69,* 250–260.

Gabel, D., & Bunce, D. (1994). Research on problem solving: Chemistry. In D. Gabel (ed.), *Handbook of research on science teaching and learning.* (pp. 301–327). National Science Teachers Association. New York: Macmillan Publishing Co.

Grossman, P. L. (1989). *The making of a teacher.* New York: Teachers College Press.

Grossman, P. L., Wilson, W. M., & Shulman, L. S. (1989). Teachers of substance: Subject matter knowledge for teaching. In M. Reynolds (ed.), *Knowledge base for the beginning teacher* (pp. 23–36). New York: Pergamon.

Harel, I. (1991). *Children Designers.* Norwood, NJ: Ablex Publishing Corporation.

HyperStudio (1995). El Cajon, CA: Roger Wagner Publishing.

Kagan, D. M. (1992). Professional growth among preservice and beginning teachers. *Review of Educational Research, 62,* 129–169.

Krajcik, J. S., Blumenfeld, P. C., Starr, M. L., Palincsar, A. S., Coppola, B., & Soloway, E. (1993). Integrating knowledge bases: An upper elementary teacher preparation program emphasizing the teaching of science. In Peter Rubba (ed.), *Excellence in educating science teachers.* Columbus, Ohio: AETS Yearbook.

Lee, O., Eichinger, D., & Blakeslee, T. (1993). Changing middle school students' conceptions of matter and molecules. *Journal of Research in Science Teaching,* 30(3), 249–270.

Lehrer, R., Erickson, J., & Connell, T. (1993). The restless text. Student authoring with hypermedia tools. Paper presented at the annual meeting of the American Education Research Association, Learner Interactions in the New Electronic Writing Space. Atlanta, GA, April, 1993.

Linn, M. *International handbook of science education.* Netherlands: Kluwer Publishers. (in press).

Linn, M. & Songer, N. (1991). Teaching thermodynamics to middle school students: What are appropriate cognitive demands? *Journal of Research in Science Teaching*, 28(10), 885–918.

McDiarmid, G. W. (1990). Challenging prospective teachers' beliefs during early field experience: A quixotic undertaking? *Journal of Teacher Education*, 41(3), 12–20.

McDiarmid, G. W., Ball, D. L., & Anderson, C. (1989). Why staying ahead one chapter just won't work: Subject-specific pedagogy. In M. C. Reynolds (ed.), *Knowledge base for the beginning teacher* (pp. 193–205). New York: Pergamon Press.

Nakhleh, M. (1992). Why some students don't learn chemistry. *Journal of Chemical Education*, 69(3), 191–196.

Novak, J. D., & Gowin, D. B. (1984). *Learning how to learn*. Cambridge: University Press.

Novik, S., & Nussbaum, J., (1978). Junior high school pupils' understanding of the particulate nature of matter: An interview study. *Science Education*, 62(3), 273–281.

Novik, S., & Nussbaum, J., (1981). Pupils' understanding of the particulate nature of matter: A cross age study. *Science Education*, 65(2), 187–196.

Osborne, R., & Cosgrove, M. (1983). Children's conceptions of the changes of state of water. *Journal of Research in Science Teaching*, 20(9), 825–838.

Papert, S. (1980). *Mindstorms: Children, computers, and powerful ideas*. New York, NY: Basic Books.

Papert, S. (1991). Situating Constructionism. In I. Harel, (ed.) *Constructionism*. Norwood, NJ: Ablex Publishing Corporation.

Perkins, D. N. (1986). *Knowledge as design*. Hillsdale, NJ: Lawrence Erlbaum.

Raizen, S. A., & Michelsohn, A. M. (eds.) (1994). *The future of science in elementary schools: Educating prospective teachers*. San Francisco: Jossey-Bass Publishers.

Smith, D. C., & Neale, D. C. (1989). The construction of subject matter knowledge in primary science teaching. *Teaching & Teacher Education*, 5(1), 1–20.

Spitulnik, M. W. (1995). Students modeling concepts and conceptions. Paper presented at the National Association for Research in Science Teaching Annual Meeting, April 23, 1995, San Francisco, CA.

Spitulnik, M. W., Stratford, S., Krajcik, J. S., & Soloway, E. Using technology to support students' artifact construction in science. *International handbook of science education*. Netherlands: Kluwer Publishers. (in press)

Starr, M. L., Zembal-Saul, C. M., & Krajcik, J. S. Preparing elementary science teachers: An application of pedagogical content knowledge. In Julie Guess-Newsome (ed.), *Pedagogical content knowledge*. Boston: Kluwer Academic Publishers. (in press)

Stavy, R. (1990). Children's conception of changes in the state of matter: From liquid (or solid) to gas. *Journal of Research in Science Teaching*, 27(3), 247–266.

Weinstein, C. S. (1990). Prospective elementary teachers' beliefs about teaching: Implications for teacher education. *Teaching and Teacher Education*, 6, 279–290.

Zembal, C. M., Blumenfeld, P. C., Krajcik, J. S., & Palincsar, A. S. (1994). Preservice elementary teachers' emerging understanding of how to select, represent, and teach science content. Paper presented at the annual meeting of the National Association for Research in Science Teaching, April, Anaheim, CA.

Zulich, J., Bean, T. W., & Herrick, J. (1992). Charting stages of preservice teacher development and reflection in a multicultural community through dialogue journal analysis. *Teaching and Teacher Education*, 8(4), 345–360.

# CHAPTER 10

# Small Groups and Shared Constructions

M. GAIL JONES

University of North Carolina

GLENDA CARTER

North Carolina State University

The use of student groups in science instruction has continued to grow as educators have been able to identify and understand the processes students use when they work together to develop understandings of science phenomena. Group work has been used in the context of cooperative learning, peer tutoring, laboratory experiences, and collaborative teams. These various instructional groupings differ in distinct ways but share the common thread of student–student discourse that involves sharing ideas, challenging hypotheses, providing assistance, and motivating peers through working together on common learning tasks. This chapter explores the use of instructional groups within a constructivist framework and considers those critical questions outlined in Chapter 2 regarding the nature of knowledge, the roles of teachers and learners, and the organization of classroom experiences.

## WHY USE INSTRUCTIONAL GROUPS IN SCIENCE INSTRUCTION?

The popularity of one grouping strategy, cooperative learning, rose rapidly during the early 1980s as the use of individualized "mastery learning"

*Teaching Science for Understanding: A Human Constructivist View*

declined. Mastery learning was based on behaviorist philosophy of instructional design. Educators eventually realized that what was missing from individualized mastery instruction was the motivational and mediating impact of peer–peer interactions. The cooperative learning movement provided educators with new models that emphasized achievement of objectives (including the use of rewards and recognition for achievement) while also including the diversity of perspectives and learning strategies that group work provides. Educators viewed cooperative learning to be a more efficient way of meeting the wide range of needs of students in a heterogeneous science classroom.

Today there are a wide number of cooperative learning models that extend beyond the original behaviorist instructional frameworks. Research that has emerged from the cooperative learning movement has led us to better understandings of the myriad of complex roles, interactions, and communities that arise when students work together to learn science. Cooperative learning is now viewed as an effective bridge between the traditional narrow focus on achievement and the broader social constructivist view of learning.

In the sections that follow we describe how learning in student groups evolved from Piagetian and Vygotskian theoretical perspectives. We explore knowledge construction when two or more students work together on an instructional task. The roles that students play in dyads and small groups are examined, including how these relationships mediate learning, scaffold the construction of knowledge, and facilitate critical thinking. Finally, the implications of using small groups to create shared meanings and understandings is described, as well as how these communities of learners can be valuable for teachers and educators seeking to reform science education.

## THEORETICAL PERSPECTIVES OF GROUP INSTRUCTION: PIAGET AND VYGOTSKY

The increased popularity of groupwork as an instructional strategy has paralleled the shift in educators' focus from the individual (a Piagetian theoretical perspective) to the larger social context (a Vygotskian theoretical perspective). Piaget's work as a psychologist focused primarily on understanding the cognitive development of the individual. Piaget's theory maintained that the child becomes progressively more social, whereas for Vygotsky the child is social from the start (Tudge & Rogoff, 1989; Tudge & Winterhoff, 1993). Piaget recognized that other individuals can play an important role in promoting one's cognitive growth (Piaget, 1926). From a Piagetian perspective, the greatest advantage of group work is the role that another individual plays in creating a cognitive conflict or dissonance. Piaget noted the power of others in promoting conceptual growth as students disagree about ideas and then subsequently resolve disputes. Piaget argued that as students work through conceptual conflict, the negotiations and the articulation of ideas lead to the development of more complex cognitive constructions (Linn & Burbules, 1993). Piaget's theory also stressed that peer interactions, unlike adult interactions, influence the individual's development of rule-based play and perspective taking (Tudge & Winterhoff, 1993).

Unlike Piaget's focus on the development of the *individual*, Vygotsky was a psychologist whose work focused on the role of *others* in learning. Vygotsky believed that higher mental thinking is a result of social interactions, whereas Piaget focused his research on understanding the sequence of development that takes place within the individual child. While Piaget recognized that children could provide disequilibrium for other children by means of verbal interaction, Vygotsky viewed the child's social world as paramount to the learning process. Vygotsky suggested that all higher mental functions originate as a direct result of interactions between and among individuals. In other words, learning takes place on an interpsychological plane (between people) before it becomes internalized on a personal, intrapsychological plane (within the individual) (Wertsch, 1991).

## SOCIAL MEDIATION OF KNOWLEDGE

Vygotsky described several social mediators of learning, maintaining that the most powerful mediator of learning is language. He recognized that children first imitate the word usage of others without understanding the meaning represented by the words. It is through long-term sociocultural interactions that word usage takes on expanded meaning with a concurrent expansion in conceptual understanding (Dixon-Krauss, 1996). A second critical component of social cognition was described by Vygotsky as the "zone of proximal development." This "zone of proximal development" has been defined in multiple ways, but in essence the phrase refers to the learning potential of the individual when assisted by an adult or more capable peer. Vygotsky argued that our interest as educators should not lie in what we can measure as an individual's past achievement, but instead, our efforts should focus on understanding what the individual can do when provided with assistance from others. His theory focuses on an individual's *potential* for learning. Vygotsky (1978) wrote: "The zone of proximal development defines those functions that have not yet matured but are in the process of maturation, functions that will mature tomorrow but are currently in an embryonic state" (p. 86).

From a Vygotskian perspective the sociocultural nature of learning suggests that work with other individuals is a critical component of the process of knowledge construction. Researchers looking at classrooms through the constructivist lens have reported that the context and the socially-rich environment in which children interpret and solve problems, influences the strategies children select to solve these problems (Girotto & Light, 1993; Saxe, 1992). This is congruent with Vygotsky's (1962) description of the two sources of knowledge in an individual. One source of knowledge comes from interaction with the environment and has been called everyday knowledge, "gut" knowledge, intuitive knowledge, or spontaneous knowledge. This type of knowledge is influenced by peer interactions, language, and experience as the individual attempts to make sense of the environment (West & Pines, 1985). The other source of knowledge is the type derived from formal instruction that occurs in classrooms. Vygotsky concluded that children use their everyday life experiences as well as school experiences to construct meaning. Both types of experiences originate in culture and constructed understanding takes place as children move back and forth through these events in an effort to merge their more formal school experiences with their out-of-school experiences (West & Pines, 1985). In this way the sociocultural environment of both the "everyday world" and the "school world" influences how knowledge will ultimately be constructed.

As Mintzes and Wandersee noted in Chapter 2, in order for learning to be more than rote recall it must be incorporated into the learner's cognitive structure in a nonarbitrary, nonverbatim way. Peer–peer discussion assists the learner in translating new experiences and information into meaningful, nonverbatim learning. Peers assist each other in seeing how new knowledge has potential meaning, a critical component of learning as defined by Ausubel (1963). In fact, Vygotsky argued that peers are sometimes more effective than adults in helping an individual construct meaning because peers are at similar developmental levels. That is, they are in the same zone of proximal development. In the classroom, a peer may be successful in assisting a confused student by rewording the teacher's explanation.

In the sections that follow, Vygtosky's theories are applied to the sociocultural construction of knowledge and the mechanisms students use to assist each other through the concept-building process. A building analogy is useful as we think about ways the learning experience can be structured so that knowledge construction or intellectual growth is possible. The first step in any construction process is contingent upon the blueprint or building plans for construction. In order to participate in the building of a viable structure, the builder must understand the building plan as provided by the architect (the teacher) and have some fundamental idea of how the building task will be accomplished. Within an educational context, the blueprints specify a scries of unified learning tasks that the architect envisions will lead to a useful construction as delineated by preset specifications (i.e., course goals, curriculum guidelines, national standards). The architect must supply blueprints that are intelligible to the builder. That is, the blueprints must include a system of common words and symbols that are used within the building community. A solid foundation is another prerequisite for the building process. Being able to recognize relevant prior experiences as related to the building task at hand provides the learner with this solid foundation. Within the building context there are also construction tools whose usage have been culturally determined. In the science classroom these tools include science equipment used for scientific inquiry. Students must be able to select and utilize the appropriate tools in the knowledge construction process.

Many students come to the construction site deficient in one or more of the skills needed to fully engage in the construction process. Other students can mitigate the impact of these deficiencies by serving in mediating roles during the construction process. Peers can scaffold one another's knowledge construction by serving as a master builder to an apprentice. Peers can also cooperate as cobuilders, working as equal participants to create a product that is better than that which would have been built by either individual alone.

## THE LANGUAGE OF CONSTRUCTION

From a Vygotskian perspective we recognize that students can't engage in the process of constructing knowledge unless they understand the task or blueprint for construction. On the most basic level, in order to construct meaning students must share some common understandings of the words and symbols that are used in the context of the science classroom. These symbols and words are embedded in both our school culture and our science culture. Students who don't understand the language of construction often engage in off-task behavior, focus on trivial aspects of the learning task, and fail to develop viable concepts (Jones & Carter, 1994).

### Verbal Interactions

Verbal mediation of knowledge may come about as a more capable student interprets the directions, defines unfamiliar terms, and functions as a verbal interpreter during discourse. For example, in one class that we observed (Jones and Carter, 1994) two fifth-grade students worked on a series of activities with levers, the goal being to formulate a generalization about how to get a lever to balance. Larry was confused about the task. Billy provided Larry with an interpretation of the plans that allowed Larry to proceed with the building process.

> Larry: Do we place the three blocks on the same side of this thing?
> Billy: No, we are supposed to figure out how to balance these two blocks using this other block.
> Larry: How do we know when its balanced?
> Billy: The lever will be straight out. Neither side of the lever will be touching the table. That means it is balanced.

In this exchange Billy interpreted the written directions of the worksheet, provided the term "lever" to describe the equipment they were using, and explained the meaning of the concept "balance" for Larry.

The verbalization component of peer interaction may be critical for cognitive development even in situations where students are working as co-builders. Peers working together on more equivalent planes have been described by Rogoff (1991) as engaging in participatory appropriation. Participatory appropriation includes "people participating in coherent events (where one could examine each person's contributions as they relate to each other, but not define them separately), and development is seen as transformation. Inherent to the participatory appropriation view is the *mutual* (emphasis added) constitution of personal, interpersonal, and cultural processes, with development involving all planes of focus in sociocultural activity" (Rogoff, 1991, p. 156–157). In this type of peer relationship, there isn't an obvious expert or novice, but instead two or more individuals work together, participating mutually in the learning task as they use common language to create meaning.

Driver (1987) suggested that the exchange of ideas in small groups promotes the development of complex conceptions. Even the process of putting into language one's thoughts may affect cognitive growth. Durling and Schick (1976) reported that college students who vocalized during problem-solving were more successful in concept attainment than were students who did not vocalize. Both Piagetian and Vygotskian theories support the need for verbal reciprocity with peers mutually respecting and attending to the opinions of others (Cannella, 1988).

## Sharing Metaphors and Analogies

Lakoff and Johnson (1980) contend that "any human conceptual system is mostly metaphorical in nature." That is, basic concepts emerge as a result of experiences. As noted in Chapter 7 on analogies by Dagher, these experiences are used to arrange and interpret new experiences. Using metaphors or analogies is one way to create the parallel conceptualizations necessary for conceptual growth (Gurney, 1995). From a Vygotskian perspective, this is another aspect of the reciprocal interweaving process that must take place between everyday experiences and school experiences. Through the use of metaphors and analogies, peers can provide bridges between other students' two intellectual worlds. For example, we observed three fifth-grade boys experimenting with hot and cold water as they worked together exploring patterns related to convection currents. One of the students, James, described a convection current as being like a tornado. He shared this explanation: "Think about when hot air makes a tornado. The hot water in our experiment went up and the cold water went down like in a circle." One of the other boys, Charley, responded: "Oh, like a tornado, now I understand."

In this example, Charley didn't understand how to relate the movement of the warm water in the experiment to the question about defining a convection current until James used the analogy of the tornado. This analogy, like most instructional analogies, is never a perfect conceptual comparison (or the analogy would be the same as the original concept). Analogies promote conceptual understanding by bridging the new concept to a familiar concept. Analogies "help students transfer their existing knowledge to the understanding, organizing, and visualizing of new knowledge. The result is often a high order, relational understanding; that is, the students see how the features of a concept fit together and how the concept in question connects to other concepts" (Glynn, Duit, & Thiele, 1995, p. 255).

Students also spontaneously use metaphors with peers when discussing their ideas about science phenomena. Metaphors contain symbolic similarities to an unfamiliar concept and can promote students' conceptual understandings. Although teachers often use metaphors in instruction, student-generated metaphors can be equally or more powerful. Metaphors that students use often build on their common experiences and can serve as effective tools. When observing pond water, Carol, a middle school student, shared this observation: "Look Marie! It (the protozoan) is a Pac Man eating up that other little guy." For Marie and her partner, the Pac Man metaphor from their experiences playing videogames gave them instant shared understanding of the protozoan's behavior.

## TOOLS OF CONSTRUCTION

The National Science Education Standards (National Research Council, 1996) describe an effective learning environment as one in which the appropriate science tools are available for students to use as they build understandings of science. These tools and their usage are culturally determined by the science community (Brown, Collins & Duguid, 1989). To undertake the building process of a science construction, students must know not only how to choose but how to use the tools provided in the context of scientific inquiry. We have observed that using science equipment for data collection in the science laboratory may be problematic for students for a variety of reasons. Some students have not had many opportunities outside of school to use science-related equipment. Therefore, they do not have necessary prior experiences, nor do they have the psychomotor skills necessary to manipulate the equipment. Unassisted attempts to use the equipment can be intimidating and frustrating for these students. Even students with some prior experience outside of school may have had limited opportunities to use the basic tools of science in elementary school. Therefore, they may have a difficult time using equipment in the context of scientific investigation in later years. On another level, students in an inquiry-based classroom are not only expected to use the equipment but are expected to recognize attributes of objects that makes them useful as tools for collecting data about targeted phenomena. The National Science Education Standards stresses that the use of hands-on activities alone is not sufficient to promote intellectual growth. Unless the tools of science are used appropriately in the knowledge construction process, meaningful learning will not occur.

## Focusing on the Relevant Aspects of Tools

At the most basic level, peers can assist each other by focusing attention on the relevant aspects of science tools. When one student is experienced and familiar with the use of a tool and the other student is not, the dynamics of the learning context may vary according to how the students work together to accomplish the learning task. For example, when first using microscopes students are often more interested in how to tilt the microscope backward, how to spin the mirror, or remove the eyepiece than in using the microscope as a tool to examine small organisms or tissues. The more experienced peer can facilitate the less experienced student's construction of knowledge by helping to focus attention to efficient use of the tool to create meaning; that is, to use the microscope as a tool to develop understandings of a microorganism.

In a study of fifth-grade students (Carter & Jones, 1994), we observed two girls using colored blocks to balance a lever. The less experienced student focused on the color of the blocks as the critical factor that would balance the lever. The more experienced student recognized that the blocks differed in color but were the same weight and, as a result, knew that color would not impact the balancing of the lever. The more experienced girl was able to focus the less experienced student's attention on the distance of the blocks from the lever fulcrum and away from the block color as a significant variable in balancing the lever.

## Selecting and Using the Appropriate Tool

In many laboratory situations tools and their usage are quite clearly specified by the teacher. Students are able to collect data using the tools, but an understanding of the tools remains quite limited. The practice of putting out only the equipment that is needed for a lab may be efficient in terms of time and effort but does not allow students to choose the relevant tools for themselves. An example of this deficit was shared by a high school teacher who was implementing performance assessment. As she observed her students she was amazed to realize that although students had completed a number of prior tasks using balances, graduated cylinders, and overflow cups, when given the opportunity to select the appropriate equipment to make elementary measurements many students were unable to proceed without intervention.

"Tool experts" that emerge in student groups are often able to claim their expertise on the basis of prior experiences. These tool experts determine how the tools are used in the context of data collection. From a Vygotskian perspective these students become the tool experts because they have the "everyday" experience in which to anchor the formal school structured experience. A particularly striking example of this phenomenon was observed in the verbal and nonverbal interactions of a group of ninth-grade students in the context of working through a circuit unit. This particular group was composed of two males and two females of similar abilities and motivation. For most of the activities the males claimed the right to manipulate equipment because they could propose everyday analogies to the science tools. "This is like hooking up the car battery . . . this is like the circuit breaker in my house . . . this is like the light switch at home." Although the females in this group continually made attempts to use the equipment, the males continued to assert their ownership. This ownership was challenged several days into the unit when students were assigned the task of solving an application question about the arrangement of batteries in a golf cart by using bulbs and dry cells. One of the males announced that he didn't know what a golf cart was and therefore couldn't say anything about it. Immediately one of the females declared that her brother had a golf cart and she could help. Then, with a great deal of effort, she removed the "tools" from the resisting males. Despite repeated attempts by the males to reestablish ownership of the equipment, the females claimed ownership for that 1 day and directed the activity.

Tool usage is inherently culturally and contextually determined. The tools that individuals select in their problem-solving process is determined situationally (Girotto & Light, 1993; Saxe, 1992). How students perceive unfamiliar tools is important to the way in which they will use these tools to mediate understanding. Vygotsky concluded that students work out of their everyday life experiences concurrently with the more structured school experiences. If students must have experiences with both the "everyday tools" and the "science tools" in order to mediate understanding, students who can access an analogous "everyday tool" are able to internalize the selection and usage of the science tools to construct understanding. Since many students are deficient in tool use, an important consideration in group selection is structuring the group to include a peer who is more "capable" with tools.

## SCAFFOLDING CONSTRUCTIONS

The metaphor of scaffolding can be used to describe the way in which adults or more capable peers assist other students as they participate in the construction task. Roth (1995) described the task of scaffolding as providing support for any part of the assignment that individuals are unable to carry out on their own. This type of dependent relationship has also been described as an expert–novice or peer-tutoring type of cognitive apprenticeship. Rogoff (1991) defined cognitive apprenticeship as "a plane of community activity involving individuals participating with others in a culturally organized activity that has as part of its purpose the development of mature participation in the activity by the less experienced people" (p. 142). The traditional example of cognitive apprenticeship is seen when a higher achieving student assists a "less able" student in developing understandings of concepts. Therefore, a cognitive apprenticeship is defined by a relationship where one individual possesses more knowledge than the other (Kutnick, 1994).

In the following description of a science lesson that we observed, the actions of two fifth-grade girls illustrate this scaffolding process as they worked together to make sense of a demonstration of convection currents in air. The teacher placed a candle in front of an overhead projector so that the convection currents in the air above the candle were dramatically visible to the class. Anna, one of the students, noted that the wavy pattern visible above the candle was not a shadow. Her partner Nicole, said, "Yes, it is!" To this Anna explained, "No, it's not. It's actually the air moving." Nicole argued that it was a shadow and that when you looked through the flame you could see shadows. In response Anna explained: "No, I don't agree. A convection current is . . . like a cycle through which air moves up and down. Remember in the other experiment we did where we put the food coloring in the cup and it went up over the hot place, when to the top and then went back down after it cooled off? It's that cycle." At this point Nicole was able to make sense of what she had seen and replied, "Oh, it's the same thing, air going up over the candle! We just couldn't see it come back down like we could with the water."

In this excerpt Nicole was guided through the task by Anna who was scaffolding Nicole's understanding. Anna assisted Nicole with her construction of knowledge by clarifying the task. She also helped Nicole link her prior observations of convection currents with the new experience. Without this assistance, it is likely that Nicole may not have been able to integrate the demonstration into her understanding of convection.

In the context of the science classroom, scaffolding can be provided in a number of different ways, depending on the strengths of the peer being assisted. Scaffolding by a more capable peer may involve providing verbal mediation through instruction, providing explanations, supplying relevant metaphors and analogies to promote understanding, linking new ideas with prior knowledge.

## Prior Experiences as Bridges
## for Conceptual Development

As previously described, Vygotsky envisioned the conceptual growth process as an intricately interwoven system by which students make sense of everyday (spontaneous) concepts in terms of school (formal) concepts and school concepts in terms of everyday understanding (Howe, 1996). West and Pines (1985) described this reciprocal process through a metaphor of vine growth. The students' understanding of everyday concepts are represented by a vine

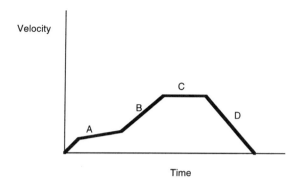

**FIGURE 1**
Students were asked to interpret this graph by writing a story about a student on a bicycle.

growing upward indicating that the growth is promoted by their experiences. Formal concepts are represented by the vine growing downward indicating that the vine doesn't originate from the individual but originates in a top-down fashion. The eventual intertwining of the individual vines into a thick cord represents the formation of a cohesive concept. Connecting relevant prior experiences with new knowledge provides the mechanism by which the vines can intertwine. Consider the following example that took place as two students waited in the school parking lot for their bus. Notice how Betina linked the observed phenomena to prior experiences, bridging understanding for both herself and Sally.

Sally:    It's so hot . . . Look at the steam coming up from the road.
Betina:  It's not steam because the road isn't wet.
Sally:    I still think it's steam.
Betina:  We saw the same thing in class when the teacher put the hotplate in front of
          the screen. Remember? Hot air rising!
Sally:    Oh, so it must be heat.

Prior experiences used in the building process may bridge formal knowledge to everyday phenomena as in the preceding example. In some cases, students are able to offer other students examples from their own common "everyday" experiences. This was observed in a physical science class when a group of students were having a great deal of difficulty interpreting an acceleration graph. The students were given the task of illustrating their interpretation of the graph by writing a story about a student on a bicycle (Figure 1). One of the students, Tina, described a bike path at a nearby park. She noted: "You know where you enter the bike path at the lake? Well, because the entrance is narrow the path is really crowded and you can't get up any speed. So you are just going along at the same speed for a while. This part [pointing to A] shows that velocity isn't changing over time. Then the path gets wider and you come to the top of the hill. You pick up speed going downhill faster and faster. That's what this part of the graph is showing [pointing to B]."

Tina's description of the motion of a bicycle on this trail and the other group members' common experiences with the bike trail mediated their understanding about the meaning of the graph.

## Cognitive Conflict and Conceptual Change

As noted previously, cognitive growth occurs as students try to integrate and make sense of everyday and more formal, school-based knowledge. When these two types of knowledge are in opposition, cognitive conflict occurs. For example, most young people start out thinking that the world is flat by observing the appearance and disappearance of the sun and moon. It is only by formal instruction that the conception of the earth is altered from flat to spherical. Conceptual resolution, or assimilation, occurs as new knowledge is incorporated into a new concept. "Conceptual change views . . . emphasize the transformations of conceptions in the process of learning. New ideas are not merely added to old ones; they interact with them, sometimes requiring the alteration of both" (Strike & Posner, 1985, p. 215).

Research has shown that students often hold a number of naive concepts, or alternative frameworks, that they have developed in an attempt to explain the world around them (Novak, 1987). Cognitive conflict training has been shown to be effective in altering these naive concepts in experimental or quasi-experimental situations, especially for students in transition states between two cognitive structures (Stavy & Berkovitz, 1980). This technique involves exposing the misconception through an "exposing event," creating conceptual conflict, and encouraging cognitive accommodation (Nussbaum & Novick, 1982). For additional information on the role of conflict in learning see Chapter 6 written by Nussbaum.

Posner, Strike, Hewson, and Gertzog (1982) have suggested four prerequisites for conceptual change:

1.  Students must experience dissatisfaction with their current conceptions.
2.  Students must develop a minimal understanding of the concept.
3.  The concept must be plausible.
4.  Students must see the concept as useful in several different situations.

Several research studies have documented the role of dissonance in effecting conceptual change (Jones, 1990; Stavy & Berkovitz, 1980). This dissonance can be promoted by the perspectives of other individuals and can result in cognitive conflict and conceptual change (Cannella, 1988). Peer interactions can be valuable in the conceptual change process (Posner et al.,

1982) by helping students experience dissatisfaction with existing concepts, develop plausible new concepts, and see the relevance of new knowledge in different contexts. This impact of peer interactions was noted previously in the example in which one student's experience with a bike path helped the group understand the relationship between time and velocity as illustrated in Figure 1.

## MONITORING THE CONSTRUCTION PROCESS

Providing students the opportunity to work collaboratively in the science classroom does not ensure individual cognitive growth (Rogoff, 1991). However, research findings in the area of peer collaboration do provide some insights into effective group structuring. For example, it has been reported that effective groups have grounded experiences, share a common language, and are motivated to work together (Dixon-Krauss, 1996). Lumpe and Staver (1995) suggest that cognitive growth is more likely to occur if teachers assign cognitive group roles such as executive, skeptic, educator, and record keeper (Brown & Palinscar, 1986) in place of managerial roles. Vygotskian theory proposes that collaboration will lead to intellectual growth if the learning task is inside of the group's zone of proximal development and there is not too great a discrepancy of cognitive development within a dyad or group (Perret-Clermont, Perret, & Bell, 1991). This means that peer interaction is effective in promoting cognitive growth when students working within one another's proximal zones of development are able to model group behaviors more advanced than those they could perform alone as individuals (Slavin, 1987).

Within a sociocultural context there are many variables that can affect the learning that takes place in a group setting. Recognizing and assessing these factors can assist the classroom teacher in structuring effective learning groups. For example, the type of experience that the students will have may be dependent on group size. Having students work in pairs can be advantageous because each student has a greater opportunity to express ideas verbally. The potential drawback to dyad grouping is that there may be fewer ideas generated within the dyad. In small groups, individual students have a greater opportunity to manipulate equipment and use the tools of science. However, having larger groups increases the chances that the expertise required to accomplish a given assigned task will be available. This availability of expertise can be critical for group construction of knowledge. From our observations of dyad interactions (Jones & Carter, 1994) it is apparent that pairing two students operating at a low cognitive level is not fruitful because there are virtually no cognitive resources available to the pair. If no one in the group can provide the necessary kinds of expertise needed to complete a task, the construction process is suspended.

Therefore when forming groups it is important to consider the many ways in which students can help each other as they work together to construct new concepts. Expertise can fluctuate as students operate at different levels for different parts of the task and at different levels dependent on the content. It is important to note that in some learning situations, the expert can be the lower-ability student. In a previous study of ability-grouped science instruction (Jones & Carter, 1994; Carter & Jones, 1994) we found that in some contexts the lower-ability student was able to quickly pick up a new concept and would teach or serve as the "more capable peer" to the higher-ability student. Because expertise can change as the context changes, the situations in which certain students will excel may be difficult to predict. For example, a ninth-grade physical science student, who had been unable to provide expertise in using laboratory equipment, unexpectedly became the group's tool expert during a circuit unit because of prior experiences with his grandfather's voltmeter.

The social climate of individual groups should also be evaluated. Students that are not accustomed to working together need adequate preparation in order to understand what it means to work together to achieve a common goal. An appreciation for group member contributions and a sense of responsibility to the group fosters an atmosphere where peers can assist one another with learning. One aspect of effective collaboration is that of respectfully listening and evaluating the views of others. In a recent study on peer collaboration we observed that, within the context of one group, a very knowledgeable student's ideas were not accepted by the group and her contributions were discounted. For the next unit she was placed in a different group that perceived her as an expert, her contributions were accepted, and she successfully mediated her own learning as well as the learning of her peers.

The Generative Learning Model proposed by Osborne and Wittrock (1983) suggests that for conceptual change to occur, teachers must ascertain students' ideas prior to instruction, facilitate the exchange of views, and challenge students to compare ideas. In order to design effective instructional groupings, teachers need to assess students' work habits, language development, manipulative skills, social skills, as well as conceptual levels. Preassessment tools such as concept maps, open-ended questions, and interviews can be used to identify an individual's prior experiences, familiarity with targeted concepts, understanding of related scientific terminology, and the presence of naive conceptions. Preassessments that include performance assessments tasks can be used to assess tool usage and identify potential "tool experts." In addition to extensive preassessment for grouping purposes, continuous assessment of group dynamics and interactions must occur if peer interactions are to stimulate cognitive growth. A rubric such as the one shown in Figure 2 can be used to assess the working effectiveness of individual groups. Having students serve as guides or coworkers in the con-

| GROUP #<br><br>Criteria | 3<br>exemplary | 2<br>satisfactory | 1<br>needs<br>improvement |
|---|---|---|---|
| **Cognitive Tasks**<br><br>• identifies problem<br>• recognizes necessary information<br>• makes connections<br>• implements appropriate strategies<br>• interprets data<br>• communicates findings | | | |
| **Psychomotor Tasks**<br><br>• proper use of materials/equipment<br>• all members use materials/equipment<br>• accurate measurement<br>• collection of data<br>• data display | | | |
| **Affective Tasks**<br><br>• members exhibit on- task behavior<br>• members show mutual respect<br>• members encourage mutual<br>  participation<br>• members recognize responsibility for<br>  group learning | | | |

**FIGURE 2**

This rubric can be used to assess group effectiveness.

struction process frees the teacher to conduct this type of on-going, on-site assessment. One elementary teacher found that having students work in groups was not only good for the students, but it also gave her the opportunity to observe the students in a new way.

> It has taken a lot of energy to sit back and let the children work together. It has taken restraint on my part to keep my mouth shut. I am quieter and let the children do the talking. In the past I tried to let my students do activities, but I used to give directions and tell them what to do. I think that the idea that children need to be engaged in groups led me to the idea that they could be more responsible. They could use each other as resources. Many times now I am the last person they come to. It used to be that all the little hands would be up and I would think I was going to go crazy. It took me a while to wean them. Now I get to watch them more than I did in the traditional role. When students take the responsibility for each other's learning I get to watch what they do and hear what they say.

## TEACHING TOMORROW'S STUDENTS: CHANGING DEMOGRAPHICS

The National Science Education Standards calls for teachers to guide and facilitate student learning by orchestrating discourse among students about scientific ideas while recognizing and responding to student diversity and encouraging all students to participate fully in science learning (National Research Council, 1996). The Standards specifically suggest that by "using a collaborative group structure, teachers encourage interdependency among group members, assisting students to work together in small groups so that all participate in sharing data and in developing group reports" (National Research Council, 1996, p. 3).

Although the Standards make a clear recommendation for reform, the reality of putting these recommendations into practice will become an increasing challenge as the demographics of American schools changes over the next 20 years. By the year 2000, it is estimated that minority students will comprise the majority in over 50 major cities throughout the United States and by 2010 almost one out of every three Americans will be nonwhite (Suzuki, 1987). These changing demographics mean that educators who want to teach from a constructivist perspective will have to adopt a variety of strategies to meet their students' diverse needs.

Research has shown that females, African American, and Native American students prefer cooperative small group learning experiences to competitive or individual learning structures (Owens & Barnes, 1982; Owens & Stratton, 1980). In addition, Lew, Mesch, Johnson, and Johnson (1986) found that cooperative learning strategies promoted positive relationships and higher achievement for mainstreamed socially and academically handicapped students.

Although researchers have not fully unscrambled the complex relationships between culture and instructional strategies, small group instruction assists educators in building on diverse views, perspectives, experiences, and skills of students. The roles peers play in promoting cognitive growth of others' which was discussed previously, provide insight into why these strategies are particularly effective for diverse student groups. When students for whom English is not their primary language encounter difficulty, peers can provide the needed verbal assistance. Sharing diverse experiences enriches a group's problem solving and creativity. Complex instructional tasks that involve students working in small groups encourages students to draw on the variety of skills and abilities of each member. A student who has had prior experiences with a microscope, balance, or other science tool can facilitate the other members' knowledge construction. Similarly, a student who has a language disability may be unable to contribute to the written products of the group, but instead may be able to provide artistic or organizational skills to the group's work. If carefully engineered, the diversity of the group can facilitate the construction of meaning that emerges from collaborative inquiry.

# INSTRUCTIONAL GROUPING
# AND THE SCIENCE TEACHER

Even with the wide array of educational advantages we have noted, group instruction can break down at any number of points and be of little value to the learner. Science educators must recognize that when two or more individuals come together for instruction there are complex dynamics and interactions that need careful orchestration. Students' access to power and authority within the group can vary according to a myriad of variables that include gender, race, personality, and socioeconomic-related prior experiences. Although cultural experiences and ethnic perspectives may serve as diverse strengths of the group, without careful monitoring one or more of these variables can isolate and restrict a member's access to materials, ideas, and peer assistance. This can be observed when students prevent others from fully participating in investigations and discussions based on gender, ethnicity, or socioeconomic levels.

In summary, the potential benefits of grouping students for instruction are enormous. Students who work together are generally more successful than students who work alone (Ames & Murray, 1982; Dansereau, 1988; McDonald, 1985). Small groups provide opportunities for students to share ideas and experiences, argue hypotheses, and develop understandings of different perspectives. Peers can mediate each other's learning in ways that are distinctly different from the teacher's methods. As noted earlier in this chapter, peers can provide cognitive conflict that can promote reconstruction of another person's knowledge. Peers can assist each other in the planning and execution of science investigations. One peer may help another as they collaboratively select and use the tools of science to collect and analyze data. When a student encounters difficulty, one student can scaffold, or provide additional structure, to the learning task to make it accessible for the other student to use in building understandings. The verbalizing of ideas and strategies that takes place as students work together has been shown to be of benefit as a mediator of learning. Additionally, group instruction is very useful in helping students learn to value each other's talents, abilities, skills, and diversity of views. Small instructional groups can help us meet the goals set out in the National Science Education Standards for *everyone*:

> To use scientific information to make choices that arise everyday.
> To be able to engage intelligently in public discourse and debate about important issues that involve science and technology. And . . .
> To share in the excitement and personal fulfillment that can come from understanding and learning about the natural world.
>
> (National Research Council, 1996, p. 1)

# References

Ames, V., & Murray, F. (1982). When two wrongs make a right: Promoting cognitive change by social conflict. *Developmental Psychology*, 18, 894–897.

Ausubel, D. P. (1963). *The psychology of meaningful verbal learning*. NY: Holt, Rinehart and Winston.

Brown, A., & Palinscar, A. (1989). Guided, cooperative learning and individual knowledge acquisition. In L. Resnick (ed.), *Knowing, learning, and instruction: Essays in honor of Robert Glaser*. Hillsdale, NJ: Erlbaum.

Brown, J., Collins, A., & Duguid, P. (1989). Situated cognition and the culture of learning. *Educational Researcher*, 18(1), 32–42.

Cannella, G. (1988). *The nature of dyadic social interaction producing cognitive growth in young children*. Paper presented at meeting of the American Educational Research Association, April, New Orleans, LA.

Carter, G., & Jones, M. G. (1994). Relationship between ability-paired interactions and the development of fifth graders' concepts of balance. *Journal of Research in Science Teaching*, 31(8), 847–856.

Dansereau, D. (1988). Cooperative learning strategies. In C. E. Weinstein, E. T. Goetz, & P. A. Alexander (eds.), *Learning and study strategies: Issues in assessment, instruction, and evaluation* (pp. 103–122). New York: Academic.

Dixon-Krauss, L. (1996). *Vygotsky in the Classroom: Mediated literacy instruction and assessment*. White Plains, NY: Longman Publishers.

Driver, R. (1987). Promoting conceptual change in classroom settings: The experience of the children's learning in science project. In J. Novak, (ed.), *Proceedings of the 2nd international seminar "misconceptions and educational strategies in science and mathematics"* (Vol. I., pp. 26–31). Ithaca, NY: Cornell University.

Durling, R., & Schick, C. (1976). Concept attainment by pairs and individuals as a function of vocalization. *Journal of Educational Psychology*, 68(1), 83–91.

Glynn, S., Duit, R., & Thiele, R. (1995). Teaching science with analogies: A strategy for constructing knowledge. In S. Glynn & R. Duit (eds.), *Learning science in the schools: Research reforming practice* (pp. 247–243). Mahwah, NJ: Lawrence Erlbaum.

Girotto, V., & Light, P. (1993). The pragmatic basis of children's reasoning. In P. Light & G. Butterworth (eds.), *Context and cognition: Ways of learning and knowing*. Hillsdale, NJ: Lawrence Erlbaum.

Gurney, B. (1995). Tugboats and tennis games: Preservice conceptions of teaching and learning revealed through metaphors. *Journal of Research in Science Teaching*, 32(6), 569–583.

Howe, A. (1996). Development of science concepts within a Vygotskian framework. *Science Education*, 80(1), 35–51.

Jones, M. G. (1990). *Cognitive Conflict and Cooperative Learning*. Paper presented at the National Association for Research in Science Teaching Annual Conference, April, Atlanta, Georgia.

Jones, M. G., & Carter, G. (1994). Verbal and nonverbal behavior of ability-grouped dyads. *Journal of Research in Science Teaching*, 31(6), 603–619.

Kutnick, P. (1994). Use and effectiveness of groups in classrooms: Towards a pedagogy. In P. Kutnick and C. Rogers (eds.), *Groups in schools* (pp. 13–33). London: Cassell.

Lakoff, G., & Johnson, M. (1980). *Metaphors we live by*. London: Chicago: University of Chicago Press.

Lew, M., Mesch, D., Johnson, D., & Johnson, R. (1986). Components of cooperative learning: Effects of collaborative skills and academic group contingencies on achievement and mainstreaming. *Contemporary Educational Psychology*, 11, 229–239.

Linn, M., & Barbules, N. (1993). Construction of knowledge and group learning. In K. Tobin (Ed.), *Practice of constructivism in science education* (pp. 91–119). Washington, DC: AAAS.

Lumpe, A., & Staver, J. (1995). Peer collaboration and concept development: Learning about photosynthesis. *Journal of Research in Science Teaching*, 32(19), 71–98.

McDonald, B. (1985). Cooperative dyads: Impact on text learning and transfer. *Contemporary Educational Psychology*, 10, 369–377.

National Research Council (1996). *National Science Education Standards*. Washington, DC: National Academy Press.

Novak, J. (ed.) (1987). *Proceedings of the second international seminar: Misconceptions and educational strategies in science and mathematics*. Ithaca, NY: Cornell University.

Nussbaum, J., & Novick, S. (1982). Alternative frameworks, conceptual conflict and accommodation: Toward a principled teaching strategy. *Instructional Science*, 11, 183–200.

Osborne, R., & Wittrock, M. (1983). Learning science: A generative process. *Science Education*, 67(4), 489–508.

Owens, L., & Barnes, J. (1982). The relationships between cooperative, competitive, and individualized learning preferences and students' perceptions of classroom learning atmosphere. *American Educational Research Journal*, 19(2), 182–200.

Owens, L., & Stratton, R. (1980). The development of a co-operative, competitive, and individualized learning preference scale for students. *British Journal of Educational Psychology*, 50, 147–161.

Perret-Clermont, A-N., Perret, J-P., & Bell, N. (1991). In L. Resnick, J. Levine, & S. Teasley (eds.), *Socially shared cognition* (pp. 41–62). Washington, DC: American Psychological Association.

Piaget, J. (1926). *The language and thought of the child*. New York: Harcourt Brace.

Posner, G., Strike, K., Hewson, P., & Gertzog, W. (1982). Accommodation of a scientific conception: Toward a theory of conceptual change. *Science Education*, 66(2), 211–227.

Resnick, L. (1991). Shared cognition: Thinking as a social practice. In L. Resnick, J. Levine, & S. Teasley (eds.), *Socially shared cognition* (pp. 1–22). Washington, DC: American Psychological Association.

Rogoff, B. (1991). Social interaction as apprenticeship in thinking: Guided participation in special planning. In L. Resnick, J. Levine, & S. Teasley (eds.), *Socially shared cognition* (pp. 349–364). Washington, DC: American Psychological Association.

Roth, W. (1995). *Authentic school science: Knowing and learning in open laboratories*. Dordrecht, Netherlands: Kluwer Academic Press.

Saxe, G. (1992). Studying children's learning in the context: Problems and prospects. *The Journal of the Learning Sciences*, 2(2), 215–234.

Slavin, R. (1987). Developmental and motivational perspectives on cooperative learning: A reconciliation. *Child Development*, 58, 1161–1167.

Stavy, R., & Berkovitz, B. (1980). Cognitive conflict as a basis for teaching quantitative aspects of the concept of temperature. *Science Education*, 64(5), 679–692.

Strike, K., & Posner, G. (1985). A conceptual change view of learning and understanding. In L. West & A. Pines (eds.), *Cognitive structure and conceptual change* (pp. 211–231). New York: Academic Press.

Suzuki, B. (1987). *Cultural diversity: Increasing achievement through equity*. Paper presented at the Los Angeles Multicultural Conference, October, Los Angeles, CA.

Tudge, J., & Rogoff, B. (1989). Peer influences on cognitive development: Piagetian and Vygotskian perspectives. In M. H. Bornstein & J. S. Bruner (eds.), *Interaction in human development* (pp. 17–40). Hillsdale NJ: Lawrence Erlbaum.

Tudge, J., & Winterhoff, P. (1993). Vygotsky, Piaget, and Bandura: Perspectives on the relations between the social world and cognitive development. *Human Development*, 36, 61–81.

Vygotsky, L. (1962). *Thought and language*. Cambridge, MA: MIT Press.

Vygotsky, L. (1978). *Mind and society*. Cambridge, MA: Harvard University Press.

Wertsch, J. (1991). *Voices of the mind*. Cambridge, MA: Harvard University Press.

West, L., & Pines, A. (eds.) (1985). *Cognitive structure and conceptual change*. New York: Academic Press.

CHAPTER

# 11

# Interactive
# Historical Vignettes

JAMES H. WANDERSEE
*Louisiana State University*

LINDA M. ROACH
*Northwestern State University of Louisiana*

## WHAT DOES THE TERM
## "NATURE OF SCIENCE" MEAN?

Just what is the *nature of science*? Don't expect agreement (either within or between groups) if you ask philosophers of science, historians of science, sociologists of science, or science educators. Then, can't we just ask some scientists? (After all, they are the ones who *do* science every day.) Unfortunately, today's busy scientists often have little time to reflect on such issues and, furthermore, most see little practical value in doing so. This is not to say that there are not many fascinating and helpful books addressing aspects of the nature of science, books by each kind of specialist just mentioned— including some introspective scientists. However, no one has a perfect understanding of the nature of science—that is a lifetime project, not an endpoint.

In addition, these academic communities are gradually coming to realize that, in some ways, the nature of science may be too all-encompassing a construct—that it may be more accurate to speak of the nature of biology, for example, than to speak of the nature of science *in toto* (Rosenberg, 1985). They are coming to realize that what used to be called the history of science was predominantly the history of physics—the presumed prototypical science that all others should emulate (Mayr, 1988). Now, each branch of science is more likely to be considered independently and within the context of the kinds of problems it addresses.

For our purposes in this chapter, we define the nature of science as discipline-specific knowledge of the natural objects, events, and properties to be studied, the presuppositions and assumptions about them, the theories used to decide what the important unresolved questions are, the methods and instruments the discipline employs to gather valid and reliable data, the habits of mind associated with practitioners of the discipline, the kinds of knowledge and value claims that typically are made, the ways in which such claims are adjudicated by that community of scholars, and what constitutes "progress" in that scientific discipline.

Thus, in applying our definition, it is possible for a student to enroll in a particular science course, memorize a teacher-selected set of scientific information, and find answers to exercises (routinized problems) using traditional instructional algorithms, yet have virtually zero knowledge of the nature of that science! We see such instruction as both tragic and woefully inadequate—at best, it is mere *training*, rather than *education* in that science. It is limited knowledge with a short shelf life and near expiration date. In short, it is both less meaningful and less generative than we would recommend. Duschl (1990) calls such science teaching the presentation of *final form science* and warns of its dangers: namely, (1) all knowledge claims may be treated as equal; (2) knowledge claims may be decontextualized; and (3) theory change in science may be inaccurately portrayed. In contrast, we see a sound understanding of the nature of science as a more durable *meta*knowledge about a particular science—knowing both what that science knows and how that science knows what it knows.

## WHAT IS THE ROLE OF THE NATURE OF SCIENCE IN CONTEMPORARY SCIENCE TEACHING?

While there have always been some science educators who advocated incorporating perspectives from the histories and philosophies of science into science teaching, their numbers have been growing of late. There have been three major, recent international conferences on the use of history and philosophy of science in science teaching (now abbreviated HPSST, formerly HPS or HPST). These were held in 1989, at Florida State University; in 1992, at Queen's University in Kingston, Ontario (Canada); and in 1995, near the campus of the University of Minnesota. We have attended and presented papers at all of these conferences. Large volumes of scholarly proceedings were generated by each conference and the next one [at this writing], to be held at the University of Calgary in the summer of 1997, promises to be no different. These published conference proceedings offer a finely sculpted portal into the work of the HPSST movement (Finley, Allchin, Rhees, & Fifield, 1995a,b; Herget, 1989, 1990; Hills, 1992a,b). They also represent a significant amount of scholarly work; we weighed the six volumes and found they totaled 16 pounds! Factor in Duschl's (1994) panoramic Chapter 15 in the *Handbook of Research on Science Teaching and Learning*, plus the special issues of the *Journal of Research in Science Teaching* (the April, 1992 issue) and *Science Education* (the January, 1991 issue) devoted to this topic and you have the beginnings of a significant corpus.

The members of this international scholarly community also support a journal called *Science & Education*, which is published by Kluwer Academic Publishers (based in the Netherlands) and is edited by Professor Michael R. Matthews, University of New South Wales, Australia. One of the authors of this chapter has been a member of that journal's editorial board since its inception and we can both attest to the quality of the articles it contains. It is, however, challenging reading that deals with substantive content issues and is not intended to be an HPSST *teaching* journal. The latter is a need that remains unfulfilled at this writing.

If we had to choose one person who personifies the HPSST scholarly community and has done more than anyone else to breathe life into it and keep it flourishing, it would be Professor Michael R. Matthews. Besides serving as journal editor, Matthews has edited/written two important books that we think all who wish to understand the contributions HPSST can make to science education ought to read. They are: *History, Philosophy, and Science Teaching: Selected Readings* (1991) and *Science Teaching: The Role of History and Philosophy of Science* (1994).

In the first article in the first issue of the first volume of *Science and Education*, Matthews (1992) explains why history and philosophy of science is useful for teaching school science. The title of his article is: "History, Philosophy, and Science Teaching: The Present Rapprochement." The "rapprochment" (i.e., establishment of cordial relations) to which Matthews refers is the inclusion of HPSST in the national curricular reforms of school science taking place worldwide. We have constructed a concept map that sets forth some (but not all) important propositions we have extracted from that article (see Figure 1). The reader who is unfamiliar with concept maps should be aware that such maps are to be read from the top down, one branch at a time.

A major component of science education reform is teaching the nature of science (AAAS, 1993; NRC, 1996; Rutherford & Ahlgren, 1990). This is not a new idea (Duschl, 1994). For example, in 1951, Conant recommended providing nonscience majors with an understanding of science, and furthermore, he suggested using histories of science as tools for accomplishing this task. In 1954, Wilson advocated the teaching of the attitudes of scientists to college nonscience majors. These sentiments were echoed in scholarly

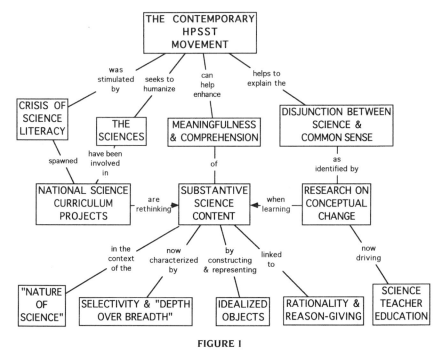

**FIGURE 1**
Concept map of propositions that the authors extracted from editor M. R.
Matthews' introductory article for issue 1(1) of *Science & Education*.

publications by Klopfer in 1969, by Anderson in 1978, by Shahn in 1988, by
Duschl in 1990, by Brown in 1991, by Matthews in 1992, and by Roach and
Wandersee in 1993.

Despite these continuing calls to action, Ray (1991) and Bybee, Powell,
Ellis, Giese, Parisi, and Singleton (1991) reported that there were few curriculum materials available and few projects actively engaged in developing
materials to achieve these propositions. This finding was confirmed at a
higher level of generality by Dr. Albert Shanker (1996), the late president of
the American Federation of Teachers, who complained that reforms recommended by the educational research community often fail to deal with the
realities of classroom instruction.

We have noticed that many science teachers, who are themselves products of a university system which values scientific knowledge more than the
history and philosophy of science, show the same lack of understanding of
the nature of scientific knowledge that scientists do. Perhaps an analogous
observation is that great players of a sport seldom make the best coaches of
it—they "do what they do" almost implicitly.

However, our epistemological studies (Abrams & Wandersee, 1995a,b), historical analysis (Wandersee, 1992), and educational research (Wandersee 1986a) indicate that there is a relationship between how *scientific communities* and *science students* construct increasingly more powerful models of how the world works (over time). Wandersee (1986a) provided evidence of this in a benchmark, cross-age study that compared over 1400 U.S. elementary, secondary, and tertiary students' understanding of photosynthesis with the historical milestones of scientists' progress in understanding plant nutrition. Some noteworthy parallelism was detected. This does not mean that science learners recapitulate the historical development of scientific concepts as their understanding of them grows, he points out, but it does indicate that becoming familiar with the cognitive barriers encountered by scientists of the past may serve as a heuristic device for anticipating the instructional barriers faced by, and the alternative conceptions (a.k.a. misconceptions) held by, some of today's science students. Thus, this study represents an uncommon link of research to teaching, and it proposes a new application of history and philosophy of science in science teacher education.

Roach (1993) reports that numerous studies provide evidence that teachers themselves do not understand the nature of science. This raises an important question: How can a science teacher teach what he/she does not fully understand? If teachers are to actualize the reform goals, they must understand not only what scientists know, but also how science works—and we think they ought to use research-tested instructional tools appropriate for this new task.

The American Association for the Advancement of Science (AAAS, 1990) has defined *science literacy* to include a basic understanding of the nature of science—which it divides into (1) the scientific world view, (2) scientific methods of inquiry, and (3) the nature of the scientific enterprise.

The AAAS (1990) proposes that the scientific enterprise may be best illustrated by using historical examples of exceptional significance to the development of science (e.g., the clockwork universe, plate tectonics). We heartily concur, although we think there is merit in moving the student's gaze beyond what Kuhn (1970) called historical cases of *revolutionary science*, toward important but more evolutionary-than-revolutionary histories of science. In addition, we think that the history of science can *also* be used to teach the scientific worldview—primarily, by providing relevant examples of scientists who demonstrated it via their life histories.

In contrast, we have noted that many existing curriculum materials that address the nature of science misrepresent it as inherently positivistic; this essence is sustained by teaching practices such as "cookbook" laboratory activities and finding the predetermined correct answer to a so-called "experimental" activity. Even science fairs reinforce this outdated, positivistic view of science (cf., the critical research study on science fairs published by C. L. Cummins [1995]). Students who follow the recipe-like "scientific method" of stating the problem, formulating a hypothesis, doing a controlled experiment, confirming or rejecting the hypothesis, and drawing a valid conclusion are rewarded with first-place ribbons—while students who perform exploratory or naturalistic, observation-based research usually go home empty-handed.

The imagination of research design and the excitement of discovery is also diminished by science teachers who offer mindless, step-by-step, failure-free laboratory activities intended to verify the teacher's lectures (such activities become merely an expensive, time-consuming, expectation-laden "See, I *told* you so!"). No wonder students are opting out of elective science courses or jettisoning their intended science majors at their earliest opportunity (Seymour & Hewitt, 1997).

Stinner (1989) contends that we must provide students with insights into how people such as Galileo and Einstein used intuition and imaginative processes to help them make breakthroughs in science. In so doing, students need to have some understanding of the cultural and political temperaments of their time in order to fully understand that science is an integral part of society (Roach, 1993).

For example, if the preeminent physics genius Albert Einstein (1879–1955) had not been Jewish, he might have remained in Germany and the outcome of World War II may even have been different. Since he was a Jew, he fled Nazi Germany and immigrated to the United States, taking with him his scientific knowledge and his brilliant thoughts as well. Most of today's science students have no idea that Einstein was a political activist or that he had profound thoughts about science and religion, for instance. Yet he published countless articles in *Mein Weltbild* of Amsterdam, providing us with his thinking about international cooperation, world peace, the atomic bomb, and economic crisis leading up to WWII. For example, Einstein wrote that because the scientist is possessed by the sense of universal causation . . . his religious feeling takes the form of utter amazement at the harmony of natural law. Thus, we claim that if you want to fully understand a scientist's scientific accomplishments, you must not fail to factor in the variables of historical context and circumstance.

And, while Einstein's name is almost synonymous with science to today's students, a talented female contemporary of his, physicist Lise Meitner (1878–1968), is not. It is safe to assume that virtually none of your students will know of her or her contributions to science. Why that is so is also revealing of the current limited curriculum inclusion of history and philosophy of science. Meitner, also a brilliant Jewish (female) physicist at the time of Hitler's regime who was forced to flee Germany and immigrated to Sweden, made significant contributions to our understanding of uranium fission—publishing the first scientific report about it and, later, winning a share of the 1966 U.S. Atomic Energy Commission's Fermi Award—the first woman ever to do so. It is sad (but important, we think) to note (from a gender-bias perspective) that, in Germany, Nobel laureate Emil Fischer allowed Lise Meitner to work for him *only* if she promised never to enter a laboratory where males were working (Asimov, 1972)! Her devotion to science was total; nearly all of her years were spent pursuing an understanding of the physical world. Why have science textbooks failed to reveal the stories of quests for knowledge in the natural sciences and the historical trails of such inquiry, choosing only to present the resulting intellectual products in print? Simplification of a subject for instruction purposes is good only if it does not omit information vital for knowledge construction by the learner. By skipping ahead to the ending, the story becomes meaningless; to the learner, science becomes what Joseph J. Schwab has called a *rhetoric of conclusions* (Schwab & Brandwein, 1962, p. 24).

## WHAT ARE INTERACTIVE HISTORICAL VIGNETTES (IHVs)?

Wandersee has demonstrated a sustained interest in using history of science to teach science (Abrams & Wandersee, 1995a,b; Good & Wandersee, 1992, in press; Trowbridge & Wandersee, 1995, 1997, in press; Wandersee, 1981, 1983, 1985, 1986a,b, 1987, 1990a,b, 1992, 1995).

In 1989, at the first International Conference on History and Philosophy in Science Teaching held in Tallahassee, Florida at Florida State University, Wandersee (1990a,b) introduced his instructional technique of *constructing historical vignettes*. Immediately after his conference presentation, he was greatly encouraged by the supportive comments of the noted physics educator Arnold Arons about the promise of the technique, and because of Arons' remarks that day, Wandersee has continued to develop and expand it.

Wandersee invented interactive historical vignettes in 1989 in response to a problem voiced by science teachers enrolled in one of his graduate-level science education courses at Louisiana State University: "How can we incorporate the history of science into the science courses we teach when our curriculum guides already mandate such a large amount of science content that we can barely address it?" His answer: Administer a carefully chosen "slice" of the history of science (now called an IHV), present it in an interactive way, design and use each IHV to illustrate a single aspect of the nature of science, and spend only 10–15 minutes of class time on each one, but do it, once every week, without fail, throughout the science course. In addition, always tell students where they can read more about the central characters of each vignette if they want to dig deeper into this historical case. He hypothesized that the effectiveness of spaced practice and periodic reflection about the personal challenges and intellectual roots of the science they are studying would combine to leave a lasting impression in the science student's long-term memory after the course was finished. Later, Roach (1992), in collaboration with Wandersee, advanced these ideas by writing what has proven to be a popular book of 36 vignettes for high school science teachers (one for each week of the school year) and conducting an important study of their educational impact on university "Introductory Physical Science" students (1993).

After initial collaboration with Linda Roach, at that time a Ph.D. student in science education at Louisiana State University, the two (hereafter referred to as "we") have worked to improve and provide examples of that approach, now called the interactive historical vignette (IHV). We have developed the IHV concept (etymology of vignette: French for "little vine") to make our vignettes orally presented, docudramatic, attention-span considerate, incident-driven, and audience interactive. Every IHV incident is based on an actual historical predicament extracted the life of a real scientist but the dramatization speaks to contemporary youth. Recent research indicates that, when used throughout an existing science course on a weekly basis, interactive historical vignettes help to accomplish the nature of science goals set forth in the science education reform literature (Roach, 1993).

The science education literature has established the need for development of curriculum materials to facilitate the balanced inclusion of histories of science in existing science courses for nonscience majors in order to teach the nature of science (Roach, 1993). Duschl (1990) recommends that at least one content-related, history-of-science unit be designed for insertion into each existing science course. These units are to be intensive and focus on a particular aspect of the nature of science, using history to demonstrate key points. It is, indeed, reasonable to anticipate that the student will assume there are similar, existing, detailed historical accounts for the other science topics in the course—but time precludes their consideration in a science course. However, our concern is that pupils' memories are short and that large-interval time spacing of instructional events may not yield a discernible pattern for human cognition to detect.

In contrast to the single, major, annual transfusion approach, occasional, "boxed," history-of-science-based essays are not uncommon in contemporary science textbooks and vignettes from histories of science may be found in such journals as *Science* and the *Journal of College Science Teaching*. The term "vignette" has recently acquired a certain cachet and apparently comes to terms with the fact that few readers, learners, or even science teachers will spontaneously "devour" entire histories of science. When we first began using the term, it was rarely used in science education. Now, it has become synonymous with "little science stories" that are easier to read.

The fact remains that many students do not even read what is assigned by the teacher—much less the extraneous copy placed outside the text stream in their textbooks. In addition, the content of the other kinds of vignettes typically has no nature-of-science focus—often it meanders between scientific repartee and scientific aphorism. In contrast to the reading habits of science aficionados, most students have no strong intellectual appetite to partake of such historical tapas buffets—even though they (the textbook vignettes) are, admittedly, lighter and "less filling" than six-course meals (scholarly, history-of-science tomes).

As we have worked with the IHV strategy, we have labored under the assumption that *Mooer's Law of Information Retrieval* (Garfield, 1997) also holds for science students: It is the *quality* of the information, not the *quantity* of the information that makes a difference—"the more relevant the information [we choose to share with them]. . . , the more it will be used" (p. 9).

Figure 2 shows a process diagram of our current strategy for teaching the nature of science (NOS) using interactive historical vignettes (IHVs). Note that key features of the process that differentiate it from conventional historiography include: (1) choosing a scientist of personal interest to the vignette's author and audience; (2) gaining multiple historical perspectives of the chosen scientist; (3) selecting a pivotal incident in the life of that scientist that has potential for teaching an aspect of the nature of science (or of *a particular* science); (4) writing the IHV in a standard format in docudrama style; (5) letting students make a personal intellectual investment in the vignette by predicting how the story will end; then (6) telling the rest of the story and discussing how the NOS aspect(s) that emerged from guided discussion of how the IHV relates to contemporary science.

We have developed a (nonexhaustive) list of critical attributes of scientific thought that we use as a heuristic for historical incident selection and development of nature-of-science IHVs (Good & Wandersee, 1992; Schrock, 1989). We agree that there are exceptions to all of these attributes, but we think that higher learning always involves further elaboration and differentiation of basic propositions that one learns in any introduction to a topic area. We are currently in the process of making a detailed comparison of the list items to the contents of the National Science Education Standards (NRC, 1996) and Benchmarks for Science Literacy (AAAS, 1994). However, we anticipate that many of the following attributes listed here that we have found useful for IHV construction in the past will remain unchanged after that comparison:

1. Empiricism
2. Determinism
3. Belief that problems have solutions
4. Parsimony
5. Ruling out of possible causes
6. Skepticism
7. Precision
8. Respect for what science already knows
9. Respect for the power of theory
10. Willingness to change one's opinion

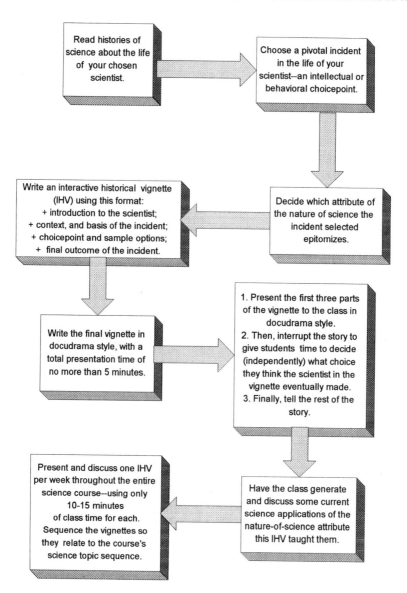

**FIGURE 2**

Process diagram explaining how to teach the nature of science using interactive historical vignettes. (© 1997, Wandersee & Roach.)

11. Loyalty to evidence
12. Preference for scientific explanations of natural phenomena over supernatural explanations
13. Thirst for knowledge
14. Suspended judgment
15. Awareness of one's assumptions
16. Ability to tease apart fundamental concepts
17. Respect for quantifying and measuring
18. Appreciation of probability and statistics
19. Understanding all knowledge has limits
20. Empathy for the human condition

Once the teacher has presented a series of IHVs to the science class across the first month of the course, we have found it may be appropriate to ask the students to construct their own vignettes (aligned with the course objectives), using the standard IHV format, with the resulting vignettes to be presented before the entire class. In this case, it is important to provide a hand-out explaining the IHV format and a sample reading list drawn from available library resources, both to provide some initial structure and to make it easier for students to begin. We have found that videotapes of exemplary presentations of IHVs done by previous students also help to convey the ideas of structure, content, and flow of an IHV.

The cummulative experience of one teacher who has tried this (the chemistry and physics instructor at Louisiana State University's Laboratory School, Helen Headlee) has been that students not only are capable of doing so, but enjoy such intellectual inquiry immensely. In fact, the same students who had constructed and presented IHVs when enrolled in her junior-level chemistry course asked her at the beginning of the following school year if they could do it again in her senior physics course, because, they said, it helped them to get interested in and to better understand the science content.

While some of Ms. Headlee's students prepared costumes and scientific props for use in their vignette presentations and even videotaped them for posterity, not all students may be so highly motivated or have the resources to do that. In order to provide a less artistically demanding alternative, we have proposed that students make and use large IHV character masks (see Figures 3–7 for photographs of actual IHV presenters using home-made IHV character masks to create an exotic character environment for their in-class, docudramatic narratives).

The character masks are made from large ($\sim3 \times 3$ ft.) stiff pieces of corrugated cardboard (or foamboard from an art supply store) on which an enlarged photocopy of a drawing or photograph of the head and shoulders of scientist is glued. (Copy shops have special photocopiers [zoomers] capable of making large copies or a conventional enlarging photocopier can be

**FIGURE 3**
An IHV character mask and costume presentation by a teacher and students
from an all-girl school in the deep south. Subjects, from left to right:
scientists R. Franklin, F. Crick, J. Watson, and M. Wilkins. Note how tiny the
openings on the mask are and that it is held by handles in the back.

used to enlarge sections of the scientist's head and shoulders and these
sections can then be pasted together somewhat seamlessly. Inconspicuous
eye, nose, and mouth openings are cut-out of the image so the presenter
can see, breathe, and talk through the openings in the cardboard, while
grasping the cardboard on its sides with his/her hands. Our students have
also enjoyed adding wigs, stethoscopes, binoculars, neckties, and so forth to
the surface of their two-dimensional poster to make it somewhat three-
dimensional. We have recently found that costumes or IHV character masks
are very important in lowering the inhibitions of presenters who may be
hesitant about facing their classmates and/or portraying a scientist. With the
character masks, students arrive in the classroom eager to impress their
peers and surpass previous masks. These theatricalities are also helpful in
creating a dramatic mood and signaling an imaginative break from the daily
routine of the science classroom.

## WHAT PERSPECTIVES ON IHVs DO LEARNING
## THEORY AND SCIENCE EDUCATION RESEARCH
## HAVE TO OFFER?

Influenced initially by James B. Conant (1947), learning theorist Joseph D.
Novak (1977) has always used the history and philosophy of science as a
reference point for understanding science and contemplating its learning. In

**FIGURE 4**

An IHTV character mask presentation by a teacher at a large urban public high school in the deep south. The subject is scientist/technologist George Washington Carver. Note the use of just a head-and-collar image which permits larger openings in the mask.

1988, Novak wrote, "Any attempt to teach the content of science that does not consider its complex 'conceptual web,' its evolving nature, is destined to failure, provided our objective is *meaningful*, rather than verbatim, rote learning" (p. 317).

The theory of Human Constructivism suggests that meaningful learning is aided by the use of cognitive bridges which allow students to incorporate new experiences into their existing cognitive structure in a meaningful, non-arbitrary way. If appropriate for the learner's prior knowledge, IHVs can act cognitive bridges built in narrative form from histories of science, allowing students to make connections between what they already know and what they need to know (Roach & Wandersee, 1995). The stories themselves may serve as conceptually compressed, sequence-based examples that can serve to trigger activation of related concepts across the learner's conceptual hierarchy and thus facilitate reconstruction of knowledge learned in the past. Over time, details of the story are lost from conscious recall, but the key propositions remain intact—bolstered by the evidence of similar instances.

**FIGURE 5**
An IHV character mask presentation by a chemistry professor at a 2-year
public college in the midwest. The subject is scientist Linus Pauling.

Stories are typically intended to be retold by audience members at a later
date and carry both a surface and a deeper meaning—the latter requiring
reflection and discussion to become evident and empowering. We hypothesize that progressive conceptual change regarding the nature of science does
not occur from one-shot treatments of the topic, but requires making closely
spaced, partially overlapping, multiple passes at it within a given science
course. That's why we favor the narrative approach underlying the IHV
strategy.

Smith (1990) contends that one function of a culture is to perpetuate the
stories that people need to make sense of the world. Egan (1986) calls the
story form a kind of "cultural universal." Elwell (1993) argues that to gain a
pupil's authentic interest in science requires hooking each lesson to prior
knowledge and telling a coherent story instead of just teaching discrete topics. Arons (1989) has even suggested structuring an entire science course
around a unifying story line. Bruner (1990) argues that it is the "push" to
construct narratives that drives the young child to master grammatical forms;

**FIGURE 6**
An IHV character mask presentation by an elementary teacher at a public
school in the deep south. The subject is scientist/technologist/artist
Leonardo da Vinci. Note how the mask was designed to visually match the
seated teacher's body.

without stories to listen to and tell, little language learning would occur. Stories, "by native endowment and exposure" (Bruner, 1990, p. 138) are an important feature of childhood and primary school, but in later schooling we are weaned from narrative and cold abstraction takes its place—especially in science and mathematics classes.

We wonder why this must be so—especially in light of Turner's (1996) assertions that our mind makes sense of the world by telling itself little stories—that story and parable are the basis of all human knowledge. Turner's thesis seems to be supported by research being done at the Neurosciences Institute in San Diego where neuroscientist Gerald Edelman hypothesizes that simultaneous activation of many different neural maps blends (parable-like) to form our thoughts and sensations (Caldwell, 1997, p. 86). McMillen (1996) points out that successful lawyers are good storytellers and the law implicitly acknowledges the power of stories by regulating what

**FIGURE 7**

An IHRV character mask presentation by a high school teacher at a public school in the deep south. The subject is Jane Goodall's work at the Gombe Stream Chimpanzee Reserve in Africa. Note that this character mask does not attempt to duplicate the field scientist's actual face because the teacher herself is a young woman about the age of the scientist (at the time of the vignette) that she wishes to portray; the mask features shocks of wig hair surrounding the head opening to create a 3D effect.

stories the jury can hear. Just as legal studies are rediscovering narrative, so is science education.

Design of the current IHV strategy was informed, in part, by *conceptual change theory* which asserts that learning is not a simple accumulation of information but an interactive process in which the learner must be actively involved in revising his or her ideas when confronted by new information (Posner, Strike, Hewson, & Gertzog, 1982; Strike & Posner, 1992). The learner's ideas are embedded in a conceptual structure that serves to explain experiences in the world around him or her. This structure and the learner's "conceptual ecology" are continually changing, as new information interacts with past experiences. An increase in understanding involves rearrangements of existing conceptual structures to allow forming, elaborating, and integrating the new ideas—provided they meet certain prerequisites for conceptual change (e.g., intelligibility, plausibility, fruitfulness). As Southerland (1997) observes, conceptual change, for the science learner, is seldom wholesale, but rather intermittent and *cascading*—often dependent on the learner's successfully negotiating what Trowbridge and Wandersee (1994) have called *critical junctures* in learning.

## HOW HAVE PARTICIPANTS RESPONDED TO IHVs?

An instrument called the Nature of Science questionnaire (NOSQ) was developed by Roach (1993) in conjunction with a panel of national experts experienced in studying the nature of science. After determining through statistical analysis that it was valid, reliable, sensitive to alternative conceptions about the nature of science, and useful for inferring whether or not students understand the nature of science, it was administered as a pretest to two sections of Science 1010, an introductory college physical science course for nonscience majors at a regional state university in the deep south.

Both sections were taught the same science topics over the same time period (one university summer session). Both sections were taught by the same instructor using lecture (50%), discussion (15%), demonstration (20%), and question-answering (15%) methods. In the treatment section, the 15% question answering was subdivided into 5% end-of-chapter questions and 10% working with IHVs. The IHVs were infused into the course at appropriate breaks in the topical discussions. In the comparison section, the entire question-answering component was based on end-of-chapter questions.

Both class sections completed the NOSQ as pretests and posttests, and both sections also responded to journal-writing prompts designed to elicit more information about the student's understanding of the nature of science. Pretest–posttest scores were compared within groups and a dependent $t$ test was conducted. Quantitative evaluation provided evidence that the treatment induced statistically significant conceptual change about the nature of science. Roach's (1993) findings appear to show that IHVs are useful in helping students attain a clearer understanding of the nature of science. The posttest NOSQ scores of the treatment group seem to indicate a greater understanding of the nature of science by that group; journal-writing responses to nature-of-science prompts also seem to support the quantitative results. We hypothesize that conventional teaching does not provide the opportunities and the time required for analysis and reflection about the nature of science.

What has been the students' response to IHVs? In Roach's 1993 study, after the students had completed their physical science course, they were asked (1) to write a short paragraph describing what they thought of IHVs as an instructional strategy and (2) to submit these paragraphs anonymously. This writing approach was selected because it had been shown to foster honest expression of students' views (Mead & Metraux, 1957).

The data collected from the students who had experienced the IHV strategy for an entire college science course revealed that nearly all of them liked the vignettes, typically describing them as interesting and informative. Some representative student comments are included here; each comment is from a different student:

1. It changed my attitude about scientists—I now think of them as being more human.

2. They [IHVs] tried to put you in the mindframe of the person being discussed.

3. I hope you continue using vignettes because they really are helpful in learning.

4. I feel they were helpful to me mostly because they steered me straight to who was being talked about and made it easier to study that person or phenomenon.

5. They made me believe, whether it's true or not, that you really enjoy what you do—you are genuinely interested in it, and you want us to be.

6. They shed light on ideas which could be left to question. I liked the way you presented, especially because you always started reading and then asked us some questions about who or what we thought you were reading about.

7. I really looked forward to your stories. I thought they were very creative and provided a great deal of information that helped the class understand the material better.

8. I found the stories very informative. I think this is an excellent idea. More teachers need to use them. They give lots of information.

9. The stories were great at first, but sometimes I felt like I was in the first grade. It might have been because we heard them quite often, instead of once a week in a regular [nonsummer session] class. Don't get me wrong, quite a few are really helpful in making the point get across, and striking up discussion in the classroom. It's just not every day that you want to hear them.

In-service science teachers who have attended our workshops on writing and using interactive historical vignettes in the classroom have also been asked for their anonymous reaction to IHVs as a teaching strategy. What follows are representative teacher comments:

1. These vignettes are a useful tool for bringing a historical perspective about famous men and women of science.

2. Vignettes will be useful for motivation and for teaching concepts. Storytelling, or teaching by parable, has proven to be powerful.

3. I enjoyed these and feel they could be helpful in stimulating some students' interest. I don't feel that they are quite as good for math as for science.

4. This method of teaching can inspire any subject area. Getting the attention of the student early and then building on it is a wonderful way to teach.

5. I thought writing vignettes was very interesting. It was a new experience for me and I plan to try this format in my classroom.

6. This vignette idea was fun and a very different slant for science. I doubt I will use it every week but will use it as a treat.

Chan (1997) recently reported on a study he conducted in Taiwan that infused IHVs into two high school physics classes at an all-girl high school taught by the same teacher, with 91 young women randomly assigned to control and treatment groups. Pre–post understanding of the nature of science was assessed using a Chinese version of Rubba and Andersen's (1978) Nature of Scientific Knowledge Scale. MANCOVA and follow-up ANCOVAs were employed to analyze the data for significant differences between groups on the posttest measures, using pretest scores as covariates. Chan found that, overall, pupils who received the IHV treatment achieved a significantly better understanding of the nature of science than those who did not. He noted that his study's relatively large effect sizes indicated large differences between control and treatment groups on three dimensions of the nature of science, the creative, developmental, and parsimonious aspects, using Rubba and Andersen's (1978) six-dimension model. He also found that the IHV instructional strategy, which combines storytelling and guided discussion, can facilitate students' dissatisfaction with their extant, inadequate views of the nature of science through comparison with the characteristics of science reflected in the IHVs and thus foster conceptual change.

## WHAT ARE SOME OF THE NEWEST APPLICATIONS OF THE IHV INSTRUCTIONAL STRATEGY?

Abrams and Wandersee (1995a,b) have described construction and use of interactive historical research vignettes (IHRVs) to teach precollege students how scientific research is actually conducted today. Contemporary accounts of research, including funding pressures, are to be used as the basis for the IHRV. Both field and bench settings for IHRVs should be employed in order to show students that scientific research is conducted at many sites, not just within the confines of a laboratory. A range of IHRV scientist ethnicities, including both males and females, is also recommended as desirable for demonstrating that contemporary science is international and *transcultural* rather than multicultural. Sample IHRVs are included in the article to show how students can vicariously confront such contemporary science-related issues as intellectual property rights within a research team, externally driven vs curiosity-driven research, the paradox of proprietary research at public universities, and the pressure to demonstrate progress in research according to a predetermined funding timetable. The point is made that schools teach primarily ideal (prescriptive accounts) science rather than real-world (descriptive accounts) science and thus create an unrealistic career image for future science students and provide a rose-colored lens for voting citizens. IHRVs can help students become aware of the social and economic factors that impinge on scientific research. Although they use the same *context setting/point-of-conflict/interrupted story/prediction/denouement/guided discussion* design as IHVs, they are intended to accomplish another goal: to understand

```
TECHNOLOGY--------TECHNOSCIENCE-----------SCIENCE
0% Science----->-----------50/50----------<--------0% Technology
The World: Modifies-------------- BOTH----------------Explains
Lab Activity: paper towel testing----hydrometer making----Archimedes' bucket
Key Words: create, design, solve,build----------------interpret, theorize, describe
Historical Order: 1.-----------------------------------3.----------------------------------2.
```

**FIGURE 8**

The technology-science teaching/learning continuum. Note: Consider the
nature of science and the nature of technology. This diagram demonstrates
the learning tool we use with students and teachers to provoke their
thinking about the differences between science and technology and the
relative emphases of science and technology for a given learning activity—
with regard to both the *processes* and the *products* of science and technology.
The center of the continuum uses Bruno Latour's term *technoscience* to
represent a relatively even mixture of both. We think the central question
participants should ask is: What is the goal of the activity we are
considering? We think the debate (and subsequent awareness) that
emerges is more valuable than the somewhat arbitrary placement of the
activity at a given position on the continuum. Verbs like *create, solve, modify,
build,* and *construct* characterize technological processes whereas verbs like
*describe, interpret, theorize,* and *explain* characterize scientific processes. A typical
science laboratory teaching activity can fall anywhere on the continuum,
depending on how it is conducted and analyzed by the participants.
However, we suggest that the set of related laboratory activities which is
presented on the diagram, if taught as is common practice at present,
distributes itself at different positions on the continuum. The diagram also
emphasizes that, historically, technology emerged before science or
technoscience and that both science and technology can and sometimes do
occur without the presence of the other. Sometimes science leads
technology's advancement, and, at other times, the opposite occurs.

science as a "social enterprise" and to see how funding influences the direction of science (AAAS, 1993, pp. 19–20).

We are also beginning work on what we call Interactive Historical Technology Vignettes (IHTVs), given the mandate of the science education standards movement to include technology in the science curriculum. We have
found that students have great trouble distinguishing between science and
technology (cf. Trowbridge & Wandersee, 1997) and we have developed a
giant classroom continuum chart with technology on one end (100% technology, 0% science), science (100% science, 0% technology) at the other, and
technoscience (50% technology, 50% science) in the middle (Figure 8). We

have found that the exercise of discussing where to place a particular person's work (based on that stated goal[s] of that project) on our continuum is a good way of learning the T–S distinction. We are pioneering the use of contemporary newspaper obituary articles of technologists and technoscientists who made important contributions to everyday living through their work and have recently passed away as a starting point for teachers' and students' IHTV development. Initial results appear promising, as both students and teachers seem quite enthusiastic about opportunities for learning the *problem-solving* and *design* stories behind the products they use daily.

## HOW CAN IHVs ADVANCE SCIENTIFIC LITERACY GOALS?

Who needs scientific literacy, anyway? Showman P. T. Barnum (Early, 1996, p. 4) once said, "The people love to be humbugged." Barnum saw their ignorance as the gateway to exploiting them financially. For example, from 1842 to 1856, he exhibited what he claimed was a preserved specimen of an organism called the "Feegee Mermaid." Barnum charged a steep admission fee to countless gullible spectators. What the duped observers saw was a 16-inch dried creature with monkey-like arms, head, and torso morphing into the rear half of a fish. Detailed examination of Barnum's actual dried specimen in 1990 by conservator Scott Fulton at Harvard's Peabody Museum revealed it was really made of carp (fish) parts embedded in cleverly molded papier-mâché. Rubie Watson, Associate Director of the Peabody Museum, has learned that these "mermaids" were actually handicrafts of Southeast Asian (e.g., Javanese) fishermen who sold them to 19th-century seamen and other visitors as exotic souvenirs. This makes us ask two questions: "Which group, the supposedly more sophisticated American exhibition-goers or the rustic Javanese fishermen, were more scientifically literate?" and "Are Americans any more scientifically literate today?" Having been deceived by the mermaid hoax, scientists were subsequently reluctant to accept that the platypus of Australia actually existed. Sometimes, the truths of nature can, indeed, be stranger than fiction.

We hope that today's high school graduate knows enough about biology to (1) question the plausibility of a chimerical organism that is purported to be half human and half fish, (2) rank the credibility of a showman below that of reputable scientists, and (3) understand that scientists' illustrations and accounts of the unusual egg-laying mammals of Australia are intellectually compatible with the rest of mammalian zoology.

*Science for All Americans* (1990) and *Benchmarks for Science Literacy* (1993), both publications of the American Association for the Advancement of Science (AAAS), have devoted several chapters to the nature of science and its allied disciplines. Chapters entitled "The Nature of Science," "The Nature of Technology," "The Nature of Mathematics," "Historical Perspectives," "Common Themes," and "Habits of Mind" provide many ideas for incorporating the nature of science into the K–12 classroom. While it is not the intent of these publications to serve as curriculum materials, experienced science teachers will probably be able to modify existing science exercises, content, and activities to meet some of the new benchmarks just mentioned. In 1996, the National Research Council issued the *National Science Education Standards*. These present a vision of a scientifically literate U.S. population that gives an even greater mandate to the U.S. science education reform movement.

One problem students face in learning science is the unfamiliarity of the discourse. Scientists feel most comfortable when they are using the full spectrum of scientific terms to explain natural phenomena. Sometimes those terms are the same as words in everyday speech (e.g., work, energy) but carry science-specific definitions. At other times, the terms are virtually unpronounceable, polysyllabic, and/or words of Greek and Latin origin (Wandersee, 1988). Finally, some science terms are the logical products of complex nomenclature systems (e.g., chemical names, animal names) that appear cryptic to an outsider. It's no wonder students think that *theories* are wild ideas, green plant cells contain "Chlorasceptic" (confusing *chlorophyll* with a common, over-the-counter medicine for treating sore throats), and the chemical symbol P*b* (Latin) stands for "pure brass."

IHVs, IHRVs, and IHTVs are ways of: (1) ameliorating the terminology problem by priming the cognitive pump so that terms are more than rote memory items on examinations, (2) letting scientific and technological biography influence the student's emergent autobiography so that scientific and technological domains seem less daunting and strange, and (3) explaining the complexity in the contemporary nature of science and exploring the pathways that led to today's scientific understanding—by way of a series of carefully crafted stories and opportunities for "talking science."

Joel Shurkin, a well-known science writer (Finn, 1996, p. 15), says that two things are necessary for a good scientific biography: (1) the person involved must be fairly interesting and (2) he or she must have done something that people think is important. Since vignettes are extracted from such historical accounts; we think those criteria are worth remembering.

Shurkin (Finn, 1996, p. 16) has also concluded, "Biography makes scientists look like humans. . . . in a good scientific biography, you get that across. You get to the person behind the science." We hypothesize that most of us both like and need a look "behind the scenes" to understand what's really going on. We are convinced that "You can't become scientifically literate if science seems like magic to you!" IHVs are opportunities for demystifying and demythologizing science.

# References

Abrams, E., & Wandersee, J. H. (1995a). How does biological knowledge grow? A study of life scientists' research practices. *Journal of Research in Science Teaching, 32*(6), 649–663.

Abrams, E., & Wandersee, J. H. (1995b). How to infuse actual scientific research into science classroom instruction. *International Journal of Science Education, 6,* 683–694.

American Association for the Advancement of Science (AAAS) (1990). *Science for all Americans.* New York: Oxford University Press.

American Association for the Advancement of Science (AAAS) (1993). *Benchmarks for science literacy.* New York: Oxford University Press.

Anderson, H. O. (1978). The holistic approach to science education. *The Science Teacher, 45*(1), 27–28.

Arons, A. B. (1989). What science should we teach? In *Curriculum development in the year 2000* (pp. 13–20). Colorado Springs, CO: BSCS.

Asimov, I. (1972). *Asimov's biographical encyclopedia of science and technology.* New York: Avon Books.

Brown, R. A. (1991). Humanizing physics through its history. *School Science and Mathematics, 91*(8), 357–361.

Bruner, J. (1990). *Acts of meaning.* Cambridge, MA: Harvard University Press.

Bybee, R. W., Powell, J. C., Ellis, J. D., Giese, J. R., Parisi, L., & Singleton, L. (1991). Teaching history and nature of science in science courses: A rationale—Integrating the history and nature of science and technology in science and social studies curriculum. *Science Education, 75*(1), 143–155.

Caldwell, M. (1997). The science of fiction. *Discover,* March, 84, 86.

Chan, K.-S. (1997). *Effectiveness of interactive historical vignettes in enhancing high school students' understanding of the nature of science.* Paper presented at the annual meeting of National Association for Research in Science Teaching, March, Oak Brook, IL.

Conant, J. B. (1947). *On understanding science.* New Haven, CT: Yale University Press.

Conant, J. B. (1951). *Science and common sense.* New Haven, CT: Yale University Press.

Cummins, C. L. (1995). The nature of science as communicated by science fairs: Is experimentation really the only scientific method? In F. Finley, D. Allchin, D. Rhees, & S. Fifield, (eds.), *Proceedings volume 1: Third international history, philosophy, and science teaching conference, Minneapolis, Minnesota* (pp. 277–287). University of Minnesota, College of Education.

Duschl, R. A. (1990). *Restructuring science education: The importance of theories and their development.* New York: Teachers College Press.

Duschl, R. A. (1994). Research on the history and philosophy of science. In D. L. Gabel (ed.), *Handbook of research on science teaching and learning* (pp. 443–465). New York: Macmillan.

Early, A. (1996). The little mermaid? *Harvard University Gazette,* October 17, 1, 4.

Egan, K. (1986). *Teaching as story telling.* Chicago: University of Chicago Press.

Elwell, L. P. (1993). Let's teach biology with a hook and a story. *The American Biology Teacher, 55*(6), 324.

Finley, F., Allchin, D., Rhees, D., & Fifield, S. (eds.) (1995a). *Proceedings volume 1: Third international history, philosophy, and science teaching conference, Minneapolis, Minnesota.* University of Minnesota, College of Education.

Finley, F., Allchin, D., Rhees, D., & Fifield, S. (eds.) (1995b). *Proceedings volume 2: Third international history, philosophy, and science teaching conference, Minneapolis, Minnesota.* University of Minnesota, College of Education.

Finn, R. (1996). Opinions differ on the features of a well-done scientific biography. *The Scientist,* September 30, 15–16.

Garfield, E. (1997). A tribute to Calvin N. Mooers, a pioneer of information retrieval. *The Scientist,* March 17, 9.

Good, R. G., & Wandersee, J. H. (1992). A voyage of discovery: Designing a graduate course on HPST. In S. Hills (ed.), *The history and philosophy of science in science education: Proceedings of the second international conference on the history and philosophy of science and science teaching* (Vol. 1, pp. 423–433). Kingston, Ontario, Canada: Queen's University, the Mathematics, Science, Technology and Teacher Education Group and the Faculty of Education.

Good, R. G., & Wandersee, J. H. Cognitive travels via the H.M.S. Beagle: A study of Darwin's voyage of conceptual change and its implications for teaching about evolution. *Proceedings of the 1997 HPSST conference: Toward scientific literacy.* Calgary, Alberta, Canada: University of Calgary, Faculty of Education. (in press)

Herget, D. E. (ed.) (1989). *The history and philosophy of science in science teaching: Proceedings of the first international conference.* Tallahassee, FL: Florida State University.

Herget, D. E. (ed.) (1990). *More history and philosophy of science in science teaching: Proceedings of the first international conference.* Tallahassee, FL: Florida State University.

Hills, S. (ed.) (1992a). *The history and philosophy of science in science education: Proceedings of the second international conference on the history and philosophy of science and science teaching* (Vol. 1). Kingston, Ontario, Canada: Queen's University, the Mathematics, Science, Technology and Teacher Education Group and the Faculty of Education.

Hills, S. (ed.) (1992b). *The history and philosophy of science in science education: Proceedings of the second international conference on the history and philosophy of science and science teaching* (Vol. 2). Kingston, Ontario, Canada: Queen's University, the Mathematics, Science, Technology and Teacher Education Group and the Faculty of Education.

Klopfer, L. E. (1969). The teaching of science and the history of science. *Journal of Research in Science Teaching, 6,* 87–95.

Kuhn, T. S. (1970). *The structure of scientific revolutions* (2nd ed.). Chicago: University of Chicago Press.

Matthews, M. R. (ed.) (1991). *History, philosophy, and science teaching: Selected readings.* Toronto: OISE Press.

Matthews, M. R. (1992). History, philosophy, and science teaching: The present rapprochement. *Science & Education, 1*(1), 11–47.

Matthews, M. R. (1994). *Science teaching: The role of history and philosophy of science.* New York: Routledge.

Mayr, E. (1988). *Toward a new philosophy of biology.* Cambridge, MA: The Belknap Press of Harvard University Press.

McMillen, L. (1996). The importance of storytelling: A new emphasis by law scholars. *The Chronicle of Higher Education,* July 26, A10.

Mead, M., & Metraux, R. (1957). Image of the scientist among high school students: A pilot study. *Science, 126,* 384–390.

National Research Council (NRC) (1996). *National science education standards.* Washington, DC: National Academy Press.

Novak, J. D. (1977). *A theory of education.* Ithaca, NY: Cornell University Press.

Novak, J. D. (1988). The role of content and process in the education of science teachers. In P. Brandwein & A. H. Passow (eds.), *Gifted young in science: Potential through performance* (pp. 307–319). Washington, DC: NSTA.

Posner, G. J., Strike, K. A., Hewson, P. W., & Gertzog, W. A. (1982). Accommodation of a scientific conception: Toward a theory of conceptual change. *Science Education, 66*(2), 211–227.

Ray, C. (1991). Breaking free from dogma: Philosophical prejudice in science education. *Science Education, 75*(1), 87–93.

Roach, L. E. (1992). *I have a story about that: Historical vignettes to enhance the teaching of the nature of science.* Natchitoches, LA: Roach Publishing Company.

Roach, L. E. (1993). Use of the history of science in a non-science majors course: Does it affect students' understanding of the nature of science? Unpublished doctoral dissertation, Louisiana State University, Baton Rouge.

Roach, L. E., & Wandersee, J. H. (1993). Short story science. *The Science Teacher, 60*(6), 18–21.

Roach, L. E., & Wandersee, J. H. (1995). Putting people back into science: Using historical vignettes. *School Science and Mathematics, 95*(7), 365–370.

Rosenberg, A. (1985). *The structure of the biological sciences.* Cambridge, England: Cambridge University Press.

Rubba, P., & Andersen, H. (1978). Development of an instrument to assess secondary students' understanding of the nature of scientific knowledge. *Science Education*, 62(4), 449–458.

Rutherford, F. J., & Ahlgren, A. (1990). *Science for all Americans*. New York: Oxford University Press.

Schrock, J. R. (1989). Pseudoscience of animals and plants: A teachers guide to nonscientific beliefs. *The Kansas School Naturalist*, 35(4), 3–15.

Schwab, J. J., & Brandwin, P. F. (1962). *The teaching of science as enquiry*. Cambridge, MA: Harvard University Press.

Seymour, E., & Hewitt, N. M. (1997). *Talking about leaving: Why undergraduates leave the sciences*. Boulder, CO: Westview Press.

Shahn, E. (1988). On science literacy. *Educational Philosophy and Theory*, 20(2), 42–46.

Shanker, A. (1996). Where we stand: The real solution. *The New York Times*, September 29, 7.

Smith, F. (1990). *To think*. New York: Teachers College Press.

Southerland, S. A. (1997). Conceptual change theory and what counts as science learning. Paper presented at the annual meeting of National Association for Research in Science Teaching, March, Oak Brook, IL.

Stinner, A. (1989). The teaching of physics and the contexts of inquiry: From Aristotle to Einstein. *Science Education*, 73(50), 591–605.

Strike, K. A., & Posner, G. J. (1992). A revisionist theory of conceptual change. In R. A. Duschl and R. J. Hamilton (eds.), *Philosophy of science, cognitive psychology, and educational theory and practice* (pp. 147–176). New York: SUNY Press.

Trowbridge, J. E., & Wandersee, J. H. (1994). Identifying critical junctures in learning in a college course on evolution. *Journal of Research in Science Teaching*, 31(5), 459–473.

Trowbridge, J. E., & Wandersee, J. H. (1995). Agassiz's influence on marine science teaching: Promoting nature study by direct observation. In F. Finley, D. Allchin, D. Rhees, & S. Fifield (eds.), *Proceedings volume 2: Third international history, philosophy, and science teaching conference, Minneapolis, Minnesota* (pp. 1217–1224). University of Minnesota, College of Education.

Trowbridge, J. E., & Wandersee, J. H. (1997). Can students distinguish between science and technology? Paper presented at the annual meeting of National Association for Research in Science Teaching, March, Oak Brook, IL.

Trowbridge, J. E., & Wandersee, J. H. Deep sea observation: Seeing in the dark. *Proceedings of the 1997 HPSST conference: Toward scientific literacy*. Calgary, Alberta, Canada: University of Calgary, Faculty of Education. (in press)

Turner, M. (1996). *The literary mind*. New York: Oxford University Press.

Wandersee, J. H. (1981). A letter from Leeuwenhoek. *The American Biology Teacher*, 43(8), 450–451.

Wandersee, J. H. (1983). Be quick on the draw—Use chalkboard templates. *The American Biology Teacher*, 45(5), 271–272.

Wandersee, J. H. (1985). The history phone. *Science and Children*, 23(1), 15–17.

Wandersee, J. H. (1986a). Can the history of science help science educators anticipate students' misconceptions? *Journal of Research in Science Teaching*, 23(7), 581–597.

Wandersee, J. H. (1986b). Estimating the size of "little animals." In H. L. Schoen & M. J. Zweng (eds.), *1986 Yearbook: Estimation and mental computation*. Reston, VA: National Council of Teachers of Mathematics.

Wandersee, J. H. (1987). Francis Bacon: Mastermind of experimental science. *Journal of College Science Teaching*, 17(2), 120–123.

Wandersee, J. H. (1988). The terminology problem in biology education: A reconnaissance. *The American Biology Teacher*, 50(2), 97–100.

Wandersee, J. H. (1990a). On the value and use of the history of science in teaching today's science: Constructing historical vignettes. In D. E. Herget (ed.), *More history and philosophy of science in science teaching: Proceedings of the first international conference* (pp. 277–283). Tallahassee, FL: Florida State University.

Wandersee, J. H. (1990b). Concept mapping and the cartography of cognition. *Journal of Research in Science Teaching*, 27(10), 923–936.

Wandersee, J. H. (1992). The historicality of cognition: Implications for science education research. *Journal of Research in Science Teaching*, 29(4), 423–434.

Wandersee, J. H. (1995). Latour's "inscription device" concept: Is it useful for teaching biology? In F. Finley, D. Allchin, D. Rhees, & S. Fifield (eds.), *Proceedings volume 2: Third international history, philosophy, and science teaching conference, Minneapolis, Minnesota* (pp. 1277–1285). University of Minnesota, College of Education.

Wilson, L. L. (1954). A study of opinions related to the nature of science and its purpose in history. *Science Education*, 38(2), 159–164.

# Talking and Doing Science:
# Important Elements in a
# Teaching-for-Understanding Approach

ELEANOR ABRAMS

*University of New Hampshire*

Talking science is not simply a teacher talking about science, but students doing, learning, and communicating through a specialized process and language. Jay Lemke (1990) argues that

> Talking Science means observing, describing, comparing, classifying, analyzing, discussing, hypothesizing, theorizing, questioning, challenging, arguing, designing experiments, following procedures, judging, evaluating, deciding, concluding, generalizing, reporting, writing, lecturing, and teaching in and through the language of science. (p. ix)

The essence of this definition is that for students to learn science, the teaching of science should happen in the context of scientific inquiry.

The latest national science standards such as *Benchmarks for Science Literacy* (American Association for the Advancement of Science (AAAS), 1993) and the *National Science Education Standards* (National Research Council (NRC), 1996) concur that students need to learn science through real-world scientific experiences to become scientifically literate.

This knowledge of the scientific process is not an intuitive or natural outcome (Wolpert, 1993). Students do not develop an understanding about the nature of scientific enterprise without repeated exposure and experiences to scientific investigations. However, somehow we have come to the belief that participating in scientific inquiry is supposed to come later, such as in college—after learning certain knowledge.

Ultimately all scientific knowledge is rooted in the experiences of the learner, and the processes involved in scientific investigation and organization are an integral part of what science is (see Figure 1). Thus, an essential feature of science education is that the precollege student participate in these processes (Mullis & Jenkins, 1988).

## PERSONAL AND PUBLIC SCIENCE—CONCEPTUAL CHANGE AND SOCIAL CONSTRUCTION

Science educators need to portray scientific research practices and the resulting conclusions drawn from such research endeavors accurately to their students. A classroom view of science that depicts scientific knowledge as a simple extension of the data collected objectively during research is clearly misleading. Philosophers of science and sociologists' reports that modern scientific research departs substantially from the traditional Baconian scientific view taught in schools.

Martin and Brouwer (1993) suggest that the world of a scientist is composed of both a public and a personal side. The personal side is divergent and employs literary devices such as stories, plays, and narratives to evoke meaning. A novice researcher acquires a narrative mode of knowing by dwelling in a situation or in a field of knowledge such as biology. Skilled practitioners through prolonged and intimate contact with his or her ideas acquire an intuitive or tacit sense of understanding and coherence of their chosen field of study. Students can see this narration and informal dialogue through scientists' field journals or diaries. The *Voyage of the Beagle* (1962) which Charles Darwin wrote during his 5-year journey around the world on the sailing vessel the *Beagle* is one of the more famous examples available.

From the writings of scientists, a reader can visualize the struggles before the famous "aha" moments that occur during scientific discoveries. These are private and solo times in a scientist's professional life that accompany the "back-of-the-head," itchy feeling that occurs when something does not fit with existing scientific knowledge. At these times, scientists collect more data or try to find more evidence as they develop a new way of accommodating the data before voicing those feelings in a public forum.

An analogous thought process in education called conceptual change occurs in meaningful learning. Cognitive growth happens as students try to integrate and make sense of everyday and more formal school-based knowledge. When these two types of knowledge are in opposition, cognitive conflict occurs. Posner, Strike, Hewson, and Gertzog (1982) suggested four prerequisites for conceptual change:

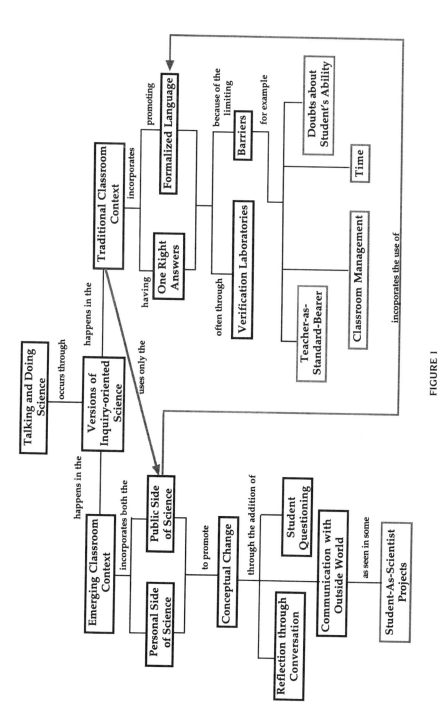

**FIGURE 1**

Talking and doing science in precollege classrooms.

1. Students must experience dissatisfaction with their current conceptions.
2. Students must develop an alternative understanding of the concept.
3. The new concept must be plausible.
4. Students must see the concept as fruitful or useful in several different situations.

This dissonance can be promoted by the perspectives of other individuals, conflicting data sets, and/or ideas, and may result in cognitive conflict and conceptual change (Cannella, 1988). Learning to reason and think about problems in common terms that translate into the formalized voice of language is a skill most students do not get a chance to practice. However, peer interactions can be valuable during the conceptual change process (Posner et al., 1982) by helping students experience dissatisfaction with existing concepts, develop plausible new concepts, and see the relevance of new knowledge in different contexts.

In a study that compared the beliefs of scientists about the nature of science, the scientists agreed that there is a tension that exists between the private process of science and the public view of the scientific method, as formally reported to colleagues, leaders, and the general public (Pomeroy, 1993). They stated they did not necessarily have an accepted public vocabulary with which to express the private side of their work.

Mitroff (1974) found that the most credible scientists tend to be seen by their peers as operating with values associated with private science such as being subjective, closed-minded, and biased. Mediocre scientists tend to be seen as operating solely with values associated with public science (being objective, open-minded, and unbiased).

However, all scientists' communicate in a stylized fashion when communicating their conclusions to the public. This standardized format allows the presenting scientists to define, refine, and modify their ideas from advice given from other experts in the scientific community.

In the view of many researchers, science classrooms should include both informal discussions that simulate the private side of science as well as traditional activities that promote the formalized public side. This view is founded on the belief that all knowledge is socially constructed. Social constructivism has gained credence in the science education community as an epistemological viewpoint that values the way students coconstruct, or build, ideas together about the world through dialogue (Tobias, 1990).

The *National Science Education Standards* (NRC, 1996) states that working collaboratively with others not only enhances the understanding of science, it also fosters the practice of many of the skills, attitudes, and values that characterize science. The Standards also recommend that teachers should encourage informal discussion and should structure science activities so that students are required to explain and justify their understandings, argue from the data and defend their conclusions, and critically assess/challenge the scientific explanations of one another. This public side requires students to formally verbalize (via the vernacular of science) what still might be a hunch, an unformed thought, or an intuitive leap through the lens of science.

## THE TRADITIONAL CLASSROOM CONTEXT

There is an old saying that when a pebble is dropped in the center of a pond the ripples spread throughout the pond. However, if there is an island in the middle of the pond, the waves from the disturbance leave the land mass essentially untouched. Often science education reforms wrap around various educational communities like ripples on a pond—leaving most teachers' classrooms untouched. In spite of the new national standards describing the nature of science as varying from the Baconian scientific method, teachers may still teach the traditional sanitized view. There are several factors involved in this decision to maintain the status quo. The teacher may not know about the new national standards, read the latest educational journals, or attend any conferences. Therefore, they teach the same material and employ the methods they experienced in college science courses.

Both *Science for all Americans* (AAAS, 1989) and the *National Science Standards* (NRC, 1996) state that students should be involved in scientific research starting in elementary school. By the end of fourth grade, students should be able to ask questions about objects, organisms, and events in the environment; plan and conduct a simple investigation; employ simple equipment and tools to gather data and extend the senses; use data to construct a reasonable explanation; and communicate and defend explanations. By the eighth grade, students should be able to identify questions that can be answered though scientific research; design and conduct a scientific investigation; use appropriate tools and techniques to gather, analyze, and interpret data; develop descriptions, explanations, predictions, and models using evidence; and to think critically and logically to make the relationships between evidence and explanations. By graduation, students should be able to identify questions and concepts that guide scientific research, design and conduct scientific investigations, use technology and mathematics to improve investigations and communications, formulate and revise scientific explanations and models using logic and evidence, recognize and analyze alternative explanations and models, and to communicate and defend a scientific argument.

However, the constraints of the typical science classroom limits the way the scientific process is taught to students (Hodson, 1993). Besides the oft-heard problems of time and classroom management (Fleury & Bentley, 1991), there are few curriculum materials based on the new understanding of the nature of science, leaving teachers alone in trying to integrate it into their classrooms. A review of the literature reveals the inadequacy of instructional materials in regard to facilitating students understanding of the nature of science and scientific knowledge (Meichtry, 1993). Griffiths and Barry (1995) concluded that a curriculum that does not adequately portray these issues will most likely have a negative effect on student understandings.

Another limiting factor in the way science is depicted is the teacher's own beliefs in the nature of science. In one view, teachers hold that they are charged with the task of upholding the scientific standard. Pomeroy (1993) found that scientists and secondary science teachers were scientistic and positivistic in their views of science. These findings may be attributed to the scientists' and secondary science teachers' deep initiation into the "norms of the scientific community" through university courses. These secondary science teachers' self-image is as a role model, foundation layer, recruiter, and/or gate keeper to the world of science. This causes them to present a more normative rather than realistic, or descriptive, view of the nature of scientific research.

Often, such teachers' primary goal is to help students experience the traditional scientific method (i.e., question, theory, hypothesis, data collection, analysis, and conclusions). Verification labs are common and designed to corroborate known scientific knowledge. The teachers remain in complete control of the class and help students avoid making too many "unnecessary" detours. Hodson (1993), in a study of secondary science teachers' practices, was surprised to find that teachers were reluctant to entertain alternative explanations of data by students and were casual in the way they dismissed data that seemed to indicate different patterns, trends, and categories. Those teachers seemed to have an "ideal model" of science and a strict sense of what is possible in a school laboratory, given the constraints of time, resources, pressure of the syllabus, and examinations (Hodson, 1993).

Teachers who tend to present only the public side of science also see it as an appropriate domain only for few talented students, the less skillful students need to be led to the right answers. As a consequence, there had to be one answer with good clear conclusions. Thus, in planning laboratory work, all else is subordinated to the content issue and to "getting the right results." Despite the national reform effort calling for science for *all* Americans, it seems that teachers still tend to teach the way they were taught.

## THE EMERGING CLASSROOM CONTEXT

The other side of the continuum consists of teachers who believe that they and their students can participate in and/or contribute to the growth of scientific knowledge. These educators view research not as a meticulous path to enlightenment, but a winding lifelong trip with only temporary stops along the way. From this perspective, students become joint partners in the quest for knowledge. Dissonance in students occurs naturally as they strive to make sense of the data. There are no right or wrong answers, but communal perspectives that are coconstructed and based on the data at hand. Therefore, a teacher's understanding of where students fit into the scientific community shapes the type of experiences that students encounter in a science class.

This is not a new idea. Many studies investigated the effectiveness of introducing concepts on the nature of science in the 1960s curriculum projects (see Chapter 2). These curricula were designed to promote inquiry and process skills. It was accepted that a laboratory approach to the teaching of science would enhance understanding of the scientific enterprise regardless of the knowledge domain (Ramsey & Howe, 1969). We now recognize that just as scientists perform their work in the context of a chosen field such as ecology or astrophysics, the student must also investigate science within a real-world-problem context.

Teachers who subscribe to this emerging view do not question whether inquiry should be taught in precollege classrooms, but how and how much. For example, how much of "real-world" science should be in the science classroom? Should students be exposed to the social pressures often inherent in research, such as the ever-increasing time it takes to acquire funding, the publish or perish dilemma, or the pressure to find solutions to problems? If so, how much? These are the decisions the teacher has to make based upon the students' experience levels.

Lederman (1992) argues that the nature of science cannot be separated from the doing of science. He also asserts that there needs to be continued stress on higher-level thinking skills, problem solving, inquiry-oriented instruction, and frequent higher-level questioning within a supportive, risk-free environment if we desire changes in students' conceptions. The question teachers should ask themselves is, "are we to remain '. . . the keeper(s) of the information, the one(s) who know all the answers' (Tobias, 1990, p. 21) or are teachers willing to share with their students the grand adventure of science and explore together their own personal science"? The following sections illustrate some examples of how the curriculum might be implemented in such emerging science classrooms.

## THE USE OF "STUDENT AS SCIENTIST" PROJECTS

The new reform efforts have resulted in curricula developed to give students real-world experiences in scientific research. GLOBE (Global Learning to Benefit the Environment), Journey North, and Green are just a few examples of the K–12 environmental monitoring programs in which students collect quality data along specific guidelines for scientists. GLOBE is an international program where students monitor environmental conditions in their local area and have access to every other school's data. In Journey North students follow the migration of monarch butterflies and in *Green*, they monitor water quality of their local watersheds.

There are common elements in most of these student-as-scientist programs. Students are asked a scientific question couched in a real-world environmental problem that a scientist is striving to answer; the students are trained to collect data through a series of systematic protocols; the collected data are sent to the scientist. The class has access to every other class's data, thereby allowing the students to draw their own conclusions. All these programs educate the teacher through workshops and offer web sites on the World Wide Web.

Scientists and educators involved in the development of these projects assume that students learn the nature of science through "authentic" scientific research. The version of the nature of science portrayed, while not a complete picture of the context of research, has many of the elements that cookbook verification laboratory exercises lack. Those components include: variability in data, how to develop conclusions from data, and the tentative nature of those conclusions. Some of the missing aspects of the private world of the scientist are the pressures of funding sources upon setting a research agenda, developing a researchable question, the social communication of findings and further research directions, and the demand to publish those findings (Abrams & Wandersee, 1995a,b).

Student-as-scientist projects should not be confused with inquiry-oriented labs that are based on consensual knowledge. In a study about inquiry labs, Solomon (1991, p. 97) found that students have doubts about their own ability to do science:

> . . . It has been the recent trend in curriculum rhetoric to call for more teaching of the processes of science in the hope, perhaps, that by learning observation, experiment, data analysis, and pattern-seeking in their own learning, the students would come to associate related features with scientific knowledge. The argument that student learning, however open-ended, will be seen to resemble accepted scientific knowledge, or even its manufacture, is not entirely convincing. Attitude research shows that students rate science as very difficult, and other studies show that scientists are popularly thought to be unusually clever. Would students readily assume that their own faltering attempts to learn what they see as already known were similar to the processes by which science has advanced?

Solomon also believes that the current research, though scant, does not give much hope that a student diet of laboratory work would automatically yield an understanding of the nature of science.

Meichtry (1992) developed, for Biological Science Curriculum Study (BSCS), a five-stage model to teach the nature of science by engaging the student, allowing exploration through the use of hands-on experiences, providing students and teachers the opportunity to explain and elaborate on the experiences, and focusing on evaluation. This curriculum was tested on

11 teachers and 1004 students at the middle school level (sixth-, seventh-, and eighth-grade students). The study found no significant differences between the students taught with the BSCS curriculum and those in a control group, with respect to their understanding of the nature of science.

Solomon's and Meichtry's work reveal the limitations of attempting to recreate through laboratory experiments what is already known. The latest "student-as-scientist" projects offer an improvement over earlier "inquiry-based" efforts in that they don't seek to lead students to "correct" answers, but instead they allow students to coconstruct new knowledge with the teacher.

However, the teacher's behavior in class determines the efficacy of these projects. Lemke (1990) suggests that teachers should not seek to control student behavior by directly telling them what to do. Explicit orders, directives, and even requests should be fairly rare. Behavior is basically controlled by the expectations built into the activity structure patterns. Teachers need to step aside as the leader of the class in student-as-scientist projects to become a facilitator and coach (Wolk, 1994). Otherwise, they may discourage student-dominated activity in order to control the pacing. Students do need feedback and teachers do need to keep students on task. However, it has been demonstrated that students and teachers become engaged in and excited about their work when they start coconstructing their own findings about a local environmental problem and *this takes time.*

For example, seven students' understandings of the scientific process were tracked across the school year in a conservation biology class at Scientist High School (a pseudonym) (Abrams, Moss, & Kull; in preparation). The class completed a series of five projects during the school year, all based on the "student-as-scientist" model. The students monitored water quality along a local watershed, modeled population growth on a computer, developed a land cover map from a TM satellite image for GLOBE, and tracked the health of the white pine (*Pinus strobus*) forest for *Forest Watch.* All the projects except the modeling were prepackaged curricula developed by scientists and teachers to allow students experience being scientists.

These projects comprise a significant response to Clough and Clark's (1994) criticism that most laboratories are "cookbook" because they are artificial and the teacher has the correct answer. The projects were based on real-world environmental problems that have no "right or wrong" answers. In fact, Scientist High students knew the scientists were interested in their data.

In the course of completing their projects, students were encouraged to become proficient in many measurable research skills (e.g. collecting data from a variety of sources, analzing the data, and communicating findings formally through presentations to mentors and peers) (AAAS, 1993). All projects were scored on various aspects of those skills by assessment rubrics.

The format of such projects confused the students at first. They were used to having the "right" answer, but by the end of the year the students felt more confident about their own conclusions as illustrated in this portion of an interview:

> I:  Did you feel like a scientist?
> S:  Yeah. I kind of did.
> I.  Why? I mean, what did you do that a scientist does?
> S:  We went out and we went out to our site that we made. We went out with a purpose, an objective. And with that purpose and objective, we step-by-step systematically collected data and that eventually measured up to a single meaning which is the health of our forest. So we go up there, we'd clip samples, we'd core our tree out so we can get the age of it.
> I:  Do you feel confident in the conclusion that it is healthy?
> S:  I only know, I feel confident in our conclusion. I don't know if the forest is extremely healthy or healthy, but it varies. Whatever the conclusion is I know I feel confident. I think it's healthy. It's in my papers.                (Eleventh-grade male)

The class was heterogenously grouped and one student who did not feel she could do science at the beginning of the year voiced some interesting comments about the scientific process by the end of the school year.

> S:  For science, you know, you have to be extremely thorough and you can't, you know, whatever, grade student-wise, it doesn't really matter. If you are an A-student or a C-student, you have to be precise with your results and whatnot, so there has to be consistency with being thorough and taking the time to do the testing right. It was a lot different than science courses in my past because it was a lot more hands-on, really testing; they're (scientists) going to do something with the results.                           (Eleventh-grade female)

At Scientist High, students were provided the context and question in which to conduct the research. Students at the beginning of the year were often unaware of the essential question driving their data-gathering activities. Here is one student's quote after completing two out of the five projects.

> I:  Did you ask your own questions or were you sort of following questions that were given to you?
> S:  I did ask my own questions. I asked why these were, why we were doing this to be basic and then that was answered. And then what does this mean? If there's a certain characteristic that I don't understand or just some things I can't even put down about, yeah, we did ask our own questions.
> I:  Could you give an example of one?
> S:  I really can't.                                    (Eleventh-grade female)

One of the concerns about the student-as-scientist projects is that students will become data technicians and not see the overall context of the project. The coconstruction of conclusions based on a question and the resulting data appears critical to students' understanding of the nature of the scientific process.

Toward the end of the year, students would have liked to have had time to answer some of their own questions rather than just the ones given to them within the project curricula. One student voiced her objections:

S: I think that's good that we're helping people out (scientists), we're doing research, but I think it would be cool if we re-analyze the results too and maybe compare it to last year's results. I'd love to see last year's results and see what happened. You know? . . . What will happen here? (Eleventh-grade female)

Another student had noticed something about the growth of white pine needles and would have liked time to explore that question. This is a limitation that educators should be aware of in student-as-scientist instructional models. However, these projects offer students the scaffold to support other areas of student-directed research.

## THE NEED FOR STUDENT QUESTIONING

Despite the national science standards (AAAS, 1989; NRC, 1996) and the proliferation of curricula to support student inquiry, teachers, scientists, and curriculum developers hesitate to give students freedom to investigate research questions that arise from their own findings and interests. Among the reasons often cited for this are classroom management issues, time, doubts about students' ability to originate a feasible research project, and distrust that students will follow through to the end of the investigation.

However, what better place to start an inquiry dialogue between students than at the point of their own questions? Karen Gallas (1995), a first- and second-grade teacher, studied the patterns of discourse between students during her science class for 5 years. Throughout the typical school week, Gallas sets aside certain times for student-generated questions and dialogue called *Science Talks* as part of her science curriculum. She believes that when a community of learners begins with the act of dialogue about the world, and when that dialogue occurs outside of the influence of the teacher, it moves naturally and vitally toward theory and a readiness for instruction and study. In this process, the students take on the voice and the authority of scientists. They begin to bring their world of experience to the classroom in the form of personal narratives (private science) and important questions (vital to conceptual change), realizing (as they do those things) what they observe, wonder, and imagine has importance in a science classroom. In this way, teachers and children move purposefully together toward an inclusive kind of "talking science" where everyone is admitted. In fact, she found that the students who typically excelled at science, often because of their increased scientific vocabulary, did not outshine other students during her *Science Talks*. When pressed by other students, the vocabulary-rich students fumbled with the specialized language of science when explaining the meaning behind the words and were forced to simplify their communication and say what they thought.

However, Gallas in her elementary school experiences (1995) and Lemke in his secondary school science studies (1990) found that children don't talk science in traditional science classrooms. As a result, they are not good at doing so and they come to the conclusion that they are not "good at science." Lemke argues that it is difficult for teachers to move away from the pattern of teachers asking the questions and students answering them. This communication allows the teacher to be in control of what is said. The student's remarks are filtered through the teacher's mouth, usually in the form of revoicing and questioning. In addition, most teachers are not prepared for the distress they feel when they have to be quiet. It is the teacher's natural inclination to want to facilitate discussion, to moderate who talks and for how long, to discourage digressions, and to make sure that students get the right answers.

Gallas (1995) solves this problem by setting aside a certain time each week for her students to discuss a student-generated question. Her children coconstruct, or build, ideas through dialogue. Gallas listens and reflects without immediately agonizing over what ought to be said. Instead of intervening in children's discussions at "teachable" moments when students are voicing disturbing misconceptions, she focuses on issues of language and culture and how to bridge the gap between her intentions and the students' life experiences. Her *Science Talks* also become a rich source of information on previously taught units. Students' understandings of concepts are revealed throughout the talks, focusing the teacher's attention on what she did not know about the students' conceptual frameworks.

Gallas believes her ability to listen and understand the students improved over time. She continued to coach the students on ways to make their talks more effective; how to use each other's ideas and support new theories, how to ask clarifying questions and how to apply prior knowledge. The talks also opened a window into the students' thinking through which she could see their early ideas on many topics and respond, providing for a variety of interests in her science curriculum. This student-directed activity supports the children's growing sense of what science is, of what kinds of ideas science considers, and how it feels to speak with authority and seriousness about difficult questions.

Lemke (1990) concurs and suggests that the one change in secondary science teaching that could accomplish more than any other to improve students' ability to use the language of science is to give them more practice actually using it. Students must be given opportunities to speak at greater length and to write more about science topics.

He proposes that teachers use less question-and-answer dialogue and organize more class time for student questions, student individual and group reports, true dialogue, cross-discussion, and small-group work. Teachers should make every effort to find activities that encourage students to ask questions rather than just answer questions. Also the teacher should encourage students to talk to one another during class about science topics and should be as tolerant as possible of quiet side-conversations. Project-based investigations should be frequent and used as an opportunity for informal science talk as well as practical work.

Talking to one another, in small group work or even in side-conversations, gives students an opportunity to discuss science in a different way (private science), free of some of the social pressures of talking science with the teacher (public science). The important conclusion is simply this, that *inquiry-oriented activities are not enough*. Students can construct rich meanings when presented with rich materials, but the meanings they do construct, without reflection and discussion, are often diffuse, mysterious, and laden with misconceptions. The experience of the past 30 years supports the conclusion that "hands-on" activities need to be replaced by "minds-on" work and that students need time to develop the ability to ask questions and to "talk science."

Gallas (1995) reported that during the year, her class of students grew in their ability to talk together and build theories. This observation has also been made in high school classes. Seven high school students in an interdisciplinary science class were monitored over the course of a school year as they developed individual science projects centered around a common class theme of whaling (Abrams et al., in preparation). The Landlock High (pseudonym) class curriculum is student centered, allowing students to generate their own areas of inquiry loosely based on the whaleboat theme and tightly linked to their individual science discipline. The curriculum encourages students to pursue those areas of inquiry through the completion of individual projects.

Wolk (1994) states, "When children are free to choose their own projects, integrating knowledge as the need arises, motivation—and success—follow naturally" (p. 42). This sentiment was interwoven into the structure of the Landlock High curriculum.

The results of that study reveal that one area of student difficulty is in constructing a reasonable question on which to focus their efforts. At the beginning of the year, questions were often too wide in scope and heavily influenced by the mentor teacher. The mentor or the project deadline rather than the student determined when the project was completed. Toward the end of the first semester, students were rushed for time, and the questions became narrow, diffuse, and easily answered. By the second semester, the students chose a science topic to focus on for the semester and the students constructed several questions within their selected area of inquiry. They were better able to determine when they were finished with an intellectual product and felt comfortable about their areas of specialization. Here are three students' comments that reflect their improved ability to ask questions as the year progressed:

> S: OK. I can more (easily) look at a topic now and I have a question there. It comes to me. And that first project I really had to think of what would work as a question for what I wanted to do.

I:  And what makes it a good question now?

S:  One that's fairly specific into the area that I want to learn. I don't know, a question encompasses the whole of the project.

I:  What about do-ability?

S:  Yeah, I can do, I figure if I can come up with the question, I can do it. It's just a matter of how well and to what extent you can do it. Although I have noticed now that they are easier to do than before. . . . The questions are more specific so it's easier to answer them and say 'Yes I did answer them here, here, and here.'                                                  (12th-grade female)

I:  Do you think your questions changed over the course of the year? Did they get harder, easier, more 'do-able,' less 'do-able'?

S:  I don't know about more or less 'do-able.' For me, I changed the question to fit what I was interested in. So I guess for me it would've been easier because it was something that I was interested in that I wanted to know about.

S:  Right. Even so far as the learning part, you have to always be willing to ask questions. You can't just like sit there and say well I won't do it because I don't know the answers. You have to definitely be willing to ask questions. If you don't ask questions, you'll never get the answer and you'll never get anywhere.
                                                                  (12th-grade female)

I:  Do you think it (the last project) was different from the questions you asked at the beginning of the year? . . .

S:  They've been (pause) they've all been hard. I have a problem with a real easy one to answer. I found it easier to answer because I know where to get the stuff more and like my first question, like thinking back, my first thing was on Greenpeace and I didn't really know how to do it. It was wicked hard, but now it's no harder than this one. But I know how to do it. And do it a lot faster and better.

I:  So have your questions changed or has the way you answered them?

S:  The way I answered them changed. I just researched it in a different way. Take it from a different side. There's many ways to research something and I just take it from a different way. I did my own research to back everything up.
                                                                  (12th-grade male)

One student completing her physics class in Landlock High discussed her perceptions of her peers' learning in traditional physics classes in comparison to her own experience. She recognized that it is more difficult for her to "track down information" she needs as compared to her peers who essentially have the information imparted to them through daily lectures. However, once she obtained the information, she felt that "I really learned it as compared to the other students." She stated:

> Once the year is over, I figure they (her peers) will probably only remember five or ten things from their class anyways. . . . I will only do five or ten projects throughout the year, but the difference is I will really know those things. . . . the other students will only have a vague idea of them.                          (12th-grade female)

She has verified one of the assumed advantages of the inquiry-based curriculum. She will have a well-integrated, long-term memory store of the science content once the projects are completed, because the questions and direction of her learning were self-initiated.

## COMMUNICATION WITH THE OUTSIDE WORLD

As Lemke (1990) points out, not only do students need arenas to voice their private science talk, but forums to practice translating their personal knowledge into the formalized public language of science. This communal expression of scientific knowledge allows the presenter to test the soundness of his/her ideas within the classroom's "scientific community." Traditionally in a science class, this has meant written laboratory reports handed to the teacher or oral reports presented in front of the class. For the entire year, secondary science students, in our study, resoundingly wished for opportunities to test their knowledge with other students outside the class (Abrams et al., in preparation). Landlock High students began a magazine and started visiting an elementary school to mentor younger students; Scientist High students started several community service projects.

With the advent of the Internet, classroom communication can easily reach beyond the confines of the school. Electronic experiences can come in a variety of formats: (1) electronic journals containing student articles, (2) Web pages displaying student work, (3) chat rooms for scientific discussion, and (4) on-line conferences. Opportunities for students "talking science" have never been greater!

## SUMMARY

Many science educators believe that science teaching needs to move away from the impersonal, scientistic, and socially sterile depiction of science that is the current norm of North American high schools toward a more humanistic approach in harmony with contemporary epistemology (Ryan & Aikenhead, 1992; Aikenhead, 1985; Bybee, 1987; Duschl, 1988; Hodson, 1988; Hurd, 1987). Lemke (1990) thinks that teaching students the specialized language of science through actually speaking, writing, and reasoning scientifically is essential to every goal of science education. Students need to develop their own private and public worlds of science. Inquiry-oriented approaches are again being touted as the way for students to learn *how* scientific knowledge is developed and the nature of that construction. Instead of repeating the mistakes of the 1960s curriculum movements, science educators should build upon that foundation.

The contexts of the scientist, the teacher, and the student must be examined and understood before the science education community can help students become scientifically literate. Paul Feyerabend (1981) maintains that science is too much in the control of experts (the scientists) and that for science to avoid stifling dogmatism there must be a place for both the expert and the amateur. What better place to allow amateur scientists to flourish than in science classrooms?

# References

Abrams, E., & Wandersee, J. H. (1995a). How to infuse actual scientific research practices into science classroom instruction. *International Journal of Science Education*, 17(6), 686–694.

Abrams, E., & Wandersee, J. H. (1995b). How does biological knowledge grow? A study of life scientists' research practices, *Journal of Research in Science Teaching*, 32(6), 649–663.

Abrams, E., Moss, D., & Kull, J. K. Examining conceptual change in students in a project-oriented secondary science class. (in preparation)

Aikenhead, G. S. (1985). Collective decision making in the social context of science. *Science Education*, 64(4), 453–475.

American Association for the Advancement of Science (AAAS) (1989). Projet 2061: Science for All Americans. Washington, DC: Author.

American Association for the Advancement of Science (AAAS) (1993). *Benchmarks for science literacy*. Washington, DC: Author.

Bybee, R. W. (1987). Science education and the science-technology-society (STS) them. *Science Education*, 71(5), 667–683.

Cannella, G. S. (1988). The effects of environmental structure on writing produced by young children. *Child Study Journal*, 1813, 207–221.

Clough, M. P., & Clark, R. (1994). Cookbooks and constructivism: A better approach to laboratory activities. *The Science Teacher*, 61(2), 34–37.

Darwin, C. (1962). *The voyage of the Beagle*. New York: Doubleday & Company, Inc.

Duschl, R. (1988). Abandoning the scientistic legacy of science education. *Science Education*, 72(1), 51–62.

Feyerabend, P. (1981). *Philosophical papers*. Cambridge, UK: Cambridge University Press.

Fleury, S.C., & Bentley, M. L. (1991). Education elementary science teachers: Alternative conceptions of the nature of science. *Teaching Education*, 3(2), 57–67.

Gallas, K. (1995). *Talking their way into science: Hearing children's questions and theories responding with curricula*. Columbia University, New York: Teachers College Press.

Griffiths, A. K., & Barry, M. (1995). High school students' views about the nature of science. *School Science and Mathematics*, 95(5), 248–255.

Hodson, D. (1985). Philosophy of science, science and science education. *Studies in Science Education*, 12, 25–57.

Hodson, D. (1988). Toward a philosophically more valid science curriculum. *Science Education*, 72(1), 19–40.

Hodson, D. (1993). Philosophic stance of secondary school science teachers, curriculum experiences, and children's understanding of science: Some preliminary findings. *Interchange*, 24, 41–52.

Hurd, P. (1987). A nation reflects: The modernization of science education. *Bulletin of Science Technology Society*, 7(1), 9–13.

Lederman, N. G. (1992). Students' and teachers' conceptions of the nature of science: A review of the research. *Journal of Research in Science Teaching*, 29(4), 331–359.

Lemke, J. L. (1990). *Talking science: Language, learning, and values*. New Jersey: Ablex Publishing Corporation.

Martin, B., & Brouwer, W. (1993). Exploring personal science, *Science Education*, 77(4), 441–459.

Meichtry, Y. J. (1992). Influencing student understanding of the nature of science: Data from a case of curriculum development. *Journal of Research in Science Teaching*, 29(4), 389–407.

Meichtry, Y. J. (1993). The impact of science curricula on student views about the nature of science. *Journal of Research in Science Teaching*, 30(5), 429–443.

Mitroff, I. (1974). Norms and counter-norms in a selected group of the Apollo moon scientists: A case study of the ambivalence of scientists. *American Sociological Review American Sociological Review*, 39, 579–595.

Mullis, I., & Jenkins, K. (1988). *The science report card: Elements of risk and recovery* (Rep. No. 17-S-01). Princeton, NJ: Author.

National Research Council (NRC) (1996). *National science education standards*. Washington, DC: National Academy Press.

Pollak, V. L. (1993). Science Education—I: The spirit of science. *Journal of Science Education and Technology*, 2(4), 513–519.

Pomeroy, D. (1993). Implications of teachers' beliefs about the nature of science: Comparison of the beliefs of scientists, secondary science teachers, and elementary teachers. *Science Education*, 77(3), 261–278.

Posner, G. J., Strike, K. A. Hewson, P. W., & Gertzog, W. A. (1982). Accommodation of a scientific conception: Toward a theory of conceptual change. *Science Education*, 66, 211–227.

Ramsey, G., & Howe, R. W. (1969). An analysis of research on instructional procedures in secondary school science. *The Science Teacher*, 36(4), 62–70.

Ryan, A. G., & Aikenhead, G. S. (1992). Students' preconceptions about the epistemology of science, *Science Education*, 76(6), 559–580.

Solomon, J. (1991). Teaching about the nature of science in the British national curriculum, *Science Education*, 75(1), 95–103.

Stanley, W. B., & Brickhouse, N. W. (1994). Multiculturalism, universalism, and science education, *Science Education*, 78(4), 387–398.

Tobias, S. (1990). *They're not dumb—they're different: Stalking the second tier*. Tucson, AZ: Research Corporation.

Wolk, S. (1994). Project-based learning: Pursuits with a purpose. *Educational Leadership*, 52(3), 42–55.

Wolpert, L. (1993). *The unnatural nature of science*, Cambridge, MA: Harvard University Press.

# PART III

# Epilogue

# Epilogue: Meaningful Learning, Knowledge Restructuring and Conceptual Change: On Ways of Teaching Science for Understanding

JOEL J. MINTZES
*University of North Carolina—Wilmington*

JAMES H. WANDERSEE
*Louisiana State University*

JOSEPH D. NOVAK
*Cornell University*

In this book we have advocated a view of science teaching and learning that focuses on *quality over quantity; meaning over memorizing and understanding over awareness*. In so doing, we have been motivated by an abiding conviction that the economic engine of the twenty-first century is likely to be substantially different from the twentieth; that the age of the agrarian/manufacturing society is rapidly disappearing and that our primary role in the future will depend on our collective capacities as meaning makers and knowledge builders (Novak, 1993a). This view is supported by a host of recent global events including among others the collapse of the Soviet Union, the rise of China and other East Asian manufacturing centers, the establishment of the European Union, and the conclusion of NAFTA and other international

*Teaching Science for Understanding: A Human Constructivist View*

economic agreements. It is further substantiated by the rapid growth of multinational corporations as well as the revolution in computer technology and advanced telecommunication linkages. Clearly, we now find ourselves in the midst of a "Knowledge Age" and those who teach science are on the cutting edge of that revolution.

In Chapters 1–3 we presented a brief introduction to theory and research in science education based on a *Human Constructivist* view of learning. Chapters 4–12, authored by an internationally recognized group of leading science educators and researchers, offered a set of promising new, theory-driven, intervention strategies that have immediate applicability to a wide range of science learning environments. In our view, these chapters provide some of the best advice currently available to practitioners who wish to encourage meaning making and understanding in the science classroom.

In this concluding chapter we summarize this advice and present a model designed to help teachers reflect on and evaluate new ways of teaching science for understanding. The model is based on a convergence of evidence from a number of closely related disciplines and draws heavily on the findings of cognitive scientists, applied learning theorists, epistemologists, as well as historians and philosophers of science. The model emerges directly from our Human Constructivist perspective and seeks to focus attention on the critical relationships among meaningful learning, knowledge restructuring and conceptual change. The chapter concludes with some speculation on the future of science teaching.

## TEACHING SCIENCE FOR UNDERSTANDING: A SUMMARY OF INTERVENTIONS

In the early chapters of this book we reviewed the evolution of some of the significant ideas and practices in the history of attempts to improve science teaching and learning. While much teaching and learning in science classrooms remains focused on memorization of facts and application of algorithms, research conducted over the past half century supports instructional practices that depart widely from these approaches. Here we summarize briefly some of the suggestions offered in Chapters 4–12 which aim at teaching science for understanding.

Trowbridge and Wandersee (Chapter 4) present some of the history of graphic organizers. They point out that the idea of a "map" has a long history, and the field of cartography grew out of both necessity and invention. Analogous to maps for geographic locations, concept maps provide a kind of "cartography of knowledge." Concept maps may represent composite ideas of experts on knowledge in some domain or they may represent a "cartography of the mind" for an individual, showing the concepts and propositions held by that individual for any specific domain of knowledge. Concept circle diagrams and other representations may also provide a "cartography of knowledge," but concept maps, when well-done, are more explicit.

One of Ausubel's (1968) propositions that has enjoyed wide acceptance was given in the epigraph of his book: "Ascertain what the learner already knows and teach him accordingly." Graphic organizers can help to achieve both of these objectives; they can assist in ascertaining what the learner already knows, and they can help organize instruction that builds upon and extends that knowledge. Analogous to the role of catalysts in chemical reactions, graphic organizers can facilitate meaningful learning by reducing common barriers to teaching and learning for meaning. Overwhelmingly, the research supports this claim. Unfortunately, the use of graphic organizers remains an uncommon practice in most science classrooms.

Gunstone and Mitchell (Chapter 5) look more broadly at metacognition, emphasizing the need for both teachers and learners to recognize how they are thinking about problems they are thinking about. If you say the upward force exerted by a table is the same as the downward force exerted by a book on that table, just what does this mean? Wrestling with a problem rather than memorizing an answer is augmented by metacognitive strategies. Dealing with "real world" problems in ways that help teachers and learners recognize both faulty and valid ideas can do much to facilitate meaningful learning.

In Chapter 6, Nussbaum traces some of the history of ideas concerning the particulate nature of matter. Given that brilliant minds wrestled for centuries with the question, "What are things made of"?, is it any wonder that students too continue to struggle with the particulate nature of matter, the relationship of energy to states of matter, and the concept of "empty space"; ideas that seem to defy common sense! We expect ordinary students to build robust, valid models of the nature of matter and energy not in centuries, but in a few years of schooling. Obviously, this can be done only if we apply the best we now know about teaching and learning. In the appendix to his chapter, Nussbaum provides an excellent example of this.

Teaching with the use of analogies is another method supported by research that shows promise for encouraging meaningful learning. Dagher (Chapter 7) provides an excellent overview of research in this area. In her own work, Dagher has used "stories" to help students understand science. For example, through a story on people in a lifeboat, Dagher has helped students understand concepts of floating and sinking. Stories such as these may be ongoing throughout a school year, providing conceptual "anchorage" for new concepts encountered in the curriculum. Each new elaboration of the story helps build new analogies for understanding.

Biblical parables make use of stories and analogies to teach basic ethical precepts. The problem is that society has changed so much since these parables were written that they often fail to teach the "lessons" without the skillful interpretation of excellent religious educators. One of the problems with analogies is that they are subject to multiple meanings that depend on the learner's prior knowledge. It takes a skillful teacher to design, use and evaluate analogies that will be highly successful in communicating valid science concepts, with little or no elaboration of invalid ideas. Nevertheless, most of us can recall the power of one of our teacher's analogies for helping us to understand a difficult, abstract scientific idea.

The explosive development of the computer and related technologies presents new opportunities for education. In Chapter 8, Good and Berger sample some of the research on computer-based learning; research which suggests that these approaches can significantly enhance meaningful learning in science. Unlike movies, introduced in the first half of this century, and television, introduced in the 1950s, computer-based instruction provides an interactive medium. Each learner may, at least to some extent, pursue a unique train of learning experiences, while the computer selects and paces these experiences according to the student's previous responses. Furthermore, computers can simulate experiences that would be difficult, dangerous, or expensive to provide in any other format (e.g., a simulation of an airplane crash). Students can generate unique sets of data, and the computer can help the learner table, graph, or in other ways transform these "raw" data.

Another promising aspect of increased use of computers in education is the potential for gathering large data sets on learning successes and difficulties from learners with diverse traits. However, this potential for data gathering can obfuscate rather than clarify our understanding of learning processes unless the research is well grounded in a solid theoretical framework. Much of this potential is yet to be realized.

Finally, access to the Internet provides the theoretical potential for interacting with virtually all extant knowledge. This too can be a bane as well as a blessing unless learners are carefully and selectively guided in their search of knowledge sources. To assist teachers in this task we might expect to see new kinds of search engines designed expressly for use in the science classroom.

In Chapter 9, Spitulnik, Zembal-Saul, and Krajcik describe the use of hypermedia to represent student understandings by combining the use of analogies, metaphors, and computer-based data sources. The high school students and preservice teachers who built "computer artifacts" to illustrate their ideas of science concepts provide a rich representation of their knowledge. Unfortunately the computer artifacts they created revealed some serious misconceptions of basic scientific ideas. However, critiques from classmates and the teacher may help these students restructure their thinking and, subsequently, their artifacts.

Here again we see illustrated a data source for research on science learning made possible by the computer. It might be interesting to speculate on how the use of metacognitive ideas and tools could augment and enhance the construction of such artifacts. We look forward to reading studies of this type in the future.

While meaning making is necessarily an idiosyncratic process, the necessity for "negotiating meanings" can be enhanced and enriched when learners work in small groups, at least part of the time. Jones and Carter (Chapter 10) provide an excellent review of the pertinent literature on the theoretical foundations and practical issues of learning science in small groups. As they point out, stories, metaphors, and analogies are commonly used by learners to explain their ideas to one another. It is clear that learners bring shared experiences to their groups through the use of these devices, and this common contextual element enhances their meaning-making potential. Of course, the teacher still must play an important role in monitoring and evaluating the learning. Little purpose is served if students reach consensus on ideas or explanations that are patently incompatible with current scientific understandings.

The challenge for teachers is finding ways to devise questions, experiments, and demonstrations that require students to rethink their ideas without unnecessarily emphasizing that their current ideas are "wrong." In this role the teacher must develop or borrow creative strategies that are appropriate to the particular needs of each small group and their specific misconceptions. As a result, this kind of teaching demands both a high level of subject matter knowledge and the skills and experience necessary to devise appropriate conceptual "challenges."

It is now widely recognized that students do not become "scientifically literate" by learning concepts, principles, and theories alone. They also need to learn how science works and how scientists create new knowledge. The history of science is a necessary component of learning to understand science. This history reveals the human struggle of scientists to solve problems, create theories, and occasionally to see some ideas die. Wandersee and Roach (Chapter 11) describe their work to develop an instructional model based on the "Interactive Historical Vignette." These teaching episodes offer a glimpse of pivotal incidents in the life of a scientist revealing critical choices made by the scientist. Presented with a sample of such vignettes, students may move on to create their own vignettes. Those with talent and interest in drama may create highly engaging and informative episodes, thus gaining recognition and approbation in science classes where they might otherwise founder.

Research done by Wandersee, Roach, and others suggests that a modest commitment of time and effort devoted to the history of science can have highly significant effects. Interactive Historical Vignettes also have some of the qualities of metaphors and analogies for conveying the meaning of scientific concepts. Since they deal with "actual events" they may even offer a more powerful vehicle for helping students construct meanings. When it comes to understanding scientific ideas on the one hand and understanding the nature of science on the other, we have a real case of "one hand washing the other." Teachers can achieve a real synergy of effects by creating teaching episodes that focus on both "what scientists know" and "how they come to know."

Another way to help students acquire an understanding of the nature of science and scientists is to increase opportunities for students to "talk science." Abrams (Chapter 12) suggests that teachers involve their students in "real-world" science projects and encourage them to discuss their work. For example, students may team up with scientists and gather data on water or air quality, weather patterns, and bird or insect migration routes. Alternatively, students may work together in teams and develop their own research agendas focusing on questions that have strong personal meaning for the participants. Small group discussions and other peer exchanges help to encourage productive "science talk" among students who might otherwise lack interest in the natural sciences.

Concept maps and Vee diagrams can be very useful tools for encouraging "science talk." For example, in a study of junior high school students we found that the use of concept maps and Vee diagrams facilitated sharing and discussing of science concepts among peers (Novak, Gowin, & Johansen, 1983). Even in more traditional classrooms where "cookbook" laboratory work predominates, making and sharing concept maps and Vee diagrams facilitates the learning of scientific concepts and helps students learn to appreciate the nature of scientific inquiry (Robertson-Taylor, 1985).

Studies of discourse patterns in science classrooms are still in their infancy (Lemke, 1990). Yet, the results of early work in this area are particularly intriguing and we expect to see useful ideas emerging from this work in the future.

## TWO LESSONS IN SCIENCE

In a paper delivered several years ago at the *Third International Seminar on Misconceptions and Educational Strategies in Science and Mathematics*, Novak (1993b) drew attention to meaningful learning as "the essential factor" in conceptual change. Although the *Proceedings* of that meeting (Novak, 1993c) have been widely disseminated in electronic form and are currently available on the Internet (http://meaningful.education.cornell.edu), the message of that paper seems to have been lost except to a small handful of readers. Here we elaborate on that paper, presenting a model that compares and contrasts two lessons designed to encourage understanding in science.

In the past we have repeatedly stressed the important differences between meaningful and rote learning and have advised teachers to adopt or create strategies that encourage the former and subordinate the latter. In this section we focus attention on a pair of lessons that serve to illustrate the psychological and epistemological issues underlying successful practice in science teaching. Our intention is to explore *meaning-making* as the principal mecha-

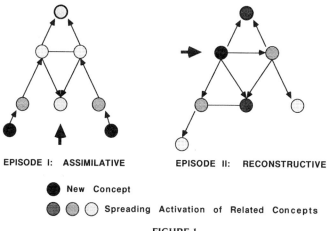

EPISODE I: ASSIMILATIVE          EPISODE II: RECONSTRUCTIVE

⬤ New Concept

⬤ ◉ ◯ Spreading Activation of Related Concepts

**FIGURE 1**

Assimilative and reconstructive teaching episodes. Assimilative episodes introduce new and less inclusive concepts in order to encourage learners to extend and elaborate upon or constrain and qualify a framework of knowledge they already possess. Reconstructive episodes introduce more general and inclusive concepts that become an integral part of the learner's cognitive structure only after a significant reordering of the existing framework of knowledge. New concepts introduced into cognitive structure change the meaning of existing concepts through a process of "spreading activation." Because cognitive structure is hierarchically arranged, concepts introduced at higher levels have a substantially greater modifying effect than concepts introduced at lower levels.

nism or "driving force" underlying knowledge restructuring and conceptual change and to speculate on ways to facilitate these processes.

We use the phrase "teaching episode" in this chapter to designate a classroom event of indeterminate length that serves as the basic unit of instruction. Such episodes when linked together in a coherent and well-integrated manner provide the raw material for lessons and units of instruction. For purposes of clarity and simplicity we have chosen to label one type of teaching episode *Assimilative* and another, *Reconstructive* (Figures 1 and 2). An assimilative teaching episode is one in which new and less inclusive concepts are introduced into the classroom in order to encourage learners to extend and elaborate upon or to constrain and qualify a framework of knowledge they already possess. The teacher's intention is that the new concepts become an integral part of the learner's existing framework of related concepts and the assumption is that this process will require minimal reorganization of cognitive structure.

| Lesson characteristics | Lesson | |
|---|---|---|
| | Animal diversity | Evolution |
| Dominant teaching episode | Assimilative | Reconstructive |
| Meaningful learning process | Subsumption | Superordination |
| Meaningful learning set | Moderate to strong | Very strong |
| Relevant concepts in cognitive structure | Well-Differentiated Scientifically acceptable | Limited or inappropriate Propositions (alternative concepts) |
| Inherent meaningfulness of new concepts | Moderate to high Strong explanatory potential | Very high Very strong explanatory potential |
| Resistance | Low to moderate | High to very high |
| Cognitive demand | Dispersed | Concentrated |
| Latent period | Brief to moderate | Extended, prolonged |
| Level of hierarchy | Low | High |
| Knowledge restructuring | Weak (tuning, accretion) | Strong (radical) |
| Conceptual change | Incremental, cumulative, limited | Wholesale, abrupt, extensive |
| Historical analog | Normal science | Revolutionary science |
| Biological analog | Natural selection | Punctuated equilibrium |
| Proponents | Toulmin Darwin | Kuhn Gould |
| Activation energy of intervention strategy | Low to moderate | Very high |

**FIGURE 2**

Two lessons in science. A summary of the psychological and epistemological factors underlying knowledge restructuring and conceptual change in science, illustrating the essential role of meaning making as the driving force in these cognitive events.

In contrast, a reconstructive episode introduces "higher-order," more general, and inclusive concepts that become an integral part of the learner's cognitive structure *only after* a significant reordering of the existing knowledge framework. The teacher's intention is to encourage a significant and lasting change or shift in the relationships among existing concepts and/or to offer new concepts that possess enhanced explanatory potential.

Assimilative and reconstructive teaching episodes are but two of many avenues to high-quality science teaching. Another is the *integrative* episode which serves to help students make connections between separate but related domains of knowledge. In this discussion, however, we wish to suggest that much about good teaching in school science can be understood by comparing and contrasting assimilative and reconstructive episodes and coming to understand the psychological and epistemological factors that underlie them (Figure 2).

To elaborate on these factors we have chosen to compare and contrast the teaching of two closely related conceptual domains in biology; for example, animal diversity and evolutionary theory. Equally relevant comparisons could be made in physics, chemistry, and the earth and space sciences; however, our formal education and extensive teaching experience in biology provide us with greater insight into conceptual problems arising within biology.

Helping students learn the fundamental principles of animal diversity is an experience common to virtually all biology teachers. And, despite its deemphasis by curriculum reformers of the 1960s (Biological Sciences Curriculum Study, 1963), a general descriptive understanding of organismic diversity is essential to grasping those broad, explanatory principles that provide a cohesive framework in the life sciences. Among the concepts typically introduced at the elementary and middle school levels and elaborated on at the high school are the following: animal, vertebrate, invertebrate, protozoa, sponges, jellyfish, worms, molluscs, arthropods, echinoderms, and chordates. With some exceptions (Trowbridge and Mintzes, 1989), the evidence suggests that these concepts are widely taught and often well-understood, although many students continue to resort to rote mode learning in this domain.

In contrast to these descriptive concepts are the higher-order, general, and inclusive ideas that comprise modern evolutionary theory. To Dobzhansky (1973), "Nothing in biology makes sense except in the light of evolution," and virtually all contemporary biologists concur with that assessment. To biology educators, "The modern concept of evolution provides a unifying principle for understanding the history of life on Earth, relationships among all living things, and the dependence of life on the physical environment" (AAAS, 1989). And yet, despite its explanatory power, there is good evidence that many biology teachers shy away from teaching evolution, and even more evidence that it is poorly understood when it is taught (Good, Trowbridge, Demastes, Wandersee, Hafner, & Cummins, 1993). How can we account for these observed differences in teaching preferences and learning success?

By the time children begin the formal study of animal diversity most have had a wide range of intense, personal, and often emotionally laden experiences with living organisms. Typically these experiences include interactions with pets, a range of insects, spiders, worms, zoo or farm animals, and other familiar vertebrates. Commonly the understandings and misunderstandings arising from these personal interactions are reinforced and extended by the mass media, toys, games, and tradebooks. The most frequent alternative conceptions seem to be of two types (Trowbridge & Mintzes, 1985, 1989): the *undergeneralization* in which children construct a highly restricted meaning for certain concepts (e.g., the concept *animal* is reserved for four-legged, furry creatures) and the *overgeneralization* in which an animal belonging to one group is assigned to another based on conspicuous and sometimes ambiguous external features (e.g., a penguin is classified as a *mammal* because its down feathers resemble fur).

Despite these conceptual difficulties, experience has shown that many students manage to learn and retain a great deal about animals as a result of repeated exposure at successive grade levels to well-planned, high-quality, conventional instruction. When successful, this instruction typically includes both assimilative and reconstructive episodes. The reconstructive episodes serve to introduce or to significantly modify the meaning of higher-order concepts such as animal, vertebrate, invertebrate, and mammal. The assimilative episodes extend or elaborate and qualify or constrain the vast framework of knowledge that young children bring with them to their first formal instruction in biology and commonly focus on the defining attributes of animal phyla and the natural history of diverse groups of organisms. Based on the success many teachers report, it appears that significant and lasting change in conceptual understanding is well within the ability level of most students, and consequently the majority of instructional time is typically devoted to the assimilative function.

In marked contrast, teachers who attempt to introduce ideas on evolutionary theory often report limited success. The evidence suggests that the limiting factors are of two principal types: (1) the strong commitment by many students to a set of alternative viewpoints (i.e., Lamarckian views; "young Earth" hypotheses) and (2) the complex, abstract and substantially novel ideas that must be incorporated into cognitive structure (i.e., chance/probability, genes [dominance, recessiveness], mutation, migration, gene flow, genetic drift, recombination, natural selection [stabilizing, disruptive, directional], species, allopatric speciation, isolating mechanisms, adaptive radiation, geologic time, Hardy-Weinberg equilibrium). The combined effects of these factors seem to undermine any reasonable probability of lasting conceptual change in conventional classrooms. In truth, when viewed in this light, it seems remarkable that any student might ever come to understand evolution or to internalize its meaning except as a nod to the teacher's authority! Consequently it now appears that successful instruction in evolutionary theory may depend critically on developing a set of well-planned and executed reconstructive teaching episodes.

As suggested earlier, a similar case could be made in the physical sciences. In physics itself, teachers report limited success in helping students develop a conceptual understanding of topics in Newtonian mechanics (Chapter 5) even though many are able to solve simple problems by applying algorithmic solutions. Chemistry teachers experience comparable problems with atomic molecular theory (Chapters 6 and 9) and Earth science teachers have great difficulty with plate tectonics.

To understand the difficulties that science teachers experience we must take a closer look at the underlying mechanisms responsible for meaning-making in the natural sciences. Why do so many teachers report on successful experiences with assimilative episodes in contrast to reconstructive episodes, where at best partial success is the general rule? Viewing this problem through a Human Constructivist lens enables us to elaborate on the contributions of learning theory, cognitive science, epistemology, and the history and philosophy of science to the improvement of science teaching. It also provides a framework for thinking about the types of intervention strategies that are most likely to result in significant and lasting change in students' ideas.

We begin with the basic proposition of Human Constructivism, that *meaning-making is the fundamental adaptation of the human species and the driving force underlying all forms of conceptual change*, whether that change occurs in the mind of the experienced, professional scientist or a young child confronting the wonders of nature for the first time (Chapter 2). On this view, our understanding is resonant with (and predates) those who now look to the nascent field of evolutionary psychology for explanations of cognitive processes (Gopnik and Meltzoff, 1997):

> . . . .we can think of organized science as taking natural mechanisms of conceptual change, designed to facilitate learning in childhood, and putting them to use in a culturally organized way. To explain scientific theory change, we may need to talk about culture and society, but we will miss something important if we fail to see the link to natural learning mechanisms. (p. 21)

We interpret this position to mean that ". . . creating new knowledge is, on the part of the creator, a form of meaningful learning" (Novak, 1993). Consequently, we look to *subsumption* and *superordination* as the principal mechanisms of conceptual change.

Returning once again to our example of lessons in animal diversity and evolution (Figure 2), it is our view that successful teaching of the former depends largely on constructing a set of assimilative teaching episodes while the latter is substantially dependent on the teacher's ability to artfully shape critical episodes of a reconstructive nature. Furthermore, we argue, from the student's perspective, that meaningful learning of concepts in animal diversity is essentially an exercise in subsumption, while the learning of evolutionary theory requires multiple instances of superordination involving reconstruction of a vast network of concepts under a few new, highly abstract, explanatory concepts.

Ausubel, Novak, and Hanesian (1978) tell us that success in meaningful learning, whether by subsumption or superordination, is dependent on three critical factors: (1) a meaningful learning set, (2) a store of relevant concepts in cognitive structure, and (3) inherent meaningfulness of the new concepts. Our collective experience with thousands of students over many decades suggests these factors operate with differential impact across knowledge domains in the natural sciences. For example, we have found that understanding concepts in evolutionary theory demands a substantially stronger meaningful learning set (i.e., "motivation to learn meaningfully") than that required to understand concepts in animal diversity. In part, this reflects the necessity of "unlearning" or delimiting the boundaries of a host of "preconceptions" (i.e., Lamarckian views; theology), but equally significant is the strenuous intellectual work needed to import a significant number of higher-order, abstract, and substantially novel (e.g., "relevant") concepts. In our view, the strongly "endergonic" nature of superordinate learning is perhaps the single most significant constraint on understanding. Once this feat has been accomplished, however, the evidence suggests that the "inherent meaning" of the new concepts provides a very strong explanatory framework for subsequent learning. Consequently, we find that resistance to learning evolution is generally quite high; that the domain poses a high threshold of concentrated demand requiring students to navigate a series of "critical junctures" early in the learning period (Trowbridge and Wandersee, 1994) and that the "incubation or percolation time" needed to assimilate and make sense of the knowledge is quite extended (i.e., months or years). For these and other reasons many students report that understanding, when it comes, arrives in a flash of insight that is reminiscent of the well-documented "ah-ha!" moments scientists occasionally experience in their work. The effect is sometimes described as "pieces of a puzzle falling into place."

In contrast, learning concepts in animal diversity demands considerably less cognitive effort. Generally students arrive with a reasonably well-differentiated framework of prior knowledge. The task itself often meets with only moderate levels of resistance; the cognitive demand is generally dispersed over a period of days to weeks, and typically the latent period (i.e., from instruction to understanding) is quite brief. Consequently students tend to "build up" frameworks of knowledge in a piecemeal fashion much as a mason constructs buildings with bricks and mortar.

Viewed through the lens of cognitive science (Carey, 1987), the type of meaningful learning we ascribe to superordination results in a "strong" or "radical" form of knowledge restructuring with significant alteration involving the highest levels of the knowledge framework. From an epistemological viewpoint, the "ah-ha!" moments are an indication of wholesale, abrupt, and extensive change in conceptual understanding; the type of change that Kuhn (1962) calls "revolutionary," and one that is reminiscent of the "punctuated equilibrium" model of speciation (Gould, 1977). In contrast, subsumption is a learning process that produces a "weak" form of knowledge restructuring involving lower levels of a knowledge framework and ultimately producing an incremental, cumulative, and often limited change in conceptual understanding. This form of conceptual change may be likened to Kuhn's "normal science" or Toulmin's (1972) "evolution of concepts." It is exemplified in the biological sciences by "natural selection," the mechanism of evolution proposed by Darwin.

With these preliminary ideas as a framework, we turn now to the problem of instructional intervention. How can a Human Constructivist analysis (such as the one just described) help us select appropriate and potentially successful teaching strategies?

## TEACHER AS CATALYST

In recent years it has become fashionable in some science education circles (Tobin, 1993) to analyze instruction through the self-selected metaphors teachers use to describe their roles in the science classroom. Among the metaphors teachers commonly employ are: gardener, entertainer, quiz master, ship's captain, comedian, and preacher. An apt metaphor we have heard less frequently is that of *catalyst*.

A catalyst is an agent used in small quantities that changes the velocity of a chemical reaction but does not become part of the final product. In living systems, most catalysts are organic compounds (composed principally of protein) that speed up the rate of a chemical reaction by lowering the energy required to make the reaction "go." These organic catalysts are known as enzymes.

For example (Figure 3), in a simple hydrolytic reaction occurring within the human digestive system, the common table sugar sucrose is cleaved into smaller absorbable sugars, glucose and fructose, by the enzyme "sucrase" which is secreted in the inner lining of the small intestine. This reaction is a strongly "exergonic" or energy-releasing event. However, in order to make this reaction go, a small amount of energy (activation energy) must be added to the system. The function of an enzyme is to lower the activation energy of a chemical reaction; a feat accomplished by providing an "active site" where chemical bonds are formed or broken. In the case of sucrase, the active site places stress on the covalent bond linking the simple sugars and thereby facilitates cleavage of the larger molecule.

Several characteristics of enzymes are important to an understanding of their functions in living cells. Among these characteristics are the following: (1) in comparison to the reacting molecules, enzymes work in small quantities; (2) enzymes are not "used up" in chemical reactions but may be reused many times; (3) enzymes are quite specific; they generally catalyze only one kind of chemical event; (4) because they are composed mostly of protein, the physical shape (i.e., conformation) of an enzyme molecule may be altered by changes in environmental conditions; these alterations may significantly effect their efficacy; (5) the action of an enzyme may be inhibited or facilitated by

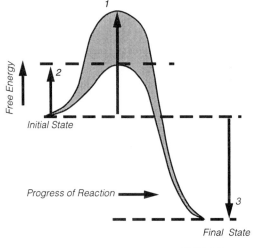

1. activation energy for uncatalyzed reaction

2. activation energy for catalyzed reaction

3. energy released by reaction (catalyzed or uncatalyzed)

**FIGURE 3**

Profile of enzyme kinetics. Many chemical reactions in living systems are energy-releasing events. However, in order to make the reactions "go" a small amount of activation energy must be added to the system. Enzymes lower the activation energy of a chemical reaction by providing an active site where chemical bonds are broken or formed.

other molecules (i.e., inhibitors, coenzymes); and (6) in biochemical pathways, enzymes tend to be compartmentalized and must work in well-orchestrated groups to produce a final product.

As with all metaphors [and analogies (Chapter 7)] this one is far from perfect. However, for us it offers a useful way of thinking about the teacher's role and ultimately about ways of selecting appropriate intervention strategies in science classrooms. It's value lies in the implicit similarities between the making and breaking of chemical bonds and the essential role of the classroom teacher which, in our view, centers on the making and breaking of connections in cognitive structure.

In its simplest form, our argument is that the teacher's role is to facilitate meaningful learning; that is, to help students form connections between new concepts and concepts that are part of their existing framework of prior knowledge. We view cognitive structure as strongly hierarchical and suggest, for reasons previously described, that concepts found at higher levels tend to be more stable and that connections between them tend to be substantially stronger and more numerous than those at lower levels. As a result, the teacher's role in reconstructive teaching episodes is significantly more arduous than that in assimilative episodes.

Using the teacher-as-catalyst metaphor, we view the teacher as a human agent whose principal function is to initiate and accelerate the rate of conceptual change and who accomplishes this feat by reducing the "activation energy" required to restructure knowledge. The teacher and all of the knowledge and resources (s)he brings to the classroom serve as the "active site" where cognitive linkages are formed and reformed; and her effectiveness can be measured in the relative success her students experience as a result of her active intervention. As with biological catalysts, teachers are generally found in small quantities (i.e., one teacher to every 25 students) and are "reused" annually, typically teaching the same subjects for 25–30 years.

Rather than completing this metaphor, we wish to challenge reader(s) to reflect on ways it informs and/or constrains our understanding of the teacher's primary roles (and possibly to suggest a more powerful metaphor, if necessary). In so doing, we wish to pose the following questions to stimulate further thought: (1) In what ways does an outstanding teacher exhibit (or fail to exhibit) the "specificity" of a biological catalyst? For example, should we encourage secondary school teachers to become "experts" in the teaching of a specific science discipline or rather is it better to educate "generalists" in science? Should we endorse the notion of the "science specialist" at the elementary school level?; (2) In what ways are good science teachers affected by changes in the classroom or school environment? What characteristics of classroom or school environments are most conducive to excellence in science teaching?; (3) What factors in the school or classroom environment inhibit or facilitate the work of science teachers? What can be done to diminish the inhibiting factors and enhance the facilitating factors?; (4) What can be done to reduce the isolation of classroom teaching? Does "departmentalization" work in the best interests of science teachers and students?; (5) Does a teacher's professional preparation have a maximum catalytic life? Is "reeducation" a necessary part of the "life cycle" of all science teachers?

These questions of course are not exhaustive and are merely meant to suggest some of the provocative issues posed by a teacher-as-catalyst metaphor. Finally, we wish to briefly address the ways in which a teacher-as-catalyst metaphor, embedded within a Human Constructivist perspective, can help in the practical business of selecting appropriate intervention strategies.

Selecting intervention strategies and sequencing teaching episodes are clearly among the most important decisions science teachers make. Each teaching episode poses a unique challenge but the job itself is made less overwhelming by the recognition that all teaching is ultimately a matter of assisting students as they work to make and break connections in cognitive structure. To exemplify this issue we return to the problem of teaching evolution.

As we view it, the problem of teaching within this domain can be reduced essentially to two major challenges: (1) providing a "safe", nonthreatening, supportive environment where students feel free to express and elaborate

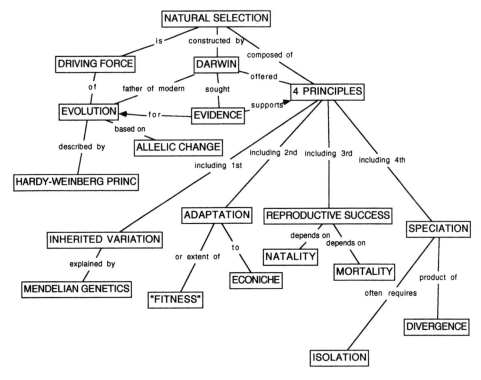

**FIGURE 4**
A micromap for a series of lessons on evolution.

on their prior scientific knowledge (i.e., in contrast to theological explanations) while considering the viewpoints of others, and (2) introducing and encouraging students to reflect on a set of new, more powerful, explanatory concepts and, where possible, helping them resolve contradictions in their thinking. We will limit our brief remarks to the second of these challenges.

To guide us in our planning, we begin with a basic, unelaborated concept map (i.e., a "micromap"; Trowbridge and Wandersee, 1994) that depicts the most important concepts and relationships we intend to consider (Figure 4). Using the map as a kind of "thinking tool," we begin at the top and gradually work our way down, considering each concept and each relationship as we proceed. At every step in the process we ask ourselves the following questions:

1. Does the concept label represent an "object" or an "event"?
2. Is the object or event covert or readily observable? Is it "concrete" or "abstract"? Can it be "seen" with the naked eye?
3. Is the concept counterintuitive, counterperceptual, or novel?

4. Is the concept label used in a different way than it is in common, everyday language?

5. Has the concept played a significant role in the history of the discipline? Will its elaboration reveal important characteristics about the nature of science and scientists? Do the historical, social or cultural characteristics of the scientists have special meaning for students in my class?

6. What is the nature of the relationship between this concept and the concepts to which it is linked: "identify," "whole-part," "set-member," "has characteristics," "time or space sequence"? Is the relationship qualitative or quantitative?

7. How much experience do my students have with the objects or events? Is it likely that they subscribe to some "alternative conceptions"? Which ones?

8. Is the concept emotionally laden? Is it related to an alternative belief system or a personally significant event? Does it have powerful, idiosyncratic meaning for the students in my class? Is the meaning likely to be significantly influenced by the student's gender, age, socioeconomic status, ethnic or cultural identity, place of origin?

9. How much "unpacking" is required? Which concepts do my students need to know before they can understand this one?

10. Within the constraints of my role, how much time, energy, physical and financial resources can be allocated to an elaboration of this concept?

This list of questions is not exhaustive but it does provide a starting point for thinking about interventions and sequencing of teaching episodes. Unlike many instructional issues that teachers are often asked to consider, these questions are driven by a strong concern for meaning making and the role of teachers as catalysts in the construction of knowledge. Perhaps you can think of some additional questions that might be added to the list.

As we reflect on these questions we develop a planning sheet that summarizes our thinking (Figure 5). In the case of evolution, we think that substantial effort must be invested in sequencing of teaching episodes and investing superordinate concepts with meaning. Among the most important concepts are: cells and cellular reproduction, Mendelian genetics, and molecular genetics.

It seems to us that the domain of cellular reproduction lends itself well to interventions that rely on the visual mode of representation. Here we introduce concepts through direct observation (i.e., microscopy) and interactive CD-ROM technology. At the conclusion of this sequence (as in all others) we set aside time for reflection, consolidation, and integration of knowledge through metacognitive strategies, including concept mapping.

In the domain of Mendelian genetics we rely heavily on "hands-on" laboratory work and computer simulation. More than any other area in biology, Mendelian genetics offers an opportunity for students to examine and model

| Conceptual domain | Teaching episode | Intervention strategy |
|---|---|---|
| Reproduction | Cells | Microscopic observation |
| | Mitotic division | Hypermedia |
| | Meiotic division | Hypermedia |
| | Summary | Concept mapping |
| Mendelian genetics | Chance/probability | Small groups (coin flipping) |
| | Mendel's pea plants | Interactive vignette ("Mendel") |
| | Monohybrid cross | Computer-based ("fly lab")/Vee |
| | Dihybrid cross | Fly lab |
| | Codominance | Fly lab |
| | Multiple alleles | Wet lab (blood typing) |
| | Summary | Problem sets/concept mapping |
| Molecular genetics | DNA Structure | Rope ladder analogy |
| | Transcription/translation | Court reporter analogy |
| | Mutation | Wet lab (bread mold) |
| | Summary | Simulation/concept mapping |
| Evolution | Darwin/HMS Beagle | Interactive vignette ("Darwin") |
| | Science and religion | Small groups/debate/conflict |
| | Lamarck | Small groups |
| | Definition | Talking science |
| | Variation | Vee diagram; wet lab (seashells) |
| | Adaptation | Wet lab (bird beaks; skulls; feet) |
| | Reproductive success | Simulation |
| | Speciation | Hypermedia |
| | Evidence | Small groups/debate/conflict |
| | Summary | Concept mapping |
| Population genetics | Phenotype frequency | Human traits in classroom |
| | Genetic drift | "Dunkers"; Internet search |
| | Hardy-Weinberg principle | Colored-bead analogy/simulation |
| | Summary | Problem sets/concept mapping |

**FIGURE 5**

Planning sheet for lessons on evolution.


dynamic processes by manipulating a set of independent variables. The opportunity to "meet" Gregor Mendel and ponder his pea experiments provides another potentially meaningful event.

Molecular genetics has proven to be an especially difficult domain for many students. Whole-class discussions that make judicious use of well-chosen analogies have been successful in many instances. We make use of a rope ladder analogy to model some of the characteristics of DNA and have found that students understand transcription and translation more easily when we liken these processes to the duties of a court reporter. Also valuable are direct experiences with laboratory tools and genetic material.

Our introduction to evolutionary theory begins with a "visit" from Charles Darwin who discusses his own education and family background, his voyage aboard the HMS Beagle, his years of reflection and discussions with pigeon breeders and natural historians, his feelings about other "ways of knowing," and his painful experiences in writing. This vignette is followed by several small-group discussions and debates on science and religion and the "inheritance of acquired characteristics." The core of "natural selection" is introduced through a sequence of episodes that rely on whole-class discussion, "wet" labs, simulation, microworlds, and interactive CD-ROMs. A culminating activity focusing on the physical evidence for evolution lends itself to small groups where the discussion inevitably returns to the nature of science in contrast to other ways of knowing.

The set of teaching episodes concludes with a sequence in population genetics where the quantitative aspects of evolution are considered. We introduce notions of phenotypic frequencies through a whole-class study of human traits focusing on common inherited characteristics such as hair color, eye color, tongue-rolling, and middigital hair. An Internet search introduces the concept of genetic drift through a reading selection on the "Dunkers," an isolated population in Pennsylvania. Finally, the Hardy-Weinberg principle is considered. Here we make use of a laboratory activity that simulates a population of interbreeding organisms and relies on a gene pool of colored beads.

## THE PROMISE OF AN INTERACTIVE SOCIETY:
## A CAUTIONARY NOTE

Futurists tell us that the U.S. is becoming an interactive society, supported by interactive technologies, both wired and wireless. Already, up to 40 million of us telecommute to work every week (Eder, 1997, p. 43). Even more of us use the Internet and the World Wide Web to carry on personal and professional tasks. So it is only natural to think that education too will be radically improved by an infusion of interactive technologies. Many futurists claim that "learning will be easier" and "education will be more effective" (Eder, 1997, pp. 43–44). However, we remain skeptical of such claims. The three of us have lived long enough to see numerous technological marvels make grand entrances accompanied by sweeping claims for improving student learning and later take quite an ordinary place in the classroom teacher's tool kit.

We do see great value in the Internet-linking of whole classrooms of science students and teachers at widely separated geographic locales. Sharing data and graphics, pooling research results, "talking science" as findings emerge, proposing laboratory and field experiments, and talking shop cannot only improve the cognitive aspects teaching and learning but also the affective. Electronic mail is still the major (and least expensive) attraction for today's Internet users.

Software magnate Bill Gates (1995, p. 184) writes, "The [information] highway is going to give us all access to seemingly unlimited information, anytime and any place we care to use it. It's an exhilarating prospect, because putting this technology to use to improve education will lead to downstream benefits in every area of society." We agree with him that the potential to improve educating is there; provided everything else remains constant.

However, the visionary's glowing view of interactive technology in the public schools assumes that infusion of these devices is not accompanied by a concomitant reduction in spending on more prosaic but essential elements such as teacher salaries and conventional teaching materials. Given the current propensity of voters nationwide to reject school bond issues and tax increases, it is far from certain that they will be inclined to adopt expanded school budgets. If they do, it will undoubtedly come with the expectation of greater teacher accountability for student performance; an expectation that might be substantially unrealistic.

When administrators (with technology bills to pay) seek to reduce the costs of offering *science* courses, we anticipate they will challenge the range of current course offerings; current needs for laboratory space, experiments and activities, and the importance of field trips. They will also question the size of the science teaching faculty, arguing that computer software and interactive technologies provide equally effective yet safer and more cost efficient "delivery systems."

In response, we assert that if the time ever comes that the natural sciences are taught primarily *without* opportunities for students to directly experience actual natural objects and events, and if these natural objects and events are available only on computer screens through the visual, auditory, and conceptual filters devised by hypermedia makers and instructional technologists, then the American leadership in science and technology is in jeopardy. We think interactive technologies should be used only to provide experiences that the science teacher finds impossible to provide through direct interaction with nature. Natural objects and events are the benchmarks of science, the referents and principal arbiters of our knowledge. You can't take *nature* out of *natural science* and still call it that.

However, the cost-cutters will be tempted to go for the replica rather than the real thing. As Negroponte (1995, p. 31) points out, digital bits are cheaper to make and to move than matter is, especially with "economy of sales" that distributes their cost across thousands of schools. For example, if software simulating the growth of bacterial populations is for sale at below-laboratory prices and no one complains about the switch to "on-screen organisms," administrators (and even some lethargic science teachers) may be tempted to use them in lieu of the genuine thing. This makes us wonder whether some visionaries are driven more by the corporate "bottom line" than the educational value of their products.

Even cyberseer Bill Gates (1995, p. 197), in one of his more reflective moments, admits that:

All this information, however, is not going to solve the serious problems facing many public schools today: budget cuts, violence, drugs, high drop-out rates, dangerous neighborhoods, teachers more concerned about survival than education. Offering new technology won't suffice. Society will also have to fix the fundamental problems.

MIT's educational visionary Seymour Papert (1993, p. 104) observes: "The metaphor of learning by constructing one's own knowledge [metaphor 1] has great rhetorical power against the image of knowledge transmitted through a pipeline [metaphor 2] . . ." We think so too. We see the so-called Information Highway [metaphor 3] as more like an unregulated pipeline [metaphor 2] leading from sources to end user, providing an indiscriminate mixture of high- and low-quality products in volumes no single consumer can adequately evaluate.

As Gowin (1981, p. 197) pointed out, the ultimate goal of educating is self-educating, but it is a hard-won, time-consuming goal that requires one to *learn how to learn*. If teaching were simply a matter of pairing students with knowledge or remote experts, we wouldn't have to build schools; we could just send our youngsters to libraries! After all, isn't the World Wide Web basically an electronic library? Isn't e-mail essentially a high-speed postal system?

While each of us is ultimately responsible for his or her own learning, we usually need a teacher's help to, as Gowin (1981, p. 24) puts it, "crack the code" of the documents in a field, to help us select learning materials that meet external standards of excellence, to share and negotiate meanings with us, and to guide and check our emerging understandings. Gowin (p. 78) warns: "Just as the teacher can be overcome by an overload of information unscreened by criteria of excellence, so too can the student be burdened by personal meanings unfiltered by standards of the field being studied." Herbert Spencer (1820–1903) perhaps best captures our concerns about the educational applications of some interactive technologies and their potential effects on student understanding when he says, "For the man [sic] whose knowledge is not in order, the more he has of it, the greater will be his confusion."

The obverse of that which causes confusion is *clarity*. For many years we thought if only we could communicate science more clearly, we could improve student learning. There is a large body of research on instructional clarity (Feldman, 1976, 1989) that suggests clarity is indeed important, but not sufficient, for student learning. Figure 6 is a composite, research-based concept map depicting the findings of Feldman and other researchers (Mintzes, 1979, 1982) in this field, and Figure 7 summarizes some of the positive characteristics of clear instruction. It has not eluded us that many of these findings are consistent with our view of Human Constructivism and Gowin's theory of educating. But remember, the *student* has the central role to play in learning! Admittedly, if the teacher plays his or hers well, the

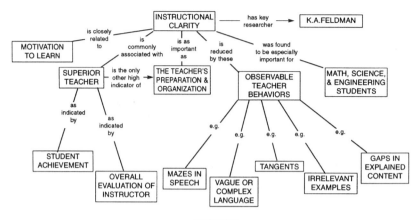

**FIGURE 6**

Concept map of the general research findings on college students' ratings
of instructional behavior with respect to instructional clarity.

probability of meaningful learning improves. But the final factor in science
learning is the learner him- or herself and what the learner does to make
meaning out of the natural world.

We close as we began [JHW and JJM] at the beginning of this book, with a
word of grateful recognition to Joseph D. Novak. Throughout his professional
career Professor Novak has focused on helping science teachers help science

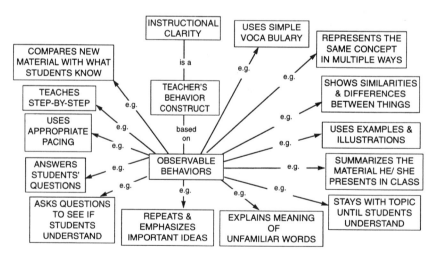

**FIGURE 7**

Concept map of the specific, positive research findings on college students'
ratings of instructional behavior with respect to instructional clarity.

students to *clarify* and *organize* what they know, to reflect on what they learn, to seek *meaning* in their pursuit of high grades, and to forge relevant *connections* by semantically linking new science concepts to those they already know. He has repeatedly advised that money alone cannot solve all the problems of education and that schools might profit substantially through the implementation of research-based recommendations. In our view, the precipitous and uncritical move toward *interactive technologies* in our nation's schools may well be premature. For, as Novak has argued, when schools and classrooms are finally organized around sound principles of knowledge construction and focused on meaning making, then and only then will additional investments in schooling effect a significant yield in learning. At that point we can affirm that our schools do indeed have an authentic commitment to *teaching science for understanding*.

## References

American Association for the Advancement of Science (AAAS)—Project 2061 (1989). *Science for all Americans*. Washington, DC: AAAS.

Ausubel, D. (1968). *Educational psychology: A cognitive view*. New York: Holt, Rinehart and Winston.

Ausubel, D., Novak, J., & Hanesian, H. (1978). *Educational psychology: A cognitive view*. New York: Holt, Rinehart and Winston.

Biological Sciences Curriculum Study (1963). *Biology teacher's handbook*. New York: Wiley.

Carey, S. (1987). *Conceptual change in childhood*. Cambridge, MA: MIT Press.

Dobzhansky, T. (1973). Nothing in biology makes sense except in the light of evolution. *American Biology Teacher*, 35, 125–129.

Eder, P. F. (1997). The emerging interactive society. *The Futurist*, 31, 43–46.

Feldman, K. A. (1976). The superior college teacher from the student view. *Research in Higher Education*, 5, 243–288.

Feldman, K. A. (1989). The association between student ratings of specific instructional dimensions and student achievement. *Research in Higher Education*, 30, 583–645.

Gates, B. (1995). *The road ahead*. New York: Viking Penguin.

Good, R., Trowbridge, J., Demastes, S., Wandersee, J., Hafner, M., & Cummins, C. (1993). *Proceedings of the 1992 evolution education research conference*. Baton Rouge: Louisiana State University.

Gopnik, A. Z., & Meltzoff, A. N. (1997). *Words, thoughts and theories*. Cambridge, MA: MIT Press.

Gould, S. (1977). *Ontogeny and phylogeny*. Cambridge, MA: Harvard University Press.

Gowin, D. B. (1981). *Educating*. Ithaca, NY: Cornell University Press.

Kuhn, T. (1962). *The structure of scientific revolutions*. Chicago: University of Chicago Press.

Lemke, J. (1990). *Talking science: Language, learning and values*. New Jersey: Ablex Publishing Co.

Mintzes, J. (1979). Overt teaching behaviors and students ratings of instructors. *Journal of Experimental Education*, 48, 145–153.

Mintzes, J. (1982). Relationships between student perceptions of teaching behavior and learning outcomes in college biology. *Journal of Research in Science Teaching*, 19, 789–794.

Negroponte, N. (1995). *Being digital*. New York: Alfred A. Knopf.

Novak, J. D. (1993a). Human constructivism: A unification of psychological and epistemological phenomena in meaning making. *International Journal of Personal Construct Psychology*, 6, 167–193.

Novak, J. D. (1993b). Meaningful learning: The essential factor for conceptual change in limited or inappropriate propositional hierarchies (LIPHs) leading to empowerment of learners. In J. Novak (ed.), *Proceedings of the third international seminar on misconceptions and educational strategies in science and mathematics* (distributed electronically). Ithaca, NY: Cornell University.

Novak, J. D. (1993c). *Proceedings of the third international seminar on misconceptions and educational strategies in science and mathematics* (distributed electronically). Ithaca, NY: Cornell University.

Novak, J. D., Gowin, D. B., & Johansen, G. T. (1983). The use of concept mapping and knowledge vee mapping with junior high school science students. *Science Education, 67,* 625–645.

Papert, S. (1993). *The childrens' machine: Rethinking school in the age of the computer.* New York: Basic Books.

Robertson-Taylor, M. (1985). Changing the meaning of experience: Empowering learners through the use of concept maps, vee diagrams, and principles of educating in a biology lab course. Unpublished Ph.D. thesis, Cornell University, Ithaca, New York.

Tobin, K. (1993). *The practice of constructivism in science education.* Hilldale, NJ: Lawrence Erlbaum.

Toulmin, S. (1972). *Human understanding, vol. 1: The collective use and evolution of concepts.* Princeton, NJ: Princeton University Press.

Trowbridge, J. E., & Mintzes, J. (1985). Students' alternative conceptions of animals and animal classification. *School Science and Mathematics, 84,* 304–316.

Trowbridge, J. E., & Mintzes, J. (1989). Alternative conceptions in animal classification: A cross-age study. *Journal of Research in Science Teaching, 25,* 547–571.

Trowbridge, J. E., & Wandersee, J. (1994). Identifying critical junctures in learning in a college course in evolution. *Journal of Research in Science Teaching, 31,* 459–473.

# Index